Exploring the
APPALACHIAN TRAIL™

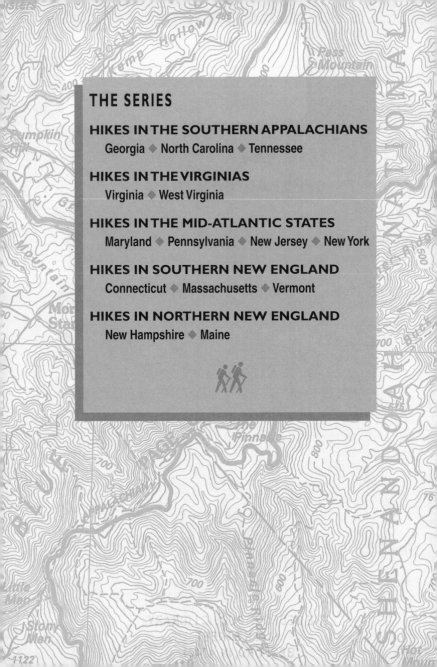

THE SERIES

HIKES IN THE SOUTHERN APPALACHIANS
Georgia ◆ North Carolina ◆ Tennessee

HIKES IN THE VIRGINIAS
Virginia ◆ West Virginia

HIKES IN THE MID-ATLANTIC STATES
Maryland ◆ Pennsylvania ◆ New Jersey ◆ New York

HIKES IN SOUTHERN NEW ENGLAND
Connecticut ◆ Massachusetts ◆ Vermont

HIKES IN NORTHERN NEW ENGLAND
New Hampshire ◆ Maine

Exploring the
APPALACHIAN TRAIL

HIKES in the VIRGINIAS

Virginia   West Virginia

DAVID LILLARD

GWYN HICKS

STACKPOLE BOOKS

Mechanicsburg, Pennsylvania

Exploring the Appalachian Trail™ Series Concept: David Emblidge
Series Editor: David Emblidge
Researcher and Editorial Assistant: Marcy Ross
Fact checking, 2nd edition: Sheila McMillen
Volume Editor: Susannah Driver
Book design and cover design: Walter Schwarz, of Figaro, Inc.
Cartography: Jean Saliter and Lisa Story, of Figaro, Inc. (topo maps); Peter Jensen, of Open-
Space (trail drawing); Carol Hutchison, of SpectraComp, using Maptech's TopoScout®
CD-ROMs (trail profiles)
Cover photograph: Nancy Hecker
Page viii: photograph by David Emblidge
Page xii: photograph of Springer Mt. AT plaque (southern terminus) by Doris Gove
Interior photographs: See credits with each image.
Indexer: Letitia Mutter

Library of Congress Cataloging-in-Publication Data

Lillard, David.
    Hikes in the Virginias / David Lillard, Gwyn Hicks.— 1st ed.
         p. cm.— (Exploring the Appalachian Trail)
    ISBN 0-8117-2670-3
         1. Hiking — Virginia — Guidebooks.   2. Hiking —
West Virginia — Guidebooks.   3. Hiking — Appalachian Trail —
Guidebooks.   4. Virginia —Guidebooks.   5. West Virginia — Guidebooks.
8. Appalachian Trail — Guidebooks.   I. Hicks, Gwyn.   II. Title. III. Series.
    GV199.42.V8L55   1998
    917.5504 ' 43 — dc21   97-50085
                                                            CIP

ISBN 978-0-8117-1066-4
Printed in the United States
10 9 8 7 6 5 4 3 2 1

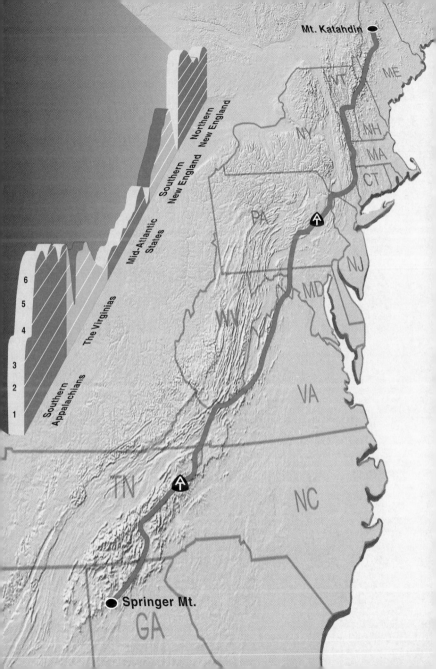

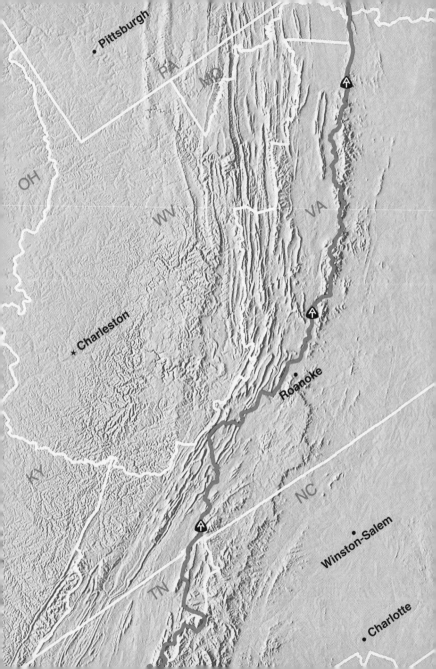

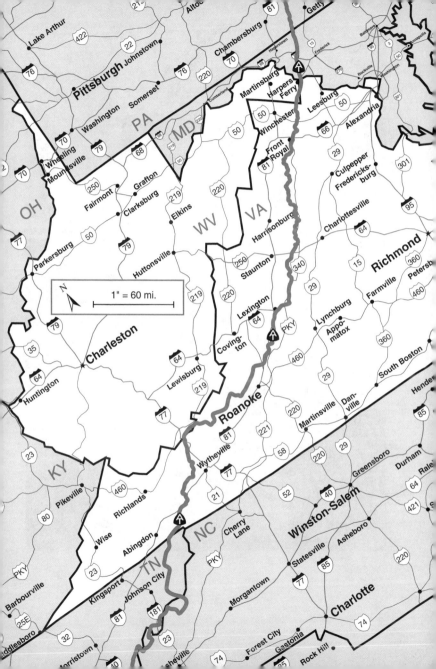

Contents

Virginia / West Virginia

APPALACHIAN
TRAIL
GEORGIA   TO MAINE
A Footpath for
Those who seek
Fellowship with
the Wilderness

1934

The
GEORGIA APPALACHIAN TRAIL CLUB

Introduction

Welcome to *Exploring the Appalachian Trail.* We're glad to have you join us for what promises to be a fine outdoor adventure.

You may not have realized it when you bought or borrowed this book, but if the truth be told, it's all about a long-standing love affair. The authors of the hiking guides in this series have been in love with the Appalachian Trail since before we can remember. And we've come to believe that if you truly love something, you will probably act positively to protect it. So when we invite you to join us in walking on the trail, we're also inviting you to let yourself be seduced, indeed to go ahead and take the leap into a sweet and enduring love affair of your own. But then be sure to act on the responsibility created as a by-product of that love. It's called service and support. In the section below called "Joining Up," you can read more about how each of us can contribute to the health and continuing life of the trail. The Appalachian Trail will give you many gifts. Be sure you give some back.

Unlike other good books about walking the Appalachian Trail, this one will encourage you to slow down, to yield to the many temptations offered up freely by nature and by the social-historical world along the trail. Benton MacKaye, considered by most to be the chief visionary of the early Appalachian Trail, once defined the purpose of hiking on the AT as "to see, and to see what you see." MacKaye was something of a romantic, and we know he read Emerson, who instructs us all to "Adopt the peace of Nature, her secret is patience." We can't improve on that.

Our intention is to help you plan and carry out a wide variety of hikes on the nation's longest continuously marked footpath, surely one of the most famous walking trails in the world. We'll guide you from point A to point B, to be sure, but as far as this book is concerned, it's what happens for you *between* points A and B that counts the most.

If the goal of hiking on the Appalachian Trail is to come home refreshed in body, rejuvenated in mind, and renewed in spirit, then along with the fun of being outside in the mountains, a little work will be required. The most obvious work is of the muscular variety. Less obvious but just as rewarding is the mental kind, and it's here that the books in this series will help you the most. The famous world traveler Sven-Olof Lindblad said, "Travel is not about where you've been but what you've gained. True travel is about how you've enriched your life through encounters with beauty, wildness and the seldom-seen."

In these AT hiking books, we'll pause to inspect the rocks underfoot and the giant folding and crunching of the entire Appalachian landscape. We'll take time to listen to birds and to look closely at wildflowers. We will deliberately digress into the social history of the area the AT passes through, thinking sometimes about industry, other times about politics, and now and then about a well-known or an obscure but colorful character who happened to live nearby. We'll explore trail towns and comment on trail shelters and campsites (they're not all alike!). And to help make you a savvy hiker (if you aren't already), we will offer up some choice bits of hiker wisdom that just might get you out of a jam or make your load a bit lighter to carry.

This is a participatory book. You will enjoy it and profit from it most if you carry a small notebook and a pen or pencil, if you bring along a camera and perhaps a birding book or a wildflower guide or a guide to some other aspect of the natural world (see the Bibliography for suggestions). Bring a compass and use our maps, or better yet, supplement the maps in this book with the more detailed ones available from the

Appalachian Trail Conference and other local sources (see page 9 and the Bibliography).

Chatting with your walking companions is a delightful thing to do some of the time while out on the trail, but the more noise you make, the less wildlife you'll see, and besides, it's hard for anyone to be both in conversation and simultaneously in close observance of the real details of the natural realm. Try hard to make some part of every hike a *silent walk,* during which you open all your senses and your imagination to drink in the marvelous environment of the Appalachian Trail.

The Appalachian Trail in Virginia and West Virginia

Most of the Appalachian Trail's 545 miles in Virginia and West Virginia lie in Virginia. The exceptions are an interlude into West Virginia near Pearisburg, along the northern Blue Ridge where the trail straddles the state line, and a few miles in and around Harpers Ferry, home of the Appalachian Trail Conference.

For thru-hikers, Harpers Ferry is considered the emotional halfway mark, but the true halfway point is in Pennsylvania (see *Exploring the Appalachian Trail: Hikes in the Mid-Atlantic States,* Hike #8). At 440 feet above sea level, Harpers Ferry marks the low elevation point on the AT in "the Virginias." As it meanders south along the Blue Ridge toward Mt. Rogers, at 5507 feet the highest peak on the AT in these two states, the trail seems never far from rhododendron and mountain laurel. From Harpers Ferry to the entrance to Shenandoah National Park, the trail passes near growing residential communities as eastern seaboard cities expand outward. However, the faint sounds from nearby roads and the increasing light in the nighttime sky are testaments to the success of the trail's supporters in preserving the experience of nature so close to so many people.

Most of the AT in these states travels through Shenandoah National Park and George Washington and Jefferson national forests. The SNP's 500 miles of trails invite seemingly endless diversions to waterfalls and remote ridges, all accessed via about 100 miles of the AT in the park. The AT here rarely strays more than a mile, usually less, from the Skyline Drive. Still, it is possible to enjoy solitude and sweeping views of farmland and the Allegheny Mts. More than 300 black bears live within the park's 300 square miles, the highest concentration in the eastern United States. South of the park, the trail ambles through mature forests and wildernesses in two national forests. Hikers can walk bald summits and enchanting, narrow stream valleys, then stroll through the "friendliest town on the trail," Damascus. Virginia is also the place on the AT where ecological north and south meet— southern and northern species of trees meet, then go their own ways. If you have never visited the region, a colorful armchair traveler's introduction awaits you in *Virginia and the Capital Region* in the *Smithsonian Guide to Historic America* series.

The Best of the AT in the Virginias

With fully one-quarter of the AT passing through Virginia, there are several stretches where the trail crosses developed areas or busy roads. We've omitted some of those miles to help you explore the very best of the AT in Virginia. In wilder areas, where there are few exit opportunities over many miles, we've picked our favorite miles and presented them as day hikes. At the ends of these hikes are brief descriptions of how to turn them into overnight trips.

Joining Up

We urge you, our fellow hikers, to honor the thousands of volunteers and paid workers who built and who nowadays maintain the Appalachian Trail by becoming a volunteer and a financial supporter yourself. Join your local hiking club (see pg. 395) and join any or all of the following organizations, each of which contributes to the survival of the Appalachian Trail:

Appalachian Trail Conservancy, P.O. Box 807, Harpers Ferry, WV 25425

Appalachian Mountain Club, 5 Joy St., Boston, MA 02108

American Hiking Society, 1422 Fenwick Lane, Silver Spring, MD 20910

Potomac Appalachian Trail Club, 118 Park St., SE, Vienna, VA 22180

Walking Lightly on the Land

On behalf of the hiking community, we urge all hikers to manage their behavior in the woods and mountains so as to have a minimal impact on the land. The old adages are apt: Take only pictures, leave only footprints. Pack out whatever you pack in. Leave no trace. Indeed, be a sport and pack out some other careless hiker's garbage if you find it along the trail. The National Park Service, which maintains a protective corridor along the Appalachian Trail, estimates that between 3 and 4 million people use the trail every year, and the numbers are growing. In many places the ecology of the AT landscape is fragile. But fragile or not, every one of its 2150 miles is subject to abuse, even if unintended. Leave the trail a better place than you found it, and you'll take home better memories.

NOLS Soft Paths is a good general introduction to the principles of leave-no-trace hiking and camping. See the Bibliography.

We wish you good weather, warm companionship, and a great adventure, be it for 6 hours, 6 days, 6 weeks, or 6 months on the trail. The Appalachian Trail belongs to all of us. Treat it as you would something precious of your very own.

Reader Participation

Readers are invited to respond. Please correct our mistakes, offer your perspectives, tell us what else you'd like to see in the next edition. Please also tell us where you bought or borrowed this book. Write to: Editors, Exploring the Appalachian Trail™, Stackpole Books, 5067 Ritter Rd., Mechanicsburg, PA 17055.

Acknowledgments

This project was made possible by the help of many people. First and foremost are those who make sure we continue to have an Appalachian Trail: the volunteers and staff of the AT maintaining clubs. We are also grateful to club members for information on the trail's condition, history, and lore. To people like Bill Foote of Natural Bridge ATC and others busy caring for the trail, pointing out relocations or explaining construction of a rock wall to passing hikers like us is all in a day's work. Their knowledge helped us ensure accuracy and offer colorful commentary. Thanks to Brian King and compatriots at ATC for information and resources, especially the staff in the ATC bookstore, and to Bob Proudman for insight into the complexities of operations and management on the world's longest greenway.

We are obliged to acknowledge other authors who are a part of the continually evolving Appalachian Trail library, especially Vaughn Thomas, the late Jack Albright, Andy Hiltz, Jean Golightly and their colleagues—field editors of and contributors to the *Appalachian Trail Guides to the Virginias,* without which our own navigation would have been impossible. As well, the writing of Jim Chase, Dan Bruce, Frank and Victoria

Logue, V. Collins Chew, and David Emblidge often sparked a new discovery in a local library or in a hidden spot along the trail.

We're grateful for the exacting technical eye of our Editor, Susannah Driver, whom readers of this volume can thank as they confidently find their way from place to place; for the skill and grace with which Marcy Ross, Editorial Assistant, kept the whole series coordinated; Peter Jensen and Kathy Orlando, of Open Space Management, for carefully drawing the corrected AT on our maps; thanks to Austin Sass and the employees of Maptech for their assistance in creating the trail profiles used in this book.

Maptech's TopoScout® CD-ROMs allowed us to illustrate the trail's topography with detailed accuracy. Thanks also to Indexer Letitia Mutter, who did a fine job; Carolyn Golojuch, for quick and accurate keyboarding; and Sheila McMillen, fact checker; and thanks to each photographer. Many thanks to series creator and Editor David Emblidge, ever dedicated to learning more about the AT, its history, and its community.

Finally, special thanks to our spouses, Lauren Clingan and Steve Hicks, and to other friends who drove us to the trailhead and enjoyed with us many miles of exploring the Appalachian Trail.

HOW TO USE THIS BOOK

USE THIS BOOK as you would the counsel of a wise friend. Absorb the information that seems noteworthy to you; take heed of opinionated statements; consider the logic behind suggested strategies for getting into, and through, the kind of hike you want. But remember that your own personal preferences for length of hike, amount of effort, and things to see along the way will be just as important as—or even more than—any information you may find in these pages. Walking and hiking in the forest and mountains are intensely personal activities. There are few rules to follow, and it's not a competitive

game with winners and losers. What works well for Hiker A will be a disappointment for Hiker B. Wallace Stevens gave us a poem called "Sixteen Ways of Looking at a Blackbird." This book should indicate that there are at least that many ways to complete and enjoy a hike on the AT.

How Hike Information Is Displayed Here

INFORMATION BLOCK: The hike's first page, a snapshot of the hike in the form of data and directions. Here you'll find road access information, elevation gain, distance to be walked, names of shelters, and so on. This first section gives an objective overview of the hike.

NARRATIVE: The full story—the hike you're likely to have on this section of the AT. Conditions vary widely depending on season and weather, depending on whether you're a robust 18-year-old, a tottering little kid, or a slow-but-steady octogenarian. Our description of the hike aims for a middle-range hiker, in good shape, with modestly ambitious goals but not with an eye on the stopwatch or the pedometer.

Throughout the hike's narrative we cite mileages at the major way points and landmarks. Occasionally we indicate the amount of time needed to go from one point to another. Generally, however, we stick to mileage as a reference point because each hiker's pace is different.

The narrative also pauses to describe rocks, plants, animals, vistas, and social history seen along the way . . . and then picks up the hike again with further directions toward its destination.

TRAIL PROFILE: A rendering of the trail's up-and-down travels over the landscape, suggesting graphically how easy or challenging sections may be. The profiles are based on USGS digital elevation maps and were created using Maptech TopoScout® CD-ROMs, developed by Maptech of Greenland, New Hampshire. The linear scale on the profiles does not match the scale

on the hike's topographic map (see below). Instead, the profile gives a cross-section view of the mountains and valleys with the trail running up and down as if on a straight line across the landscape. Trail profiles entail a certain degree of vertical exaggeration to make the rendering meaningful, and they do not show every hill or knob in the path.

TOPOGRAPHIC MAP: Based on USGS 1:100,000 scale maps, the hike topo map also draws on information provided on AT maps published by the Appalachian Trail Conservancy and its member trail clubs. Our scale is usually 1 inch to 1 mile—or as close to that as the page trim size and length of the hike will allow. These maps show actual elevations (read about contour lines on page 9), usually in feet. They also show the compass direction (north) and important waypoints along the trail. See the map legend on page 8. For most day hikes, the maps in this book will serve well. For extended backpacking in the wild backcountry or high mountains, we recommend using Appalachian Trail Conservancy or Appalachian Mountain Club maps.

Note: Some USGS maps have not been updated for several years and may not show recent trail relocations. Follow the dark green line of the AT on the maps in this book. You may see the old AT outlined in gray on the map. In some cases the old path is open and usable, but in many it's not. Check the narrative and consult local trail clubs before hiking on discontinued sections of the AT.

ITINERARY: A summary of the hike in table format, listing important waypoints noted in the narrative and shown on the topo map and/or the trail profile. Both the narrative and the itinerary describe the hike as either a south-to-north (most common) or north-to-south walk. Thus, in a S-N itinerary, directions to turn left (L) or right (R) mean "left when walking northward on the trail" and "right when walking northward on the trail," respectively. On a N-S itinerary, the reverse is true.

Bear in mind that "north" and "south" as used along the AT are not always literally true. The trail is said to run north from Georgia to Maine, but at any given point, even if you're walking "northward toward Maine," the footpath may veer to the west or east, or even southward to skirt a difficult mountain before resuming its generally northward direction. That's why in the narrative and itinerary we generally use "left" and "right" rather than compass directions. Inexperienced AT hikers simply have to orient themselves correctly at the start of the hike: Make sure you know whether you're following the trail to the north or south, and keep that in mind as you proceed. Then, "left" and "right" in the narrative and itinerary will be easy to follow. In any case, always carry a compass.

Note: In keeping with the tradition of showing north at the top of maps, we structure the itineraries with north always at the top of the table, south at the bottom. Thus, for a S-N hike, you will find the "Start" at the bottom (south) end of the itinerary, and you should read upward. "End" will be at the top (north) end of the table. We give mileage in both directions: the left-hand column goes S-N; the right-hand column goes N-S. Remember that *access trail* mileage must be added to miles walked on the AT itself. We total both mileages for you on the itinerary. Elevations are given in both feet and meters (feet elsewhere in this book). To construct our itineraries, we relied on walking the trail, taking careful notes, and then verifying by reference to other trail guides, especially the Appalachian Trail Conference and member club trail guides. Published trail guides, USGS maps, and ATC maps sometimes disagree by as much as a few tenths of a mile (distance) or a few feet (elevation).

SIDEBAR: In some hikes, special topics are discussed in a box set off from the narrative. The sidebars are listed in the table of contents.

Abbreviations
Abbreviations commonly used in this book:

AHS, American Hiking Society

AMC, Appalachian Mountain Club

ATC, Appalachian Trail Conservancy

BRPMP, Blue Ridge Parkway milepost

CCC, Civilian Conservation Corps
NBATC, Natural Bridge AT Club
Natl. Rec. Area, National Recreation Area
NF, National Forest
NHP, National Historical Park
NPS, National Park Service
OVT, Outing Club of Virginia Tech
PATC, Potomac Appalachian Trail Club
SDMP, Skyline Drive milepost
SNP, Shendoah National Park
SP, State Park
USFS, U.S. Forest Service

👫	Start or End of hike
℗	Trailhead parking
V	Viewpoint
▲	Camping
🏚	Lean-to (a.k.a. Shelter) (anything three-sided)
🏠	Cabin, Lodge, Hut (anything enclosed)
Ⓦ	Water (spring or other source)
⊤	Toilet (outhouse, privy, or better)
El.	Elevation
🍁	Natural History Site
🏛	Historic / Cultural Site
▬🔺▬	Appalachian Trail
▬ ▬ ▬ ▬	Appalachian Trail—before Start and after End of hike
▬▬▬	Appalachian Trail—planned relocation
• • • • • • •	Access Trail (to/from AT) or side (spur) trail

Geographic Organization

The hikes included in this volume follow the Appalachian Trail from south to north. Most of the hikes are described as south-to-north walks, but many are suitable to walking the opposite way, too. A few hikes are best done from north to south. Pay attention to the suggested direction. We have avoided some wicked climbs by bringing you down, rather than up, certain nasty hills.

Maps: Legends, Skills, Sources

SCALE—Unless otherwise noted, approximately 1 inch = 1 mile.

COMPASS DIRECTION AND DEVIATION— The scale bar shows the compass direction North. The north shown on the map is "true" or "grid" north, essentially a straight line to the north pole,

whereas the north you see on your compass is "magnetic" north, usually a few degrees different due to the earth's magnetic field. Along the AT, magnetic north deviates from true or grid north by several degrees west. The farther north one goes, the greater the deviation. At the North Carolina/Virginia state line the deviation is about 2.5° west; at the West Virginia/Maryland line it is about 9 – 10°.

CONTOUR INTERVAL—See "Contour Lines" below. Contour intervals on the USGS topographic maps used as the base for the hiking maps in this book are either 10 meters (33 ft.) or 20 meters (66 ft.) depending on the map (see "List of Maps" under "Useful Information").

Reading and planning your hikes with topographic maps can be fun and is certainly useful. Every hiking party should have at least one competent map reader. Often, if there are children aboard, they will be eager to follow the hike's progress on the topographic map. Here are a few pointers for beginning map readers.

CONTOUR LINES—All the hiking maps in this series of guides are based on official topographic maps which represent the three-dimensional shape of the land with contour lines (CLs). Typically, CLs are drawn at fixed intervals, for example, 20 meters, meaning that between each pair of lines in our example there is a rise or fall of 20 meters in the landscape.

In this example, the CLs are close together, suggesting a steep climb or descent:

In the next example, the CLs are farther apart, suggesting a gently sloping or nearly flat landscape:

LINEAR SCALE—To understand CLs fully, they must be related to the *linear scale* of the map. This relationship gives a sense of vertical rise or fall as it spreads out horizontally across the landscape. Thus, if 1 inch = 1 mile and if there are many CLs clustered in, say, a ¹/₂-inch section of trail, then it's safe to assume that this ¹/₂-mile section of the trail will be steep, going up or down depending on your direction.

MAP SOURCES—All maps in this series are derived from United States Geological Survey topographic maps. Each of our maps is a small slice of a USGS topo map. We have updated relevant AT information (some USGS maps are 10 or more years old; the AT has moved at several points). The original map scale of 1:100,000 is enlarged here generally to about 1:62,000 (around 1 inch = 1 mile) for readability. A 1:100,000-scale map is not practical to carry on the trail. USGS maps scaled at a more convenient 1:62,000 are easy to read as trail maps, but a day's hike may cut across several maps or use only a tiny portion of one large map, an unwieldy affair when hiking.

For short day hikes, we recommend using the maps in this book. For longer hikes, overnight trips, or serious backpacking, we advise using official AT maps from the Appalachian Trail Conservancy or supplementary maps from the Potomac Appalachian Trail Club (see below for information).

Bookstores and outdoor outfitters near the Appalachian Trail usually stock the USGS quadrangles (1:62,500) for the local area. USGS maps can also be ordered by telephone (see "Useful Information" and the Bibliography). If you do not know the USGS map number (see the "Useful Information" list for maps used in this book), be sure to indicate (a) the portion of the AT you want to hike by providing nearby cities, towns, rivers, or other landmarks and (b) the scale you prefer. Anything over 1 inch = 1 mile will be impractical for hiking.

The Appalachian Trail Conservancy publishes a set of color-shaded topographic hiking maps for almost the entire length of the trail (excluding the national parks through which the AT passes). The scale is generally 1:38,750. This translates to about $1^5/8$ inches = 1 mile. In other words, much more detail than on the USGS quadrangles and more than we can show in a book of this size. See your local bookseller or outdoor outfitter, or call the ATC (see "Useful Information"). A catalogue is available. For serious hikers and for any overnight or backcountry hiking on the Appalachian Trail, we strongly recommend these fine maps.

For the AT in Shenandoah National Park and northern Virginia/West Virginia, you'll want the fine maps published by the Potomac Appalachian Trail Club. PATC maps 9, 10, and 11 cover SNP, while their map 8 is the only available map of the AT trail system north of SNP to the Maryland line. PATC also publishes regional maps and hiking guides, many of which contain circuit hikes utilizing part of the AT. ATC maps 1 through 5 cover the southwest and central portions of the Virginia AT. The ATC and PATC maps are meticulously researched and frequently updated by trail volunteers, and proceeds from their sale go toward AT protection and maintenance. The scale is 1:62,500, or 1 inch = 1 mile; the contour interval is 100 feet. For a catalogue of maps from PATC, see "Joining Up," page 3.

Driving Time to the Trailhead

A factor frequently overlooked when planning a hike is the driving time required to reach the trailhead or to get back to civilization at day's end. When a substantial number of miles must be traveled from a major highway or town to get up into the mountains to the trailhead, we tell you in the information block. You must be sure to leave sufficient time to get to the starting point. Positioning two cars (finish and start) takes even longer.

Remember that many Appalachian Trail access roads are "secondary" at best. Some are decidedly unkind to low-chassis, two-wheel-drive cars. Some are impassable in wet weather (the entire spring mud season). Travel to the trailhead can be slow and dicey. Read our instructions carefully. Plan ahead.

Choosing Your Hike / Effort Required

In this book we rate hikes by three levels of "effort required": easy, moderate, and strenuous. Some hikes are a mix of easy, moderate, and strenuous sections.

If little kids or folks with disabilities might find a hike too rugged, we tell you. If there are difficult water crossings, perhaps varying seasonally, we say so.

But remember, our judgments are somewhat subjective.

Easy: gentle ups and downs, fairly smooth path, few obstacles

Moderate: elevation gain or loss of up to 1000 feet; narrower, rocky path; some obstacles (for example, brook crossings with no bridge)

Strenuous: elevation gain or loss of more than 1000 feet; steep ups and downs; difficult, challenging path; numerous obstacles; possibly unsuitable for young children or the infirm.

Blazing

A "blaze" (from the Old English *blœse,* meaning "torch") is a bright painted mark (about 6 inches x 2 inches) on a tree, post, or rock indicating the path of a hiking trail. The Appalachian Trail is blazed in white (rather easy to see even in fog, though tough to follow in brightly dappled sunlight), all the way from Georgia to Maine. It's the same in

each direction, south–north or north–south.

Side trails are often but not always blazed in a different color—generally blue, orange, or yellow. AT blazes are usually spaced 30 to 50 yards apart. In some sections overzealous trail maintainers have blazed at shorter intervals, while in other areas blazing has faded and may be hard to follow. If you haven't seen a white blaze for several minutes, backtrack and make sure you're still on the white-blazed AT, not an unmarked side trail or logging road.

Two blazes, one above the other, indicate a turn coming in the trail. If the upper blaze is positioned to the left, look for a left turn, and vice versa.

Estimating Hiking Times

An average adult hiker's pace is about 2.0 miles per hour on the flat. For every 1000-foot gain in elevation, add 30 minutes of time to your estimate. Thus an 8-mile hike up a 2500-foot mountain might take you 5 1/4 hours. This formula does not account for rests, mealtimes, or lollygagging to smell the flowers or talk to the bears. With a full backpack, little kids in tow, or slippery conditions, obviously you would add more time.

We recommend that you keep a record of your time and distance and the hiking conditions for a half dozen hikes, and then compare your averages to ours. You'll soon see whether our numbers match yours and if not, how much time you need to add or subtract from our estimates.

Day Hikes / Overnight Backpacking Hikes

The majority of the hikes in this book can be done as day hikes. Some day hikes can be conveniently strung together to make overnight backpacking trips of 2 or more days' duration. And some hikes are manageable only as overnight backpacking trips. The general rule: the more wilderness there is to traverse, the less likely it is that you can pop in and out for a day hike only. Read the information block carefully, and look at the hike south or north of the one you're considering to see whether a linkage is feasible.

Avoiding the Crowds

A great debate is raging: Is the AT now overused, too busy to be enjoyable, too tough on the land to be justifiable? Are we approaching, or are we already at, the point where reservations will have to be made for floor space in an AT shelter? (In fact, in some southern sections—Shenandoah National Park, for example—shelters are reserved for thru-hikers or other long-distance hikers only, not the casual weekender.) We don't mean to equivocate, but the answer seems to be yes and no. Collectively, the authors of this series have hiked thousands of AT miles over several decades. Far more often than not, we have had the trail essentially to ourselves, passing only a few people per

day. Inevitably, however, certain sites on the trail (beautifully located shelters, or summits with great views or symbolic significance, for example) attract crowds, especially on weekends, and most especially in midsummer or at fall foliage time. The southern section of the AT is busy with hundreds of would-be thruhikers in early spring. Don't expect to be alone on Hawksbill Mt. in April.

It does not require a graduate degree in engineering to figure out a plan to avoid these crowds or to avoid swelling them yourself. The best times to be alone on the trail are midweek. No offense to kids or parents (we love 'em all), but June, before the kids leave school, and September, after they're back in, are great times to find warm-weather solitude on the AT. If you can swing it, hiking during the week is the best way to capture solitude on the trail. Heading out on a Sunday can work equally well. We spent a Sunday evening at Gravel Springs Hut, only steps from the AT and only 500 yards from Skyline Drive, without seeing another soul.

If you cannot hike midweek and are headed for peaks or shelters likely to be overcrowded, start out early enough to permit you to move on to another site in daylight if your first target has already hung out the "No Vacancy" sign. When the shelter or official tent sites are full, accept the bad news and walk on. Even if you're planning to spend the night in a shelter, it's a good idea to take along a tent in case the shelter is fully occupied.

Circuit or Loop Hikes / Shuttle Services

Ideally you have a limousine with built-in hot tub and cold drinks awaiting you at the end of the trail. Short of that, you may have to improvise a way to get back to your starting point. Whenever it's convenient and sensible from a hiking viewpoint, we have suggested how to make the hike into a circuit or loop, bringing you back, on foot, to your car or pretty close to it. There are many hikes, however, especially those in wilderness areas, where this is simply not feasible.

It's usually best if you can work out a two-car team for your hike, with one car dropped at the finish line and another driven to the starting trailhead.

Out and back: Most of our hikes are described as linear—from A to B to C. Hikers with only one car available can make many fine hikes, however, by simply going out to a well-chosen point (the mountaintop, the pond) and then reversing direction to the starting point. The mileage indicators in the Itineraries will help you decide on a turn-around point. You may be pleasantly surprised to find that when walked in the opposite direction, the same section of trail yields a very different experience—especially if one direction is steeply up and the other sharply down.

Shuttles: In some areas, and through the auspices of some local hiking clubs, shuttle services are available. For example, the Green Mountain Club in Vermont provides to its members a list of shuttle drivers, although they are few in number and require early notice and modest fees. In this book, when we know there is a reliable shuttle service that is useful on a particular hike, we tell you. If we don't make a shuttle suggestion, it's often worth asking your motel or bed-and-breakfast keeper, or calling the local Chamber of Commerce or even the local taxi company. A hunting-lodge manager helped us one time at a good price. Ask around, make new friends.

Some hikers like to position a bicycle (locked) at the end of a hike so they can ride back to their car at the starting point.

If your hiking group consists of, say, four or more people and two cars, you might swap extra car keys at the beginning of the day and send people, a car, and a key for the other car to each end of the trail. You all meet somewhere in the middle of the hike, trade stories, and perhaps share lunch. And each group finds a car waiting at day's end. Depending on roads and distances to trailheads, this system can shave a good deal of time off the car travel at the start and end of your hiking day. This is especially helpful for very long day hikes and even more so in early spring or late fall when days are short. Besides, meeting friends deep in the forest or on a mountaintop is great fun.

Early Exit Options

Our hikes range from 5 to 15 miles per day. When road crossings and parking facilities permit, we indicate points where you could leave the AT before finishing the entire hike. Sometimes such exits are convenient and safe; sometimes they should be used only for emergencies. Heed our advice. If we do not say good parking is available, don't assume there's a parking lot.

The Early Exit Options can often be used to make a loop hike out of an otherwise longish linear hike. To see your options clearly, study a good local road map.

Camping

Camping is generally permitted anywhere in SNP and George Washington and Jefferson national forests, except in areas designated for no camping.

Backcountry permits are required in SNP. They are free of charge (however, a $1 donation is appreciated) and are available at park road entrances, at self-registration stations near trail entrances to the park, and from SNP headquarters, Rte. 4, Box 348, Luray, VA 22835. Campfires are permitted in the national forests, but prohibited in SNP except in public campgrounds and other designated areas.

There are three zone designations for backcountry camping in SNP:

Dispersed campsites are in areas that receive light or moderate use, may be impromptu, are usually away from the trail, and camping must not occur on a pre-existing campsite. In fact, there should be no trace of previous campers, nor of your party once you've departed. Your campsite must be more than 0.5 mile from a paved park road or a park facility, except a shelter, and must be at least 50 yards from any trail, park boundary, shelter, or camping prohibition sign and 100 yards from a previous campsite. In *established sites,* which receive moderate camping and heavy day use, tenting is restricted (in an attempt to minimize the impact on the environment) to existing, informal campsites established through repeated use. No Trace camping ethics still apply, as do the rules of distance described above. In *designated campsites,* tents are permitted only at specific sites, each marked by a post, and all cooking and camping activities must take place within 10 yards of the post. Public campgrounds, many of which have amenities such as showers or supplies, are pointed out in the hike narratives. For these facilities, reservations are often required and fees are charged. Complete backcountry camping regulations and permits are available from the SNP information office (703- 999-2266).

Camp only in designated camping areas unless you know for sure that free-for-all camping is permitted. In most sections of the AT the land is too heavily used to permit improvisatory camping. We indicate official campsites.

Shelters and Cabins

The names may vary but the accommodations are much the same: Along the AT, about every 10 to 15 miles, you'll find three-sided lean-tos with minimalist interior decorating. Bunk beds or no beds at all, just floor space. Possibly a picnic table, a fire ring, an outhouse, a water source nearby. Many of these shelters have well-maintained facilities, charming names, and equally charming views. Some you wouldn't let your dog sleep in. We tell you which ones we like. Shelters usually have a few tent sites surrounding them.

For shelters in the national forests and north of SNP, the "reservations policy" is first come, first served, with a 3-night limit. In SNP, the shelters, called "huts," are for those out for at least 2 nights of backcountry travel and for AT thru-hikers (usually traveling through SNP mid-May to mid-June). Using the honor system, hikers deposit a nominal fee into a pipe safe at the hut. Only 1 night is permitted in an SNP hut. During the work week and the off-peak season, it is possible to find room at most huts even when you're out only for a night. However, be prepared to move on if it is full or needed by long-distance travelers, who, most often, do not carry tents.

PATC operates and maintains six primitive cabins in SNP. Because they are equipped with cooking and eating utensils, axes, and saws, cabins offer a less complicated way to camp. Most have fireplaces and outdoor cooking pits; a few even have front porches. Hikers supply their own food and sleeping bags and gather their own firewood. Each cabin also has a nearby water supply. A backcountry permit is not required but reservations are and a fee is charged. To rent, call 703-242-0315.

Trail Registers

At shelters and occasionally at trail junctions, you'll find notebooks where you can, and should, write a few words for posterity and for practicality's sake. Logging in your arrival and departure time will help searchers find you if, unluckily, you get lost or hurt on the trail. But the real fun of the trail registers is adding your own thoughts to the collective wisdom and tomfoolery other hikers have already scribbled in the notebooks. The registers make great reading. A whole new literary genre! Go ahead, wax poetic or philosophical. Surely there's at least one haiku in you to express your joy at the view from the mountaintop or the first time you shook hands with a moose.

Trail registers also sometimes provide helpful warnings about trail conditions (recent mud slides or bridge washouts, for example). If the weather has been wild of late, read back a few days in the register to see what previous hikers may have said about what lies ahead of you.

WHILE IT'S TRUE that we go to the woods and the mountains to get away from the trappings of civilization, few of us really want to put our lives in jeopardy. Here are some recommendations every adult hiker (and Boy or Girl Scout–age youngster) should follow.

When the subject is equipment, we suggest you visit your outdoor outfitter to ask for advice or that you read back issues of *Backpacker* magazine, in print or on-line (see "Useful Information"). *Backpacker's* annual "gear guide" sorts through hundreds of choices and makes useful recommendations. For the truly hiking/camping gizmo-obsessed, there are on-line chat rooms (again, see *Backpacker*) where you and other similarly gadget-crazed friends can compare notes.

Boots / Shoes

Nothing is more important to a hiker than the condition of his or her feet. From this axiom derives an important rule: Wear the right boots or shoes for hiking, or stay home. Some of the easier sections of the AT can be hiked in firm running shoes or high-top basketball sneakers, but most sections require a tougher, waterproof or water-resistant boot providing nonslip soles, toe protection, and firm ankle support. Shop carefully. Go to an outdoor outfitter rather than a regular shoe store. Try

on several pairs of boots, with the actual socks you intend to wear (two pair: one thin, one thick). If you buy boots by mail, trace your foot size with those socks on your feet. Save your pennies and buy the best you can afford. Gore-Tex or one of its waterproofing clones is worth the money. Check the hiking magazines' annual gear reviews (in print or on-line) for ratings of comfort, weight, durability, and price. Think of the purchase as a multiyear investment. Shop long before the hiking season starts, and wear your boots for a good 10 to 20 miles of everyday walking before hitting the trail. Your feet will thank you.

Caveat for kids: The better discount stores carry boot brands that are quite sufficient for a season of hiking by young people whose feet are still growing. Parents, buy your own boots first and then use your shopper's savvy to find inexpensive boots for the kids.

Clothing

Bring sufficient clothes, appropriate for rain and cold. Layers work best. Gore-Tex and other waterproof fabrics are miraculous, but a $3 emergency poncho will do in a pinch. Think about what you would need to get through a rainy night, even if you're just out for a short, sunny day hike.

A visored hat: The top of your head is the point of major heat loss, whether you're bald or not. Inexpensive Gore-Tex hats can be found. Cruise the catalogues.

Sunglasses, in a protective case. Rhinestone decorative motif not required.

Cotton socks, sweatshirts, and T-shirts: avoid them. Blue jeans (essentially cotton): avoid them. Cotton is comfortable until it gets wet (from rain or perspiration). Then it's your enemy. It dries slowly and does not wick away perspiration. There are extraordinary synthetic fabrics nowadays for shirts, underwear, and long johns that will keep you warm or cool and will let the moisture leave your body. Visit your outdoor outfitter for a wardrobe consultation. Money well spent.

Wool is a miracle fabric from nature. Especially good for socks and gloves. Polartec is a miracle fabric from the high-tech world (recycled plastic bottles!). Jackets and pullovers in these miracle fabrics are what you want.

Food

Hiking eats up calories. Cold weather demands body heat, which demands calories. Diet at home. Eat high-energy foods on the trail. Carbohydrates are best. Sweets are less helpful than you might think, though a chocolate or energy bar to help you up the hill is sometimes right. It's better to eat several smaller meals en route than to gorge on a big one, unless you plan for a siesta. Digestion itself takes considerable energy. You'll

find it hard to climb and digest at the same time. The hiker's fallback snack plan: (1) "Gorp," a mix of nuts, granola, chocolate chips, dried fruit, and whatever else you like. Mix it yourself at home—much cheaper than the ready-made variety at the store. (2) Peanut butter on anything. (3) Fruit. Heavy to carry but oh so refreshing. The sugar in fruit is fructose, high in energy but it won't put you to sleep.

And remember the miracle food for hikers, the humble banana. Or dried banana chips (crunch them or add water). High in potassium, bananas are your muscles' best friends because the potassium minimizes aches and cramps.

Planning menus and packing food for extended backpacking trips is a subject beyond the scope of this book. Several camping cookbooks are available, and *Backpacker* frequently runs how-to articles worth reading. Search their Web site for articles you can download. Advice: Whatever you plan to cook on the trail, try it out first, on the backpacking stove, at home. Make a list of cooking gear and condiments needed, and if the list looks long, simplify the menu unless you have willing friends along who will carry a gourmet's kitchen for you. Over time you'll find camp food tricks and tastes to add to your repertoire, such as bagging breakfast granola with powdered milk in self-seal bags (just add water and stir), or choosing tough-skinned veggies like carrots, celery, or snow peas that can be eaten cooked or raw and won't turn to mush in your pack. The ever popular macaroni and cheese (available nowadays in many fancy permutations from Lipton, Kraft, et al.) can be dressed up in countless lightweight, quick-cook ways. The camper's most important kitchen tool is imagination.

Whatever you plan to eat or cook on the trail, be prepared to clean up spotlessly. Leave no mess—indeed, no trace.

Food Storage

You're not the only hungry critter in the woods. Everyone from the bears to the squirrels and mice would like to breakfast on your granola and snack on your Oreos. Never keep food in your tent overnight. It's an invitation for unwanted company in the dark. Use a drawstring food sack, wrapped in a plastic garbage bag, which you hang from a sturdy branch on a nearby tree, keeping the sack several feet out on the branch, about 10 feet off the ground and several feet below the branch. Obviously this means you must carry about 50 feet of lightweight cord (useful in emergencies too).

Don't store your food in your backpack, either, indoors or out. Those cute little chipmunks and their bigger friends will eat a hole right through that expensive high-tech fabric.

Water

Keep drinking a little at a time all day while you hike. Dehydration is the major cause of hiker fatigue. Double or triple your normal daily intake of water.

Sadly, most of the water flowing in streams the AT crosses is polluted to one degree or another, sometimes by industry or agriculture, often by wild animals such as beavers upstream. The most common problem is a nasty protozoan known as giardia from which we get stomach cramps, fever, and the runs. Trust us: you don't want it. The rule is, unless an official sign says the water has been tested and is pure, assume the water must be treated with either iodine tablets or a water filter. Iodine is cheap and lightweight but slow, and it leaves a somewhat unpleasant taste in the treated water (Potable Aqua is an iodine treatment that minimizes the bad taste). Hiker water filters are faster-acting but more cumbersome. They are useful elsewhere too—on boats, at freshwater beaches, and so forth. A good investment. Look for one that screens out most bacteria, is lightweight, and pumps quickly. The most convenient water bottles are (a) wide-mouth, facilitating refill and filter attachment, and (b) equipped with a drinking tube or nipple, eliminating the need to open the bottle itself.

When Nature Calls

Every hiker—day only or overnight backpacker—must come prepared to deal appropriately with disposal of human waste in the woods. At most shelters and many campsites along the AT there are outhouses. Please help to keep them clean. Gentlemen especially are encouraged to urinate in the woods, a few hundred feet off the trail. Urine in the outhouse pit adds to the bad aroma.

Believe it or not, there's an entire book on the subject of defecating in the woods (see the Bibliography). Good reading on a slow day in camp, perhaps. This much you must know to do: Bring biodegradable white single-ply toilet paper in a plastic bag. Bring a little shovel (a plastic garden trowel will do). Bring a strong self-seal plastic bag to carry out used toilet paper, tampons, etc. If the woods is your toilet, get at least 100 feet off the trail and at least 200 feet away from any water. Dig a hole at least 8 inches deep, and cover your waste firmly. A squat is the time-tested position.

Weather

Basic precautions include a careful review of weather forecasts and typical conditions in the area you're hiking—before you pack your pack or leave home. See "Useful Information" for a weather Web site. If you go adventuring outdoors frequently, you'll enjoy and benefit from a lightweight battery-operated weather radio that provides access to several NOAA (National Oceanic and Atmospheric Administration) channels, offering detailed forecasts 24 hours a day, with special recreational forecasts emphasizing conditions at elevations of 3000 feet and above.

Learn to forecast weather yourself by reading the clouds (particularly cumulous clouds with towering thunderheads) and by noticing changes in animal and plant behavior that may telegraph the advent of a storm. Make it a habit to do a 360-degree sky check every hour or so to see what's coming and from which direction. If trouble is heading your way, plan ahead for emergency shelter. Get off the mountaintop or exposed ridge, where high winds and lightning are most likely to hit. Don't sit under a big rotting tree with branches waiting to clunk you on the head. When lightning is likely, avoid all metal objects (fire towers, tent poles, pack frames, etc.). Do find a dry, wind-protected spot (the downwind side of overhanging boulders is good), and lay a plan to make it your home for a few hours.

Wet weather often brings cool or cold temperatures. Wet clothing or a wet sleeping bag can exacerbate your sense of chill. Hypothermia can set in quickly, especially if you're fatigued or anxious. Even day hikers should carry extra clothing and something, if only a big plastic garbage bag, to cover themselves and their pack. Overnight backpackers, anywhere on the AT, must be ready for the worst. Keep rainwear light and simple so you won't resent carrying it on a sunny day.

First Aid

Outfitters such as Campmor and REI (excellent catalogues) offer first-aid kits for everyone from the day hiker to the Mt. Everest climber. Buy from them or patch together your own kit, based on the contents listed in the catalogues. A waterproof container is a must. Be prepared for cuts, scrapes, burns, blisters, sprains, headache. Sunscreen if exposure is likely. A very lightweight first-aid manual is not a bad idea either.

One essential is moleskin, a skin-covering adhesive, thicker than a Band-aid but soft enough to wrap around an unhappy toe. Many a hike has been ruined by blisters. At the first sign (heat, burning, tingling feelings on toes or heels), slap on the moleskin and leave it there until you're back home. Insurance against blisters is cheap: two pairs of (dry!) socks. And break in your new hiking boots *thoroughly* before you hit the trail.

Further insurance: bring a few feet of dental floss. If your teeth don't use it, a sewing job might.

Include a little but loud whistle in your first-aid kit. You might need to call for help. (Three successive whistles signal trouble.)

If first aid is foreign to you, by all means take a course, with CPR (artificial respiration) training, from the local Red Cross. For parents hiking with kids, this is a must. For kids, join the Scouts and earn that First Aid merit badge.

Hiking Alone
There are real pleasures to be had from hiking alone. Generally, however, it's not recommended. Whether you hike alone or in a group, take pains to let someone know your plans (route, estimated times of departure and arrival, what to do if you don't check back in). Often a hiker who wants to

walk alone can have that pleasure, letting fellow hikers know that by day's end he or she will rejoin the group.

Hiking in Groups
Keep your group size down to fewer than ten people. Even that many is stretching what the trailside facilities can bear. Large groups tend to overwhelm smaller ones, yet everyone has the same rights to enjoy the space and the quiet on the trail. Don't take a busload of kids on the trail. Find volunteers who will lead sections of a group with at least a mile or 30 minutes between them.

Women Hikers
Statistically, the Appalachian Trail is one of the safest places a woman (or a man) can be in the United States. But there have been some problems with harrassment, and there have been some cases of violence, even a few tragic murders. Play it safe. Don't hike alone. Be sensible—inappropriate clothing may attract the wrong kind of attention. Avoid the rowdy set sometimes found at shelters near road crossings or towns. If you arrive at a shelter and find suspicious people there, move on.

Taking Children on the Trail
By all means, do take the kids. The environment of the Appalachian Trail and the activities of climbing, exploring, and camping will engage the imagination and channel the energies of almost every kid, including those whose regular turf is the city street.

Adult hikers just need to remember that a few things are different about kid hikers. Kids' attention spans are (usually) shorter than grown-ups'. Plan to break your hike into smaller units with something special to do in each part—birds here, lunch there, rock collecting next, photography from the mountaintop, writing messages in the trail registers. Give a kid a short-term achievable project linked to today's hike (such as collecting as many different-shaped leaves as you can from the ground beneath the trees), and you'll probably have a happy, satisfied kid hiker by evening.

Most kids love hiking and camping gear. Get them involved in planning, shopping, packing for, and executing the hike, especially the camping portion. Let them make breakfast. Teach them to set up the tent; then get out of the way. Take pictures and make a family hiking photo album: it's a memory bank for years to come. Put a map on your children's wall at home and mark the trails they have hiked, the peaks they have climbed. A sense of accomplishment is priceless.

Be realistic, too, about what kids can endure on the hiking trail. Their pain (and boredom) thresholds are lower than most adults'. Don't let blisters happen to kids; check their feet at lunchtime. Bring a book to read in case of rain, or a miniature chess set if they're old enough to play. Anticipate your own behavior in an emergency situation. If you panic, the kids will. If you're calm, know where to go for help, and know how to keep dry and warm, most kids will rise to the occasion and come home strengthened by the adventure.

Parking

Do not leave a sign on your car saying where you're going or when you'll return. Try not to leave anything (visible) in your car that might interest burglars. Avoid camping at shelters located very close to easily accessible parking lots. Respect the AT's immediate neighbors by not parking on their private property.

PACKING YOUR PACK

Backpacks and Day Packs

It's not quite a science but it's certainly an art. An incorrectly loaded backpack (badly packed on the inside or poorly fitted or adjusted to your torso and shoulders) can wreck even a sunny day on the world's loveliest trail. Some tips: Fanny packs, worn at hip level, are fine for short day hikes as long as you can carry sufficient water, food, clothing, first aid, and map and compass. Less than that and the pack is too small.

Day packs carry proportionately more but without the frame that supports a backpacking pack. For both day packs and true backpacks, similar packing rules apply. Start at the outdoor outfitter. Have a knowledgeable salesperson fit the pack (with realistic dummy weights inside) to your specific torso. Walk around, bend over, squat, and be sure you're comfortable and stable.

At home, make a packing list with items categorized carefully (food, kitchen, first aid, clothes, stove and fuel, etc.). Jettison anything unnecessary. Roll your clothes. Pack one thing inside another (the Chinese box method). Then use the following scheme for stuffing the pack.

Keep weight distributed equally on the horizontal plane, but on the vertical, pack the lightweight items (such as sleeping bag) down low and the heavyweight items (food, water, tent) up high. Keep the heavier items close to your body. But be sure to pad any sharp-edged items so as not to poke you or to rip the pack fabric. Use the pack's outside pockets for a water bottle, fuel bottles, and smelly garbage.

Last, buy a rainproof pack cover or make one from a heavy-duty plastic garbage bag. Your clothing and sleeping bag will be glad you did.

Flashlight

Even a day hiker ought to carry a lightweight flashlight, just in case. In winter, early spring, and fall, daylight can disappear quickly, especially if the weather turns bad or you lose time by being temporarily lost. A slim flashlight that's portable in an elastic headband is a good investment.

Check the batteries before leaving home. Bring an extra bulb.

Matches

Even if you do not intend to cook or camp out and have a campfire, bring a supply of waterproof matches or a cigarette lighter. If you're forced to overnight in the woods, a fire may be good company indeed.

Jackknife

A multipurpose pocketknife will do. It needn't have a built-in chain saw or an eyebrow pencil, but a can opener, a Phillips screwdriver, and a tweezers are handy.

Weapons

We strongly discourage hikers from carrying any kind of weapon.

Cellular Phones

People have been hiking safely and contentedly in the woods for several thousand years without the aid or comfort of cellular phones. This is still possible. Many people come to the trail to get away from the electronic web in which we all are increasingly caught up. Here's a way to win friends on the trail: Keep your cell phone, if you bring one, out of sight, beyond earshot, and out of mind for everyone else. Don't use it except for emergencies, and do use it only when you're far away from other hikers. Domino's Pizza does not deliver to most AT shelters anyway. So why even call them?

Map and Compass

Don't go hiking without a map and compass and the skills to use them. In the fog, in the dark, in a storm, even familiar territory can seem like a directionless wilderness. Many hiking clubs offer map and compass (a.k.a. "orienteering") workshops. Map skills are fun to develop and highly useful. Many of the best natural history observations described in this book depend on your ability to locate a spot on the map and to orient yourself once you're there.

At the very least, be sure everyone in your party knows the compass direction of your intended hike, the cars' locations on the map, and the most likely way toward help in an emergency. *Backpacker* has run articles on map and compass skills (check the index on their Web site). The venerable *Boy Scout Handbook* has a good chapter on these skills. Or see Karen Berger's *Hiking & Backpacking: A Complete Guide.*

Being Lost and Getting Found

If you have studied your map before starting the hike, and if you faithfully follow the AT's white blazes or the access trails' blue (or red or yellow) blazes, the chances of getting lost are just about zero. With a map and compass in hand, there's no good excuse for being lost while you're on the AT itself. Your group should have a leader and a backup leader, and both

should know the route. Because hikers sometimes get separated on the trail, everyone should know the direction of the hike, the major landmarks to be passed, the estimated timetable, and how to use the sun and the clock to keep themselves oriented.

But mistakes do happen. Inattention and inadequate planning are the enemies. Sometimes nature conspires against us. Fog (or snow) may obscure the blazes or the cairns above treeline. Autumn leaves or a snowfall may obliterate the well-worn trail that otherwise would guide your eyes as clearly as the blazes themselves.

If you are lost, the first thing to do is to decide that you will not panic. You probably have not been off the trail for long. Stay where you are and think. Keep your group together. Study the map and note the last landmark you're sure you passed. Get reoriented with the map and compass, and try to go in a straight line back toward the trail. Do not wander. Be especially observant of details until you regain the trail.

If all else fails, let gravity and falling water help you out. Except in the deepest wilderness of Maine or the Smoky Mts., at most places along the AT streams flow eventually to brooks, then to rivers, and where there's a river there will soon enough be a house or even a village. If you have to bushwhack to get out of the woods, and if you're really not sure where you are on the map, follow the water downstream. Patience and a plan will get you out.

Common Sense / Sense of Humor

Taking care of yourself successfully in the woods and on the mountains is not rocket science. It starts with preparedness (physical and mental), appropriate equipment, sufficient food and water. It continues with a realistic plan, guided by a map and compass, a guidebook, a weather report, and a watch. It gets better if you and your companions resolve ahead of time to work together as a team, respecting each other's varying needs, strengths, and talents. And it goes best of all if you pack that one priceless essential hiker's tool: a ready sense of humor.

APPALACHIAN TRAIL HISTORY

AT LEGEND HAS IT that the 2150-mile footpath from Georgia to Maine is an ancient Native American walkway. Not so. In fact, the AT, as a concept, leapt from the imagination of one federal government civil servant who in 1921 had already recognized that Americans were too citified for their own good and needed more nearby, convenient opportunities for outdoor recreation.

In 1921, Harvard-educated forester and self-styled philosopher Benton MacKaye, of Shirley, Massachusetts, published an article ("An Appalachian Trail, A Project in Regional Planning") in the *Journal of the American Institute of Architects*. His was a revolutionary idea: a linear park, extending from Georgia to Maine. The concept germinated in a hotbed of idealistic left-wing social thinking that called into question many of the assumed values of the capitalist workaday world. Look a little more deeply into MacKaye's thinking and the roots lead directly to the 19th-century romantics and Transcendentalists, Thoreau and Emerson. MacKaye had read his John Muir, too.

A whirlwind of self-promoting public relations energy, MacKaye set the ball rolling to develop the AT. Thousands of volunteers and many legislators helped make it a reality. Two other key players were Judge Arthur Perkins of Hartford, Connecticut, who helped found the Appalachian Trail Conference in 1925, and his successor as president of the Conference (1931–1952), Myron Avery, of Maine and Washington, D.C. By 1937, with major assistance from Civilian Conservation Corps workers under President Roosevelt's New Deal Works Progress Administration, the complete trail was essentially in place, though by today's standards much of it was unblazed.

Thru-hikers are an admirable but increasingly common breed these days. Yet it wasn't until 1948 that anyone walked the entire trail in one season. The first thru-hiker was Earl Shaffer. The first woman to thru-hike in one season was Emma "Grandma" Gatewood, in 1955. By the mid-1990s the National Park Service was estimating that between 3 and 4 million people per year used the trail. In its first 75 years, from MacKaye's brainstorm to today, the AT has gone from a concept about escaping urban crowding to the point where crowding on the trail itself is a big issue.

In 1968, Congress put the AT under the authority of the National Park Service by passing the National Trails System Act. Overall, the story of the AT is a sweet tale of success. Occasionally there has been a sour note when the government's right of eminent domain has been used to take land required to create a 1000-foot-wide corridor of protection for the trail. By 1995 fewer than 44 miles of the trail remained unprotected by the Park Service corridor. In 1998 funding for the final miles became imminent. In the 1990s, environmental impact concerns (wear and tear, sustainability) and hiker management issues (overuse, low-impact camping and hiking, safety) fill the pages of AT magazines and spark many a late-night campfire conversation. While the educational and environmental protection efforts of the Appalachian Trail Conference (now Conservancy), the Appalachian Mountain Club, and all the regional hiking clubs improve yearly, adding strength to an admirable history, the erosion of financial support from Congress in a budget balancing era threatens to undermine many good efforts at a moment when user demands are growing exponentially. It is a time of fulfillment and challenge for all who use and manage the Appalachian Trail.

Note: A more detailed history of the AT can be found in any of the Appalachian Trail Conservancy's hiking guides. *The Appalachian Trail Reader,* edited by David Emblidge, contains a diverse collection of writings about the AT.

Appalachian Trail History in Virginia and West Virginia

AT founder Benton MacKaye's vision for the trail was that it be close enough to population centers to be a viable weekend escape. It was just after development of the AT began that the search for a national park site in the area started. By the time the National Park Service began development of the SNP and the parkway atop it, Skyline Drive, the AT was in place. Many hikers were outraged, believing that the road would obliterate the trail experience, while others saw in the road an opportunity to make the AT accessible to more people. Today, with some 5 million people living within an hour's drive of the AT in SNP, the trail draws quite a crowd. It also enjoys a strong, passionate constituency of hikers. With the trail under continuous pressure from growing use and encroaching suburbs, retaining the sense of wilderness and solitude is the challenge of AT proponents.

The southern stretches of the trail through George Washington and Jefferson national forests point to nature's reclamation of the landscape from people. Like the northern Blue Ridge, the forests in southern Virginia were once largely cleared of trees or extensively mined. Today, to the casual observer, there are few traces of the extractive industries that operated there. Like the Adirondacks to the north, and many other forested areas in the mid-Atlantic states, these forests, while still shadows of themselves in pre-Columbian days, are much healthier and more removed from the pressures of civilization than they were only a generation ago.

Those actively involved in caring for the trail know well that the history of the AT is a history of the clubs that maintain the trail. We owe their existence to Myron Avery. As a founder the Potomac Appalachian Trail Club and initiator of AT trail building in Virginia in 1927, Avery was The Organization Man. He recruited hundreds to help build the trail. Later, as chair of the Appalachian Trail Conference, he encouraged the formation of AT-based clubs from Georgia to Maine. In Virginia and West Virginia, every contemporary hiker benefits from the labor of these clubs. Although not all have been around since Avery's days, they are all a part of the Avery AT legacy: Mt. Rogers AT Club, Piedmont AT Hikers, the Outing Club of Virginia Tech, Roanoke AT Club, Natural Bridge AT Club, Tidewater AT Club (whose members must travel nearly 200 miles to maintain their trail section), and PATC. Volunteers and members are welcome and needed—even club dues help take care of the trail.

Lost Mt. and Whitetop Laurel Creek

Map: ATC Va. #4, Southwest Virginia

Route: From VA 859 over Straight Mt. along Whitetop Laurel Creek to Feather-camp Branch at US 58

Recommended direction: N to S

Distance: 9.0 mi.

Elevation +/-: 3500 to 2200 ft.

Effort: Moderate

Day hike: Yes

Overnight backpacking hike: Yes

Duration: 5 to 6 hr.

Early exit options: At 2.9 mi., Bear Tree Gap-Shaw Gap Trail; at 4.1 mi., logging road

Natural history features: Whitetop Laurel Creek Gorge; Bear Tree Gap; Straight Mt.

Social history features: Creek Junction railroad depot; Luther Hassinger Memorial Bridge

Other features: Virginia Creeper Trail; Bear Tree Day Use Area

Trailhead access: *Start:* From Damascus, go 14.6 mi. E on US 58, then S on VA 859 1.0 mi. to trailhead. Limited overnight roadside parking is available near the AT crossing. *End:* From Damascus, go 5.6 mi. E on VA 58 to trailhead parking (overnight permitted) for 6 cars on R, 200 yd. W of AT.

Camping: Saunders Shelter and campsites; permitted along trail

T his hike is a day trekker's dream. The trail visits the wild Whitetop Laurel Creek Gorge, crosses the creek on the magnificent Hassinger railroad bridge, opens to the panoramic views from Straight Mt., then meanders alongside a mountain stream just above the Virginia Creeper National Recreation Trail. Following the abandoned Norfolk and Western Railroad bed, the Virginia Creeper is designed to accommodate horses and bicycles as well as foot travel.

After the hike, there are pizza, sweets, and ample dining opportuni-ties in Damascus, known as the friendliest town on the Appalachian Trail. The trail actually travels through the heart of town, allowing ambitious hikers to step an additional 5.6 mi. to complete this hike at a favored eatery. From there, it's another 3.3 mi. to the Tennessee state line. These two legs, totaling 8.9 mi., are traveled mostly by AT long-distance hikers and are not covered here.

Damascus is a town that understands its assets. Hikers are welcomed with open arms, particularly during the annual Appalachian Trail Days, which celebrate the arrival of several hundred thru-hikers each May. The festival may not be the best time to find solitude on the AT, but it is a rare opportunity to witness and join the antics of a subculture that is to hiking what beatniks were to the 1950s. There are several inns and bed and breakfasts in the area that cater to hikers, and one could spend weeks in the area without hiking the same trail. A call to the friendly staff at Appalachian Outfitters on Laurel Avenue in Damascus will provide a line on Trail Days information and any special equipment needs for a trip along the AT here.

The hike begins at the VA 859 trailhead, easily visible from the road, and heading south descends Lost Mt., then quickly finds Whitetop Laurel Creek emerging on the right. The steep descent is just enough to warm up hiking legs when, just after the AT merges with the Virginia Creeper Trail (0.6 mi.), suddenly there is good reason to stop and marvel at both nature and humanity where the 500-ft. Luther Hassinger Memorial Bridge crosses the extraordinary Whitetop Laurel Creek at 0.7 mi.

Ironically, in the early 1900s, a timber company owned by the bridge's namesake cleared the area of nearly every twig, and to haul this bounty built the railroad and the bridge to carry it. That's ancient history now, with the bridge and the former Creek Junction station, at 1.2 mi., the only remnants that nature has yet to reclaim. Decked for foot travel and lined with handrails that provide emotional support as well as physical safety, Hassinger's bridge, like the millponds scattered about the east-

Caboose information booth, Jefferson National Forest, Damascus

Trail Days in Damascus

With such renowned spots along Virginia's Appalachian Trail as McAffee Knob and Marys Rock, it might seem odd that one of the most talked-about rest stops in the state is the town of Damascus. To many hikers, especially the legions who have attempted a thru-hike of the entire trail, the AT is as much a social experience as a journey through the natural world. The highlight of the AT social season, without doubt, are the Appalachian Trail Days held each May in Damascus.

Begun in 1987 by hiker-author Dan "Wingfoot" Bruce and organized since by the town, Trail Days (a.k.a. Trail Daze) has all the ingredients of a classic small town fair—a festival queen, hot dogs, a talent show, as well as antics you might expect from a fraternity party. On the Saturday, the backpackers' parade, in which an army of thru-hikers follow the AT white blazes right down Main Street, brings to life the connection between the town and the trail. The festival doubles the town population to about 2400, and is for merchants there a kind of Christmas in May.

You don't have to be a thru-hiker to be welcome in Damascus. Town boosters tout the hamlet as the "friendliest town on the trail," and many hikers would agree. With all due respect to Damascus, however, heavy helpings of southern hospitality are served up by the other trail towns in Virginia, so that casual day hikers anywhere can enjoy small-town charm along the AT.

ern hardwood forests, illustrates the odd role resource extraction has played in contemporary conservation efforts. Built to take from nature, they now enhance our enjoyment of it.

Just across the bridge, the trail crosses VA 728 and roughly follows it until the road ends at Creek Junction. Leaving the creek and the Virginia Creeper, the AT begins a rocky ascent of Straight Mt. toward Bear Tree Gap, amid bleeding-hearts in May and nodding wild onions in summer. Following a series of old logging roads and railroad grades (other Hassinger legacies now enjoyed by hikers), the trail finds open woods of fir and white pine as it continues climbing, more gradually now. The trail rises to level ground at a small pond, at 2.8 mi. This trailside pond is a popular spot for backpackers to take a break and a dip. But, according to *The Thru-Hiker's Handbook*, swimmers should keep an eye open for snakes near the dam. The spring that feeds the pond is unprotected but its water is potable after treatment. Tent sites are nearby.

Just beyond the pond, the purple-blazed Bear Tree Gap-Shaw Gap Trail provides an early exit, leading 0.3 mi. to US 58. Parking is available 0.2 mi. west on US 58 at the Beartree Day Use Area. The purple blazes then follow USFS 837 for 0.7 mi. before breaking north at Beartree Group Camp, with Beartree Family Campground 1.5 miles further northeast on USFS 837. The Beartree Day Use Area offers canoe rentals on the lake, equestrian trails, picnicking, and shower facilities. The family campground has both tenting and camper sites, for extended stays in the Mt. Rogers region. The Bear Tree Gap-Shaw Gap Trail also leads 3.0 mi. from the AT to Iron Mt. Trail, a former route of the AT and the keystone of a dozen or more circuit hikes through the region.

Just beyond Bear Tree Gap, the world seems to open up all around as the trail follows the Straight Mt. ridge above Straight Branch to the north and Whitetop Laurel Creek to the south. Looking back, Mt. Rogers, the highest peak in Virginia, looms tall 9 mi. east. To the north, the cliffs of Iron Mt. seem just out of arm's reach. The cliffs along the 30-mi. ridge are the results of the erosion of soft, sandy soils that once formed the southeast fold of Iron Mt. The erosion-resistant crest, the cliffs, and the northwest slope of quartzite are the result of folding that took place beneath the earth's surface as the Iron Mt. fault drifted north to form the valley below. Beartree Lake, visible to the north, is a fine spot for a summer swim after a day of hiking.

Past a logging road at 4.1 mi. that leads 0.6 mi. to US 58 then 0.4 mi. to Beartree Day Use Area parking

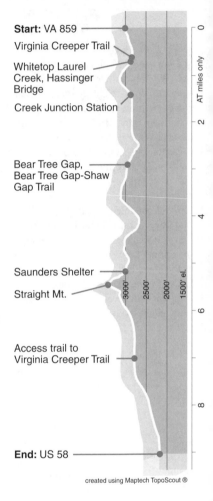

Start: VA 859
Virginia Creeper Trail
Whitetop Laurel Creek, Hassinger Bridge
Creek Junction Station
Bear Tree Gap, Bear Tree Gap-Shaw Gap Trail
Saunders Shelter
Straight Mt.
Access trail to Virginia Creeper Trail
End: US 58

AT miles only

3000' 2500' 2000' 1500' el.

created using Maptech TopoScout ®

(another exit option), the terrain becomes steep and challenging, but only for a few hundred yards, before dipping into a sag, then finishing the ascent of Straight Mt. The views along the way are well worth the energy, so

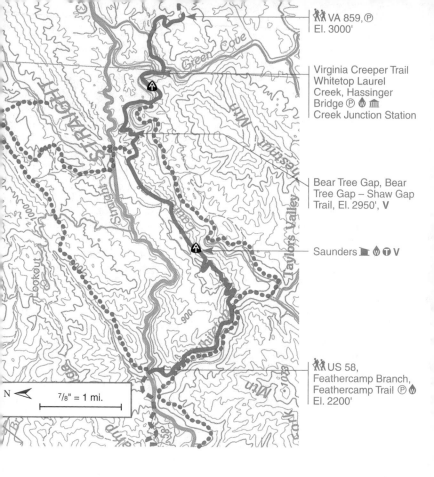

笊笊 VA 859, Ⓟ
El. 3000'

Virginia Creeper Trail
Whitetop Laurel
Creek, Hassinger
Bridge Ⓟ ◍ 血
Creek Junction Station

Bear Tree Gap, Bear
Tree Gap – Shaw Gap
Trail, El. 2950', **V**

Saunders ▰ ◍ ◉ V

笊笊 US 58,
Feathercamp Branch,
Feathercamp Trail Ⓟ ◍
El. 2200'

N ◄   ⁷/₈" = 1 mi.

even hikers planning an early exit to Bear Tree Day Use area at 4.1 mi. should consider pressing on another mile, then backtracking to exit via the logging road. From an open overlook on Straight Mt. (4.6 mi.), the view south over Taylors Valley is of Chestnut Mt. and the Great Smoky Mts. in Tennessee. To the southwest is the southerly route of the AT over Holston Mt. And it only gets better.

The blue-blazed trail at 5.2 mi. leads 0.2 mi. to the Saunders Shelter and a potable spring just beyond. The shelter is itself a work of art. Constructed by the Mt. Rogers Appalachian Trail Club and the Appalachian Trail Conference's professional trail builders, the Konnarock Trail Crew, the shelter is named for Walter T. Saunders, an outdoorsman whose parents contributed the funds for the shelter in his memory. It is a fitting memorial to a hiker, a veritable log home that will withstand the test of high winds and winters for many years.

In another 0.3 mi. the trail finds the crest of Straight Mt., where the view of the thousand-foot walls of Whitetop Laurel Gorge brings this hike to rest for a long look. The gorge is carved from glacial rock, which was formed from sand, gravel, and silt left by a receding glacier. In his comprehensive geologic history of the Appalachian Trail, *Underfoot*, V. Collins Chew writes that the maroon stone was a pebbly, powdery mix of rock and ice that hardened after the ice melted. The soft rock was the perfect raw material for the lovely gorge carved by Whitetop Laurel Creek.

Descend through a series of switchbacks to a side trail at 7.0 mi. that connects in 300 yd. with the Virginia Creeper Trail. The AT route continues largely within sound of water as it winds around the western slope of Straight Mt. in the hollow between Straight and the base of Fork Mt. At 7.7 mi., a footbridge over a tumbling branch of Whitetop Laurel Creek is a fine spot for a rest amidst the mountain laurel. The waterfall below the bridge invites the shedding of shoes and a good cooling off.

For the final 1.3 mi., the AT closely parallels the Virginia Creeper and the creek until a break 0.3 mi. from Straight Branch at US 58. Hollies join rhododendron, clinging to the rocky, steep slope of Straight Mt. as it bottoms out at the creek. A fitting end to a hike so generous in water views and sounds awaits, as the trail breaks from Whitetop Laurel Creek to emerge onto US 58 at the confluence of Straight Branch and Feathercamp Branch, 0.25 mi. above the main creek.

Parking for six cars is visible 200 yd. west on US 58. Picnic tables and fireplaces are also available. Overnight hikers continuing to Damascus will enjoy several small stream crossings and views of the town from Hall Ridge. Camping is permitted along the way, but the steep terrain offers few opportunities. The hardiest hikers may go 1.8 mi. up Feathercamp Trail from the US 58 trailhead to Sandy Flats Shelter for a steadily rising but scenic hike along the creek.

Hike #1   Itinerary

Miles N	NORTH	Elev. (ft/m)	Miles S
9.0	**Start:** VA 859, roadside parking, 14.6 mi. E of Damascus; trail descends.	3000/914	0.0
8.4	Join **Virginia Creeper Trail.**		0.6
8.3	Cross **Luther Hassinger Bridge** over **Whitetop Laurel Creek.**		0.7
7.8	Reach **Creek Junction Station,** parking; begin ascent of Straight Mt.; leave Virginia Creeper Trail.	2700/823	1.2
6.2	Pond, campsites.		2.8
6.1	Junction **Bear Tree Gap-Shaw Gap Trail;** leads 0.3 mi. to US 58, parking 0.2 mi. W, early exit option.	2950/899	2.9
4.4	View of **Whitetop Laurel Gorge.**		4.6
3.8	Trail to **Saunders Shelter,** 0.2 mi. to L, water, privy.		5.2
3.5	Crest of **Straight Mt.**	3500/1067	5.5
2.0	Pass access trail to **Virginia Creeper Trail** (300 yd. L).	3000/914	7.0
1.3	Footbridge over branch of Whitetop Laurel Creek, waterfall.	2400/732	7.7
0.0	**End: US 58, Feathercamp Branch,** 5.6 mi. E of Damascus; parking for 6 cars 200 yd. W of trail.	2200/671	9.0

SOUTH

HIKE #2
Whitetop Mountain and Buzzard Rock

Map: ATC Va. #4, Southwest Virginia

Route: Elk Garden at VA 600 over White-top Mt. and Buzzard Rock to Summit Cut at US 58

Recommended direction: N to S

Distance: 6.9 mi.

Elevation +/-: 4430 to 5350 to 3160 ft.

Effort: Moderate

Day hike: Yes

Overnight backpacking hike: Optional

Duration: 4 hr.

Early exit option: At 2.4 mi., Whitetop Mt. Rd.

Natural history features: Endangered salamanders; balds of Whitetop Mt.

Other features: Many stream crossings

Trailhead access: *Start:* From Damascus, go 20.0 mi. E on US 58, then L onto VA 600. Overnight trailhead parking is 3.5 mi. ahead in Elk Garden. *End:* From Damascus, go 16.9 mi. E on US 58; at marked AT crossing, park in picnic area.

Camping: Whitetop Mt. picnic area; permitted along trail

The views from Buzzard Rock and the bald crest of Whitetop make this moderate hike a popular one, but it is the subtle working of nature in the streams underfoot and the upper story of the forest that attract the savvy hiker to Whitetop. Trickling, unassuming streams, most unworthy even of names, are home to endangered salamanders, and the hiker who takes time to explore under rocks and water-soaked logs will find a treat. Above the trail, the observant hiker might catch a glimpse of the northern flying squirrel in its unusual act of aeronautics. Subtler still, for the observant hiker, Whitetop Mt. is a tale of two ecosystems, marking the southern limits of the red spruce and the northern limits of the Fraser fir.

The hike begins at the AT trailhead at an elevation of 4430 ft. on VA 600, just west of the Lewis Fork Wilderness Area, and makes quick work of a strenuous 600-ft. ascent of the northeast slope of Whitetop, Virginia's second-highest peak at 5520 ft. Even though there is still more ascending ahead, when the trail finds gentler terrain at 0.5 mi., the hardest hiking of the day is done. The AT does not visit the summit, but passes just a few hundred trail-yards and 150 ft. in elevation below it.

That first 0.5 mi. can challenge the lungs of the ablest hiker, and makes the small streams along the way, as well as the salamanders that inhabit them, seem strategically placed to lure hikers into rest stops. The headwaters of one small stream, at 0.6 mi., are a reliable, but unprotected, water source. The rest of the ramble around Whitetop is more moderate, leading to a 2300-vertical-ft. descent to Summit Cut. Take note that choosing to hike south to north instead of north to south as we recommend would require a 2300-ft. ascent of Whitetop.

The next mi. continues a gradual ascent, almost imperceptible at times, leading to an open view of Mt. Rogers, the tallest mountain in the Virginia Commonwealth (elev. 5729 ft.) at 1.9 mi. The peak has a way of making surprising appearances; when sights and sounds of any hike in this region make one forget about the world beyond the footpath, there is Mt. Rogers, as though the mountain itself continually changes positions to find the hiker's viewshed.

At 2.3 mi., the trail leaves the woods of Whitetop and finds the open balds below the crest. For everyone lured here by descriptions of the Appalachian Trail's southern balds, to walk below the crest of Whitetop is to understand why hikers find the balds so captivating. Picture yourself ambling through a wide, open meadow; below are the tops of mountains that seemed giant from the road below them, while above is the forested crest of the mountain. Walking south, there is an open view of the trail, resplendent in June with wildflowers, covering more than a mile toward Buzzard Rock.

The views below and beyond the bald are of the forested lower slopes of red spruce. Above the trail, along the crest, are the last Fraser fir a thru-hiker would see in abundance if traveling north. Even more fetching, and certainly more immediate for the hiker, are the patches of white flowers on this mountain meadow: ox-eye daisy and the clustered, tiny petals of flowering spurge in June, then starry campion nearly 4 ft. high, which all summer long blooms in white, daisy-like flowers grouped at intervals along its tall stalk. Slender ladies' tresses, an orchid whose flowers are braided into its stalk like cornrows, blooms in mid and late summer.

At 2.4 mi., the trail joins Whitetop Mt. Rd., in place to service the communications towers that somewhat disfigure this idyllic spot. After breaking with the AT at 2.6 mi., the road climbs 300 yd. to the right to the summit of Whitetop, which has picnic grounds, parking, and camping but offers no views. Hikers taking this exit option are urged to press on to Buzzard Rock, then return to Whitetop parking. It's an easy, 1.0-mi. stroll there and back, and the view is certainly worthy.

The woods near the picnic area offer an abundance of ramps, a Virginia/West Virginia delicacy, to spice up a hiker's lunch. The ramp, like its herb cousins the onion and garlic, is a member of the lily family. It is found along the edges of woods, where they meet meadows. The town of Whitetop hosts one of what must be a hundred annual ramp festivals that take place in Blue Ridge small towns. Day hikers out to enjoy the people and places of the Blue Ridge, in addition to days on the trail, can enjoy the Whitetop Ramp Festival and Appalachian Trail Days (see Hike #1) in back-to-back weekends.

At 2.6 mi., leaving Whitetop Mt. Rd. as it breaks toward the summit and picnic area, Buzzard Rock looms 0.5 mi. ahead above open fields. The utter peacefulness of the walk to the big rock belies the violent geologic upheaval that created the bald and extensive views beyond. The Whitetop-Buzzard Rock formation is a transition zone from one geologic event to another. The meadow leading to the overlook has grown over soils of quartz crystals, the scattered remnants of volcanic activity 700 million years ago. South of Buzzard Rock, glaciers carved the steep south slope from billion-year-old granite, leaving red, white, and dark green cobbles in their wake.

Arriving at Buzzard Rock at 3.1 mi., it is impossible to move on without stopping to enjoy the view (although some weekend days it's also impossible to find some time alone to enjoy it). To the north beyond the prominent ridge of Iron Mt. lie the Clinch Mts., and to the south the view extends 40 mi. to Grandfather Mt. From Buzzard Rock, the trail begins a 3-mi. descent, first through the short

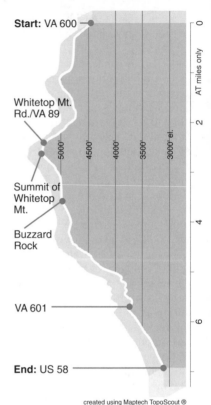

created using Maptech TopoScout ®

sag separating Whitetop from Beech Mt., then, at 3.6 mi., around the southern slope of Beech amid low shrubs and trees hardy enough to withstand the windy blasts from the southwest: cedar, witch hazel, gooseberry.

For the next couple of miles, the trail is a classic representation of the "green tunnel" for which the Appalachian Trail is known. It is the kind of terrain that thru-hikers

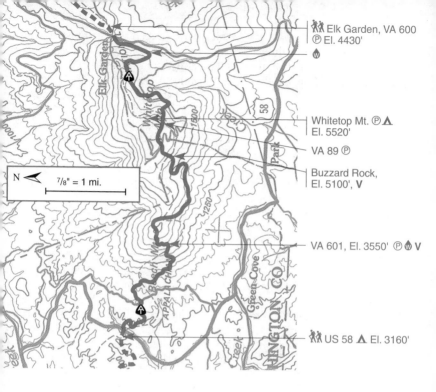

Elk Garden, VA 600
Ⓟ El. 4430'
Ⓦ

Whitetop Mt. Ⓟ ▲
El. 5520'

VA 89 Ⓟ

Buzzard Rock,
El. 5100', **V**

VA 601, El. 3550' Ⓟ Ⓦ **V**

US 58 ▲ El. 3160'

N ◀ ⁷/₈" = 1 mi.

speed past on their way to the next shelter, hurrying to make the mileage to the day's destination. For the day hiker, there are subtle pleasures. One that is particularly enhanced by slow-poking the 1940-ft., 3.8-mi. descent from Buzzard Rock to Summit Cut Rd. (at US 58) is the climate. On a typical day, the temperature difference between Buzzard Rock and the US 58 crossing could be 15 to 20 degrees.

Hikers with a mind to can literally feel the temperature changing.

At about 4.4 mi., the trail finds gentle terrain, ever descending, but casually. This is a real walk in the woods, and a welcome break from the ceaseless, steep drop. Going down the mountain may be easier on the lungs and heart, but it tests the legs and backside as much as a climb. Here, the ramble allows the eyes to focus on red spruce and the yellow flowers of downy foxglove in their favored habitat beneath the scattered oaks.

At 5.2 mi., before another steep descent begins, there is an excellent campsite with an unprotected spring. In recent years, other impromptu campsites have taken shape nearby. As a point of no-trace camping, hikers are urged to make use of this and other existing campsites whenever possible, rather than creating random new ones. Although camping is permitted throughout the national forest, except where otherwise noted, the temptation to "improve" a favored spot for successive hikers may be well intentioned, but it is misguided.

Still descending, at 5.7 mi. there is a reliable spring to the right near the crossing of gravel VA 601. Parking for several cars is available here, providing an early exit option for this hike. Just beyond the road, there are views of Lost Mt. and the Green Cove Creek watershed from a pastured sag. Over next 1.2 mi. between VA 601 and US 58, the trail will reveal a lovely, intimate passage through pastures and mature woods and over several streams that quickly gather steam as they rush toward drainages for Green Cove Creek.

From 6.3 to 6.7 mi., several intermittent, small streams signal the bottom of Beech Mt. In spring thaws and rains, the way can be wet, but is always manageable. There are a handful of spots offering enough level ground for camping — a good one at 6.6 mi. — but the nearness of US 58 (only 200 yd. below) and the proximity to private property do not promise quiet and solitude. The most reliable water source for camping here is the spring at the base of Lost Mt., about 300 yd. beyond the AT's dip to US 58 and the end of this hike at 6.9 mi. The picnic and parking area is visible from the trail.

Optional Extended Hike: You may want to plan to spend a night in the Lost Mt. Shelter, at 7.8 mi. If so, you will have the Mount Rogers Appalachian Trail Club and the ATC's Konnarock Trail Crew to thank for their fine feat of shelter construction in 1994. The water source is a spring 150 yd. behind the shelter. It is an easy ascent from Summit Cut to the shelter, and a steep but short descent from there to VA 859, at 9.2 mi. The final 0.4 mi. follow a small stream, which the trail crosses just before leaving the woods. There is limited roadside parking near the trailhead, which is 1.0 mi. south of US 58 and 14.0 mi. east of Damascus.

Hike #2   Itinerary

Miles N	NORTH	Elev. (ft/m)	Miles S
6.9	**Start:** Elk Garden trailhead parking at VA 600, 3.5 mi. N of US 58, 20 mi. E of Damascus; ascend steeply.	4430/1350	0.0
6.4	Reach level terrain.	5000/1524	0.5
5.0	View of **Mt. Rogers.**		1.9
4.5	Trail joins **Whitetop Mt. Rd. / USFS 89;** parking 250 yd. R, early exit option.		2.4
4.3	Road bears R (E) to **Whitetop Mt.** summit, picnic area, camping, and parking; AT bears L (W).	5350/1631	2.6
3.8	**Buzzard Rock.**	5100/1554	3.1
1.7	Campsite, spring.		5.2
1.2	Cross **VA 601,** early exit option; spring is R of trail.	3550/1082	5.7
0.6	Stream crossings next 0.4 mi.		6.3
0.3	Campsite.		6.6
0.0	**End:** Cross stream to **US 58** picnic and parking area, 16.9 mi. E of Damascus.	3160/963	6.9

SOUTH

Pine Mt. and Mt. Rogers Circuit

Map: ATC Va. #4, Southwest Virginia

Route: A circuit hike from The Scales to Pine Mt. Trail, along Pine Mt. to Rhododendron Gap, and back on AT to The Scales via Wilburn Ridge on Mt. Rogers

Recommended direction: S to N

Distance: 10.7 mi. total; 8.5 mi. on AT, 2.0 mi. on side trail for loop

Access trail name & length: USFS 613, 0.2 mi.

Elevation +/-: 4650 to 5400 to 4650 ft.

Effort: Strenuous

Day hike: Yes

Overnight backpacking hike: Yes

Duration: 7 to 8 hr.

Early exit option: At 5.8 mi., blue-blazed trail

Natural history features: Rhododendron Gap; Quebec Branch; Big Wilson Creek

Social history feature: The Scales

Other features: Showers and phone at Grayson Highlands SP

Trailhead access: *Start and end:* From Troutdale, go 2 mi. W on VA 603 to L onto USFS 613. In 2.5 mi., park at gate. AT is 0.2 mi. further.

Camping: Wise Shelter; tent camping in Grayson Highland SP

E ven if you must take this hike over mountain meadows and rock ledges in a single day, you will certainly have a memorable trip: wild ponies prancing through a mountain meadow, hundreds of acres of rhododendron in bloom, open balds at 5000 ft. that recall the Alps of Europe, the tallest and third-tallest mountains in Virginia, more blueberries than could be eaten in a lifetime. But few things in a hiker's world, however, can match emerging from a tent in Grayson Highlands to glimpse wild ponies starting the day. For that reason alone, anyone who can make the time should plan to camp before or after this hike.

The hike is described here as a circuit of 10.5 mi. that includes 8.5 mi. on the Appalachian Trail and 2.0 mi. of the former AT route over the open crest of Pine Mt., at 5050 ft., Virginia's third-highest mountain. This means hikers will begin the hike on the AT by heading north, then double back on a side trail 2.0 mi. to a point on the AT that lies south of the starting point. After rejoining the AT, the hike heads north again to the original starting point. Despite its nearly 11 mi., this is a manageable day hike. We describe it as strenuous due to distance only. Wise Shelter, along the route in Grayson Highlands SP, and Thomas Knob Shelter, 0.8 mi. south of

Rhododendron Gap, offer the possibility of an overnight circuit (long-distance backpackers are afforded priority use of the shelters ahead of hikers out for a single night).

The hike also offers an optional diversion to the summit of Mt. Rogers, and a longer backpacking trip of 16.9 mi. can be created by starting from Fox Creek, 4.8 mi. north of the start of this hike, and hiking south to VA 600 at Elk Garden. We've omitted those 9.8 AT mi. here because the circuit provides the very best of the Mt. Rogers area and eliminates the need for a second car or a lift. The additional 3.4-mi. round trip to reach the forested summit of Mt. Rogers is described below. Although there are no views from the summit, its dense forest of red spruce is a favored spot for picnics.

The hike begins at the trailhead on USFS 613, an unimproved dirt road. A gate restricts car traffic to a point about 0.2 mi. from the AT junction at a split-rail corral called The Scales. Once a cattle-weighing station, it now serves more often as a staging area for equestrians riding the Bear Pen Horse Trail, which intersects with the AT here and at several other points.

Heading north, the trail ascends to the crest of Pine Mt. (1.3 mi.) gradually, then all at once at 1.4 mi., emerges into the open splendor of the Pine Mt. meadow. Were it not for Mt. Rogers, looming larger than the sun at 5729 ft., Pine Mt. would seem the top of the world. Wooded peaks and everything else appear tiny from

Pine Mt. Veering from the AT at 1.4 mi., the hike route follows a blue-blazed trail that breaks west (left) from the AT. For the next 2.0 mi., the hike follows the former AT route over the mostly open crest of Pine Mt. The trail dips and then ascends 200 ft. casually, with Mt. Rogers ever looming in the foreground.

Then, at 3.4 mi., without warning, the June-early-July hiker is rewarded with a scene out of a fairy tale: literally hundreds of acres of purple rhododendron shimmering in the mountain breeze. They just go on and on. The blue-blazed trail rejoins the AT here, but before moving north on the trail, Rhododendron Gap gives cause for a pause.

Hikers who miss the blooming shrubs of June can come in August for the abundant blueberries. A real treat is to grab a bowlful of berries, then ascend one of the spectacular rock outcroppings of volcanic ash that dot the landscape for dessert and siesta. One hiker met in the gap calls the place The Blueberry Café. As a real blueberry connoisseur, she recommends bringing along a frozen mixture of light cream and sugar. After hiking in, gathering berries and finding the perfect rest rock, the frozen mixture will have defrosted to a perfectly chilled sweet cream. Drop in the berries and enjoy the view.

For a side trip to the Mt. Rogers summit, from Rhododendron Gap follow the AT 1.2 mi. south (right) to the blue-blazed Susan Spillane Trail, which climbs 0.5 mi. to the forested summit. There are no views, but a wild, restful setting within the Lewis Fork Wilderness area awaits. Known as Balsam Mt. until 1883, the peak was renamed to honor William Barton Rogers, whose curriculum vitae includes many firsts, including first state geologist and first president of the Massachusetts Institute of Technology. No camping is permitted on Mt. Rogers within the Lewis Fork Wilderness Area, but the Thomas Knob Shelter lies 0.4 mi. from the Spillane Trail to the summit. Built with the assistance of the ATC's professional Konnarock Trail Crew by the Mt. Rogers Appalachian Trail Club, which maintains the AT in the area, the shelter sleeps ten.

Back in Rhododendron Gap at the junction with the AT, following the signature white blazes once again, the route for this circuit ramble heads northward (left, when reaching the AT from Pine Mt.). Without even leaving the trail there are panoramic views on the descent from the gap. Descending toward Wilburn Ridge, craggy outcroppings and cliffs of pink and reddish volcanic ash pose a hiker's dilemma: which one to scamper up to admire the views? These outcrops, says V. Collins Chew in *Underfoot: A Geologic Guide to the Appalachian Trail,* are not the results of erosion resistance as much as they are the remnants of crags covered by other soils and rock and compressed into their current formations.

From approximately 4.4 mi. to about 4.8 mi. the views are so extended and varied that hikers may find it difficult to keep moving. Views of Pine Mt., Stone Mt., Haw Orchard Mt., and many other ridges and peaks dominate. At 5.0 mi., a blue-blazed trail leads right 200 ft. to the cliffs of Wilburn Ridge, another place to stop and watch the world.

Moving on (eventually), at 5.3 mi. you will climb over a wooden fence on a stile and enter Grayson Highlands SP. With the opening of the Wise Shelter (at 8.0 mi.) in 1996, tent camping is permitted only in a few designated areas in the park, and a permit, which can be obtained from rangers or at the park office, is required. At 5.8 mi., in Massie Gap, a blue-blazed trail leads very steeply down 0.5 mi. to the park's parking area, an exit option for this hike. The parking area is adjacent to the trailhead, with ample parking for a dozen cars. The park also offers a picnic area with barbecue grills, a store, rest rooms, a campground with sites accommodating up to six people each, and showers. The fee for the campsites is collected at the park entrance off US 58. *The Thru-Hiker's Handbook* warns that the store hours are unreliable; unfortunately, there is no way for hikers to know until making the 2.0-mi. trek down the access trail and the road to the campground.

At 6.0 mi., alongside one of many cliff formations in the highlands, the trail enters a broad mountain meadow. The grasses and blueberries return, and the wild ponies and not-too-shy deer who feast upon the berries may emerge. Stock cattle, which graze the area seasonally, often join the horses. Hikers who did not get their fill of berries in Rhododendron Gap will find an abundance here in August. The ponies invariably want a handout, but like all animals in wilds, they should not be fed by people. It is not good for them to be overfed through the kindness of so many strangers, and processed food does them harm. However, the ponies are practically pets in the care of the state park, so getting them hooked on handouts is not a real danger. In season, some hikers will feed them blueberries from the bushes; it gives people a bonding experience without contributing to the delinquency of the ponies.

At 6.3 mi. the trail leaves the rock outcroppings behind, descends through rhododendron and scattered holly toward Quebec Branch, and continues beyond the stream through the woods until breaking into a clearing at 7.9 mi. The hike along Quebec Branch, first amidst a rhododendron thicket, then above the stream in tall grass, is as intimate and enchanting as the views from Wilburn Ridge are grand. Until the 1960s, the AT bypassed Grayson Highlands for the shorter route over Pine Mt. employed for this circuit. The addition of Grayson Highlands enhanced not only the AT experience, but the network of protected lands along the Blue Ridge.

Checking the trail register

Wise Shelter is at 8.0 mi. The shelter accommodates eight. If camping here, collect water from the spring 100 yd. south of the shelter on the AT. At 8.2 mi., the trail crosses Little Wilson Creek, then, leaving the park and crossing Big Wilson Creek, begins the ascent of Stone Mt. At 8.4 mi., the trail enters the Little Wilson Creek Wilderness, a preserve of 3800 acres. The remnants of railroad grade and logging roads the trail follows here are reminders that the area has not always been wild. In another generation or two, however, these wide pathways will be completely overgrown and, except for the minimal tending allowed in designated wilderness, the signs of human activity will all but disappear.

David Emblidge

For the next 1.2 mi. as the trail passes through the wilderness area, the occasional rose mandarin, a red member of the lily family, and showy orchis can be spotted in May and June. Easier to find due to its size is the purple-flowering raspberry, a thornless rose that grows to 6 ft.

At 9.3 mi., a small pond offers a soothing spot for a break before leaving the Little Wilson Creek Wilderness at 9.6 mi. Beyond the wilderness, the trail ascends open Stone Mt. and reaches its flat summit at 4800 ft. Cattle and cow pies occupy the ridge. While some hikers resent the bovine intrusion, others treasure the pastoral activities of the working landscape as a vital part of the Appalachian Trail experience. Children who make the hike seem to enjoy the ponies and cattle most of all. White-blazed posts mark the trail through the pasture as it descends to The Scales, ending on the ridge above the world where you began.

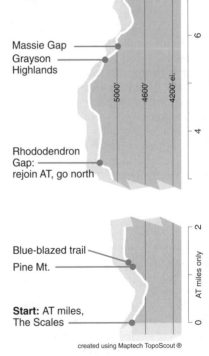

created using Maptech TopoScout ®

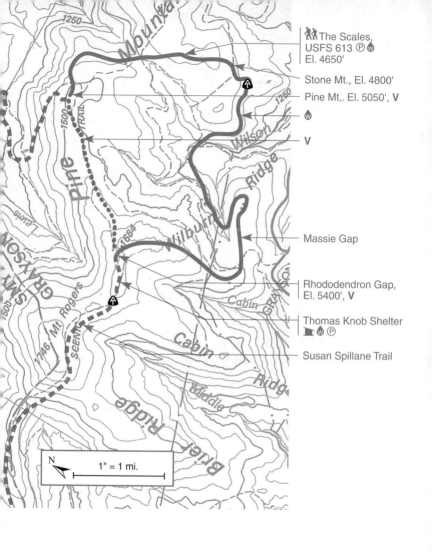

The Scales, USFS 613 Ⓟ 🚰 El. 4650'

Stone Mt., El. 4800'

Pine Mt,. El. 5050', **V**

🚰

V

Massie Gap

Rhododendron Gap, El. 5400', **V**

Thomas Knob Shelter 🛏️ 🚰 Ⓟ

Susan Spillane Trail

N

1" = 1 mi.

Miles N	Circuit Hike	Elev. (ft/m)	Miles S
	Total: 10.9 mi. with access at Start/End		
	Access: End of **USFS 613**, parking at gate; AT is 0.2 mi. N; 4.5 mi. from Troutdale.		0.2
	Start: The Scales. Head N on AT.	4650/1417	0.0
	Pine Mt.	5050/1539	1.3
	Leave AT, turn L onto blue-blazed trail; head W.	5050/1539	1.4
	Rhododendron Gap; for Circuit Hike, turn L, rejoining AT, heading N, back to The Scales; for Mt. Rogers side trip, go R (S on AT) to Spillane Trail (3.4 mi. RT).	5400/1646	3.4
	READ FROM BOTTOM UP.		
10.5	**End:** The Scales.	4650/1417	
10.2	Crest of **Stone Mt.**	4800/1463	
9.0	Spring, old sawmill.		
8.4	Enter **Little Wilson Creek Wilderness.**		
8.2	Cross **Big Wilson Creek.**	4500/1371	
8.0	**Wise Shelter,** spring 100 yd. S on AT.		
7.6	Clearing, open fields.		
6.8	Cross **Quebec Branch.**	4800/1463	
6.0	Cliffs and meadow.		
5.8	**Massie Gap;** steep descent (0.5 mi.) to **Grayson Highland SP** parking, early exit option; AT wends N.		
5.3	Rail fence, enter **Grayson State Park.**		
5.0	200 ft. trail to **WIlburn Ridge.**		

Circuit Hike

Iron Mt. and Brushy Mt.

Maps: ATC Va. #3 & #4, Southwest Virginia

Route: Through Jefferson NF from Fox Creek, over Iron Mt., through Dickey Gap to High Point, Brushy Mt., and Mt. Rogers Natl. Rec. Area headquarters

Recommended direction: S to N

Distance: 23.1 mi.

Elevation +/-: 3480 to 4200 to 3000 to 4040 to 2450 to 3350 to 3220 ft.

Effort: Moderate

Day hike: Optional

Overnight backpacking hike: Yes

Duration: 17 hr.

Early exit options: At 8.5 mi., VA 650; at 15.1 mi., VA 670; for emergencies only, at 3.9 mi., Barton Rd. Trail (seasonal) and at 6.4 mi., blue-blazed trail.

Natural history features: Dickey Gap; Iron Mt.; Comers Creek; Mt. Rogers Natl. Rec. Area headquarters exhibits

Social history features: Iron Mt. Trail (former AT route); former narrow-gauge railroad beds

Other features: Restaurant, post office and grocery in Troutdale; showers at Hurricane Campground; fishing on Hurricane Creek

Trailhead access: *Start:* From the Marion exit of I-81 go S on VA 16 12.0 mi. to Troutdale, then W on VA 603, 4.0 mi. to trailhead parking 0.1 mi. beyond junction with VA 741; overnight parking for a dozen cars. *End:* Take I-81 to Marion exit, then VA 16E 7.0 mi. to overnight trailhead parking at Mt. Rogers Natl. Rec. Area Headquarters.

Camping: Raccoon Branch and Trimpi shelters; Hurricane Campground

---

The Appalachian Trail is known as the "Footpath through the Wilderness," and in Virginia it is the Mt. Rogers National Recreation Area that gives the phrase its meaning. The AT travels through the heart of the "NRA," as it is called, as a kind of trunk line that connects to dozens of side trails to remote places like Shaw Gap and Chestnut Flats. The AT also figures prominently in many circuit hikes throughout the Mt. Rogers region.

From the beginning of the hike described here, two distinct ecological worlds of the region are clear: the moist soils near the stream valleys and the rocky, dry soils of the ridges and ledges. Down in the stream valleys, ironweed and other moisture-loving plants thrive. Lucky, observant hikers may catch a glimpse of the rare bleeding heart, a puffy, air-filled blossom only an inch long, on the steep, dry ridges of Iron Mt., which play host to a virtual forest of rhododendron, very common along the AT in southern Virginia.

From the AT trailhead parking at VA 603, the trail crosses Laurel Creek and Fox Creek and immediately begins the 720-vertical-ft. climb of Iron Mt. The tiny white lilies by the streams — Indian cucumber-root — point to a happy irony of the Appalachian Trail. When Benton MacKaye first proposed the idea of the Appalachian Trail in 1927, this area, known as Fairwood Valley, lay in waste. Timber harvests and magnesium mining had cleared the landscape of marketable resources. Today, Indian cucumber-root is evidence that the forest has recovered; you'll find this flower only in heavily wooded settings.

The trail makes quick work of the ascent of Iron Mt. No gentle slabbing along gradually sloping ledges here; the route is up. Approaching the dry rocky crest of Iron Mt., the yellow flowers of downy false foxglove and the wild pinks (actually, they are bright red) sprouting from mineral soils tell a story similar to that of the Indian cucumber-root. These flowers are parasites upon the roots of mature oak trees, so the trees and flowers together say things are okay in the forest.

At 2.0 mi., the trail crests Iron Mt. (elev. 4200 ft.) and without a pause begins its descent. Then, at 2.3 mi., is Chestnut Flats, a half-mile-wide plateau just below the crest of Iron Mt. In winter, there are views to the northeast of High Point. Here also is the junction with the yellow-blazed Iron Mt. Trail, heading west. This former AT route through the Mt. Rogers Natl. Rec. Area is maintained for its entire 21.8 mi. into Damascus. The Iron Mt. Trail and the AT, which run roughly parallel, can be combined with various side trails for a seemingly limitless number of circuit hikes. Perhaps the most ambitious is the 56.7-mi. circuit formed by the two trails from this point into Damascus and back.

As the trail leaves the plateau, it joins an abandoned logging road and discovers an unnamed stream racing downhill toward Hurricane Creek. For the next 0.4 mi., the trail drops steeply to the sound of falling water only a few feet away. When it leaves the creek, the trail slabs west for 0.3 mi., then east for the long, gradual descent into the stream valley. At 3.9 mi. the AT makes a sharp turn east (right), the overgrown Barton Rd. Trail is straight ahead. This 0.5-mi. trail provides emergency access to USFS 84 (Hurricane Creek Rd.) in winter and spring, but because it is generally not maintained, cannot be depended on in high vegetation months. USFS 84 leads north 1.7 mi. to Hurricane Campground.

At 6.4 mi., as it begins a steep ascent, the AT intersects a blue-blazed access trail that leads 0.5 mi. to Hurricane Campground, where there are tent sites, picnic tables, showers, rest rooms, and water. In his annual *Thru-Hiker's Handbook*, Dan "Wingfoot" Bruce calls Hurricane

Campground the "Mt. Rogers NRA's premiere campground for tent campers." It's a point that is hard to argue, especially for families with children — and there are a lot of them here. The picnic area close to the creek is a choice spot for a late-day snack after a long hike. In the height of summer, solitude seekers will want to stay in the woods. Past the campground cut-off trail, the trail joins an abandoned railroad bed, the sole reminder of the narrow-gauge lines that once moved a payload of timber and minerals from Iron Mt.

After cresting Iron Mt. and testing your feet and knees during the long descent, it's time for a cool dip in the best swimming hole of the Mt. Rogers AT route. At 7.3 mi., Comers Creek is the place. The 10-ft. cascade and deep pool are just the ticket for a brief siesta for backpackers. Day hikers who are packing it in at Dickey's Gap, 1.2 mi. down the trail, may as well stay even longer. One caution: enjoy the water, but don't drink it; VA 741 drains into the creek and its headwaters. Leaving Comers Creek (not an easy thing to do), ascend through rhododendron and then woods along a rocky shelf. Just as the rhythm of hiking takes over and the image of the cascades moves to the back of your mind, the AT reveals the sound of a brook bubbling toward Comers Creek. It's enough to make you turn around.

The trail emerges onto VA 650 in Dickey Gap at 8.5 mi., with VA 16 about 35 yd. to the east. For day hikers, roadside parking on VA 650 makes an early exit possible. The town of Troutdale is 2.5 mi south on VA 16. Ascending from Dickey Gap, the trail slabs north under cover of trees. It then descends into a sag at 9.3 mi. where it intersects the Virginia Highlands Horse Trail, a 68-mi. pathway for equestrians and recreational wagon trains. As it is for hikers, the Mt. Rogers area is a special place for equestrians, especially on the balds of the highlands atop Pine Mt.

The trail ascends from the sag to a craggy ridge, where there are views northwest to Hurricane Mt. and the Hurricane Creek valley. A blue-blazed trail at 10.0 mi. escorts you 0.2 mi. to the Raccoon Branch Shelter. Built and maintained by the USFS, the shelter is also used by riders of the Virginia Highlands Horse Trail, which skirts the opposite side of the hill. For backpackers en route to Mt. Rogers Natl. Rec. Area headquarters, the shelter is about 1.5 mi. short of the halfway point; Trimpi Shelter, at 12.5 mi., is a little more than halfway.

Raccoon Branch shelter accommodates eight, six comfortably, but be warned that the spring behind the shelter, which drips into Raccoon Branch, is unreliable in dry summers. There are a few similar springs downstream along Raccoon Branch. The stream itself is paralleled by the horse trail; it is not a source for drinking water.

Continued on p. 52

Whether spending the night at Raccoon Branch or forging ahead, a rest stop atop High Point, elev. 4040 ft., is in order. It's only a short, 0.1 mi.-detour west on the blue-blazed trail at 10.6 mi. From High Point, there are pretty good views of the Mt. Rogers high country: Mt. Rogers and Whitetop and Pine mountains, Virginia's three highest peaks. This is an ideal winter hike; in cool weather, water along the ridge top is less of a concern and the views are more expansive.

High Point also marks the highest elevation on this hike. From here, the trail starts a descent toward the South Fork Holston River, 4.5 mi. downhill. At about 10.8 mi., a spring trickles 100 yd. east and 75 ft. below the trail. You'll hear it if it's running. With another 1.7 mi. to go to Trimpi Shelter, it may be worth a scamper down the hill to recharge.

After your descent of more than a thousand feet from High Point, at 12.5 mi. you will find the blue-blazed trail that leads 0.1 mi. to Trimpi Shelter. The Mt. Rogers Appalachian Trail Club and the ATC's Konnarock Trail Crew performed extensive renovations on this hut in memory of Robert Trimpi, a student and AT enthusiast. Built by the USFS, the shelter accommodates eight, has a reliable spring only 100 ft. away, and is a peaceful spot for an evening on the trail. However, as with many other AT shelters located close to a road crossing (VA 670 is less than 2 mi. down the trail), you may arrive to find car campers crashing

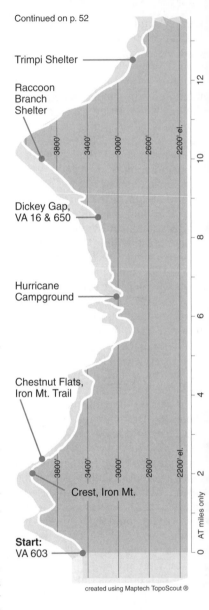

Trimpi Shelter

Raccoon Branch Shelter

Dickey Gap, VA 16 & 650

Hurricane Campground

Chestnut Flats, Iron Mt. Trail

Crest, Iron Mt.

Start: VA 603

AT miles only

created using Maptech TopoScout ®

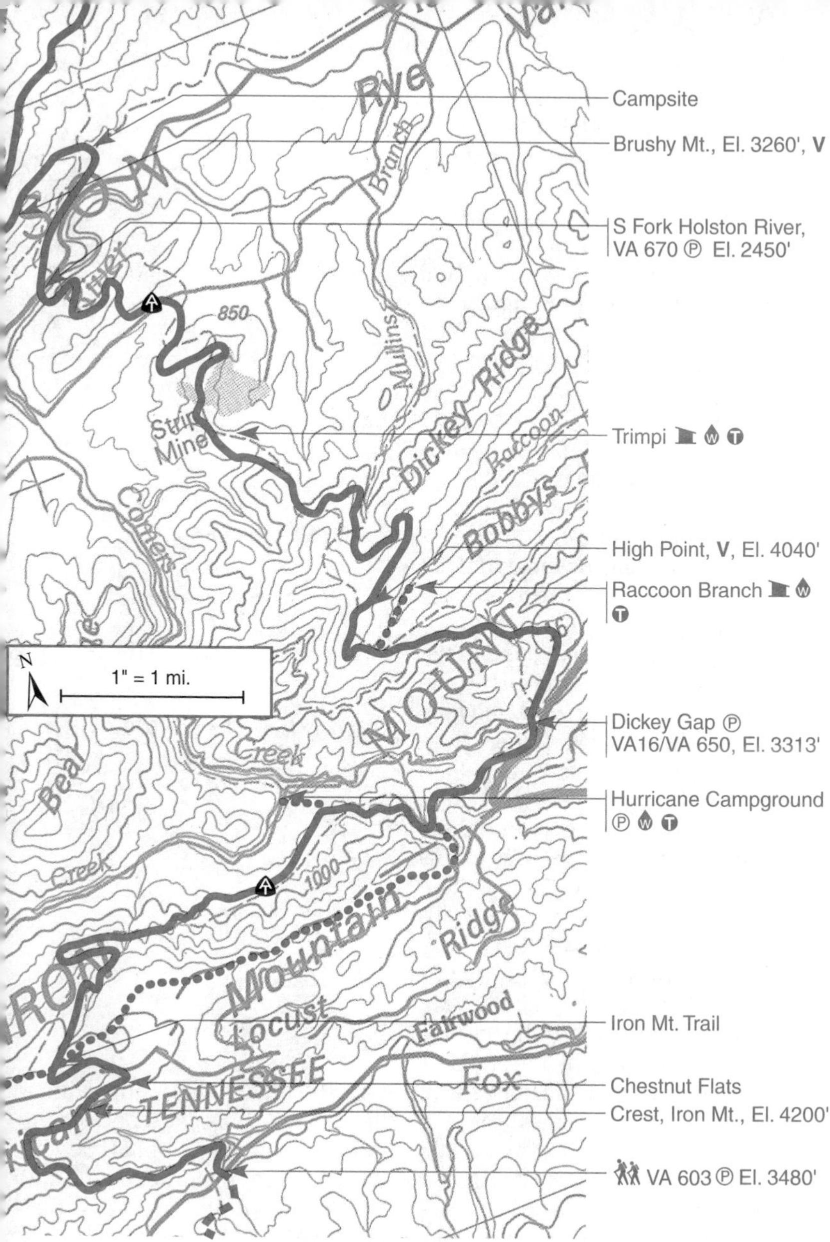
Campsite
Brushy Mt., El. 3260', **V**
S Fork Holston River, VA 670 Ⓟ El. 2450'
Trimpi
High Point, **V**, El. 4040'
Raccoon Branch
Dickey Gap Ⓟ VA16/VA 650, El. 3313'
Hurricane Campground Ⓟ
Iron Mt. Trail
Chestnut Flats
Crest, Iron Mt., El. 4200'
VA 603 Ⓟ El. 3480'
Rye
Branch
Mullins
Dickey Ridge
Raccoon
Bobbys
Strip Mine
Comers
850
1000
Creek
Bear
MOUNT
Mountain
Ridge
Locust
Fairwood
Fox
TENNESSEE
N
1" = 1 mi.

for the evening. More brazen hikers than ourselves will remind them that AT shelters are intended for use by backpackers, not partiers carrying in coolers for the night.

At 13.2 mi., the trail visits the site of a former surface mine, known as Slabtown. To support the World War II effort, manganese, iron, and, to a lesser extent, copper were hauled from the forest as quickly as they could be extracted. Mining operations began in the region in the latter decades of the 19th century and continued until 1950. The national recreation area was designated only sixteen years later, when the landscape surrounding the mines did not yet conjure images of recreation in the wilds.

With great effort on the part of the USFS and other federal agencies, the pit rims have been revegetated very successfully, although tailings from the mining operations still pollute the South Fork Holston River below. The area now is a reminder of how quickly eastern hardwood forests can recover. Slabtown is not there yet, but just as hikers from the 1960s would marvel at the forest's recovery over the last thirty years, today's young hikers who revisit the Mt. Rogers area in another thirty years will find a more mature forest still.

Half a mile beyond the mine site, at 13.7 mi., the trail emerges from the wood to an open prospect, still descending, to reveal views of Brushy and Iron mountains. Our advice here is to have a seat and enjoy the pic-

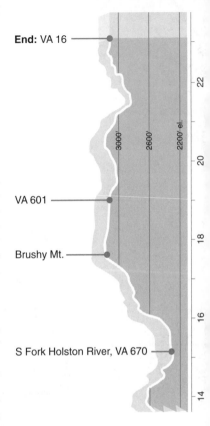

ture. The trail continues downhill to VA 672, then ascends once more, briefly, preceding a final descent through rhododendron to the South Fork Holston River and VA 670 at 15.1 mi. There is roadside parking here for

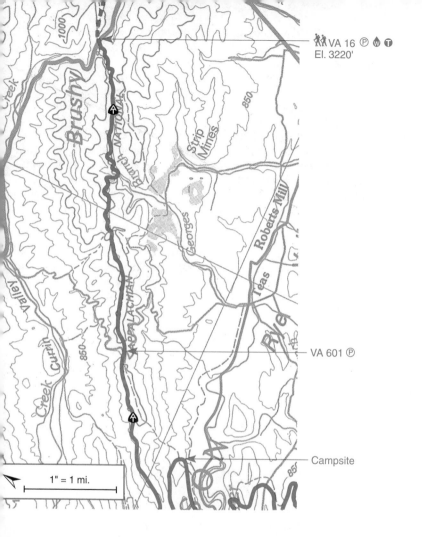

VA 16 🚶‍♂️ Ⓟ 🔥 🚻
El. 3220'

VA 601 Ⓟ

Campsite

1" = 1 mi.

several cars, allowing for a day hike of 5.4 mi. from Dickey Gap to South Fork Holston River.

Ascending northward into the woods, the trail joins another abandoned railroad bed, which it follows for 0.5 mi. through the woods, running parallel to VA 670. There is a nice campsite tucked into the hillside just after the trail crosses a brook trickling toward the South Fork at 16.2 mi. From there the trail cuts back to the west as it ascends Brushy Mt., retraces its way across the brook at its headwaters, and finds the wooded main ridge of Brushy (elev. approximately 3100 ft.) at 16.8 mi. It then climbs steadily through the canopy toward Brushy's crest (elev. 3260 ft.) at 17.6 mi.

High atop Brushy, descending only 100 ft., the trail crosses gravel VA 601, a windy, rut-ridden road that leads south 2.5 mi. to VA 670 and north 2.5 mi. to VA 16. Back up on the ridge, through a series of seemingly endless ups and downs (what thru-hikers call PUDs, for "pointless ups and downs"), the AT works its way across the ridge without revealing much of the world beyond.

It is down near the ground, beneath a hurried hiker's field of vision, that most of the action is taking place. Here are some highlights from our log of the sights and sounds along this often overlooked ridge: at a quartzite outcrop at 20.2 mi., fresh bobcat scat and the remains of what appears to have been a mouse; at a stream crossing at 21.5 mi., a spotted fawn and doe drinking (hence it's not advisable that hikers do here); at a third stream crossing, at 22.0 mi., a child playing in the mud; just beyond the stream, at about 22.4 mi., a barred owl hooting from its roost above. On a less-than-natural note, the ponds east of the trail at 22.8 mi. are the remains of pit mining during World War II.

The trail reaches the Mt. Rogers Natl. Rec. Area headquarters and the end of this trek at 23.1 mi. The huge map of the region in the visitor center alone is just about worth the trip. There are interpretive exhibits and a fine bookstore, as well as rest rooms and water.

Hike #4   Itinerary

Miles N	NORTH	Elev. (ft/m)	Miles S
23.1	**End: Mt Rogers Natl. Rec. Area headquarters on VA 16,** parking, rest rooms, water; 7.0 mi. S of Marion.	3220/981	0.0
21.5	First of three stream crossings.		1.6
19.0	Cross **VA 601.**		4.1
17.6	Peak of **Brushy Mt.,** views.	3260/994	5.5
16.2	Campsite.		6.9
15.1	Cross **South Fork Holston River** on log bridge and **VA 670;** roadside parking, early exit option.	2450/747	8.0
13.2	**Slabtown,** site of former mine.		9.9
12.5	0.1-mi. trail to **Trimpi Shelter.**		10.6
10.6	0.1-mi. trail to **High Point,** view.	4040/1231	12.5
10.0	0.2-mi. trail to **Raccoon Branch Shelter,** spring.		13.1
8.5	**Dickey Gap,** VA 16 and VA 650, early exit option.	3313/955	14.6
7.3	**Comers Creek** swimming hole.		15.8
6.4	0.5-mi. blue-blazed trail to **Hurricane Campground,** water, showers, rest rooms.	3000/914	16.7
2.3	**Chestnut Flats, Iron Mt. Trail.**		20.8
2.0	Crest of **Iron Mt.**	4200/1280	21.1
0.0	**Start:** Fox Creek, VA 603 trailhead parking, 4.0 mi. W of Troutdale.	3480/1061	23.1

SOUTH

Brushy Mt. and Glade Mt.

Map: ATC Va. #3, Southwest Virginia

Route: Through Jefferson NF from Mt. Rogers Natl. Rec. Area headquarters over Brushy Mt., Locust Mt., and Glade Mt. to the boundary at VA 615

Recommended direction: S to N

Distance: 8.8 mi.

Elevation +/-: 3220 to 3900 to 2600 ft.

Effort: Strenuous

Day hike: Yes

Overnight backpacking hike: Optional

Duration: 5 hr.

Early exit option: At 4.1 mi., USFS 86

Natural history feature: Vaught Branch

Social history features: USGS marker; Lindamood school and Settlers Museum of the Southwest

Other features: Restaurant, groceries, and lodging in Atkins, 3.0 mi. N of northern endpoint on VA 683

Trailhead access: *Start:* From the Marion exit of I-81 go E on VA 16 6.5 mi. to overnight trailhead parking at Mt. Rogers Natl. Rec. Area. *End:* On I-81, take the Groseclose/Atkins exit and go S on VA 683 0.5 mi. to US 11. Go R, then in 0.5 mi. go L on VA 683. At T in 1.5 mi., go L and come to trailhead parking on R in 0.35 mi. Overnight parking is permitted.

Camping: Louise Chatfield Shelter

This hike from the Mount Rogers National Recreation Area headquarters rambles over the crests of Brushy, Locust, and Glade mountains, following a ridgeline at about 4000 ft., and descends into the Great Valley. Because the Appalachian Trail here is a trunk line through an extensive trail system, the Mt. Rogers region has become one of the most popular hiking destinations in the AT corridor.

However, the route of this hike is not in the more-visited section of the AT or the Mt. Rogers Natl. Rec. Area, a 154,000-acre outdoor wonderland designated a national recreation area by Congress in 1966. There are few viewsheds (although in winter, when the deciduous trees have shed their leaves, the route is more generous with views) and no memorable contacts with water. But along the way are many blackberries in July and August at the northern end, a rare quiet trail through the woods where few hikers will be encountered after May, and for the knowledgeable hiker, morel mushrooms hiding in the dark. This is a hike for getting away from the crowd — even other hikers.

A visit to the Mt. Rogers Natl. Rec. Area headquarters and visitors' center before or after the hike is recommended. The oversized map of the area and exhibits on display there interpret the natural and social history in a way that can enhance understanding and enjoyment of everything to be seen along the trail. Should we expect anything less from a place named for the first president of the Massachusetts Institute of Technology and the first state geologist of Virginia? It was after his death in 1883 that William Barton Rogers's name officially replaced the former Balsam Mt.

From the Mt. Rogers visitors' center, the trail ascends through hardwoods and scattered rhododendron. Scattered young beech beneath maple in the low, moist woodland illustrate a forest gaining maturity, as hardwoods become predominant. The tree's gray bark and teethy leaves make it easy to spot. The beech is an ecosystem unto itself. The edible bolete mushroom, identified by its rust-colored cap, often grows beneath the beech in spring and summer. Silky sheath mushrooms and slimy armillarias grow on the tree itself. Surrounding the tree trunk, almost invariably, is the tiny beechdrop flower, a plant that feeds on beech roots.

At 0.7 mi., the trail crosses gravel VA 622. The next 0.5 mi. is an ascent of Brushy Mt., quite steep at times but never sustained for more than a few hundred yd. Reaching the crest at 1.2 mi., the trail continues to ascend, although gradually now, along a ridge covered by a hardwood canopy of mostly oak and hickory. There are no overlooks atop Brushy Mt., and, except in the leafless winter,

few places to stop for a view. There is, however, an interesting U.S. Geological Survey marker from 1934 at 2.1 mi. Because no overlook has been cut to encourage a rest until now, this is a good place to stop.

Over the next mile, the AT offers a repeating theme of up, down, up until reaching a distinct sag between Brushy and Locust mountains at 3.3 mi. From the sag, the 0.5 mi. ascent to the crest of Locust Mt. can only be characterized as steep and challenging. No sooner does the trail achieve the crest at 3800 ft. than it's on its way down.

At 4.1 mi., the trail bottoms at the base of Locust and Glade mountains and crosses USFS 86, an optional exit point with parking for several cars. The road leads west to a junction with VA 16, approximately 3 mi. south

Michael Warren

Blazing the trail with reflective white paint

of I-81. Three hundred yards east on USFS 86, a spring box supplies water, which should be treated before drinking. The area adjacent to the road offers the flattest most comfortable place along the hike to pitch a tent. As throughout Washington-Jefferson National Forest, camping and fires are permitted anywhere unless designated off-limits. Hikers are urged to camp in established campsites or campgrounds, where available.

For hikers out only in search of long views, the cresting of Brushy and Locust might amount to work without reward, but the dense forest and mature trees offer a splendid solitude and belie the extensive timbering that cleared the area in the early 20th century. It is along the crest of Glade Mt. that the view seekers are rewarded. From USFS 86, at 4.1 mi., the trail begins a steady, mile-long, 500-vertical-ft. ascent to capture those views.

When you need a rest from the steady climb, the white oaks scattered throughout invite a visit. These oaks, like many forest oaks, display various sacklike growths at the ends of branches, in the apexes of small branches, even on the leaves. These "galls" are manufactured housing for larvae, often of wasps or moths. Of the most common, bullet galls resemble golf balls, while club galls look like a five-wood. Taking the time to explore the twigs and branches of other hardwoods will reveal similar insect incubators.

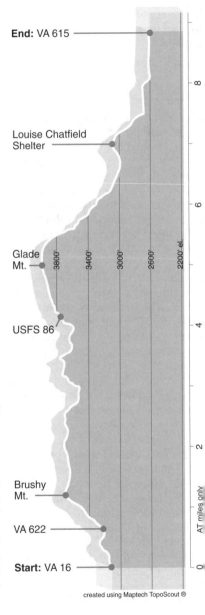

End: VA 615

Louise Chatfield Shelter

Glade Mt.

3800' 3400' 3000' 2600' 2200' el.

USFS 86

Brushy Mt.

VA 622

Start: VA 16

AT miles only

created using Maptech TopoScout ®

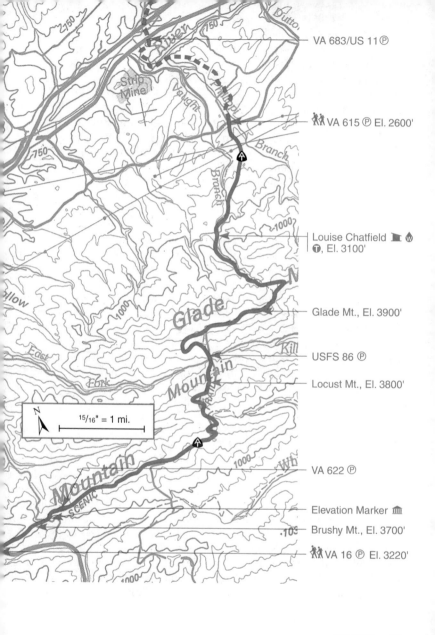

VA 683/US 11 Ⓟ

🚶🚶 VA 615 Ⓟ El. 2600'

Louise Chatfield 🏔 💧
🚰, El. 3100'

Glade Mt., El. 3900'

USFS 86 Ⓟ

Locust Mt., El. 3800'

VA 622 Ⓟ

Elevation Marker 🏛

.103 Brushy Mt., El. 3700'

🚶🚶 VA 16 Ⓟ El. 3220'

At 5.0 mi., the AT reaches the crest of Glade Mt. (elev. 3900 ft.). Continuing northwest along the ridge top, the trail on occasion breaks through the rhododendron thicket to offer views north of the Great Valley and Little Brushy Mt., which hosts the AT north of here. At one vantage point, 5.8 mi. into the hike and perfectly placed for lunch or siesta, a log bench beckons.

The Louise Chatfield Shelter, at 7.0 mi., has a privy, but no protected water source. The creek that the trail crosses here provides drinking water, but purification, as well as filtration, are absolute necessities. The shelter offers ample protection from the elements, but its proximity to VA 615, only 1.8 mi. away, regularly draws in-and-out campers who come early and frequently fill the shelter beyond capacity before the arrival of backpackers. And with the Great Valley opening below Glade Mt., the faint sound of traffic on I-81 can intrude upon the evening.

From Chatfield Shelter, the AT descends to cross gravel USFS 644 at 7.3 mi., passes farmland on the left, and continues through woodland, crossing Vaught Branch half a dozen times, first at 7.5 mi. Vaught Branch drains into the South Fork Holston River just beyond the AT junction with US 11. As you slosh through the creek beneath the trees, be on the lookout for Indian Pipe clusters. The albino plant, which grows in unusually large numbers here, is practically translucent. Its white stems grow 3 to 12 in. tall, each sustaining one pipe-bowl flower drooping toward the forest floor. Because it contains no chlorophyll, it does not rely on sunlight for nourishment; instead its food comes from other plants whose roots it taps.

After crossing a stile at 8.1 mi., the trail meanders among rhododendron until, at 8.5 mi., passing through a field and beneath power lines. The open glade here is prime habitat for blackberries. With the end of this hike near, a bag of berries is in order after feeding on them right off the bush. A note of warning: poison ivy can almost always be found in blackberry bushes, so beware of those "leaflets three." For a southern treat after the trail, cover two cups of blackberries with just enough water to submerge the berries; add two cups of sugar and simmer until the syrup and berries begin to blend; chill and eat over country biscuits with a slice of ham.

At 8.8 mi., the trail leaves the woods and the berries behind, finding VA 615 and the end of this hike. Before driving off, hikers can visit a historic restoration in progress adjacent to the trail. The Settlers Museum of Southwest Virginia, the USFS, and other partners are restoring a farm village. The Lindamood schoolhouse, built circa 1890, has been restored, as has a 19th-century farmhouse, which houses the museum office

Hike #5   Itinerary

Miles N	NORTH	Elev. (ft/m)	Miles S
8.8	**End:** Trailhead parking on VA 615 3.0 mi. from Groseclose.	2600/793	0.0
8.5	Power lines.		0.3
7.5	First of 6 crossings of **Vaught Branch.**		1.3
7.0	**Louise Chatfield Shelter,** privy.	3100/948	1.8
5.0	Crest of **Glade Mt.**	3900/1189	3.8
4.1	Cross **USFS 86;** water R (E) 300 yd.; early exit option L (W).		4.7
3.8	Crest of **Locust Mt.**	3800/1158	5.0
3.3	Gap.	3400/1036	5.5
2.1	USGS marker.		6.7
1.2	Crest of **Brushy Mt.**	3700/1128	7.6
0.7	Cross **VA 622.**		8.1
0.0	**Start:** Parking at **Mt. Rogers Natl. Rec. Area, VA 16,** 6.5 mi. S of Marion.	3220/981	8.8

SOUTH

and several exhibits. Further restoration is in progress. This living history of the valley and Blue Ridge offers glimpses of the area in the days before automobiles bore hikers to the hills for day-long rambles. It is open weekends from 10 to 4.

We have omitted the 2.7 mi. between this spot and Hike #6 because it is traveled mostly by thru-hikers to cross the I-81 corridor.

Tennessee Valley Divide

Map: ATC Va. #3, Southwest Virginia

Route: From VA 742 through Tilson Gap, over Little Brushy Mt. to VA 617, 0.2 mi. N of Atkins

Recommended direction: N to S

Distance: 9.7 mi.

Elevation +/-: 2450 to 3500 to 2450 ft.

Effort: Strenuous

Day hike: Yes

Overnight backpacking hike: Yes

Duration: 6 1/2 to 7 1/2 hr.

Early exit option: None

Natural history features: Tennessee Valley Divide; North Fork Holston River; Great Valley; Tilson Gap

Social history features: Davis family cemetery; Davis Path

Trailhead access: *Start:* From I-77, take Bland exit to VA 42W; go 17.4 mi. to VA 610; turn L and go S 1.0 mi. to gravel VA 742; turn R. AT crossing is 0.3 mi. ahead. Day parking along road. Overnight parking available at VA 42 parking area, 0.5 mi. before turning onto VA 610. *End:* From I-81 Exit 18 (Groseclose/Atkins), take VA 683N; in 1.0 mi., go R onto VA 617 to trailhead, 0.3 mi. Limited roadside parking. If no parking is available here, retrace toward I-81 to restaurant just S of exit; ask permission if parking here. *Note:* This adds 1.3 mi. of AT hiking on gentle, almost flat terrain.

Camping: Mozer homestead tenting area; Davis Path Shelter

D ue to its elevation changes, this 9.7-miler makes an ambitious day hike, but offers a fine overnight camping spot for hikers out for the evening. This rugged ramble gets little visitation from day hikers because there are no options for early exit after the VA 610 crossing at 1.4 mi. What they miss by avoiding this hike is a close encounter with a geologic phenomenon that illustrates the very evolution of life on Earth: a place where waters divide. (See sidebar.)

Along the way there is one breathtaking view of farmland and Big Walker Mt., remote Crawfish Valley, Glade Mt., the Great Valley, and rhododendron thickets so thick a bobcat might not know if it were night or day. With so much rhododendron and forest cover, this hike is a little stingy on overlooks. But when the view does open up, it's well worth the wait. Few routes are better for a quiet hike, but it doesn't come easily. There are two climbs of 800 vertical ft., the second after descending 1000 ft. from the first. Total elevation gain and loss amounts to 5000 ft. Still, to experience the pleasures of the Crawfish Valley — the hidden treasure on this hike — makes it well worth the effort.

Before setting out, a 100-yd. walk back along VA 742 (north) to the remains of the Tilson Mill offers a chance to stretch auto-weary legs and look back into the 1860s when wheat and corn were ground into flour here for residents of the North Fork Holston River valley. This mill and the river are part of a grand history that ends in the Gulf of Mexico, and to appreciate it fully hikers should tighten their laces and head south on the AT. Only a few yards beyond the trailhead, it crosses the North Fork Holston. The trail follows the river on wooden puncheons (split timbers laid like a one-track railroad corridor over cross logs) for 150 yd., then ascends through the woods. The ascent is steady, but not steep. It is also necessary to warm up legs and lungs for the many ups and downs ahead.

At 1.1 mi., the woods end and reveal a high, open meadow. In the fore view are acres and acres of bucolic farmland, punctuated by groups of cows and scattered barns. This is a fine spot at which to sit, stretch, and finish off a traveler's breakfast. From here the trail descends through a meadow to cross VA 610 at 1.4 mi. The trail next passes over a series of stiles before beginning an aggressive ascent of Big Walker Mt. by a succession of switchbacks beginning at about 1.8 mi. Purple rhododendron appear at every turn, along with the bright, white-flowering liverwort, blooming March to May, and the church bell-shaped Solomon's-seal in May and June.

The trail crosses two intermittent streams, then continues its climbs through switchbacks. Along the way, several groupings of the distinctive Dutchman's-breeches, which looks like its namesake, can be seen. In summer, trumpet creeper, a climber similar to the common hedgerow variety, but with bright red, bugle-shaped flowers fills the wood's air with sweetness. The Virginia pine and tulip poplar give the AT through here a distinctively southern feel.

At 2.7 mi., the crest of Big Walker Mt. at Tilson Gap (elev. 3500 ft.) makes the first big climb of the hike a memory of flowering shrubs. Tilson Gap is a classic "wind gap" of the Appalachian Blue Ridge — a dry gap through which, geologists speculate, ceaseless winds or water carried rock and soil away grain by grain. Viewed from the air, it resembles the river gaps formed through millions of years of surging river current. Without so much as a look-over-there, the trail begins a descent, finds the old woods road through the gap, and continues down through another thicket of rhododendron, now interspersed with mountain laurel and azalea. Then another. And another. At 3.2 mi., 0.5 mi. into the descent, an intermittent spring provides emergency water. Then it is back into the rhododendron understory beneath towering oaks, maple, and walnut. Any thoughts that hiking is easier on the descent than on the climb are dispelled by the many switchbacks.

Suddenly, at 4.3 mi., there is the sound of water, a trickle followed by a babble followed, in the wet season, by a roar just as the mountain bottoms out in the Crawfish Valley at 4.5 mi. The valley is so narrow here that it seems only a few steps further to the ascent of Little Brushy. But what's the rush, especially when all of geologic history is just underfoot? Reed Creek, tumbling from Big Walker Mt. just east of the trail, is taking its own route to the Ohio River. Like a textbook military ruse, Reed Creek runs an end-around maneuver, first to the southeast of Big Walker Mt., then to the northeast, and dumps into Walker Creek as it rolls steadily toward the north-flowing New River. Despite its name, the New is the world's second-oldest river. It seems the early settlers found it altogether "new" that a river would flow north instead of south. Where else but in the new world would one find this new kind of river? The course of the New River was set, many geologists believe, tens or hundreds of millions of years ago. The relatively recent geologic and tectonic activities that have shaped other rivers has not changed the path of the New.

If pondering all this makes a hiker want to pitch a tent a stay a while, just 0.4 mi. away the old Mozer homesite in Crawfish Valley is the place to be. To get there, cross the creek on the Walker Mt. Trail, which intersects the AT at Reed Creek. To the left, Walker Mt. Trail fords Reed Creek; to the right it descends along Bear Creek, which begins as a trickle several yards from the AT. The Walker Trail leads 20 yd. to a junction with an abandoned roadbed that heads south (right) along the creek. It is unmarked but easy to follow, eventually becoming little more than a narrow, overgrown footpath. The footpath leads another 0.3 mi. to the former homestead of James Mozer, who farmed the valley in the early 1900s. There is not much left of the place, save the rubble and old foundation walls that can be seen beneath the vegetation. But here the creek valley opens a little to an open meadow and a giant oak near the creek that offer a picturesque setting in which to pitch a tent. Water from the creek should be treated before drinking. In Crawfish Valley, the resilience of the eastern forest is apparent. Heavily logged and farmed by Mozer in the early 20th century, already the valley is again covered with green. Today's hikers see dense understory, and hikers in the late 21st century will enjoy a climax hardwood forest.

From Reed Creek (4.5 mi.), the AT begins a steep 1.1-mi. ascent of Little Brushy Mt., also known as Gullion Mt. On the lower switchbacks nodding wild onion and wild bergamot, a kind of mint, add a little pink to July and August hikes, as well as a fragrant touch to the vast volumes of air your lungs will consume to make the climb out of the valley.

At 5.6 mi., the trail reaches the crest of Little Brushy (elev. 3300 ft.) and

Where the Waters Divide

The Appalachian Trail plays a special role in this tale of two rivers. As it passes Reed Creek, it is meandering over the Tennessee Valley Divide, which, like the Continental Divide in the western United States, marks the division between two major watersheds, the New River and the Tennessee, both of which eventually flow into the Ohio, the Mississippi, and finally the Gulf of Mexico.

The AT crosses the North Fork Holston River at the northern end of this hike. After joining its south and middle forks, the Holston empties into the Tennessee River and travels another 570 miles, dipping into northern Alabama, then back north into western Kentucky before emptying into the Ohio River just upriver from its confluence with the Mississippi.

The New River cuts due northwest past Pearisburg, Virginia, then through the famous gorge that bears its name, and onward across West Virginia to join the Kanawha in Charleston. The Kanawha (pronounced ken-NAW) finds the Ohio River 97 miles farther northwest, nearly 500 miles upstream from the Tennessee River's confluence with the Ohio.

What does all this mean in its simplest terms? The Appalachian Trail, as it passes Reed Creek in Crawfish Valley, helps to tell the story. Imagine two leaves falling, one into Reed Creek and the other a few yards west into the Bear Creek drainage. The Bear Creek leaf would find its way to the North Fork Holston. As the headwaters for one of America's great rivers — the Tennessee — the North Fork Holston drains a narrow vale between Big Walker Mt. and Brushy Mt. to form the top of the Tennessee Valley. So our leaf would float 100 miles to the Tennessee River and beyond.

Our Reed Creek leaf will make an "end around" northeast of the headwaters of the Holston to find the New River, then continue on an 800-mile journey through coal country, sandstone cliffs, and the most rugged region of the oldest mountains on Earth. Its trip to the Ohio will be a mad rush of fast-moving water, leaving nothing but an ever-deepening (and beautiful) drainage in its wake.

This geologic story suggests the ultimate circuit hike — a trail following Reed Creek to the Holston and the New to the Ohio, then down the Ohio to the mouth of the Tennessee, then back up the Tennessee to the Holston, to the North Fork Holston, to Bear Creek, and this spot on the Appalachian Trail.

immediately starts back down — a temporary descent. With a series of switchbacks and ups and downs over several knolls, the ridge of Little Brushy is rarely level. It is quite steep at times, but in a few extended places the trail slabs gently down around several knolls to give weary legs a break. At 6.7 mi., it's time for a rest. Here is an open view of the settlements in the Great Valley, marred only slightly by the intrusion of I-81, which remains out of earshot. Known as the Shenandoah Valley in northern Virginia and by other identifiers in other places, the Great Valley arcs from Alabama to Canada, broken on the west by steep ridges that rise, run north-south with the valley, then disappear. Geologically, this is the Valley and Ridge Province, in which the Great Valley resembles a vast ocean, and the intermittent ridges, islands. The Appalachian Trail hugs the eastern edge of the Valley for most of its journey from Tennessee to New York. Here atop Little Brushy Mt. is a rare stretch where the trail travels west of the Great Valley, where it remains until reaching Tinker Mt. to the north.

For the next 0.5 mi. the trail follows a steep descent through oak and hickory, hardwoods overcoming the locust and black walnut that dominated the early regeneration of these fields to forest. At 7.3 mi., there is a sag between two ridges, recommended as a rest stop before beginning a climb of 250 vertical ft. over 0.4 mi. — normally no big deal, but at this point in the hike, a challenge. The

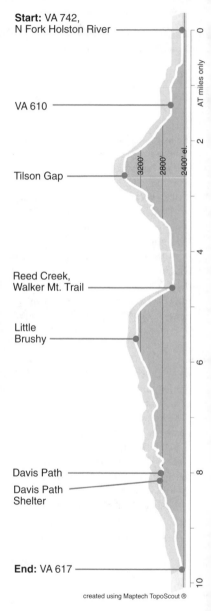

created using Maptech TopoScout ®

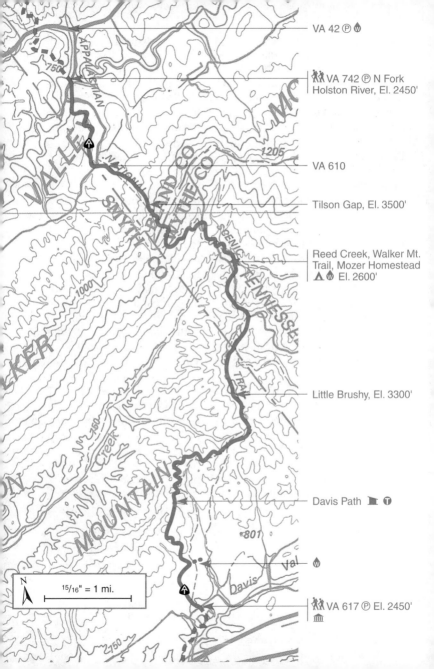

VA 42 Ⓟ Ⓦ

⚐⚐ VA 742 Ⓟ N Fork
Holston River, El. 2450'

VA 610

Tilson Gap, El. 3500'

Reed Creek, Walker Mt.
Trail, Mozer Homestead
▲ Ⓦ El. 2600'

Little Brushy, El. 3300'

Davis Path ▰ Ⓣ

Ⓦ

⚐⚐ VA 617 Ⓟ El. 2450'
🏛

N
¹⁵/₁₆" = 1 mi.

rain that drains into the sag brings patches of five-finger, a yellow member of the rose family that looks more like a daisy, in the summer months. Its name is derived from its leaves, grouped together like fingers on a hand.

The old woods road at 8.0 mi. is Davis Path, a wind-gap pass route used by 19th-century settlers. It no longer appears on most maps, but its intersection with the trail is unmistakable. While some local histories refer to Davis Path as a migration route, others refer to it merely as a local access route to farms and settlements in Davis Hollow to the east. After all, the Great Valley, more than 6 mi. wide and only 1 mi. south of here, provided an easier migration route.

The Davis Path Shelter is 200 yd. beyond Davis Path. Although the shelter has a privy, the nearest water source is a mi. further down the trail (at 9.0 mi., a blue-blazed trail leads left to the spring; backpackers heading north should collect enough water at this spring for the evening and the morning hike). Despite its proximity to the trail, the shelter offers a wondrous seclusion as it is on a section of the AT that gets few day visitors.

From Davis Path Shelter, there is one more knoll to ascend, then the gradual descent via switchbacks, first through hardwoods, then through another thicket of rhododendron. At 9.2 mi., the trail ascends into an open meadow. From its pinnacle, there are views of Glade Mt. and Brushy to the south, as well as the town of Groseclose in the Great Valley.

The final 0.5 mi. to VA 617 travels open meadow with views of farmland and the Davis Valley. The flowers of Viper's bugloss and pale-spike lobelia, common in these mountain meadows, rise among the grasses. Reaching the end of the hike, at 9.7 mi., you may want to stow your pack in your car and replace your hiking boots with sneakers before going on to the Davis family cemetery, another 175 yd. down the trail. The family of James Davis first settled the Middle Fork Holston valley in the mid-1700s. An interpretive sign by the trail marks the surrounding ground as Davis Fancy, the name of the early settlement. It is a lovely setting that provides a gradual reentry into the so-called civilized world buzzing past on I-81 less than a mile south.

Hike #6   Itinerary

Miles N	NORTH	Elev. (ft/m)	Miles S
9.7	**Start: VA 742, N Fork Holston River,** 17.4 mi. W of Bland; roadside parking.	2450//747	0.0
8.4	Cross **VA 610.**		1.3
7.7	Stream crossings.		2.0
7.0	**Tilson Gap,** crest of **Big Walker.**	3500/1067	2.8
6.5	Intermittent spring.		3.2
5.2	**Crawfish Valley, Reed Creek;** junction with **Walker Mt. Trail,** cross stream for short trail to **Mozer homestead camping area.**	2600/792	4.5
4.1	High point on **Little Brushy,** begin descent.	3300/975	5.6
3.0	View of Great Valley.		6.7
1.7	**Davis Path.**		8.0
1.6	**Davis Path Shelter,** privy, no water.		8.1
0.7	Intersect short, blue-blazed trail to spring.		9.0
0.5	Open fields, views.		9.2
0.0	**End:** Trailhead parking along **VA 617,** 1.3 mi. N of Groseclose/Atkins I-81 interchange; 0.1 mi. on AT to Davis family cemetery and historic marker.	2450/747	9.7

SOUTH

Garden Mt., Chestnut Ridge, and Brushy Mt.

Map: ATC Va. #2, Southwest Virginia

Route: Through Jefferson NF from Garden Mt. and Walker Gap over Chestnut Ridge and Brushy Mt. to VA 42

Recommended direction: N to S

Distance: 17.1 mi.

Elevation +/-: 3880 to 4409 to 2300 to 3100 to 2600 ft.

Effort: Strenuous

Day hike: Optional

Overnight backpacking hike: Yes

Duration: 13 hr.

Early exit options: At 4.9 mi., VA 727; at 10.8 mi., USFS 222/VA 625

Natural history features: Burkes Garden; Beartown Wilderness; Chestnut Ridge; Poor Valley

Social history feature: Chestnut Knob Shelter

Trailhead access: *Start:* From Bland exit on I-77, travel 4.0 mi. S on VA 42/US 52 to fork. Stay R at fork, on VA 42; go 7.0 mi. Turn R onto gravel VA 623 (slow going) for 7.5 mi. to trailhead atop Garden Mt., where there is limited parking (overnight). *For day hike start:* Continue 5.0 mi. farther into Burkes Garden and go L onto VA 727, which ends in 5.0 mi., 0.3 mi. before the AT; roadside parking at gate. *End:* From Bland exit on I-77, travel 18.5 mi. on VA 42W to overnight parking at the O'Lystery Community Picnic Area (picnic area not open to hikers).

Camping: Chestnut Knob Shelter; Knot Maul Branch Shelter; and see Camping section in Introduction.

T his saunter over Chestnut Ridge to Poor Valley and over Lynn Camp and Brushy mountains offers the kind of remote, wild feeling for which the southern Appalachian Trail is known. The American chestnut that gave the ridge its name no longer survives, but there is still plenty to enjoy: the lush farmland of Burkes Garden, a spring-fed pond for cooling off, the stillness of the deep woods of Beartown Wilderness below the ridge. For a 5.7-mi. day hike, you can start from Walker Gap (mi. 4.9) and hike into Poor Valley (mi. 10.8).

From trailhead parking on VA 623, heading south, the hike begins with a steady ascent toward the ridge of Garden Mt. At 0.2 mi., just as the trail finds the crest, an unmarked trail leads right 25 ft. to a rock overlooking the giant topographic bowl known as Burkes Garden. The "garden" is a 9-mi.-long oval that resembles a crater left by a great meteor or a city-sized Roman arena full of cows and corn. It is, however, the depression left behind after the soft limestone bedrock eroded. This porous rock allows for excellent drainage and the production of fertile soils and excellent growing conditions, hence the garden moniker (see also Hike #8).

The trail descends through rocky, rough-going terrain with towering sandstone outcroppings looming above. The fairly level roll of the ridge typically would make for easy walking, but clusters of large stones may interrupt your rhythm and bring fatigue early. The sandstone walls offer a diversion from the pounding of feet on stone, one that spelunkers are sure to enjoy. At 0.6 mi., the trail ascends the second of four distinct knolls along Garden Mt. amidst scattered laurel, which is joined by rhododendron in a dense thicket as the trail nears the crest of the knoll. At the top, at about 1.1 mi., the thicket opens to reveal another view of Burkes Garden and the several streams meandering through the fertile farmland below.

For the next 0.5 mi. the trail makes a gradual descent into a gap at 1.7 mi., still following sandstone outcrops, then heads up again through hemlock and white pine clinging to the dry soils along the ridge. At the crest, at 2.2 mi., a thicket of tall rhododenron surrounds the trail. Here begins more of the well-known "long green tunnel," as the AT descends only long enough to find a brief bowl and ascend again. Veteran thru-hikers know these continual ascents and descents as PUDs, or pointless ups and downs. For hikers attempting to cover the more than 2100 mi. of the AT, the ups and downs no doubt take their toll. For those of us out for a few days, they offer a prompting to stop and study the sandstone walls that accompany the trail until 3.8 mi.

In this rugged landscape it may be hard to imagine anyone staking out territory, but the remnants of a stone wall in a low gap at 4.3 mi. mark a time when the ridge described the grazing boundary for a Burkes Garden farmer. After crossing a final knob at 4.6 mi., the trail descends toward Walker Gap, the long green tunnel broken only by a seasonal stream just before you cross an unpaved road in the gap at 4.9 mi. The road is the tail end of VA 727, which traverses Burkes Garden. It is gated 0.3 mi. north, where there is parking. This road can be used as an early exit option or as the entry point for a 5.7-mi. day hike to Poor Valley (see Trailhead Access, above).

At the crossing, the dirt road becomes a blue-blazed ATV trail. Before you ascend the ridge, a 100-yd. trip left along the ATV trail to a spring, located near the ruins of a house, is in order. There are few opportunities for water above on Chestnut Ridge. Backpackers planning a night at Chestnut Knob Shelter especially should take note: the spring 300 yd. south of the shelter often gives out in dry summers.

From Walker Gap, the trail ascends steeply into woods of oak and hickory with scattered fir and hemlock. At about 5.2 mi., at the second intersection with the ATV trail, there is a chance to relax and admire the view south across Poor Valley to Brushy and Walker mountains. Back under the canopy, the trail continues a steady, formidable rise. The 889-ft. ascent to the crest is covered in about 1.2 mi., making a vigorous climb. But switchbacks offer places for pauses in the shade.

Moving ever upward, clinging to the hillside depressions here and there are straight lines of cedars lined up, like soldiers, in a row. Utilizing a method of regeneration uncommon on a dry peak such as this, each tree in a row sprouted from the trunk of a single fallen cedar, covered by years of humus and soil eroding from above. This method of regeneration is much more common in moist soils or swampy areas, but the hillside depressions here — whether natural or the result of logging activities — provide enough standing water annually to encourage root development underground.

The trail leaves the woods at 6.1 mi. and reaches the exposed summit of Chestnut Knob (4409 ft.), which provides a window onto Burkes Garden and the rich farmland to the north and northeast. The western ridge (the left rim of the bowl, if you will) marks the Tennessee Valley Divide, the division between the New and Tennessee rivers' watersheds. Both eventually empty into the Ohio (see Hike #6). Just a few steps farther, atop the world and in perfect position for viewing oncoming sunsets and star formations, is Chestnut Knob Shelter. It is an odd looking, squat,

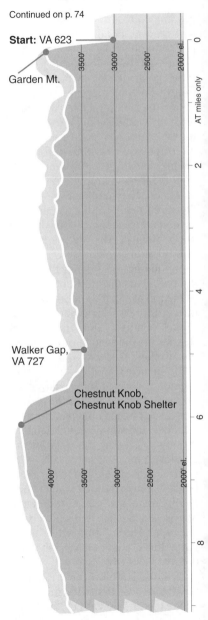

Continued on p. 74

Start: VA 623

Garden Mt.

Walker Gap, VA 727

Chestnut Knob, Chestnut Knob Shelter

AT miles only

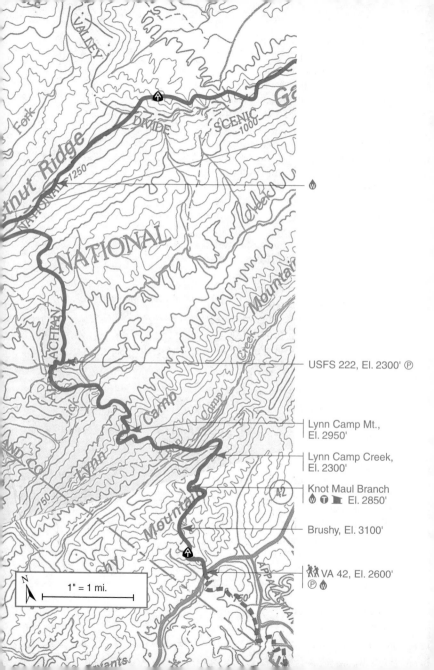

USFS 222, El. 2300' Ⓟ

Lynn Camp Mt.,
El. 2950'

Lynn Camp Creek,
El. 2300'

Knot Maul Branch
🅦 🅣 📷 El. 2850'

Brushy, El. 3100'

VA 42, El. 2600'
Ⓟ 🅦

1" = 1 mi.

stone building, more like a gunnery than shelter, but its height and construction are perfectly suited to the windy ridge. Any hiker who has spent a nervous night in an electrical storm above treeline will feel safe and snug here.

Originally used as a fire warden's cabin, the structure has found new life after a makeover performed by the Piedmont Appalachian Trail Hikers, the ATC's professional Konnarock Trail Crew, and the USFS. Perhaps somewhat tongue in cheek, and certainly stating the matter delicately, AT authors Victoria and Frank Logue proffer that the best view of Burkes Garden is obtained from the three-sided privy serving the shelter.

Although there are plenty of views and crags from here, there is occasionally no water atop the ridge. There is a good seasonal spring along the blue-blazed trail that has paralleled the AT from Walker Gap. To find it, follow the trail 300 yd. downhill; the spring emerges from an embankment left of the trail. A search in late June after a dry spring season revealed a only a trickle. However, when the area receives normal rainfall, the spring typically will dry up only in August.

From the shelter, the trail reenters the woods and begins its long descent along an old jeep road, which is wide enough, for the next 0.5 mi., that hiking companions can walk side by side through the forest, recounting the sights seen from Chestnut Knob. At 7.0 mi., the trail

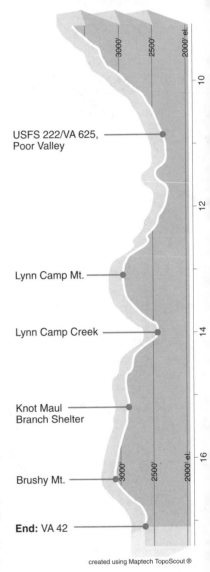

created using Maptech TopoScout ®

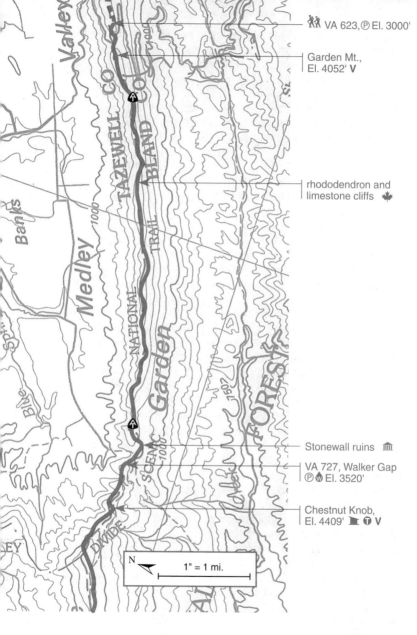

🥾 VA 623, Ⓟ El. 3000'

Garden Mt.,
El. 4052' **V**

rhododendron and
limestone cliffs 🍁

Stonewall ruins 🏛

VA 727, Walker Gap
Ⓟ 🚰 El. 3520'

Chestnut Knob,
El. 4409' 🏚 🚹 **V**

N

1" = 1 mi.

slips from the woods into the open, descending Chestnut Ridge, and offering arresting views of Big Walker Mt., Lynn Camp Mt., Clinch Mt., and many others to the south. To the north, adjacent to the trail, the Beartown Wilderness begins; the trail will travel astride the boundary for more than a mile. Beartown, 6375 acres of isolated hardwoods and pristine creeks, then stretches south of the AT and up the slope of Clinch Mt. There are few pathways into Beartown — one strategy for maintaining its pristine values. For the adventurous, an unimproved dirt road (USFS 631) leaves the parking area at the end of this hike and, at the border of the wilderness area, becomes a narrow footpath to a trout stream on Roaring Brook.

At 7.9 mi., a spring box at the north end of an unnamed pond provides water and a pleasant place for a rest and to watch clouds' shadows gaming on the field of green below. At 3900 ft., the spring is icy cold, there's usually a breeze, and getting wet and then a little chilled in the wind is the kind of summer polar fun that people who don't hike would never understand. Sun drying, some call it — it's pretty quiet and solitary up there.

Descending south, the trail reenters the woods at 8.6 mi. There are several old roads through here, and it is easy to take a wrong turn if you're still thinking about sun drying on the ridge. As ever on the AT, the white blazes show the way. At 9.5 mi., descending very steeply through switchbacks, the trail passes a junction with yet another ATV road, this one leading to USFS 631, the route into Beartown Wilderness. The valley floor is visible below, through the trees, as the trail crosses a small stream at 9.6 mi. At 9.9 mi., the trail takes a temporary respite from continuous falling, enough to rest weary feet. Sprouting from the rocky soils March to May is the tiny heartleaf flower. The green, mottled, heart-shaped leaf, growing from single stems about 6 in. tall, provide cover for the flowers, which are only an inch across and are lily shaped with red-and-white-speckled flowers that resemble those painted on rustic enamel plates and cups.

After a final, steep, 300-ft. descent, the trail emerges from the woods in Poor Valley at USFS 222/VA 625 (an early exit opportunity; there is overnight parking 175 yd. to the west) at 10.8 mi. From Chestnut Knob, less than 5 mi. back, the trail has dropped more than 2100 ft. to the low elevation point on this hike, 2300 ft.

On this side of Chestnut Ridge the underlying rock is shale, which makes for poor drainage and mineral soils that can't match the fertility of Burke Garden. Jack pines take hold among the other shallow-rooted species. The damp clay soil cannot support the delicate, needy root systems of crops nor the grasses favored by grazing livestock. Farmers found the soils here so inhospitable to agriculture they named the vale Poor Valley. On the other side of Lynn Camp Mt. you will visit a stream valley whose soils and farmers fared much better; it is known as Rich Valley. Just a kick of a boot into the earth reveals the difference between so-called rich valleys and poor ones.

Crossing USFS 222/VA 625, the trail follows an abandoned rail bed on level terrain, then jumps a narrow stream at 11.0 mi. Ascending from Poor Valley, the path makes quick work of a 100-ft. knob and drops again, quickly, to Lick Creek, crossing on a small footbridge at 12.0 mi. The trail begins a winding ascent of Lynn Camp Mt. beneath hemlock and pine, then follows an old roadbed through a narrow hollow between ridgelines. Pale touch-me-not and wintergreen dot uphill surroundings of tree trunks, before giving way to rocky, rough switchbacks up a challenging 800-ft. advance to the crest of Lynn Camp that becomes quite steep at about 12.5 mi. No sooner has the ridge been crested, at 13.1 mi., than the descent begins.

In the valley below, the trail crosses Lynn Camp Creek, then three more streams. The final creek, crossed by a log footbridge at 14.7 mi., is the last reliable source of water on the hike, particularly important for hikers planning an evening at Knot Maul Branch Shelter. Many older maps show a spring at the shelter, but it should be considered unreliable at best. The shelter, at 15.2 mi., is named for the knot branches gathered here by early settlers to make hammers (mauls) and other farm implements. There is a privy.

From the shelter, continue to ascend Brushy Mt. steeply for a few hundred ft., then descend gradually along the ridge until the woods open to the lush pastureland of Rich Valley and the end of the hike. The trail enters the O'Lystery Community Picnic Area parking area, where there is limited overnight parking. There is also limited roadside parking. A reminder: The picnic pavilion is private and is not for use by hikers.

Miles N	NORTH	Elev. (ft/m)	Miles S
17.1	**Start:** Trailhead parking on **VA 623,** 7.5 mi. N of VA 42 junction, which is 11.0 mi. W of Bland.	3880/1183	0.0
16.9	Crest of **Garden Mt.;** views of Burkes Garden (25 ft. to R on unmarked trail); sandstone rock outcroppings begin.	4052/1235	0.2
12.8	Pass ruins of stone wall.		4.3
12.2	**Walker Gap, VA 727,** early exit option; **spring** 100 yd. to L on ATV trail; ascend steeply.	3520/1073	4.9
11.0	**Chestnut Knob, Chestnut Knob Shelter,** seasonal spring, privy, views of Burkes Garden.	4409/1344	6.1
10.1	Leave woods; begin **descent of Chestnut Ridge,** views.		7.0
9.2	**Pond, spring.**	3900/1189	7.9
8.5	Reenter woods; begin **descent on switchbacks.**		8.6
6.3	**Cross USFS 222 in Poor Valley.** Ascend.	2300/701	10.8
5.1	Cross footbridge over **Lick Creek.**		12.0
4.6	Begin sharp ascent of **Lynn Camp Mt.;** switchbacks, rough going		12.5
4.0	Crest of **Lynn Camp Mt.;** start descent.	2950/899	13.1
3.1	Cross bridge over **Lynn Camp Creek.**	2300/701	14.0
2.4	Cross creek on **footbridge;** water for Knot Maul Branch Shelter.		14.7
1.9	**Knot Maul Branch Shelter,** unreliable water, privy.	2850/8687	15.2
0.8	**Crest of Brushy Mt.**	3100/945	16.3
0.0	**End:** Parking on **VA 42** and at **O'Lystery Community Picnic Area;** 18.5 mi. W of Bland.	2600/792	17.1

SOUTH

Garden Mt. and Little Wolf Creek

Map: ATC Va. #2, Southwest Virginia
Route: From Garden Mt. at VA 623 over Brushy Mt. to Little Wolf Creek and Laurel Creek
Recommended direction: S to N
Distance: 8.7 mi.
Elevation +/-: 3900 to 2500 to 3080 to 2450 ft.
Effort: Moderate
Day hike: Yes
Overnight backpacking hike: Optional
Duration: 5 hr.
Early exit option: None
Natural history features: Burkes Garden; Hunting Camp Creek; Little Wolf Creek; Laurel Creek

Other features: Views of Burkes Garden along ridge of Garden Mt.
Trailhead access: *Start:* From Bland exit on I-77, travel 4.0 mi. S on VA 42/US 52 to fork. Stay R at fork, on VA 42; go 7.0 mi. Go R on gravel VA 623 (slow going) for 7.5 mi. to trailhead atop Garden Mt., where there is limited parking (overnight). *End:* From Bland exit on I-77, travel 3.0 mi. S on VA 42/US 52. Turn R onto VA 615 and travel about 3 mi. to trailhead parking area.
Camping: Davis Farm Campsite; Jenkins Shelter; camping area just N of hike's end

---

This hike begins with a view of Burkes Garden so diverting a hiker could have trouble moving down the trail. But the beaver ponds and isolation of Hunting Camp Creek and Little Wolf Creek are worthy enticements into these wild stream valleys. For its part, Little Wolf Creek is a bewitching little world not to be missed by anyone who hikes in these parts.

Hikers should proceed prepared for the elements, however. Although the 8.7 miles, covering largely level or descending terrain, can be covered easily in a day hike, there are no early exit options along the route. For those considering an overnight trip,

there are abundant tent sites and water supplies in the valley, as well as Jenkins Shelter, tucked into the flats beside Hunting Camp Creek.

From the VA 623 trailhead, the AT follows the crest of Garden Mt., a Silurian sandstone ridge dividing the excellent agricultural soils of Burkes Garden to the north and the inhospitable, black shale of Poor Valley to the south. At about 0.4 mi., a jumble of sandstone to the north (left) side of the trail provides a long view of the Burkes Garden farmland below (see also Hike #7). The area was named for James Burke, whose association with the valley is the stuff of much folklore. According to legend, he discovered the valley while in pursuit of game, then, years later, guided British exploration parties into the valley. One explorer, Colonel James Patton, was so taken by the place and by Burke's hunting and backcountry culinary skills that he named the rich woodlands, now rich farmland, for Burke.

The blue-blazed trail at 0.9 mi. leads 0.5 mi. to Davis Farm Campsite. It may be a little early in this hike to think about making camp, but a one-mile round trip diversion to the campsite provides an expansive view of Burkes Garden with the Beartown Wilderness in the background (see Hike #7). There is a privy, and water also is available from a spring behind the campsite.

Beyond the campsite side trail, the AT meanders along the ridge amidst mixed hardwoods and seemingly ever-present rhododendron, finding level ground with minor ascents and descents until beginning a steady descent at 1.3 mi. from Garden Mt. toward Hunting Camp Creek. This stretch of the AT is a classic "long green tunnel," as the path winds through woodland. What is most striking perhaps is the complete absence of nonwildlife sounds — unfortunately a rarity along many sections of the AT. Here, descending into a steep-sided valley away from the country roads and highways on the other side of Garden Mt. to the north and Brushy to the south, the most notable sounds may be those of the wind and, for the quiet hiker, of

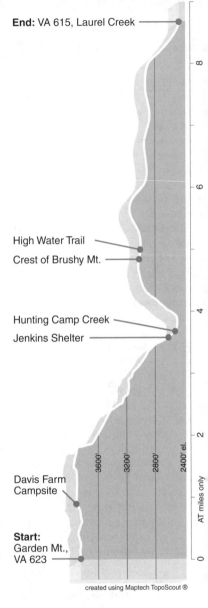

End: VA 615, Laurel Creek

High Water Trail
Crest of Brushy Mt.

Hunting Camp Creek
Jenkins Shelter

3600' 3200' 2800' 2400' el.

AT miles only

Davis Farm Campsite

Start: Garden Mt., VA 623

created using Maptech TopoScout ®

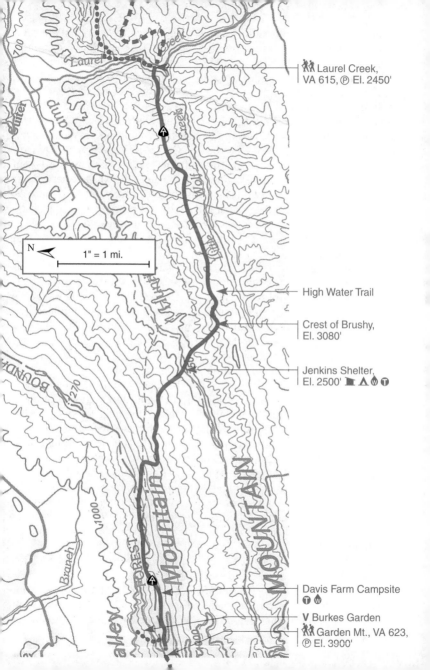

🥾 Laurel Creek,
VA 615, Ⓟ El. 2450'

High Water Trail

Crest of Brushy,
El. 3080'

Jenkins Shelter,
El. 2500' 🔲 ⛺ 💧 🚻

Davis Farm Campsite
🚻 💧

V Burkes Garden
🥾 Garden Mt., VA 623,
Ⓟ El. 3900'

N

1" = 1 mi.

deer and smaller creatures that scamper through the forest just as you discover them. At 2.6 mi., the trail crosses a small stream amid dense rhododendron.

As the trail bottoms it crosses a small stream at 3.4 mi. and reaches Jenkins Shelter at 3.6 mi. The water source is a spring 100 yd. behind the shelter on a blue-blazed trail. The shelter can accommodate about eight. The splendid surroundings are no secret to area hikers, so the shelter gets plenty of use. It is especially popular with members of the Outing Club of Virginia Tech, which built the shelter and named it in honor of David Jenkins, a professor and outing club leader at the school. Fortunately, there are adequate tenting sites another 0.1 mi. down the trail just past an old logging road, enough to accommodate the May invasion of hundreds of AT thru-hikers on their way north.

Beyond the tent sites, crossing Hunting Camp Creek at 3.7 mi., the trail abruptly begins an ascent of Brushy Mt. Backyard gardeners who have nursed rhododendron through battles with mites and fungi and root rot will marvel at the unchecked proliferation of these evergreens along the AT. The thickets are the predominant vegetational feature of the climb up Brushy Mt.

Reaching the wooded crest of Brushy, at 4.9 mi., the trail heads down again. Brushy is a defining feature of the AT in southern Virginia. For nearly 50 mi., Brushy is never far away, and is

ever being crested with little scenic reward. This particular cresting of Brushy is another one AT thru-hikers might call a PUD — for "pointless ups and downs." Once descending into the delightful Little Wolf Creek stream valley, this crossing of Brushy will seem anything but pointless, however.

On the way down, a blue blaze on the left at 5.0 mi. signals a reroute. This part of the AT once served as an alternate route when Little Wolf Creek was running high, but it is now the official route; you'll see the old route, no longer maintained, off to the right. Spring rains or extended precipitation at other times raised water levels so that the numerous crossings of Little Wolf Creek were dangerous, forcing the eventual reroute. There is no harm in going down to the creek for a look-see, even after a rainy period. The trip down to the creek and back is 1.4 mi.

Returning to the AT, the route follows the former high-water trail and climbs to the ridge for an easy 3.0 mi. walk through open woods. At 8.0 mi. the trail begins descending through rocky terrain toward Laurel Creek.

It is easy to see how Laurel Creek received its name. In spring, white and pink mountain laurel add color to the trailscape. The creek is making its way toward Hunting Camp Creek. It will eventually find Hunting Camp at a point about 5 mi. east of Jenkins Shelter.

At 8.7 mi., the trail reaches Laurel Creek 0.2 mi. north of where Little Wolf Creek washed in. Just beyond are VA 615 and the end of the hike. The bridge over Laurel Creek itself deserves a close look, perhaps even from below while dipping sore feet. It was constructed by the ATC Konnarock Trail Crew and the Outing Club of Virginia Tech using stone from the creek and masonry techniques long out of fashion. There are no concrete culverts reinforced with steel, no pylons, no mechanically sawed stone. Although built using wilderness tools and techniques, the bridge is by no means primitive. It just feels that way. It is a real work of art, and a fitting end to the beguiling ramble through the waters of Little Wolf Creek.

Miles N	**NORTH**	Elev. (ft/m)	Miles S
8.7	**End:** Cross **Laurel Creek to VA 615,** 3.0 mi. N of VA 42 junction, which is 3.5 mi. W of Bland.	2450/747	0.0
5.0	**High Water Trail** heads L (N)		3.7
4.9	**Crest of Brushy Mt.**	3080/939	3.8
3.7	**Campsites;** cross **Hunting Camp Creek;** AT ascends.		5.0
3.6	**Jenkins Shelter;** privy, water from spring 100 yd. up blue-blazed trail.	2500/762	5.1
2.6	**Cross small stream;** pass through rhododendron thicket.	3000/914	6.1
1.3	**Begin steady descent.**		7.4
0.9	Trail to **Davis Farm Campsite** (0.5 mi.), water, privy.		7.8
0.0	**Start:** Trailhead parking on **VA 623,** 7.5 mi. N of VA 42 junction, which is 11.0 mi. W of Bland.	3900/1188	8.7

SOUTH

HIKE # 9
Kimberling Creek to Laurel Creek

Map: ATC Va. #2, Southwest Virginia
Route: Through Jefferson NF from Kimberling Creek at US 21/52 over Brushy Mt. to Laurel Creek at VA 615
Recommended direction: N to S
Distance: 6.9 mi.
Elevation +/-: 2920 to 2600 to 3100 to 2400 ft.
Effort: Easy
Day hike: Yes
Overnight backpacking hike: Optional
Duration: 4 to 6 hr.
Early exit option: At 3.0 mi., overgrown woods road to USFS 282
Natural history features: Brushy Mt., Laurel Creek
Other features: Views of Burkes Garden; overnight accommodations, restau-rants, and groceries at N end of hike in Bastian and Bland

Trailhead access: *Start:* From I-77, take Exit 64 and proceed S on US 21/52, pass through Bastian, and continue 1.8 mi. to trailhead parking lot on L. *End:* From I-77, take Exit 64 and proceed S on US 21/52 for approximately 2.0 mi. to northern outskirts of Bastian. Turn R on VA 615 and continue approximately 4 mi. to sharp L. Follow VA 615 to L (road ahead becomes VA 618) and proceed 1.5 mi. further to small parking area on R.

Camping: No shelters; see Camping section in Introduction.

T his is an easy stretch of trail that, aside from a couple of dips and a mile-long descent at the end, follows a level course. Although thick stands of hardwoods restrict extensive views, the glimpses of Brushy Mt. and Hunting Camp Creek Valley that are afforded make it worth toting a camera with you. The trail follows, then runs parallel to, USFS 282 for the first half of the hike, but once the trail leaves the road and crosses into the woods, the trees keep the sound and sight of the few automobiles that pass to a minimum.

Although the cool waters of Little Wolf Creek wait for you at the end of your trek, there are no water sources along the way so be sure to pack some with you.

US 21/52, at the northern end of this hike, is a busy road, so proceed with caution as you leave your car behind and head for the trail. For the most part, however, the drivers who pass are a friendly lot who often wave or give a nod of approval that says they wish they could join you. There are several houses along the road and even a flower shop near

Galax, Wolf Creek

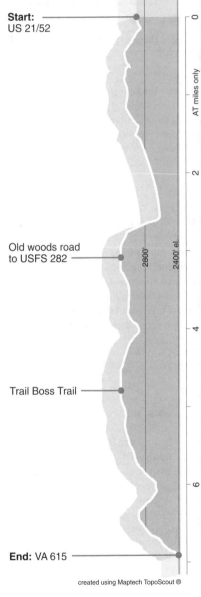

Start:
US 21/52

Old woods road
to USFS 282

Trail Boss Trail

End: VA 615

AT miles only

2800'

2400' el.

created using Maptech TopoScout ®

the trailhead. The neighbors are used to hikers, but be respectful of private property and stick to the blazed trail.

From the trailhead sign at US 21/52, the AT follows USFS 282 westward as it sets out along the crest of Brushy Mt. The gravel road is much less traveled than the highway, but remain on the look out for motorists. Thick clusters of azalea bushes keep the corridor colorful in spring. Painting a canvas of yellow, orange, and scarlet, their tubular blossoms bloom from May to June before giving way to long, bright green leaves. Many gardeners pay a high price to have these bushes blooming in their yards, but for AT hikers in the southern Appalachians, the spectacle is bountiful and free. Rhododendron bushes are also prevalent here. Once their purple blossoms have run their

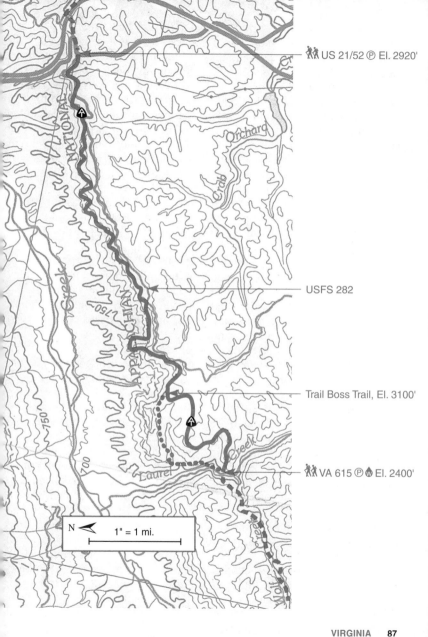

🏃🏃 US 21/52 Ⓟ El. 2920'

USFS 282

Trail Boss Trail, El. 3100'

🏃🏃 VA 615 Ⓟ ⦿ El. 2400'

N ◀ 1" = 1 mi.

course (May and June), dark green leaves keep the trail colorful year round, especially along mountain slopes.

After following USFS 282 for 0.3 mi., the AT crosses a power line right-of-way. From this sloping, grassy area there are views of Wolf Creek and Hunting Camp Creek valleys in the distant west and Garden Mt. peeking above the horizon. Beyond the clearing, at 0.5 mi. and 3000 ft., the trail bears right and begins to follow a well-graded footpath through the woods. In addition to the azalea and rhododendron, look for an occasional flowering dogwood among the high, sturdy oak trees. In spring, dogwoods blossom with starch-white flowers. In fall, they can be identified by clusters of small scarlet berries. The berries are high in fat and although their bitter taste makes them unappetizing to humans, they are a commodity for many of the forest's inhabitants including rabbits, foxes, and gray squirrels. White-tailed deer prefer to dine on the tree's foliage. Birds also feast on the berries. As they do, they also help replant the trees by dispersing the seeds in their droppings, often many miles from the original tree.

Crossing the northern side of Brushy Mt.'s crest, the AT continues along an easy course as it follows the flat, well-graded path. Just as civilization begins to feel like a distant memory, the trail crosses under a single-wire telephone line. Beyond this point (2.2 mi.) the trail comes to

a fork and bears left onto an old woods road as it descends 500 ft. in 0.4 mi., then immediately regains its previous altitude.

At 3.0 mi., an overgrown path on the left leads less than 100 yd. to USFS 282. Since the trail has been paralleling the narrow road from the beginning of the hike, 3.0 mi. of backtracking will bring you back to your starting point at US 21/52. At 3.5 mi., look to the right for a passing view of the town of Bastian. With a population of 300, the town is small and quaint, characteristics that are accentuated from this vantage point at 3000 feet.

The trail continues through thick woods, where hearty oaks keep the area colorful in spring, summer, and fall and evergreens continue to brighten the area in winter. At 4.1 mi., an old road to the right of the trail descends a spur ridge of Brushy Mt. 1.5 mi. toward Hunting Camp Creek Valley. The remote, deep valley is intersected by narrow, winding streams and shimmering blue ponds caused by beaver dams. An extensive beaver population is quite active in the area.

At 4.8 mi., the AT turns left onto a sidehill trail as the blue-blazed Trail Boss Trail continues straight ahead. Following a former AT route, the Trail Boss Trail was named for Keith "Trail Boss" Smith, a former Konnarock Trail Crew leader and member of the Outing Club of Virginia Tech. The blue-blazed trail leads 2.0 mi. to VA 615, near the southern end of this route.

After turning to the left at the Trail

Miles N	**NORTH**	Elev. (ft/m)	Miles S
6.9	**Start: U.S. 21/52** on Brushy Mt., 1.8 mi. S of Bastian and 2.5 mi. N of Bland.	2920/890	0.0
4.7	**Bear L** at fork in woods road.		2.2
4.3	Complete steep descent and begin ascending.	2600/792	2.6
3.9	**Early exit option** at old woods road leading 100 yd. to USFS 282.		3.0
2.8	**Cross** old road leading R to Hunting Camp Creek.		4.1
2.1	Blue-blazed **Trail Boss Trail** leads straight ahead 2.0 mi. to VA 615; AT bears L.	3100/945	4.8
1.3	**Bear L** and descend.		5.6
1.2	Cross **drainage area** on rock steps.		5.7
0.0	**End:** AT intersects with VA 615, 2.5	2400/732	6.9

SOUTH

Boss Trail intersection, the AT emerges into a somewhat open area as the trees thin slightly. The trail descends here, then travels back up the crest of Brushy Mt., ascending for the next 0.5 mi. A sharp switchback to the left (5.6 mi.) takes the trail down to a wide, rocky drainage area. As you use the flat rock steps to cross over the area, be careful of wet, slippery spots, especially after a recent rain.

At 5.9 mi., the trail leaves the top of Brushy Mt. and begins a 1.0-mi. descent toward Laurel Creek. A series of ten long switchbacks over a well-graded trail make this an easy 520-ft.

drop. After making a sharp right onto an old logging road, the trail meets a small arm of Laurel Creek and follows it to VA 615 and the southern end of this section of the AT.

Beyond VA 615, Laurel Creek and Little Wolf Creek intersect. Laurel Creek flows parallel to the road, while Little Wolf Creek runs perpendicular to the road, and parallel to the AT south of this section. If you're looking for a cold drink, head for Little Wolf Creek as Laurel Creek passes through a residential area just upstream and is not safe for consumption.

Lickskillet Hollow to Kimberling Creek

Map: ATC Va. #1, Southwest Virginia

Route: Through Jefferson NF from VA 608 near Crandon over Brushy Mt. to Kimberling Creek, VA 612 and I-77

Recommended direction: N to S

Distance: 12.4 mi.

Elevation +/-: 2200 to 3100 to 2800 ft.

Effort: Easy

Day hike: Yes

Overnight backpacking hike: Optional

Duration: 6 1/2 to 8 hr.

Early exit option: VA 611

Natural history features: Jenny Knob; Kimberling Creek Valley

Other features: Supplies and phone available near both ends of hike in Crandon, Bland, and Bastian

Trailhead access: *Start:* From I-77, take Exit 52 to Bland and head E on VA 42 for 10.0 mi. to VA 608 in Crandon; turn L and head N 0.8 mi. to small trailhead parking area on L. *End:* From intersection of I-77 and VA 42, continue N on I-77 for 2.5 mi. to VA 612 and turn R. Proceed 0.25 mi. to small parking area on L. Trailhead is on R.

Camping: Jenny Knob Shelter; Helvey's Mill Shelter; and see Camping section in Introduction

---

The majority of this 12.4-mi.-long hike crosses over the flat top of Brushy Mt. on old woods roads, making it doable as a day-long excursion. Or, if you're looking for an overnight trek, you can break it up at one of the two shelters along the route or the several primitive campsites. The trail reaches the highest point of the section at 3100 ft., just past the 10.0-mi. mark, but, because the 1000-ft. rise is mostly spread out over the first 2.9 mi., the climb is hardly noticeable. Stock up on water before you start, especially if you are out for a two-day affair. There are water sources at each end, but the mountain is pretty dry. If you didn't pack enough water or other staples

to get you through the hike, try the small grocery store on VA 42 in Crandon. Don't plan to pack for your entire trip here, but you should find an extra bottle of water or an afternoon snack.

Beginning at VA 608 in Lickskillet Hollow, head westward on the AT, slowly climbing on an old road that runs parallel to a rolling creek. The water tumbling over its dark shale bed helps drown the sound of traffic buzzing down VA 608. Be careful near the roadside: this can be a busy thoroughfare. The trail heads away from the traffic and passes through a small clearing, beyond which several large rocks form a pretty waterfall as the creek travels alongside the AT.

The trail continues through a forest dominated by mature red oak trees. Their pointy, bristle-tipped leaves crunch below hikers' feet in autumn and winter and provide a welcome canopy from the sun in spring and summer. The fastest-growing of all oak trees, many red oaks prosper for up to 300 years. As the name suggests, this oak's leaves turn vibrant red before falling to the forest floor, making this a particularly colorful stretch of trail in early autumn. In addition to enhancing our viewing pleasure, the trees, which produce an abundance of acorns, also provide an important food source to a variety of wildlife, especially birds. Wild turkeys, blue jays, tufted titmice, and crows are just a few of the vertebrates that feed upon these trees, which also help squirrels, bears, and other mammals stay well stocked in winter.

After this easy half-mile warm-up, the trail crosses a narrow stream and begins a much steeper ascent, leaving the old woods road and turning left onto a narrow, grassy footpath. The AT follows the footpath up a long sidehill. In the winter and early spring, look to the east for a view of Big Walker Mt., a long Silurian sandstone ridge.

In less than 100 yd. the steep uphill climb tapers to a less demanding ascent and the AT makes a more gradual climb toward Jenny Knob to reach Jenny Knob Shelter on the left, 1.2 mi. into the hike. Up to eight hikers can snuggle into the tiny structure, built by the USFS and ATC's Konnarock Trail Crew and currently maintained by the Outing Club of Virginia Tech. A blue-blazed path leads behind the shelter and past an outhouse to a small creek. Water is usually available, but it should be treated before you drink it. There is a smaller creek in the opposite direction, but, unless it has rained recently, it is likely to be dry.

At the shelter, look to see if a nesting family of phoebe have settled into the rafters. The mild-mannered, olive-gray birds are quite populous in this area and tend to build their nests under the eaves of the shelters or inside, under the roof. The birds seem at ease with hikers and will go about their business if left uninterrupted.

Beyond the shelter, the AT continues to ascend a narrow path through an old oak forest as it rises to meet the crest of Brushy Mt. The forest is similar to the one you passed through near the beginning of the hike, but as you travel further away from the water, the trees become knottier and a little less vibrant. As the trail heads up the old sandstone ridge, look for wildflowers, including violets and buttercups in spring, wild geranium in summer, and, in open areas, black-eyed Susans throughout the fall. At 1.6 mi., the trail makes a sharp right as it reaches the spur of a smaller ridge. Reaching the crest of Brushy Mt. at 1.9 mi. (3000 ft.), the AT veers to the left, following the ridge westward. The trail dips into a narrow gap, then widens as it picks up another woods road and continues to ascend, topping the wooded summit of Brushy Mountain at 2.9 mi. and 3100 ft.

The woods road begins to dwindle and soon the AT is back on a narrow footpath as it mounts a low knob and descends into a wide, unnamed gap (4.0 mi.). Continuing downward, the trail widens onto another old road, then narrows onto a footpath once again. This pattern continues throughout most of the hike.

In the gap, erosion, melting snow, and rainwater run-off have carved gullies in the sandstone that create a bit of an obstacle course. Beyond these trenches, the trail rises to meet the ridgeline of Brushy Mt. once again. Near the top of the ridge, at 4.3 mi., the AT makes a sharp right and intersects with VA 611, a gravel road that leads south 1.5 mi. to to VA 42. There is a roadside parking lot to the left of the trail, and if you are looking for a shorter day hike, this is the spot to leave a second car.

Beyond the intersection, the AT continues to climb, attaining the ridge 0.3 mi. farther on. Now the trail follows a fairly flat course for nearly a mile, passing occasional views of Kimberling Creek Valley to the north. At 5.9 mi., the trail makes a minor descent into another shallow gap. There, it crosses a rocky woods road that leads to Kimberling Creek Valley in both directions, passes under a telephone line (6.1 mi.) and makes another steep, but brief, ascent back to the ridgeline.

The AT turns left onto a prominent woods road and follows it along a

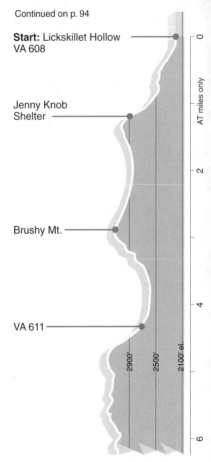

Continued on p. 94

Start: Lickskillet Hollow VA 608

Jenny Knob Shelter

Brushy Mt.

VA 611

AT miles only

2900' 2500' 2100' el.

flat course for the next mile. Then, at 7.7 mi., bear right up a hill and join a less well-defined road with limited views of the valley to the north.

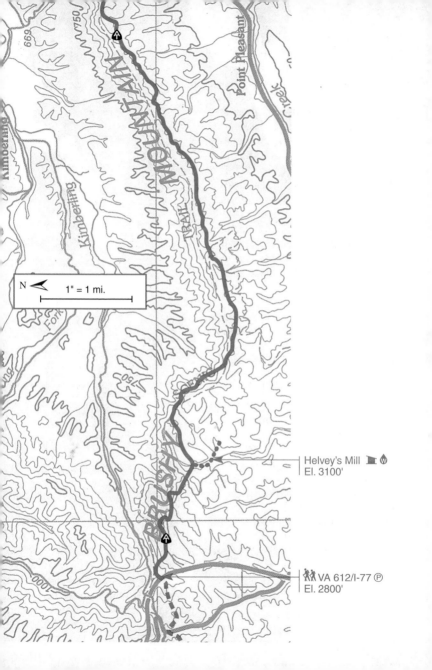

750

669

Kimberling

Kimberling

Point Pleasant

Creek

BRUSHY MOUNTAIN

TRAIL

Fork

1000

N

1" = 1 mi.

Helvey's Mill
El. 3100'

VA 612/I-77 Ⓟ
El. 2800'

Continue along this level route to the end of the ridge where, at 10.1 mi., the trail starts a descent over a series of long, sloping switchbacks. Beyond the switchbacks, the trail picks up a wide all-terrain-vehicle path and continues to descend, reaching at 11.0 mi. a blue-blazed trail leading 0.3 mi. to Helvey's Mill Shelter, another project of the OVT. The blue-blazed trail continues beyond the shelter to a narrow stream that, unless it has rained recently, is likely to be dry. At the shelter, take time to explore the mossy surroundings. The spot of sun that often breaks through the trees here makes this a good spot for a picnic, or at least a short rest.

Past the shelter, the AT intersects with a narrow footpath. As the footpath turns to the left, stick to the wide road and bear to the right, sloping slightly downward. Then, just ahead, the road turns to the left and the AT joins another narrow footpath and ascends over a small knob straight ahead.

Soon the AT is descending again, down a sidehill through a thick forest of rhododendron. As you continue downward, look to the northwest for occasional views of Kimberling Creek waiting below. The trail descends through this thicket of rhododendron for 0.6 mi. before bearing left onto an old railroad bed at 12.1 mi. From here, there is a clear view of Kimberling Creek below and to the right.

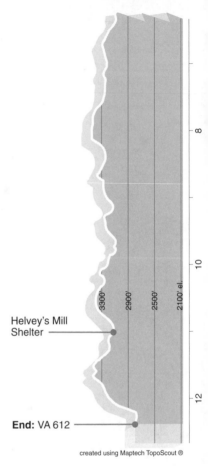

Helvey's Mill Shelter

End: VA 612

created using Maptech TopoScout ®

Over 350 million years ago this area was covered by a shallow sea that consisted of two layers of water. The top layer was fresh water that flowed off the land, covering a bottom layer of salt water. The upper

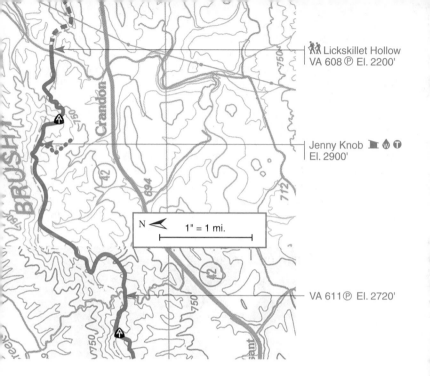

Lickskillet Hollow
VA 608 Ⓟ El. 2200'

Jenny Knob ▰ ⓦ ⓣ
El. 2900'

VA 611Ⓟ El. 2720'

N ◄ 1" = 1 mi.

layer was warm, slightly salty, and light, while the lower layer was cool, clammy, and dense. Depleted of oxygen by the top layer, the lower layer was unsuitable for animal or plant life. As organic materials flowed into the water from the land, they fell to the bottom. Resting under the lower layer of water, these materials did not decay, but, over time, transformed into a black rock known as Devonian shale. This shale now underlies the inferior farmland of Poor Valley (see Hike #7), as well as creeks throughout southwestern Virginia, including Kimberling Creek.

Keeping Kimberling Creek in its range of view, the AT continues along the old railroad bed for 0.2 mi., before bearing right and continuing its descent. After twice crossing a tiny branch of Kimberling Creek (which is often dry), turn left onto gravel VA 612 and the end of this hike. I-77 is just ahead.

If you're looking for a place to rest up after a long day of hiking, Bland, approximately 4 mi. south at the intersection of I-77 and VA 42/US 52, is a good choice. Originally known as Crab Orchard Creek, the town was also called Selden, after James Alexander Selden, for a short time. In 1891 the name was changed to honor Richard Bland, a Revolutionary War leader. Although small by many measures, Bland is a booming metropolis by trailside standards, offering grocery stores, restaurants, overnight accommodations, a hardware store, and even a laundromat. Supplies are also available in Bastian, located 3.0 mi. north, just off US 52, but the selection is much more limited.

Hike #10   Itinerary

Miles N	NORTH	Elev. (ft/m)	Miles S
12.4	**Start:** Trailhead parking on **VA 608** in Lickskillet Hollow, 0.8 mi. N of Crandon.	2200/671	0.0
11.9	Cross **stream** at culvert.		0.5
11.2	**Jenny Knob Shelter,** water, privy.	2900/884	1.2
10.5	Crest of **Brushy Mt.**	3000/914	1.9
9.5	Wooded summit of Brushy Mt.; USGS reference marker to R.	3100/945	2.9
8.1	Cross gravel **VA 611** in gap; early exit option.	2720/829	4.3
6.3	Cross **woods road** (leads both directions to valley) and pass under telephone line in gap.		6.1
2.3	Descend **switchbacks,** then bear R onto ATV road.		10.1
1.4	Blue-blazed trail leads L 0.3 mi. to **Helvey's Mill Shelter,** water.	3100/945	11.0
0.9	Bear R and descend through thick rhododendron.		11.5
0.3	Bear L onto old railroad bed; view of Kimberling Creek on R.		12.1
0.0	**End:** AT reaches **VA 612** and follows road for short distance to **I-77** and trailhead parking. Bland is approximately 4 mi. S; Bastian is 3.0 mi. N.	2800/853	12.4

SOUTH

Southern End of Brushy Mt.

Map: ATC VA #1, Southwest Virginia

Route: Through Jefferson NF from Lickskillet Hollow at VA 608 along Brushy Mt. and across Kimberling Creek to VA 606

Recommended direction: S to N

Distance: 4.9 mi.

Elevation +/-: 2200 to 2700 to 2040 ft.

Effort: Moderate

Day hike: Yes

Overnight backpacking hike: Optional

Early exit option: None

Duration: 4 to 6 hr.

Natural history features: Kimberling Creek

Other features: Supplies available 0.2 mi. NW of N end of hike, on VA 606 and in Crandon on VA 42, 0.8 mi. S of S end

Trailhead access: *Start:* From I-77, take Exit 52 to Bland and head E on VA 42 for 10.0 mi. to VA 608 in Crandon; turn L and head N 0.8 mi. to small trailhead parking area on L. *End:* From I-77, take Exit 52 to Bland and head E on VA 42 for 12.8 mi. to VA 606; turn L and proceed 0.8 mi. to small trailhead parking area on R.

Camping: There are no shelters along this hike; see Camping section of Introduction

---

This his short hike over the crest of Brushy Mt. and through the valley of Kimberling Creek is a pleasant morning or afternoon hike that family members of all ages can enjoy.

Heading north down a gentle slope, the hike begins with a downward trend before cutting up the side of Brushy Mt. The most challenging part of the day, the climb ascends 600 vertical ft. in less than 1 mi. However, a well-graded trail and the short distance of the climb ease the pain. The section ends with a steep, downward trek into Kimberling Creek Valley, a damp area dominated by moisture-loving plants including bellwort, buttercup, and trout lily, which are unable to grow on the dry mountain crest.

From the AT parking area, cross VA 608 and descend over a well-worn path through a rhododendron grove surrounded by mature birch and maple trees. The downward course continues through the forest for 2.0 mi. In spring and summer, the trees form a cool canopy over the trail; in autumn, the covering turns to a rustling shower of colorful leaves. During the first 2.0 mi., notice the lush green color of the plants at ground level and the trees above.

David Embildge

Giant oyster mushroom

As the trail climbs to drier heights, the bright color fades.

At 2.0 mi. the trail suddenly begins a steep climb up a southern knob of Brushy Mt. Rising 600 ft. over the next 0.9 mi., the ascent gets your heart pumping. On warm summer days, you'll be thankful for the shade of the hemlock trees as they reach their heavy branches over the trail and block the burning sun. The hemlock, with its thick foliage and sprawling canopies that filter out light, casts the densest shade of any forest tree. Unlike broadleaf trees, which reflect the green portion of the color spectrum, hemlock cast a "blue shade," making their surroundings seem quite dark.

In late summer and early fall, take a break from your climb and look near the base of the hemlocks for brown-capped mushrooms. The fungus is especially prevalent on dead or dying hemlocks or on the ground near rotting trunks.

As the steady climb continues, the ascent gets steeper and steeper, but, by the time you've broken a sweat, the AT reaches the wooded crest of Brushy Mt. (2700 ft.), nearly 3 mi. into your trek. The trail doesn't stay at this altitude for long and in a few yards you will find yourself descending as quickly as you rose.

On the northern side of the peak, a blue-blazed side trail at 3.2 mi. leads 50 yd. to the left where, with a boost from a large rock, you can catch good views of Kimberling Creek Valley in the north. This is a good spot for lunch, or a mid-morning snack and water break. This is also the best vantage point of the hike, so take your photographs here.

Beyond the rock viewpoint, the trail continues to fall, cutting down a steep, rocky footpath. The rocks are quite loose in many points and should be approached slowly and with some caution. The tumbling continues to 4.0 mi. where the trail enters Kimberling Creek Valley. As you pass through a small cluster of sugar maples, listen for the running water of Kimberling Creek—its swiftly rolling rapids are just ahead.

At 4.1 mi., a now well-graded trail crosses a small footbridge over a narrow stream, then, just ahead, reaches a suspension bridge that carries it, and you, across Kimberling Creek. Beyond the creek, the descent continues into the lowest part of the valley (2000 ft.). Here, the moss on trees and rocks is thick and bright green, and moisture-loving plants, including trout lilies and buttercups, thrive.

The trail winds evenly through the damp valley, then rises slightly to meet VA 606 at 4.7 mi. Turn left onto this gravel road and trace it 0.2 mi. to the parking area on left.

Note: VA 606 is an extremely busy road and should be approached and walked with caution.

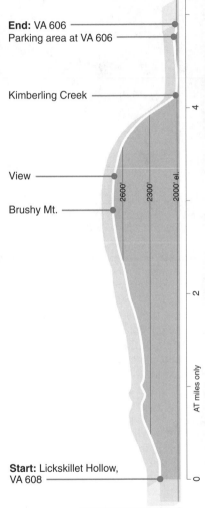

created using Maptech TopoScout ®

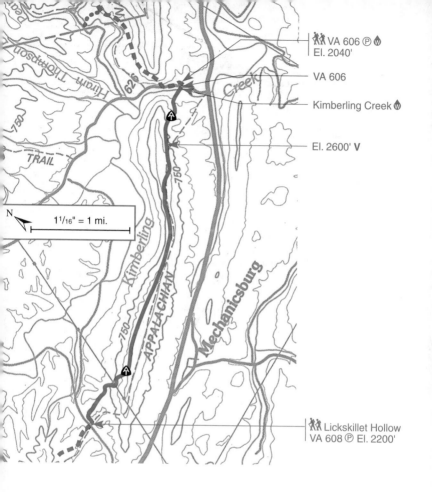

豺 VA 606 Ⓟ ⍵
El. 2040'

VA 606

Kimberling Creek ⍵

El. 2600' **V**

豺 Lickskillet Hollow
VA 608 Ⓟ El. 2200'

N

1 1/16" = 1 mi.

Hike #11   Itinerary

Miles N	NORTH	Elev. (ft/m)	Miles S
4.9	**End:** Parking area on **VA 606,** 3.6 mi. NE of Crandon.	2040/622	0.0
4.7	AT turns L and joins **VA 606.**		0.2
4.3	Low point of **Kimberling Creek** Valley.	2000/610	0.6
4.1	Cross Kimberling Creek on bridge.	2200/671	0.8
3.2	Blue-blazed trail L to **view** of Kimberling Creek Valley (50 yd.).	2600/793	1.7
2.9	Crest **Brushy Mt.**	2700/823	2.0
2.0	**Begin steep ascent** of Brushy Mt.		2.9
0.0	**Start:** Trailhead parking on **VA 608** in Lickskillet Hollow, 0.8 mi. N of Crandon; AT descends.	2200/732	4.9

SOUTH

Big Horse Gap to White Pine Horse Campground

Map: ATC Va. #1, Southwest Virginia

Route: Through Jefferson NF from Big Horse Gap over southern end of Sugar Run Mt. and through Dismal Creek Valley to White Pine Horse Campground

Recommended direction: N to S

Distance: 9.7 mi.

Elevation +/-: 3800 to 3900 to 2300 ft.

Effort: Moderate

Day hike: Yes

Overnight backpacking hike: Optional

Duration: 6 to 8 hr.

Early exit option: None

Natural history features: Summit of Flat Top Mt.; Dismal Creek

Other features: Honey Spring Picnic Area

Trailhead access: *Start:* From I-77 take Exit 52 toward Bland and proceed N on VA 42 for 12.0 mi. to VA 606; turn L and go 1.0 mi. to USFS 201 and turn R just beyond small grocery store. Follow USFS 201 to end (approx. 6 mi.); turn R onto USFS 612. Trailhead is 1.0 mi. ahead with limited roadside parking. *End:* From I-77 take Exit 52 and proceed N on VA 42 for 12.0 mi.; turn L on VA 606 and go 1.0 mi. to USFS 201; turn R and go 2.0 mi. to parking at White Pine Horse Campground.

Camping: Wapiti Shelter; White Pine Horse Campground; see Camping section in Introduction

After a slight incline up from Big Horse Gap at the beginning of this hike, it's smooth sailing as the AT cuts down the southern side of Sugar Run Mt., drops over 1300 ft. in 1.0 mi., then continues along a predominately level course. Unlike the sandstone of the ridges at the top of the mountain, the black Devonian shale in the valley creates poor soil conditions, making it difficult for plants to grow. The area was once inhabited by a large population of elk, called "wapiti," for "white," by Native Americans. With the exception of two protected herds in Pennsylvania, elk are now found only in the western United States. Toward the end of the hike, you will be glad for waterproof boots and perhaps a second pair of dry socks as you proceed through a damp forest and bog fed by Dismal Creek and its many branches. In spring, summer, and early fall, you'll also be thankful for an ample supply of bug repellent to get you through here.

From USFS 612, look for signs to the AT set back in the woods, and pick up the trail on an old woods road.

Follow this road for a short distance before turning left and beginning a gentle ascent. The surrounding area is bright green in the summer, dominated by a variety of soft, lush ferns and other low-lying plants.

The AT crosses the blue-blazed Ribble Trail at 0.1 mi.; it leads to the right 0.1 mi. to the Honey Spring Picnic Area, a small clearing that includes a picnic table and spring and, a little further down, a small pond. The Ribble Trail continues southward from the picnic area, descending to Dismal Creek and then rejoining the AT at 6.5 mi. From the intersection with the Ribble Trail, the AT continues along the southern side of Sugar Run Mt., over a narrow, well-established path. At 0.7 mi., the AT turns right on to an old woods road as it begins to ascend slightly. In late fall and winter, Flat Top Mt. is visible to the left.

Continue this easy ascent for another mile. When the road ends, the AT turns left onto another narrow footpath and heads for the crest of Sugar Run Mt. At 2.3 mi., the AT reaches a rocky outcrop on the crest, from the top of which you can catch a great view of Wilburn Valley to the north and Pearis Mt. rising above it in the distance. To the east, the New River Valley is also visible.

Sugar Run Mt. forms the middle part of an S-shaped ridge of Silurian sandstone crowned at the top by Pearis Mt. The rock, known as "Clinch" sandstone in Virginia, is several hundred feet thick and usually white or pink. Close examination of the sand-stone often reveals traces of fos-silized worms or other sand animals that once fed on the organic materials just below the surface.

The AT continues along the crest of Sugar Run Mt. for another mile, offering an occasional passing view of Wilburn Valley, but graced mostly by colorful greenery, thickets of rhodo-dendron and knobby old oak trees. An evergreen shrub with clusters of large pink or purple funnel-shaped flowers, rhododendron flowers from May to June. Its thick, leathery, oblong leaves are bright green and help keep the forest vibrant during the winter months.

At 3.4 mi. the trail veers to the right and begins a gradual but steady descent, dropping 1500 ft. over the next 1.2 mi. When the AT makes a sharp right onto an old woods road, the downhill climb toward Dismal Creek intensifies. Dismal Creek Valley is named for its poor, black shale-based soil and inhabitability. After 0.7 mi. of an increasingly steep descent, the AT (at 4.1 mi.) crosses the first of several branches of Dismal Creek that intersect the trail as it begins to level.

Following a flat course now, there is another crossing of Dismal Creek 0.4 mi. further on, then, at 4.6 mi., the junction with a blue-blazed trail that leads left 100 yd. to the Wapiti Shelter. A relatively new structure (built by the USFS in 1981), the shelter sleeps six, but there are plenty of flat areas in the immediate vicinity that, combined with the nearby creek for water, make this a good campsite —

or at least a good spot to stop for lunch or a water break.

The blue-blazed trail continues beyond the shelter and rejoins the AT at 4.7 mi. The trail remains level from here on out. Beyond the blue-blazed trail, the AT leaves the old road it has been following for the past mile, cuts to the right, and crosses another arm of Dismal Creek. Across the creek, the AT exits the woods for a short distance and enters a small clearing where it follows a levee to the left of a small pond.

In summer, you're apt to see a few hikers splashing in the pond. If you're not offended by a bit of mud, you might be tempted to slosh around a bit yourself. Past the pond, the trail reenters the woods and continues its flat-to-moderately-downward trend.

Over the next 0.5 mi. of easy hiking, the AT crosses two more branches of Dismal Creek, then heads up a slight incline to join an old woods road. The road descends toward a small, open field (5.5 mi.). Crossing the field, the AT maintains an easy downhill grade as it passes through an area overtaken by rhododendron bushes, then crosses four more segments of Dismal Creek in the next 0.3 mi.

The AT continues to cross over branches of Dismal Creek — some wide and rocky, others dry and barely visible — as it travels through a damp and misty forest. At 6.3 mi., a small pond once inhabited by a family of beavers is on your left. Beyond the pond, cross another stream as the AT approaches the southern end of the Ribble Trail on your right. The Ribble Trail continues to the left of the AT for 0.5 mi. to reach USFS 201.

Past the Ribble Trail, the AT crosses a main artery of Dismal Creek. Ahead, look for blazes on the opposite side of a wide dirt fire road and proceed over a carpet of crunching pine needles through a stand of mature white spruce trees. The white spruce, with its short, singly attached needles, is identified by its steeple shape and its one- to two-inch seed cones. Its needles are often bluish-green and sport a filmy white coating. When crushed, the needes emanate a pungent odor that also separates this pine from many of its kin. Bird watchers will want to examine the high branches for chickadees, red-breasted nuthatches, and white-winged crossbills. Gray squirrels also feed off the tree's cones. As you exit the pines you will continue through a flat, damp area. At 7.0 mi., the trail bears to the left and passes through another boggy stretch.

A mile further on, cross a small field and, on the opposite side, look for blazes leading you to a narrow footpath and continue to descend. Just ahead cross another stream and follow the trail to the right. At 8.6 mi., the AT crosses over a small bridge before carrying you 0.1 mi. up a small hill, then descending again to Dismal Creek. The trail meanders along the side of the creek, jumps a gully with assistance from a small bridge, and approaches a large field. White Pine

Horse Campground, an equestrian facility, is across the creek on the right side of the field. The campground is part of the Jefferson National Forest and is a popular recreation area. In addition to tent-camping sites, there are fishing facilities, hiking trails, equestrian trails, and rest rooms. For reservations, fee information, or permission for overnight parking, call the Blacksburg Ranger District, 540-552-4641.

Note: The next hike will pick up the AT 1.6 mi. north of the northern end of Hike #12. The stretch of trail between the two hikes we recommend runs along a rocky, wooded course, rising 225 ft. then dropping 150 ft. With no views and mostly dirt terrain, this extra climb and fall are best left to AT thru-hikers.

Optional Extended Hike: If you're up for an extended trip at the southern end of Hike #12, Dismal Creek Falls are just 1.0 mi. farther and the view is worth the extra energy. From the campground, continue along the AT for 0.7 mi. to a blue-blazed trail on the right that leads 0.3 mi. to an overlook offering a post-card view of Dismal Creek Falls crashing over large sandstone cliffs into a deep blue pool. Photo bugs, philosophers, journal-keepers, and those who just like to sit and look around will find this an engaging spot for a good long rest after a hearty day of hiking.

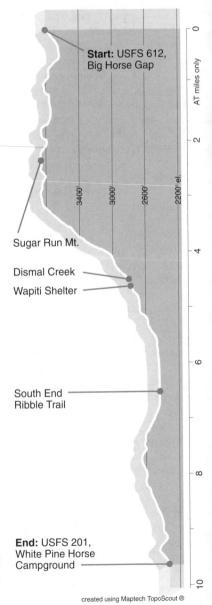

created using Maptech TopoScout ®

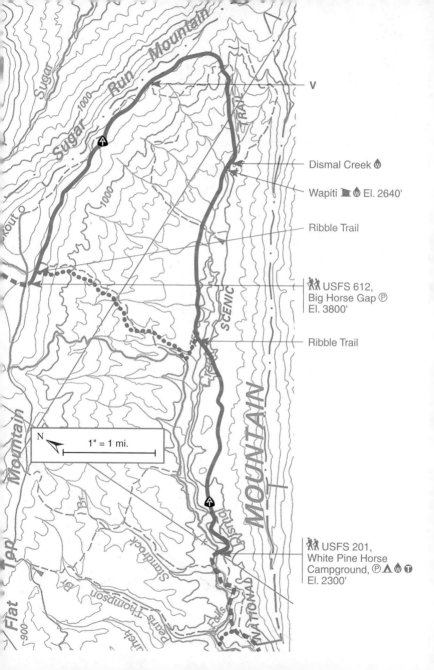

V

Dismal Creek 🌢

Wapiti ▰ 🌢 El. 2640'

Ribble Trail

🏃🏃 USFS 612,
Big Horse Gap Ⓟ
El. 3800'

Ribble Trail

🏃🏃 USFS 201,
White Pine Horse
Campground, Ⓟ ▲ 🌢 🚻
El. 2300'

1" = 1 mi.

Hike #12   Itinerary

Miles N	NORTH	Elev. (ft/m)	Miles S
9.7	**Start:** On dirt **USFS 612** at **Big Horse Gap**, approx. 7 mi. W of VA 42; limited roadside parking.	3800/1158	0.0
9.6	Cross blue-blazed **Ribble Trail,** which leads R 0.1 mi. to Honey Spring Picnic Area, then continues S 1.0 mi. to a branch of Dismal Creek and rejoins AT at mi. 6.5.	3900/1189	0.1
7.4	Rocky outcrop on crest of **Sugar Run Mt.,** with views.		2.3
5.2	Cross another branch of **Dismal Creek.**		4.5
5.1	Blue-blazed trail leads 100 yd. to **Wapiti Shelter.**	2640/805	4.6
4.9	Pass to L of small pond.		4.8
4.2	Cross field.		5.5
3.4	Former beaver pond.		6.3
3.2	Cross S end of **Ribble Trail,** which continues L 0.5 mi. to USFS 201.		6.5
3.0	Thick stand of mature white pines.		6.7
0.0	**End: White Pine Horse Campground** to R across narrow creek on **USFS 201,** parking area, 3.0 mi. N of grocery store on VA 606.	approx. 2300/701	9.7

SOUTH

HIKE #13
Sugar Run Gap to Pearisburg

Maps: ATC Va. #1, Southwest Virginia

Route: From Sugar Run Gap over Doc's Knob to Angels Rest and down Pearis Mt. to Pearisburg at VA 634

Recommended direction: S to N

Distance: 9.5 mi.

Elevation +/-: 3380 to 3990 (approx.) to 2000 ft.

Effort: Moderate

Day hike: Yes

Overnight backpacking hike: Optional

Duration: 6 to 8 hr.

Early exit option: None

Natural history features: Angels Rest; New River

Social history features: Woodshole Hostel; Holy Family Hospice

Other features: Views from Angels Rest and along Pearis Mt.; Pearisburg stores and accommodations

Trailhead access: *Start:* From Pearisburg, take VA 100 3.0 mi. S; turn R onto VA 665 and head W approx. 6 mi. Turn R onto paved and gravel VA 663/USFS 29 (Sugar Run Gap Rd.). Proceed 3.0 mi. to AT markers and roadside parking on each side of road. *End:* From intersection of US 460/VA 100 near Pearisburg, turn onto VA 100/Johnston Ave. next to Dairy Queen. Take next R onto Morris Ave., which becomes VA 634. Proceed approximately 1 mi. to trail crossing and AT markers. There is limited roadside parking (4 to 5 cars).

Camping: Doc's Knob Shelter

Heading north from Sugar Run Gap, there are a few minor elevation changes with easy ascents on the way to the crest of Pearis Mt. (3440 ft.) and the top of Angels Rest (3550 ft.) and the only major elevation change (Angels Rest to VA 634 at 2000 ft.) will be a descent. This hike features several great views, so pack plenty of film and a picnic lunch. You may also want to leave yourself enough time to explore Pearisburg and visit the New River, 1.0 mi. north of the end of this section of the AT.

Despite its name, the New River is actually the second-oldest river in the world, after the Nile. It was named "New" by early pioneers because it flowed north into the Ohio River system to empty into the Gulf of Mexico, while all older rivers flowed into the Atlantic (or so they thought). Because it was there before the Appalachians and cut through them as they formed, the New River is the only one to traverse the entire Appalachian range. The river's deep blue waters and foamy whitecaps, formed as it cascaded over large rocks, give it a savage appearance, yet it is beautiful and photographs here are a must.

In Sugar Run Gap, at 0.8 mi., a dirt road veers from the trail and heads left 0.5 mi. to Woodshole Hostel, an 1880s log farmhouse and barn that have been converted into a bunkhouse for hikers. The hostel was founded in 1986 by Roy and Tillie Wood, who discovered the homestead while studying the local elk population in the early 1940s. The Woods welcome long-distance hikers during May and June. The bunkhouse and nearby showers are free and available on a first come, first served basis. Sodas, candy, and Coleman fuel are for sale and an authentic Southern breakfast is offered to the first eight hikers who make reservations. No other meals are served here. There is a telephone on the premises.

Heading out of Sugar Run Gap, begin an easy ascent over a series of long, sloping switchbacks to a saddle between two unnamed knobs. As you climb, look to the east for passing views of Wilburn Valley and, beyond the valley, the southern end of Sugar Run Mt., which juts out to the east. (The AT follows a route along the top of this mountain described in Hike #12.) At 1.4 mi., a blue-blazed trail to the left makes a 50-yd. climb up a rock cliff for a better look at the valley below and Sugar Run Mt. in the distance. Back on the AT, beyond this interesting diversion, bear left and descend gradually over the next 0.6

Catawba rhododendron

mi. before making a sharp right onto an old road.

As you hike, look for hickory nuts along the ground. Although most of the trees are foraged by squirrels before human eyes can fall upon them, if you do happen on a nut the animals have missed, you'll also happen on a bit of history. Before modern-day baking conveniences such as almond extract were invented, Native Americans used ground hickory nuts mixed with cornmeal to make a tasty cake. They crushed the green shells and threw them into pools to stun fish and make them easier to catch. Hickory trees were also used for medicinal purposes. The Chippewas cured headaches by burning small shoots and inhaling the fumes. They also used hickory wood for their bows.

As the AT enters an area dominated by hearty rhododendrons, look for the USFS sign identifying Doc's Knob Shelter on the left (2.2 mi.). The shelter was built by the USFS in 1971 and is maintained by the USFS and the Roanoke AT Club. The structure sleeps six and water is available from a scenic stream that crosses in front. Beyond the shelter, the AT cuts up a brief incline before settling into a gradual descent over the next 2.0 mi. Look for more rich thickets of rhododendron and, in early spring, the bright-orange, tubular blossoms of the flaming azalea bushes that are also prominent throughout this section.

The AT enters another gradual ascent at 4.9 mi. as it climbs an old

road and continues through thick rhododendron and azalea bushes. Grand stands of oak trees also grace the area. Native Americans made good use of these sprawling, solid trees also. They boiled the oak's acorns, to purge their bitter taste, and then ground them into meal for bread. The Chippewas also used portions of the powdery inner bark of red oak as a main ingredient of heart medication.

Continue along the old road for over a mile before turning right onto a narrow footpath. From here, the AT ascends more steeply to the top of Pearis Mt. (7.0 mi.). This crest forms the top of an S-shaped ridge of Silurian sandstone that begins south of Sugar Run Mt. and reaches almost to Pearisburg, ending abruptly at Angels Rest. Formed over 400 million years ago, Silurian sandstone is relatively thin and usually white, pink, or buff colored.

Continue along the crest of Pearis Mt. and look to the east for passing views of Wilburn Valley. At 7.4 mi., the AT passes a rock overhang that offers unobstructed views of the valley and Sugar Run Gap Mt. to the east. The wide rock ledge makes a nice spot for a picnic lunch, or an extended water break, but if you can stave off your hunger a little while longer, the view from Angels Rest is even better. Beyond the rock ledge, a blue-blazed trail leads left 300 yd. to a seasonal spring and small campsite.

The trail now makes another easy ascent, climbing 100 ft. over the next

Continued on p. 114

0.5 mi., to reach Angels Rest at 8.0 mi. A blue-blazed trail leads left 50 yd. to the appropriately named View Rock. Standing on this wide sandstone shelf, look to the left to see the deep blue New River tumble through the valley, with the town of Pearisburg nestled along its right bank. Climbing above the river, Peters Mt. offers an exceptional viewing treat in early fall. From this vantage point, Butt Mt. and Bald Knob can also be seen to the right.

The remaining 1.5 mi. cover a steep, rocky descent, eased by a series of long switchbacks. As the AT crosses a rocky drainage area, listen for water running beneath the rocks. Beware: if you are hiking in early spring, after significant snow melt, or after a heavy rainfall, the area may be quite slick. The trail passes another seasonal spring on the left before intersecting with VA 634/Morris Ave. in the town of Pearisburg.

Named for Captain George Pearis, a Revolutionary War soldier and the first European settler in the area, Pearisburg, with a population of 2500, is one of the largest towns in the region. The city offers several chain restaurants and for cheap overnight accommodations, a motor lodge. **Note:** Holy Family Hospice is located on the northwest side of town. Operated by the Church of the Holy Family, the barn-shaped hostel is only open to hikers. Amenities include a loft with sleeping pads, a kitchen with stove and refrigerator, a bathroom with a shower, a dining

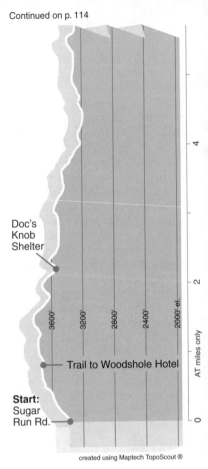

created using Maptech TopoScout ®

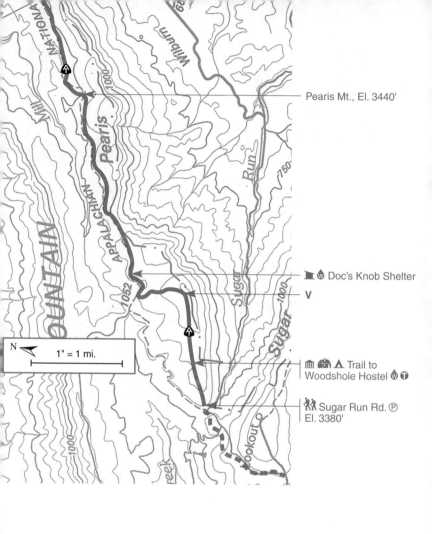

Pearis Mt., El. 3440'

■ ⊛ Doc's Knob Shelter

V

血 🏠 ⛺ Trail to
Woodshole Hostel ⊛ ⊤

👫 Sugar Run Rd. ℗
El. 3380'

N
1" = 1 mi.

area, a library, and public phones. A donation for use of the facility is requested, but the pastor often accepts yard work as payment.

Before leaving the area, head to the west side of town to explore the New River at Senator Shumate Bridge on US 460. Wade's Food Supermarket on the east side of the bridge includes a great deli and bakery.

Note: The next 2.7 mi. of the AT to the north travel along VA 100, a busy highway. We recommend skipping over these and picking up the trail again at Stillhouse Branch, at the southern end of Hike #14.

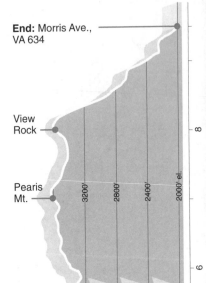

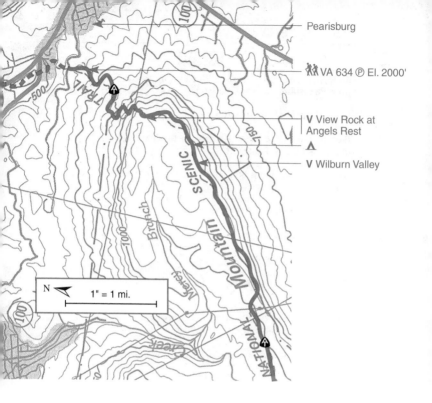

Pearisburg

🚶🚶 VA 634 Ⓟ El. 2000'

V View Rock at
Angels Rest

Ⓐ

V Wilburn Valley

N ◄ 1" = 1 mi.

Hike #13　Itinerary

Miles N	**NORTH**	Elev. (ft/m)	Miles S
9.5	**End:** AT intersects Morris Ave., **VA 634** approx. 1 mi. from Pearisburg; roadside parking.	2000/610	0.0
8.6	Begin descent of steep **switchbacks.**		0.9
8.0	Blue-blazed trail to L (50 yd.) to **View Rock** at crest of Angels Rest on Pearis Mt.	3550/1082	1.5
7.5	Blue-blazed trail leads 300 yd. L to **campsite** and **spring.**		2.0
7.4	**Rock ledge** with views of Wilburn Valley.		2.1
7.0	Crest of **Pearis Mt.**	3440/1049	2.5
4.9	Begin gradual ascent.		5.4
2.2	**Doc's Knob Shelter,** water; brief ascent, then begin 2-mi. descent.	3555/1084	7.3
1.4	**Blue-blazed trail** on L leads 50 yd. to rocky cliff with **view** of Sugar Run Mt. and valley.	approx. 3990/1216	8.1
0.8	Dirt road heads L 0.5 mi. to **Woodshole Hostel.**		8.7
0.4	Begin to ascend series of **switchbacks.**		9.1
0.0	**Start:** AT intersects **Sugar Run Rd.** in Sugar Run Gap, approx. 10 mi. SW of Pearisburg; roadside parking.	3380/1030	9.5

SOUTH

HIKE #14
Stony Creek Valley to Stillhouse Branch

Map: ATC Va. #4, Central Virginia

Route: From Stony Creek Valley at VA 635 through Peters Mt. Wilderness, over Pine Swamp Ridge, through Symms Gap meadow and The Rice Field, over the crest of Peters Mt. on the VA–W VA border, to Stillhouse Branch and VA 641 (Stillhouse Branch Rd.)

Recommended direction: N to S

Distance: 17.6 mi.

Elevation +/-: 2400 to 3900 to 1800 ft.

Effort: Moderately strenuous

Day hike: 8.7-mi. option

Overnight backpacking hike: Yes

Duration: 10 to 12 hr.

Early exit option: At 6.7 mi., Groundhog Trail

Natural history features: Peters Mt. Wilderness; Symms Gap; Dickinson Gap; Pine Swamp Branch; Stony Creek

Other features: Sugar Camp Farm; views from The Rice Field, Peters Mt.

Trailhead access: *Start:* Take US 460 E approx. 5 mi. from Pearisburg to VA 635 (just after crossing New River); go 9.0 mi. N to sign for USFS White Rocks Recreation Area. There is room for 2 to 3 cars in small parking area. *End for day hike:* Take US 460 W from Pearisburg, cross New River on Senator Shumate Bridge and proceed NW approx. 5 mi. to US 219; turn R and continue to WV 219/21. Turn R and follow blue blazes 2.0 mi. and look for sign indicating small parking area at Groundhog Trail crossing. Groundhog Trail leads 2.0 mi. to AT at 6.7 mi. on this hike. *End:* Take US 460 W from Pearisburg, cross New River on Senator Shumate Bridge, and proceed NW 1.0 mi. to dirt VA 641 (Stillhouse Branch Rd.); turn R and go 0.5 mi. to small USFS parking area.

Camping: Pine Swamp Branch Shelter; Rice Field Shelter, primitive sites along ridge of Peters Mt.

Although this is a lengthy hike, extensive sections of flat, easy trail make it a doable, albeit long, day hike if taken at a swift stride. The 8.7-mi. recommended day hike provides more opportunity to take in a variety of forest life, including large stands of chestnut oak, red maple, and yellow poplar trees. Photographers may want to consider the shorter route to allow ample time to snap some terrific shots from the crest of Peters Mt. If you decide to conquer the entire 17.6 mi., plan to get a very early start and hike in early spring, when the days are getting longer, but the foliage has not yet blocked the views entirely. This hike is dominated by a trek across the ridge of Peters Mt., which straddles the Virginia–West Virginia border. If you start in the north and head south, as we recommend, you'll put the only steep climb (a gain of 1500 ft. in 2.5 mi.) behind you early on, and will enjoy smooth sailing for most of the duration, finishing with a more gradual descent at the southern end.

From the USFS parking lot on the west side of VA 635, head toward the information display and pick up the AT approximately 100 ft. beyond it. The AT turns to the left and begins a gradual ascent up an old road. A few hundred yd. further, the trail enters the 3328-acre Peters Mt. Wilderness on the east slope of Peters Mt., with elevations ranging from 3000 ft. on Stony Creek to 3956 ft. on the crest of the mountain. Vegetation along this stretch of the AT is primarily upland oak with yellow poplar, red oak, and hickory found in the coves. Special features include the high mountain bog known as Pine Swamp and numerous sandstone outcroppings on the crest, which afford rewarding views of the surrounding countryside.

As you proceed through the forest, the mature red oaks demand attention. The fastest-growing of all oak trees, many of the red oaks surrounding this section of trail are more than two hundred years old and stand over 75 ft. high. In late spring, when its bristle-tipped leaves are still maturing, look for wind-pollinated flowers to appear as slender, dangling catkins. In autumn, as its name suggests, the tree's leaves turn a deep

wine red and even its twigs and bark develop a reddish tint. Fall will also bring a variety of wild mushrooms to examine. The reddish-brown caps found along this stretch are likely either the tawny milkcap or the wrinkled milkcap. The bittersweet bolete also grows in the forest, directly beneath the oaks. It is identified by its slightly orange hue.

At 0.3 mi., the AT passes Pine Swamp Branch Shelter on the left. A stream runs along the north side of the shelter, but unless you're desperate for a fill-up, wait until you reach a spring 0.5 mi. further down the trail. (All water in this section should be treated.) The three-walled stone shelter has a chimney, fireplace, and eight bunks. A picnic table sits out front and a well-kept outhouse is situated on a hill in back. The shelter was constructed and is maintained with funds donated by the family of the late Robert Timpi, a long-time AT maintainer. Beyond the shelter, the AT cuts to the left and begins a series of long, gradual switchbacks toward the crest of Peters Mt. Although the climb is steep, the switchbacks and the well-kept trail surface help ease the ascent.

Peters Mt. was formed from 325-to-350-million-year-old Mississippian sandstone, a combination of sand and mud washed into the area from the southeast. The sandstone and conglomerate of Peters Mt. are part of the same bed that makes up Cove Mt. (see Hikes #17 and 22). The mountains once reached even higher, but, as the rock eroded, its cracks filled with water. When the water froze, it wedged pieces of the rock apart and gravity's force sent them rolling down the hill, forming rugged cliffs on the north face of the mountain. As you ascend along the level shelf extending from the base of these cliffs, pay particular attention to the color and surface texture of the rock and compare it to the dark, Devonian shale you will encounter just a few miles further south.

At 0.9 mi., the trail bears right and crosses a stream before making a sharp left and continuing its climb. Traces of the former AT route can be seen straight ahead. Stay on the new path, following the fresh white blazes. As you continue to climb, notice that some of the trees scattered among the red oaks appear to be shedding their bark. The loose, shaggy strips make the hickory tree easy to spot. Like the red oaks and their acorns, hickories also produce nuts that are bitter to the human palate, but a tasty treat for forest wildlife. In the fall, as its leaves turn golden-yellow, the hickory's nuts are enjoyed by wild turkeys, chipmunks, and squirrels. The squirrels also bury the nuts and, in doing so, help keep the hickory population well dispersed.

After 2.6 mi. of uphill climbing, the AT begins to level and then takes a short dip into the shallow swale of Pine Swamp. Here, the air seems thicker and cooler as a dense stand of hemlocks encloses the trail. Hemlocks cast some of the densest shade of any forest tree. Their short, flat needles create thick canopies that filter out sunlight. The trees grow seed cones which ripen in the fall, drop seeds during winter, and fall off the

Pine Swamp Shelter, winter day

Henry Lafleur

following spring. Although the seeds need some shade for germination, the shade of the parent hemlock is often too dark. The parent trees also tend to deprive younger trees of moisture. As a result, hemlocks rarely grow in thick stands, making this abundant stretch of trees very unusual. Although the hemlock dominate here, they are not alone. Yellow-poplar and rhododendron are also plentiful throughout this wilderness area.

In the swale, a large yellow poplar tree denotes the head of an unmarked trail that leads from the right of the AT to an extremely unreliable spring. Unless it has rained recently, your chances for finding water here are slim. Less than a quarter of a mile on, the AT picks up its ascent of Peters Mt. again as it intersects the yellow-blazed Allegheny Trail leading north to the Mason-Dixon line. Just beyond this point, the AT reaches the crest of Peters Mt. (3900 ft.) at 2.9 mi. and continues upward, passing to the southwestern side of a 3956-ft. knob. In the fall, winter, and early spring, look to the west for panoramic views of West Virginia and to the east to catch passing glimpses of high Appalachian ridges abutting the skyline.

As the AT continues across the forested ridge, it cuts through an abundance of spring and summer wildflowers. Be on the lookout for bright yellow buttercups, the tiny white petals of the chickweed, drooping pink and white trillium blooms, deep-purple violets, and the large

Continued on p. 122

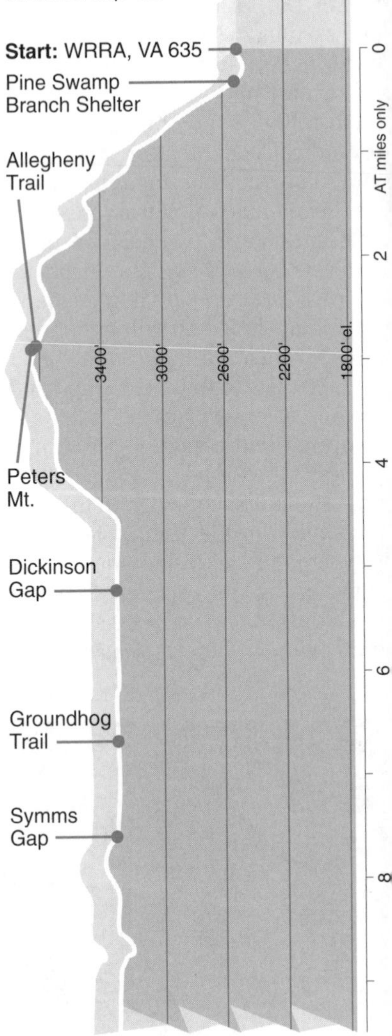

Start: WRRA, VA 635
Pine Swamp Branch Shelter
Allegheny Trail
Peters Mt.
Dickinson Gap
Groundhog Trail
Symms Gap

AT miles only

3400' 3000' 2600' 2200' 1800' el.

green leaves of the jack-in-the-pulpit that curve to cover a smaller, 2-to-3-in. club. Native Americans once gathered

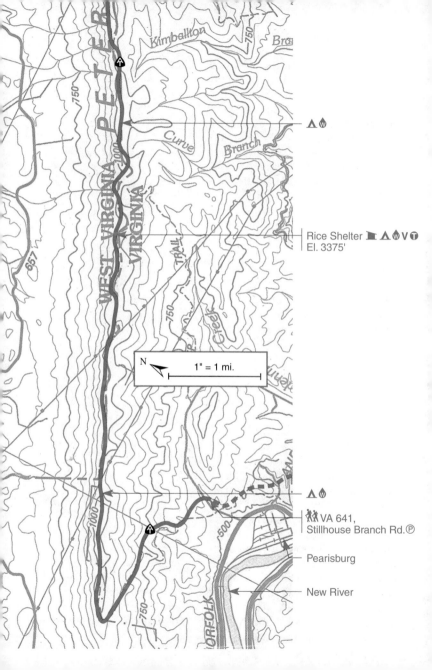

Kimballton Br...

WEST VIRGINIA PETER

Curve Branch

WEST VIRGINIA
VIRGINIA

△ ⚑

857

TRAIL

750

Creek

Rice Shelter ▰ △ ⚑ V ⊙
El. 3375'

N

1" = 1 mi.

1000

750

△ ⚑

🚶🚶 VA 641,
Stillhouse Branch Rd. Ⓟ

Pearisburg

NORFOLK

500

New River

750

the fleshy, sticklike portion of the Jack-in-the-pulpit and ate it as a vegetable.

Over the next 2 mi., the AT drops 500 ft. into Dickinson Gap, dotted with red markers designating the land as a wilderness area. At 5.2 mi., note that even the gap's stone marker is painted bright red. Beyond the marker, a blue-blazed trail to the left makes a steep, 1.4-mi. descent to join VA 635, 7.4 mi. north of US 460.

The AT forges onward, rising and falling over several small knobs over the next 1.5 mi., as more views of West Virginia are visible to the west. At 6.7 mi., the AT intersects with the blue-blazed Groundhog Trail on the right; it leads 2.0 mi. northwest to W VA 219/24. The Groundhog Trail is wooded and provides additional opportunities to view wildflowers in spring and summer and enjoy the vibrant reds and yellows of the oak and poplar trees in fall. Better parking facilities and an easier route to the trailhead make this early exit option a better choice than the blue-blazed trail 1.5 mi. earlier.

If you decided to press onward, continue along the narrow, rocky path for 1.0 mi., at which point the AT enters an old road, then cuts into an open meadow (7.7 mi.). The meadow, known as Symms Gap, was once occupied by a sprawling orchard but is now covered with wildflowers that bloom in even greater abundance here than in the colorful sections that precede it. The views of West Virginia farmlands from this point are superb. Although there

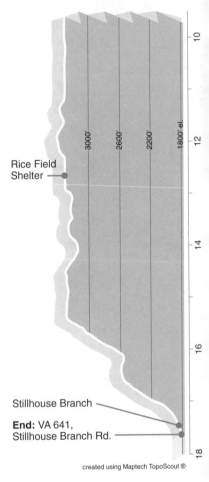

created using Maptech TopoScout ®

is no nearby water source, a large oak tree to the left of the trail makes a nice shelter for a small tent. If you have plenty of water with you, this is a good spot for an overnight stay.

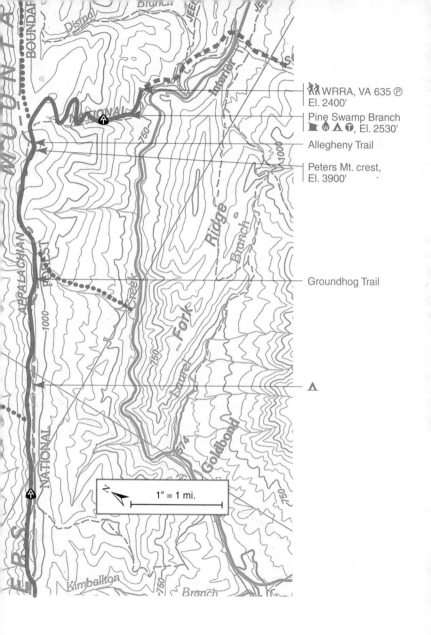

WRRA, VA 635 Ⓟ
El. 2400'

Pine Swamp Branch
▰ Ⓦ ▲ Ⓣ, El. 2530'

Allegheny Trail

Peters Mt. crest,
El. 3900'

Groundhog Trail

Λ

1" = 1 mi.

The AT continues to follow the ridge crest over old forest roads for the next 5.0 mi. A small side trail to the left at 11.4 mi. leads 150 ft. to a primitive campsite and a small spring. Beyond the spring, the AT crosses a power line access road, makes a sharp right, and crosses the power line right-of-way, which affords excellent views to the south of Angels Rest and Pearis Mt. The AT crosses Pearis Mt. on the other side of Pearisburg (see Hike #13).

At 12.6 mi., cross a stile and enter a large, open pasture known as the Rice Field, an area filled with rocky outcrops that award sweeping westward views of the deep, green valleys and colorful mountains of West Virginia. The Rice Field Shelter, also known as Star Haven Shelter, located on the right, was built in 1996 and includes a picnic table and an outhouse. In case you need to refill your canteen, a blue-blazed trail leads 0.3 mi. from the shelter to a fairly reliable spring. You will want to spend some time exploring this unusual region and enjoying, possibly even photographing, the view. As you wander through the area, look for an emu. The nonnative creature has been spotted in these parts by several hikers in the past few years.

The AT crosses another stile on the southern side of the pasture (13.0 mi.) and reenters the woods on an old forest road. The trail continues to follow this flat, wide path across the top of Peters Mt. for the next 2.3 mi.,

becoming rockier as it proceeds along this easy course. Then, at 15.3 mi., the AT makes a sharp left and begins descending the mountain over an extremely rocky trail, falling more than 1500 ft. over the next 2.0 mi. Beware of loose rocks. Just ahead you will cross a narrow stream flowing from a piped spring. Look just beyond the trail to the right for an excellent campsite among the trees.

Although water is scarce on the mountain, narrow offshoots of the New River flow freely in the valley. A mile further (16.4 mi.) make a sharp right, then a sharp left to cross a larger branch of the stream. The trail turns right again and continues downhill, following an old road for a short distance and then abandoning it for a narrower, rockier course.

With less than a mile to go (at 16.7 mi.) the AT takes a slight upward turn, ascending over a series of short knobs, then continues its steep descent. Wide switchbacks ease the fall as the trail drops 500 ft. to reach a tributary of Stillhouse Branch. The AT crosses back and forth over the stream several times (watch for blazes) before turning left onto a dirt access road. The parking area on VA 641 (Stillhouse Branch Rd.) is 40 yd. ahead.

Note: Since the approximately 2.5 mi. of the AT between Hike #14 and and Hike #15 trace VA 635 and these hikes each already offer two full days of hiking, we recommend skipping the additional miles.

Hike #14   Itinerary

Miles N	NORTH	Elev. (ft/m)	Miles S
17.6	**Start: White Rocks Recreation Area** USFS parking area on W side of **VA 635,** 9.0 mi. N of US 460.	approx. 2400/732	0.0
17.3	**Pine Swamp Branch Shelter.**	2530/771	0.3
16.7	Cross stream.		0.9
15.0	Descend into **Pine Swamp.**		2.6
14.8	AT intersects yellow-blazed **Allegheny Trail.**		2.8
14.7	Reach crest of **Peters Mt.**	3900/1188	2.9
12.9	Rocky AT descends toward Dickinson Gap.		4.7
12.4	In **Dickinson Gap,** blue-blazed trail leads 1.4 mi. to VA 635, 7.4 mi. N of US 460.	approx. 3350/1022	5.2
11.9	Blue-blazed **Groundhog Trail** leads 2.0 mi. NW to W VA 219/21, endpoint of recommended day hike (8.7 mi.), early exit option.		6.7
10.9	Enter meadow in **Symms Gap.**		7.7
10.8	Excellent campsite under large oak tree. (No water.)		7.8
6.2	Side trail leads 50 yd. to small spring and primitive campsite.		11.4
5.7	Power line right-of-way; views to S of Angels Rest and Pearis Mt.		11.9
5.0	**Rice Field Shelter** on edge of open pasture, the Rice Field.	3375/1029	12.6
4.6	Reenter woods on opposite side of pasture.		13.0
2.3	Turn L and descend Peters Mt.; rocky trail.		15.3
2.2	Excellent campsite near small stream with piped spring.		15.4
0.8	Steep switchbacks.		16.8
0.2	First of several **Stillhouse Branch** crossings.	approx. 1800/549	17.4
0.0	**End:** Small USFS parking lot on W side of **VA 641** (Stillhouse Branch Rd.), approx. 3 mi. NW of Pearisburg.		17.6

SOUTH

Map: ATC Va. #4, Central Virginia

Route: From Sinking Creek Valley over Johns Creek Mt. and Kelly Knob, through Rocky Gap and Johns Creek Valley over Wind Rock to Stony Creek Valley at VA 635

Recommended direction: N to S

Distance: 17.6 mi.

Elevation +/-: 2150 to 3740 to 2080 to 4050 to 2450 ft.

Effort: Strenuous

Day hike: 7.4 mi. option

Overnight backpacking hike: Yes

Duration: 5 to 6 hr. for recommended day hike; 10 to 12 hr. for entire distance

Early exit options: At 7.4 mi., USFS 156/VA 632; at 12.4 mi., Salt Sulphur Tpk. (VA 613)

Natural history features: Johns Creek Mt.; Big Pond; Laurel Creek; Salt Pond Mt.; Wind Rock; Mountain Lake Wilderness; Stony Creek

Other features: Views from Wind Rock and Kelly Knob

Trailhead access: *Start:* From Roanoke, take I-81 S 3.0 mi. to VA 311 and head N 20.0 mi. to New Castle. In New Castle, turn L onto VA 42 and proceed 21.0 mi. to trailhead and small parking area. *End:* From US 460 in Pearisburg, go E approx. 5 mi. to VA 635 (just after crossing New River) and turn L; go 11.5 mi. to AT markers and park on roadside.

Camping: Laurel Creek Shelter; War Spur Shelter; Bailey Gap Shelter

T his is a strenuous trek and is not recommended for first-timers. Gaining over 1500 ft. during the 3-mi. ascent of Johns Creek Mt. and then 2000 ft. over the 2.5-mi. hike to Lone Pike Peak, this route will keep you huffing. However, long stretches of level trail through Mountain Lake Wilderness allow you to catch your breath and enjoy a variety of wildlife and some great views from Kelly Knob and Wind Rock: Don't forget your camera. Pack extra water, too. This hike is sure to make you work up a seemingly insatiable

thirst and watering holes are scarce. However, Sinking Creek intersects the AT at the northern end of this hike, and Stony Creek flows approximately a quarter of a mile beyond the southern end, giving you an opportunity to wet your whistle at start and finish, provided you have packed a water filter.

You will begin with a bit of farm hiking. From VA 42, follow blazes as the AT descends a driveway and turns left to cross a wooden stile and then a pasture. A branch of Sinking Creek runs through the pasture and, after a heavy rain, the area is likely to be quite damp. Watch your step as you cross a wooden foot bridge and then exit the pasture over another stile. After climbing yet another stile, make a sharp left. On a hot, sunny day, the smell of fresh hay will tickle your nostrils. Resist the idea that a lazy catnap in the sun might be a more viable alternative for the day and press on; your head will be back into hiking soon.

In 250 ft., a stile takes you over an electric fence. Be careful here as the fence is hot. If it feels like someone's watching you, it might have something to do with the dozen or so pairs of cow eyes batting at you from the nearby fields. Cattle paths throughout this area resemble foot trails; keep an eye on the white AT blazes. Soon the smell of hay gives way to a distinct pine scent as the trail ascends through a cluster of cedars. In less than half a mile, the AT begins paralleling a barbed-wire fence. Stay to the left of it, then make a sharp left and continue up the hillside through an open pasture. In the distance, Johns Creek Mt., with Kelly Knob perched on top, is waiting.

The AT wanders up and down through the pasture, then, 0.8 mi. into the hike, passes over one more stile before entering a wooded area and beginning an at-first-gradual ascent of Johns Creek Mt. to Kelly Knob. The trail is surrounded by thick clusters of bright green rhododendron. In spring and summer, miniature iris, trout-lillies, trillium, and various violets add color to the canvas as more sweet scents fill the air. The upward climb continues for the next mile, growing steeper as the trail turns to follow an old road for a short distance, then winds back into the woods.

Just when you need a break, the AT makes an unexpected, steep descent into a lush green gorge and crosses a small branch and then the main prong of Laurel Creek at 2.3 mi. The wide stream is lined with a dark shale bottom that creates silhouettes of the surrounding rhododendron, hemlock, and laurel trees on the surface. If you are able to treat the water, this is a good place to fill your canteen.

Plenty of good "sitting" rocks and lots of shade make this a great spot to stop and rest. From this vantage point, the laurel and rhododendron may appear to be one and the same. Upon closer inspection, the laurel can be identified by its thick, leathery leaves. In spring, the contrast is most obvious as the laurel trees burst with masses of bright pink, star-shaped flowers. The mountain laurel's blooms are named "Kalmia" for Swedish botanist Peter Kalm who visited America in the late 1740s and brought the shrub back to Europe for use as a lawn decoration. The flowers are beautiful and also functional. They are spring loaded and, when an insect alights on one of their ten stamens, they release their pollen. Try touching one of the stamina with a blade of grass and watch for the tiny, sticky string of pollen to shoot upward, sometimes reaching over a

Water: It's a Real Lifesaver

Perhaps the single most essential element of a safe, enjoyable hiking trip is access to water. Although plenty of carbohydrates are an important part of keeping your energy up while out on the trail, water is the fuel you absolutely must have to keep your engine running. You can survive a surprisingly long time without food, but you can not survive without water. Approximately 70 percent of your total body mass is water, and your blood is 90 percent water. Without water, the blood thickens and causes your blood pressure to rise and your muscles to cramp. Through perspiration, breathing, and urination, the average human loses at least three quarts of water per day and much more when engaging in a strenuous physical activity. It is important to replenish this water on a daily basis — it is essential to replenish it during, and after, a hike. Experts recommend people consume between three and four quarts of water a day, or approximately half an ounce per pound of body weight. The amount increases in high temperatures, when your body loses more water through sweat, and in low temperatures, when water escapes through breath. When you can see your breath, you are exhaling a mass of tiny water droplets that need to be replaced. Altitude also affects the amount of water your body requires. You will need a minimum of three quarts of water per day up to 12,000 feet and at least 10 quarts per day in higher regions.

An adequate water supply is necessary for the body to metabolize nutrients efficiently. Water also keeps your joints lubricated, regulates your body temperature and helps flush out contaminants. It is important to continuously replenish your body's water while you hike — not only when you are thirsty.

foot. Because of this mechanism, the flowers are sometimes able to pollinate without any help from bees. (However, they are a favorite resting spot for bees, so if you do venture a closer look, proceed with caution.)

Across the creek, the AT resumes its steep ascent toward Kelly Knob, intersecting with a blue-blazed trail 0.1 mi. further. The blue-blazed trail leads left 100 ft. to Laurel Creek Shelter and an additional opportunity to funnel some water from the creek. Thick patches of mountain laurel also bring this area to life and make the shelter grounds green and inviting. Downstream from the shelter the creek deepens to form small pools that are great for a quick, cold dip. On an extremely hot day, you may see a hiker sitting on a rock, dipping his or her head back into the river as if in a beauty salon chair. At the very least, this is a good spot to splash some

Thirst is a sign that your body's water level is already low. Fatigue and headaches are also signs that you are becoming dehydrated. You may even become irritable — just like you get when your car runs out of gas. To avoid dehydration, experts recommend drinking at least one cup of fluid for every 20 minutes of vigorous hiking.

Dehydration is classified in three levels. When you are mildly dehydrated, your nose dries up, your urine is noticeably yellow, and you are mildly thirsty. In moderate dehydration, these symptoms become more severe and are compounded by a weak, rapid pulse. When your body hits severe dehydration, your mucous membranes dry up completely, you become disoriented and drowsy are unable to urinate or make tears. As this condition worsens, you will eventually go into shock. The best way to avoid dehydration is to drink regularly, even if you are not thirsty. If you start to experience early signs of dehydration, start drinking more water — quickly. More severe dehydration should be treated with salt tablets; be aware that these are difficult to digest. Other precautions include avoiding caffeine and alcohol. Both are diuretics and extract water from your system. After a long day on the trail, continue drinking large quantities of water throughout the evening to completely rehydrate.

So, how much water should you pack along? Experts maintain that a hiker will consume an average of two gallons of water per day, or as much as 3.5 gallons if the temperature climbs over the 100-degree mark. Even if you are hiking along streams and have a purification system, bring extra water. Water weighs more than 2 pounds per quart and can become a tremendous weight in your pack. But, when paring down, leave the radio and even the camera at home — don't skimp on the water.

cold water on your face. Then get ready. The next mile is a rocky one, and it's straight up hill.

At 3.3 mi., the AT reaches the crest of Johns Creek Mt. and climbs to the top of Kelly Knob at 3740 ft. Winter and fall views from this vantage point include a sweeping look into Sinking Creek Valley, which appears to be at least 30 rather than just 3 mi. away. On a sunny day, when the air is cooled by a gentle breeze, this makes a much better dozing spot than any pile of hay and is rumored to be a favorite resting spot of AT thru-hikers. It's also a great place for shutterbugs to start clicking.

The AT turns right, away from the edge of the cliff and, after tracing the crest for approximately a quarter of a mile, begins a gradual descent through tall stands of hemlock and oak trees. A blue-blazed side trail at 3.6 mi. leads left 100 yd. to White

Rock, with views of Salt Pond Mt. The AT continues downward 0.2 mi. further to Big Pond. This large bog is the only source of water on the mountain. However, its stagnant, buggy waters are unappealing and not recommended for drinking. If you are hiking in spring or early summer, lather up with some extra insect repellent before you reach this site.

The trail rises again and continues across the top of Johns Creek Mt. A mile beyond Big Pond, a wide, grassy area represents the site of a former fire tower. Today, it's a great spot for a tent. (However, there is no water.) Beyond the clearing, join a woods road and descend again. The AT intersects with Johns Creek Mt. Trail at 4.8 mi. and continues to descend, dropping 1500 ft. over the next 2.0 mi. while offering views of War Spur, Salt Pond Mt., and Potts Mt. to the northwest. Then, as the AT cuts to the left, additional views include Clover Hollow Mt., Johns Creek Mt., and the rich farmland of Sinking Creek Valley to the east.

At 5.4 mi. the AT crosses a dirt road (VA 601) in Rocky Gap (3260 ft.). As the descent continues, the narrow trail becomes increasingly steep and much rockier. Beware of loose stones and watch your footing. Ahead, high cliffs to the left of the trail offer views of Potts and Peters mountains to the west. Beyond this point, the trail is less rocky, but continues its swift downward trend over the next mile.

As the AT passes through a small stand of young pine trees at 7.0 mi.,

the descent begins to mellow. The AT crosses Johns Creek 0.4 mi. further, among densely growing rhododendron. The creek drains through the James River (see Hike #25) to the Atlantic Ocean. Several million years ago, the creek drained into the New River (see Hike #13). However, the James River has since carved out the valley and pulled the creek with it toward the ocean.

The intersection with USFS 156/VA 632 is 100 yd. beyond the creek and provides an early exit option. There is a small parking lot (for four to six cars). VA 632 (also known as Johns Creek Valley Rd.) leads north 4.2 mi. to VA 658. Turn right onto VA 658 and head south 4 mi. to VA 42, near Simmonsville.

If you decide to continue, cross the road and pick up the AT, also the War Branch Trail at this point, to the left. The trail cuts into the woods and crosses over a narrow stream and then a narrow, rutted roadway. Pass briefly through a partially open field and then bear left to reenter the woods. Spring and summer will find the ground quite muddy and the air dense and buggy as the AT skirts to the left of a boggy area and begins a gradual ascent. The trail crosses War Spur, a branch of Johns Creek, and 74 yd. further on reaches War Spur Shelter at 8.2 mi. The shelter accommodates six and is surrounded by thick stands of mountain laurel that, when in bloom in spring, make this a beautiful backdrop for a picnic. Although the creek water should be treated, its close proximity also makes this a good spot to set up camp if you're making this a two-day adventure. In addition to the shelter, there are plenty of wide, flat areas for tents.

Beyond the shelter, the AT heads up a steep incline for the next mile as it continues up the side of Salt Pond Mt. The name was given by early settlers who took their cattle up to a depression that was good for salting. The continuous tramping of cattle, apparently, closed an outlet in the floor of the depression, forming Mountain Lake, which, at the time, was a salt pond.

At 9.3 mi., the AT separates from the War Branch Trail and cuts to the right onto a narrower, less worn path. The War Spur Trail continues straight ahead for 2.0 mi. to reach the Salt Sulphur Tpk. (VA 613). The AT enters the Mountain Lake Wilderness as it continues up the steep, wooded slope of Salt Pond Mt., reaching Lone Pine Peak (4050 ft.) at 9.8 mi. As you climb, keep an eye out for white-tailed deer, which are populous throughout the wilderness area. Bear and grouse have also been spotted along this section of trail.

With 11,113 acres and elevations varying from 2200 to 4100 ft., Mountain Lake Wilderness is the largest wilderness area in the Jefferson NF. Named for the only natural lake in western Virginia, it consists of a highland plateau, which sits squarely on the Eastern Continental Divide. As you pass through the hardy stands of virgin spruce and hemlock that cover the area, look for golden-crowned kinglets, black-throated warblers, pine siskins, boreal chickadees, and red-breasted nuthatches. Search the trunks of the hemlock trees for rows of tiny holes, the work of the yellow-bellied sapsucker that often drills for food. The wilderness area also has a diverse display of wildflowers, fern, fungus, and low shrubs and is a popular spot for primitive camping expeditions. No power tools are permitted in wilderness areas. The trail is remarkably well groomed in light of this fact.

The AT crosses to the north of Lone Pine Peak, which is not as monumental as its name suggests. Don't get the camera out just yet. Better views wait at Wind Rock, not far ahead. From Lone Pine Peak, the AT crosses the flat, wooded crest of Salt Pond Mt. over a wide, easy trail. The thick shade of the hemlock trees keeps the area damp and the ground quite soft. As you pass through the swampy area, look to the left for glimpses of Little Stony Creek Valley in the north and to the right for passing views of Johns Creek Valley in the south.

At 10.5 mi., the AT makes a sharp left, turning away from an old trail that leads straight ahead to the Potts Mt. Trail. Follow the AT blazes along nice, even terrain, passing a spring 0.5 mi. ahead and, in approximately 100 ft., a semi-open area with room for two to three tents. The trail maintains its even keel, allowing you to forget the huffing and puffing you may have experienced just a few miles back and settle in to enjoying the scenery of more old hemlocks and giant spruce trees, and, in spring, a variety of wildflowers, including buttercups, violets, and dwarf iris.

Winter hikers will find the hemlock forest of the wilderness area a haven for spotting white-tailed deer. The hemlock's sturdy, dense branches can hold large amounts of snow, keeping it off the ground below. Unable to walk in deep drifts, deer often seek refuge under the hemlock's umbrella, and they dine on its low-hanging foliage. Spruce trees are less useful to deer and other wildlife. Game biologists refer to the spruce as a "stuffing" tree, because it has no nutrients. Deer can feed upon its branches, but starve with a full belly.

As the AT crosses the crest of Potts Mt. to reach Wind Rock at 12.2 mi., there are excellent views to the north of Stony Creek Valley over 4000 ft. below. Further north, Fork and Peters mountains rise above the red rock valley in the distance. This is a nice spot to rest and take some photographs. The rocky crag offers sparse cover, but the constant light breeze is refreshing.

The AT crosses Salt Sulfur Tpk. (VA 613) at 12.4 mi. This gravel road leads north 2.2 mi. to the community of Kire at the intersection of VA 635, and 11.0 mi. south to US 460. There is a large parking lot at the intersection of the AT and Salt Sulphur Tpk., making this a second viable early exit option. If you are in this one for the

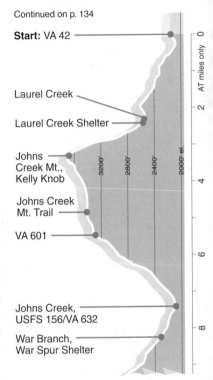

Continued on p. 134

Start: VA 42

Laurel Creek

Laurel Creek Shelter

Johns Creek Mt., Kelly Knob

Johns Creek Mt. Trail

VA 601

Johns Creek, USFS 156/VA 632

War Branch, War Spur Shelter

AT miles only

long haul, press on from Salt Sulfur Tpk. and enter a rocky descent as the trail cuts down the heavily wooded northern slope of Big Mt. The mountain lives up to its name — albeit an

War Spur Trail

Lone Pine Peak,
El. 4050'

Wind Rock **V**

Salt Sulfur Tpk.,
VA 613 Ⓟ

N ◄ 1" = 1 mi.

Bailey Gap ▰ ⓦ
El. 3525'

🥾 VA 635 Ⓟ El. 2450'

unoriginal one —and the AT's gradual downward trend continues, quite rocky at points, for 3.7 mi., reaching Bailey Gap Shelter at 16.1 mi.

The shelter is to the right of the trail and a seasonal spring passes on the left, directly across from the shelter. Do not count on this as a source for water. It is often dry, especially in the summer. The shelter was built in the 1960s, but has been well preserved by the US Forest Service and the Roanoke AT Club. It can accommodate up to six, and there is room for a few tents in the surrounding area. From Bailey Gap Shelter, the AT continues on an easy downward slope, crossing a gravel fire road (VA 734) at 16.5 mi. and an old woods road before reaching VA 635 (2450 ft.) at 17.6 mi.

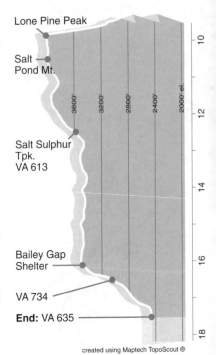

created using Maptech TopoScout ®

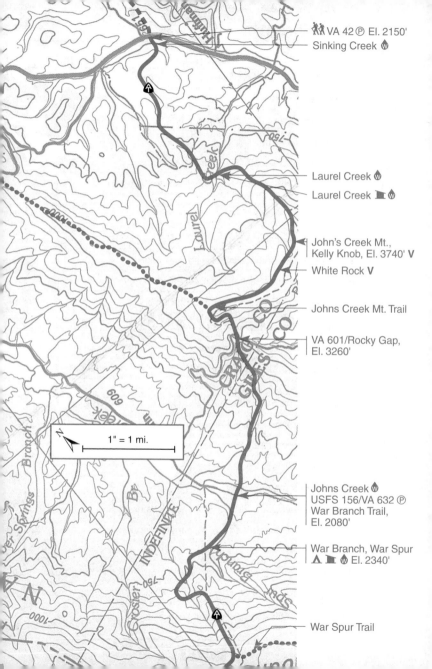

ᗿ VA 42 ⓟ El. 2150'
Sinking Creek ⬙

Laurel Creek ⬙
Laurel Creek ⬛ ⬙

John's Creek Mt.,
Kelly Knob, El. 3740' **V**
White Rock **V**

Johns Creek Mt. Trail

VA 601/Rocky Gap,
El. 3260'

Johns Creek ⬙
USFS 156/VA 632 ⓟ
War Branch Trail,
El. 2080'

War Branch, War Spur
▲ ⬛ ⬙ El. 2340'

War Spur Trail

1" = 1 mi.

INDEFINITE

CRAIG CO.
GILES CO.

Hike #15   Itinerary

Miles N	NORTH	Elev. (ft/m)	Miles S
17.6	**Start: VA 42,** driveway parking 1.6 mi. N of Newport.	2150/655	0.0
17.5	Caution: **Hot electric fence.** Cross on stile.		0.1
15.3	Cross **Laurel Creek.** Ascend Kelly Knob.		2.3
15.2	**Laurel Creek Shelter,** water.		2.4
14.3	Crest of Johns Creek Mt., **Kelly Knob;** view.	3740/1140	3.3
14.0	Descend; blue-blazed trail leads L 100 yd. to White Rock for views of Salt Pond Mt.		3.6
13.8	Big Pond.		3.8
12.9	Former fire tower site.		4.7
12.8	**Johns Creek Mt. Trail** leads R 3.5 mi. to VA 658.		4.8
12.2	**Rocky Gap** and intersection with VA 601 (dirt).	3260/994	5.4
10.2	Cross **Johns Creek** in rhododendron thicket and reach **USFS 156/VA 632,** parking lot, early exit option. AT aligns with **War Branch Trail.**	2080/634	7.4
9.7	Enter **Mountain Lake Wilderness.**		7.9
9.4	**War Branch** and **War Spur Shelter.**	2340/713	8.2
8.3	**AT turns R** and ascends; War Spur Trail continues ahead 2.0 mi. to Salt Sulfur Tpk. (VA 613).		9.3
7.8	Apex of **Lone Pine Peak.**	4050/1234	9.8
7.2	Swamp on crest of **Salt Pond Mt.;** views.		10.4
6.6	Spring on L followed by campsites.		11.0
5.8	Crest of **Potts Mt.** with view.		11.8
5.4	Pass **Wind Rock** with views of Stony Creek Valley to N.		12.2
5.2	Gravel **Salt Sulphur Tpk.** (Va. 613), early exit option.		12.4
5.1	Descend Big Mt.		12.5
1.5	**Bailey Gap Shelter,** with seasonal spring.	3525/1074	16.1
1.1	Cross gravel fire road **(VA 734).**		16.5
0.0	**End:** Paved **VA 635,** roadside parking, 16.5 mi. NE of Pearisburg.	2450/747	17.6

SOUTH

HIKE #16
Sinking Creek Mt.

Map: ATC Va. #3 & 4, Central Virginia

Route: Through Jefferson NF from Craig Creek Valley along Sinking Creek Mt. to Sinking Creek at VA 42

Recommended direction: N to S

Distance: 11.2 mi.

Elevation +/-: 1540 to 3490 to 2150 ft.

Effort: Strenuous

Day hike: Yes

Overnight backpacking hike: Yes

Duration: 7 to 9 hr.

Early exit option: At 3.7 mi., blue-blazed trail

Natural history features: Sinking Creek Mt.; Keffer Oak

Social history feature: Cemetery near Sarver Hollow Shelter

Other feature: Grocery store in Twin Oaks, 1.6 mi. from S end

Trailhead access: *Start:* From Roanoke, take I-81 S 3.0 mi. to VA 311N; follow 12.0 mi. to VA 621W, which leads 6.5 mi. to small, unmarked parking area on R with room for 3 to 4 cars. Look for trailhead on L side of lot. *End:* From Roanoke, take I-81 S 3.0 mi. to Va. 311N. Follow 20.0 mi. to New Castle. In New Castle, turn L onto VA 42 and proceed 21.0 mi. to trailhead and small parking area.

Camping: Niday Shelter; Sarver Hollow Shelter; and see "Camping" section in Intro-duction

---

This section of the AT follows the often narrow, rocky crest of Sinking Creek Mt. The scenery varies from deep woods to open fields as the trail crosses over steep ledges and rocky outcrops, offering passing views into Sinking Creek Valley and Craig Creek Valley. Early spring is a particularly good time for this hike because of the multitude of wildflowers budding throughout the area then. Aside from a steep climb at one end and a steep descent at the other, the trail follows a fairly level course.

Pick up the AT at northern side of parking area, bear left, and begin ascending through a forest of Virginia and white pine. Although there are no AT markers at the trailhead, there is a sign just out of view of the parking lot to let you know you're on the right path. Less than 10 yd. beyond the sign there is also a registration post. The trail is narrow and devoid of rocks — for now. Although the early climb is quite steep, it is also short, and begins to taper off as the trail curves to the right. As you climb, expect to feel dwarfed by the soft white pine trees that line the trail. The white pine grows more rapidly than any other northern forest tree. Averaging 15 to 18 in. per year, it is the largest pine east of the Rockies, and, next to the sugar pine of California, the largest pine in the United States. Here the towering trees shade the path, making it dark and cool.

The respite is brief and soon the trail is making another sharp ascent, over a carpet of pine needles atop dark, rich soil. As the trail continues up a series of steep inclines, interrupted by short, flat stretches, deep purple wild violets, yellow violets, and lavender dwarf iris line its edges in the spring, while wild geraniums and Jack-in-the-pulpits cover the surrounding area in summer and early fall.

The trail curves to the right and follows a narrow ridge through a forest of beech, oak, and dogwood, Virginia's state tree. The dogwoods' starch-white clusters of blooms are a splendid sight in spring, and the clusters of scarlet berries that dress the small trees in fall also produce a nice visual effect, if you're lucky enough to see them. The bright red fruit doesn't remain on the trees for long. Its extremely high fat content makes it the energy bar of the birds. Northern flickers, cardinals, and American robins are especially fond of the treat. Cottontail rabbits, foxes, gray squirrels, and Eastern chipmunks also dine on the berries, while white-tailed deer consume the twigs and foliage. Don't be tempted to pop one of the juicy red beads into your own mouth. The taste is bitter and unpalatable to humans. Next time you're out on a putting green, think back to this scene: this is how most golf club heads start out!

As the trail continues along a narrow ridge, there are passing glimpses on both the right and the left of Sinking Creek Mt. waiting ahead. At 0.5 mi., the trail bears left and descends gradually to reach a narrow stream. Keep an eye out for the blazes as the trail follows the stream to the right before crossing over large stepping-stones and continuing along its left bank.

Leaving the stream behind, the trail begins another steep ascent, through a dense forest of beech and oak. Thoreau once described the beech's leaves in autumn as a lustrous, "clear leather color, like a book bound in calf." The beech is as thin-skinned as it looks, making its smooth trunk a common target for initial carvers. Expect to see the names and initials of more than a few hikers as you pass through this area. Unfortunately, the markings often introduce wood-rot fungi into the sensitive trees. Please refrain from making your mark.

A blue-blazed trail at 1.3 mi. leads 50 ft. to the left to Niday Shelter, named for a family who homesteaded near the site in the 1800s. Just before the shelter, open areas to the right and left include ample room for one tent site each. The shelter itself is a lean-to with the open side facing away from the trail toward a fire pit and a picnic table. The shelter sleeps six and cleared alcoves nestled in the surrounding woods are great for tent camping. Be sure to clear the ground of beech nuts and pine cones before you bed down. To the right of the AT, the blue-blazed trail leads to a narrow stream approximately 50 ft. down a steep hill. If the creek is dry, head down a few hundred feet further to a larger stream. Treat its water before using.

If you are in need of a breather, this is the spot. Just beyond the shelter, a steep, rocky trek to the 3490-ft. peak of Sinking Creek Mt., part of the Eastern Continental Divide, awaits. The mountain is comprised of 410-to-430-million-year-old Silurian sandstone, the same rock that forms the Kittatinny Mt. ridge in eastern New Jersey and the Blue Mt. ridge in Pennsylvania. The sandstone is relatively thin and white, covering stretches of trail with soft, powdery sand.

At the onset of your hike up the mountain, the trail slopes to an almost vertical climb. Don't despair: it gets easier as you go. A few flat stretches on your way to the top help make the tough stretch manageable. The pine needles and sand that cover the trail are interrupted occasionally by short segments of large, loose rocks that require some careful attention to your footing. At 1.8 mi., a large, flat slab of quartzite covers the trail. It is apt to be quite slippery after a recent rain or snowfall. Proceed with caution, especially if traveling in damp conditions. When passing through rocky sections, keep an eye out for salamanders, which are prevalent throughout the area in early spring.

Near the 2.0 mi. point, the trail passes a campsite on the right with an established fire ring and room for one tent. There is no convenient water source. Just beyond the campsite, you will get your first clear view of Craig Creek Valley to the south. Several rocky ledges permit a year-round peek at its deep green, rolling pastures and spacious farmhouses with bright red barns. As you near the top of the mountain (approximately 2.8 mi.) the trail crosses over a stretch of dark, reddish-brown shale common in the Craig Creek Valley. The small, loose stones break apart underfoot and form a well-packed surface over the trail. At 3.4 mi., the trail dips into a slight sag that may have been caused by Cabin Brook, a narrow stream that is often dry. Caution: there is a small sinkhole to the left of the trail that may be camouflaged by leaves or snow in fall and winter. Stay on the path.

Continuing toward the crest of the mountain, the trail enters a laurel thicket. The low, shrublike trees permit more panoramic views of Craig Creek Valley. On a clear spring or early summer day, a slight breeze makes the air quite fragrant as the masses of rose-pink, star-shaped flowers in full bloom decorate the trees. At 3.7 mi., the AT turns left onto the crest of Sinking Creek Mt. (3490 ft.). There are "no hunting" signs to the right and a blue-blazed trail leading 2.5 mi. to USFS 209 (Old Hall Rd.), where there is limited roadside parking. Old Hall Rd. leads 1.5 mi. left to

VA 42 and 3.5 mi. right to VA 621. There are two early exit options here: the blue-blazed route or retracing your steps to your original starting point. There are enough wildflower varieties along this stretch that a repeat trip is likely to offer an opportunity to view lily-of-the-valley, buttercup, trillium, ragwort, and other blossoms you missed in your anticipation of the awaiting mountain.

Beyond the blue-blazed trail, a cluster of rocks to the left of the AT provides an excellent spot for lunch. The area is well shaded but offers views of Craig Creek Valley to the north and Sinking Creek Valley to the south. In early spring and summer, the area is vibrant green. Rhododendron and a scattering of evergreen preserve the color year round.

If you opt to press onward, continue along the crest of Sinking Creek Mt. as the AT crosses several slanting rock ledges, offering an almost continuous view of the valley. Sinking Creek was named for the way it appears to disappear as it crosses underground near Hoges Chapel on VA 42, 2.0 mi. west of the southern end of this hike. Records of European settlers along the stream date back to 1757. As you make your way along the ridge of Sinking Creek Mt., look for piles of rocks, placed here by these settlers as they prepared the land for farming.

The AT follows the crest along a flat, even grade for the next 4.0 mi., passing a 0.3-mi. side trail to Sarver

Continued on p. 142

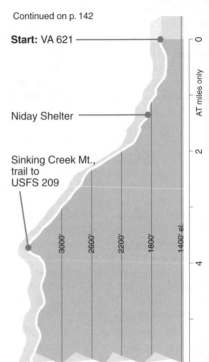

Hollow Shelter at 7.3 mi. Several homestead buildings are scattered around the area. There is room for two or three tents near the structure and a stream provides a reliable, though unprotected, water source.

Sarver Hollow Shelter
▲ 🏠 💧 🚻

Trail to Braiser's Knob

Power line

N ◄ ¹³/₁₆" = 1 mi.

Keffer Oak 🍁

VA 630, Sinking Creek
💧 Ⓟ

🚶🚶 VA 42 Ⓟ El. 2150'

Even if you're not planning to stay the night, it is worth adding the 0.6-mi. side trip to check out an old cemetery at the site with tombstones dating to the late 1800s.

Beyond the shelter, the AT continues along the flat top of the mountain, passing the 0.5-mi-long side trail to Braiser's Knob at 8.0 mi. before cutting through an open field and under a power line at 8.2 mi. Begin to descend the mountain at 8.9 mi. The descent of Sinking Creek Mt. is much more gradual than the ascent — get set for smooth sailing ahead as you pass through another forest of oak and beech. The beech tree is one of the most important sources of food for forest wildlife. Chipmunks and squirrels don't wait for the nuts to hit the ground and you are apt to hear them foraging through the trees. Having one or two dropped on your head is also not uncommon. In fall, this is a good spot for a black bear sighting. The bear feeds on the beech nuts to load up on calories for winter hibernation.

The forest gives way to a bright, grassy area as the trail crosses again under a power line at 9.6 mi. just before reaching Keffer Oak (9.8 mi.). One of the largest standing trees on the AT, this white oak is more than 18 ft. around and is estimated to be more than 300 years old. Although trees this size were common when European settlers first arrived in the area, they are a true rarity today.

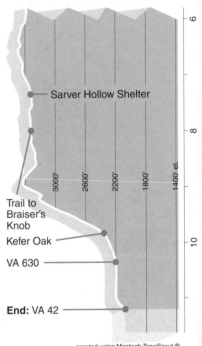

created using Maptech TopoScout ®

Continue gently downward, crossing a narrow branch of Sinking Creek at 10.2 mi. Beyond the stream, the AT crests a small hill, then reassumes its downward trend, crossing two fences to reach VA 42 at 11.2 mi.

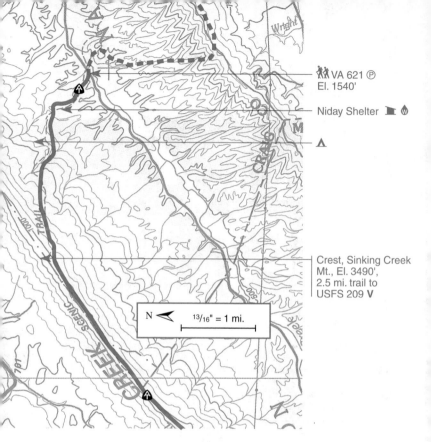

🚶🚶 VA 621 Ⓟ
El. 1540'

Niday Shelter ▰ ◍

Λ

Crest, Sinking Creek
Mt., El. 3490',
2.5 mi. trail to
USFS 209 **V**

N ◄ ¹³/₁₆" = 1 mi.

Hike #16   Itinerary

Miles N	NORTH	Elev. (ft/m)	Miles S
11.2	**Start:** Small parking area on N side of **VA 621**, 6.5 mi. W of Va. 311.	1540/469	0.0
9.9	Blue-blazed trail leads L 50 ft. to **Niday Shelter** with stream; begin ascent to Sinking Creek Mt.	1800/549	1.3
9.3	Dry campsite.		1.9
7.7	Laurel thicket; **view** of Craig Creek Valley to S.		3.5
7.5	Crest of **Sinking Creek Mt.;** blue-blazed trail leads 2.5 mi. to USFS 209 (Old Hall Rd.), early exit option.	approx. 3490/1064	3.7
3.9	Blue-blazed trail descends sharply 0.4 mi. to **Sarver Hollow Shelter.**		7.3
3.2	0.5-mi. trail to **Braiser's Knob.**		8.0
3.0	Power line in open field.		8.2
2.3	Begin descent of Sinking Creek Mt.		8.9
1.4	**Keffer Oak.**	2300/701	9.8
0.9	Turn R onto gravel **VA 630.**		10.3
0.0	**End:** Small parking area at **VA 42**, 21.0 mi. W of New Castle.	2150/655	11.2

SOUTH

Cove Mt. to Trout Creek

Maps: ATC Va. #3, Central Virginia

Route: Through Jefferson NF from VA 624 to Dragon's Tooth and along Cove Mt. to Trout Creek

Recommended direction: N to S

Distance: 7.9 mi.

Elevation +/-: 1790 to 3050 to 1500 ft.

Effort: Strenuous

Day hike: Yes

Overnight backpacking trip: Optional

Duration: 4 hr.

Early exit option: At 1.5 mi., blue-blazed Dragon's Tooth Trail

Natural history features: Dragon's Tooth; Trout Creek

Social history feature: Audie Murphy Monument (on optional extended hike)

Other feature: Grocery store 0.5 mi. from N end of hike

Trailhead access: *Start:* From Roanoke, follow I-81 S 3.0 mi. to VA 311N and proceed 10.6 mi. to VA 624. Turn L onto VA 624 and proceed 0.3 mi. to trailhead. There is room for 4 to 6 cars along roadside. Or, pass turn for VA 624 on L and continue 0.4 mi. to small USFS parking area on L. From parking area, follow Dragon's Tooth Trail 0.2 mi. to L onto blue-blazed trail for 0.2 mi. to intersect AT 0.4 mi. into this hike. *End:* From Start trailhead, follow VA 624 SW approximately 2 mi.; turn R on VA 620 and continue 3.0 mi. to 2 parking areas (for 2 cars each) on L, across from the Trout Creek footbridge.

Camping: Pickle Branch Shelter, and where permitted along trail

---

Hoisting you over towering Silurian sandstone formations and through ambushes of their smaller but still treacherous offspring, this section of the AT is not the place for a casual stroll. But for those in search of a rigorous workout, it will not disappoint. The trail rises over rocky ridges and dips into low wooded sags of pine, oak, and maple. The best views will be found in the fall, but sections are over the treeline, permitting a year-round view of North Mt. to the right (east) and Cove Mt. to the left (west). Due to the extremely rocky terrain, hiking in wet or icy conditions is not recommended.

The strenuous rock climbing that occupies much of the beginning of this hike is balanced out by the easy descent at the end, as this hike offers a little bit of something for everyone. Energetic hikers will enjoy the challenge of the foreboding boulders and will want to take advantage of the extra climbing opportunities afforded at Dragon's Tooth. Less ambitious hikers will still enjoy the crossing over Cove Mountain's crest and peering into the valleys of green pasture land below.

The 7.9 mi. from VA 624 to Trout Creek make a strenuous but satisfying day hike. Adding the 7.6-mi. optional stretch to Craig Creek provides an even greater challenge. But the hard work is rewarded. This portion of the AT has some of the best views in Virginia. Early risers could do the entire 15.5 mi. in the spring, but, with so much to see and so many rocks to climb, a long-distance hike will be more appreciated if taken as a two-day adventure.

For hikers who want to spend more than a day exploring the area, but prefer the comforts of a shower and warm bed at night, the town of Roanoke is just 16.0 mi. south of the hike's start. Roanoke is Virginia's largest metropolitan area west of Richmond. The self-proclaimed "capital of the Blue Ridge" is also known as "Star City," for the huge, lighted star overlooking the city from Mill Mt. The town is dotted with antique shops, quaint boutiques, and a wide variety of restaurants and hotels. (Beware, few restaurants are open on Sunday evenings.) Roanoke is also home to Virginia Museum of Transportation. For hike essentials closer to the trail, try the grocery store on VA 311 in Catawba, 2.5 mi. before VA 311 meets VA 624. Traveling on VA 311 from I-81, the store is on the left, just beyond the junction with VA 779.

From VA 624, climb up a log staircase and meet the AT in a mature pine grove scattered with oak and maple. In the spring, buttercups, chickweed, and various violets color the area with shades of yellow, purple, and blue. In the fall, a bed of pine needles and fallen leaves carpets the trail, crunching beneath the passing hiker's feet. Head south, and in less than 0.25 mi., the trail leaves the pine grove behind and begins a sharp ascent, continuing through a forest of oak and maple trees. Barbed wire marking the Jefferson NF boundary to the left pushes the trail to the right. If you make this climb in the fall, you can see traces of VA 311 below and to the right.

Growing increasingly narrow, the trail continues upward for the next mile to a rocky ridge. Halfway up the ridge, at 0.4 mi., a blue-blazed trail on the right leads 0.2 mi. to a stream. If you didn't stock up on water before you embarked, do so now. You'll be thankful for extra water before this hike is finished. Beyond the stream a blue-blazed trail leads right to Dragon's Tooth Trail, which leads to the parking lot at the alternate starting point for this hike on VA 311. As you make this climb, beware of loose rocks, masked by low brush in the spring and summer and by leaves in the fall. A careless step could send you tumbling down the sharp drop-off to the left of the trail.

In fall, the bright yellow leaves of the sugar maple and the deep red leaves of the red maple and red oak trees bring the area to life with a bright canvas of color. When the leaves are gone, the trees display a different kind of forest life. Rabbits, squirrels, mice, and fox feed on the sugar maple's trunk, gnawing away large strips of bark. If you notice a girdled tree, examine the size of the teeth marks to determine what type of animal fed there last.

A series of switchbacks leads to the rocky rim of Rawies Rest (1.0 mi.) where you will get your first view of Cove Mt., to the north. The trail continues a wobbly ascent along the crest of the spur. As it rises, the rocks grow from minor obstacles to maneuverable challenges. This is the first of several stretches in this hike that will find you climbing over sandstone formations much larger than yourself. The vertically challenged may need a boost and young hikers will need to be lifted.

As the trail crosses over these ominous boulders, it remains narrow, no more than a foot at its widest point, and the drop-off jumps to the right. After approximately one-half hour of hiking, you will pass a possible campsite on the left. There is room for one large tent or two small ones. A shallow fire pit is conserved by a well-constructed rock lining. There is no water near the site, but the shade of several tall oaks keeps the area cool in spring and summer.

From here, the trail becomes virtually nonexistent as the white blazes guide you over what amounts to an enormous rock pile. The tremendous

Silurian sandstone formations were created by volcanoes that erupted over 410 million years ago. But, as you make your way through the wreckage, you may feel as though you are climbing out of an avalanche. Natural rock stairwells ease small spaces of the climb, but large portions of this section are quite challenging. Beware: several of these rocks are loose, making the climb even trickier.

With some careful maneuvering, you can pull yourself up onto one of the largest rocks (some are over 20 ft. high) for another view of Cove Mt. to the north. The best of these views is available from Viewpoint Rock, 1.3 mi. into the hike. This bus-sized cluster of boulders sports a view of the gap between Cove Mt. straight ahead and North Mt. to the right. Lush maples and oak may obscure summer viewing, but won't block it entirely. The fall offers a bright mosaic of red, orange, and yellow.

From here, the trail eases and gradually widens as it passes over another ridgeline. Just beyond Viewpoint Rock, you will pass Devils Seat on the right. Also a hikers' seat, this rocky area offers a southern view of the Catawba Valley and is a good spot for a water break. Don't indulge too much—there is no water source for several miles.

The trail passes two more tent sites, each with a fire pit but no water source, then begins a steep descent into Lost Spectacles Gap. As you travel downward, keep an eye out for the white blazes. This extremely

Hiking in Fog

No views, cold and damp, too foggy. Might as well stay home, right? Wrong! Foggy hiking is fun and full of surprises.

1. Tastes and smells are more interesting in wet weather. To test this, smell or chew any of the following that you can identify with accuracy: sassafras twigs, pine or hemlock needles (the hemlock tree is not the hemlock that poisoned Socrates), bee balm and other mints, wintergreen leaves or berries, rock tripe, sourwood leaves, wood sorrel. Also, take a small piece of candy, perhaps the kind that you gobble after a hard climb, and dissolve it slowly on your tongue.

2. Talk to the owls. Barred owls and great-horned owls often call during overcast or foggy days. If you hear a call, especially the *who-cooks-for-you* call of the barred owl, answer it. Cup your hands and call toward the sound. Not loudly—you may offend the owls and other hikers, and you might even get mobbed by crows. Just get a gentle dialog going.

3. In dense fog on level trail, try an optical illusion. Walk quickly but carefully forward for 50 to 100 paces, focusing on a tree trunk or branch further ahead. Pine trees or other dark shapes work best. Then stop suddenly (warn fellow hikers beforehand), focusing on the same spot. The trees in your peripheral vision may appear to keep moving in the fog. If it doesn't work, relax and try again later. For me, this works only in dense fog and quiet woods. The effect is enhanced on foggy winter days, when snow increases the contrast in the woods.

4. If you are warm and dry, sit beside a spring or lean back on a mossy boulder and listen, smell, and feel. Taste a raindrop that rolls down your face.

5. In summer, use a flashlight to examine wet rocks, decaying logs, or leaf litter for salamanders, snails, worms, millipedes, daddy longlegs, and other animals that know good weather when they feel it.

—Doris Gove

---

rocky route takes several sharp turns. The trail opens up into a flat, low area, occupied by thin, scattered oak trees and a stone fire ring. There is space for several tents here. A blue-blazed trail on the right (at 1.5 mi.) leads 1.5 mi. back to VA 311.

Beyond this plateau, climb a stone staircase and prepare for another rocky ascent as the trail heads for the crest of Cove Mt. Offering glimpses of Catawba Valley to the left and behind you, the trail narrows as it winds around and over more towering boulders. Half-way into this latest obstacle course, you can see Dragon's Tooth, a 3050-ft.-high monolith, beckoning in the distance.

After a mile of strenuous climbing, the trail reaches the crest of Cove Mt. (3020 ft.) at 2.5 mi. and turns sharply to the right to trace the rocky silhouette. A blue-blazed trail to the left leads 200 yd. to Dragon's Tooth (3050 ft.). The massive rock offers the best photo opportunity of the hike, unobstructed views of Catawba Valley, McAfee Knob, and Big Tinker Mt. to the east. Truly adventurous hikers can pull themselves up through a crack in the Tooth and climb onto its sharp, narrow crown.

Members of the Roanoke AT Club, who care for this section of the trail, have had sometimes heated debates over whether to leave it rough or smooth it out. In the end, the rustic, albeit challenging, natural route was most appealing. Dragon's Tooth Trail, which can be picked up on VA 311 at the alternate starting point for this hike, provides a direct, 2.3-mi. climb to the top of the Tooth. This, combined with a steady flow of AT traffic, makes for a busy section of trail. Club members thought the area would become too crowded if the trip to the top were smooth. Besides, hikers love a challenge. To dissuade hikers from forging their own routes to the top (causing much greater damage to the surrounding ecosystem in the process), the club relocated some of the larger rocks to create the steps. However, the club also conserved as much of the natural state of the trail as possible.

The Tooth once was called Buzzard Rock, but Tom Campbell, a pioneer member of the Roanoke AT Club from 1947 until his death in 1986, thought the fang deserved a more poetic appellation, and renamed it. The buzzards have been replaced by hikers who bask on the Tooth's craggy surface, letting the sun beat on their faces, enjoying a cool breeze, and savoring big bites of beauty as mountains fold into the distance from a green valley. On a clear day, you can see all the way to the Peaks of Otter (south). Hikers not up to the challenge can skip the climb to the top of the Dragon and hike around it. But the smaller rock molars that cover the AT are, for the foreseeable future, inescapable.

Leaving Dragon's Tooth behind, the trail heads south along the crest of Cove Mt., reaching the 3050-ft. summit at 2.6 mi. Flanked by sharp drop-offs on both sides, the trail is blanketed with pine needles and thick patches of bright green moss. As you cross the crest and begin a steep, rocky descent, you can see North Mt. to the right and Brush Mt. to the left.

Continuing over moss-covered rocks, the trail widens as it curves to the west around Millers Cove and descends into another sag. As you enter a low, open area, the path abandons you once again and the few trees scattered about are blazed with your only directional clues. The blazes continue to guide the trail downward through a covering of lush green pokeweed. In the distant east, you can see North Mt., striped with stands of green virgin pine.

The trail changes from a gradual to an unexpectedly steep, rocky descent through a densely wooded area. Pine trees have discreetly rejoined the maple and oak over the past few miles. Popping up a few at a time, their sudden multitudes may surprise you. Their needles combine with moss, leaves, and tall grass to make a slick covering over the rocks. Watch your step: passage can be a bit tricky. At 4.2 mi., the trail passes a 2600-ft.-high unnamed knob, swoops down, and begins a second ascent of Cove Mt.

Regaining the crest of Cove Mt. at 4.4 mi., the trail follows a series of shallow dips. The up-and-down slopes are often steep, but never more than 200 yd. long. The trail continues to circle Millers Cove as it curves to the south, leaves the crest of the mountain behind, and begins its steep, rocky descent into Trout Creek Valley. It passes a small campsite on the right, then turns sharply to the left and continues downward. To the right of the trail, 30-to-50-ft.-high boulders of gray Silurian sandstone line the ridge, forming a stone fortress overhead.

At the 6.7-mi. point, the AT crosses a blue-blazed trail that leads 0.5 mi. to the left to Pickle Branch Shelter, a small wooden structure. The shelter sits on the edge of a striking, old stand of hemlocks. Their dense branches insulate the area and the tiny stream running behind the shelter is the only sound that's heard. The

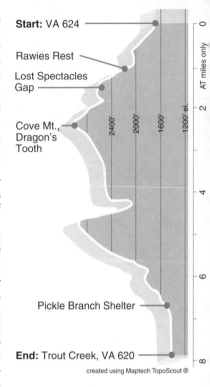

created using Maptech TopoScout ®

stream is one of the few water sources along this stretch of trail. This is also the only shelter along this hike and its optional extension, so two-day travelers not into tent camping will have to stop here.

Back on the AT just beyond the shelter, an underground stream spurts a small trickle, making the ground damp and mushy. Past this slippery area, rocks become increasingly scarce as a forest of maple, oak, hickory, and pine thickens around you. At

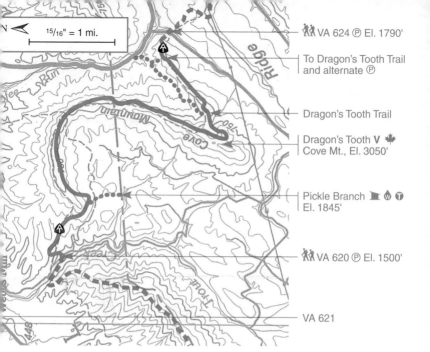

VA 624 Ⓟ El. 1790'

To Dragon's Tooth Trail
and alternate Ⓟ

Dragon's Tooth Trail

Dragon's Tooth V ❀
Cove Mt., El. 3050'

Pickle Branch ◼ ⬥ ◉
El. 1845'

VA 620 Ⓟ El. 1500'

VA 621

7.5 mi. the trail crosses under a power line, then continues an easy descent. Listen for the rushing waters of Trout Creek splashing further down the mountain. At 7.9 mi., stone steps descend to the 10-ft. wide creek. The water rolling over the rocky creek bed is inviting. The creek is less than waist deep, but it's sufficient for dunking your head or at least splashing your face. If you venture close enough to get wet, be careful. The rocks along the bed of the creek are quite slick. Wide, flat areas on both sides of the creek are softened by tall grass and provide several tent sites. A small but sturdy wooden footbridge leads across the creek to VA 620.

Optional Extended Hike: If you're not ready to call it a day, cross VA 620 and pick up the AT at a trail registration box to the right. Beyond the registration box, the trail takes a sharp right and begins a steep ascent over a series of switchbacks. The trail continues to wind from right to left as it makes the 3.8-mi., 3000-ft. climb to the Audie Murphy Monument. As you make the climb, you'll catch glimpses of North Mt. and Cove Mt., including the very top of Dragon's Tooth, to the east, and Sinking Creek Mt. to the northwest. At the top, a blue-blazed trail ascends 200 ft. to the monument, which marks the site of a 1971 plane crash that killed the most decorated U.S. soldier of World War II. A scenic overlook behind the monument affords excellent views of Sinking Creek Mt. and upper Craig Creek Valley to the north. Beyond the monument, the trail descends for 3.8 mi. to Craig Creek, ending at a parking lot for eight to ten cars on VA 621, 6.5 mi. west of its junction with VA 311.

HIKE #17 Itinerary

Miles N	NORTH	Elev. (ft/m)	Miles S
7.9	**Start:** AT ascends from roadside parking at **VA 624,** 0.3 mi. S of VA 311, 2.8 mi. S of Catawba, 14.0 mi. N of Roanoke.	1790/546	0.0
7.5	Blue-blazed trail leads R 0.2 mi. to stream and Dragon's Tooth Trail (0.2 mi. further to alternate Start of hike parking).		0.4
6.9	**Rawies Rest,** view.		1.0
6.6	**Viewpoint Rock.**	2600/792	1.3
6.4	Descend steeply into **Lost Spectacles Gap.** Blue-blazed trail in gap leads R 1.5 mi. to USFS parking lot on VA 311. Early exit option.		1.5
6.3	Begin steep ascent.		1.6
5.4	Crest of Cove Mt.; blue-blazed trail leads L 200 yd. to **Dragon's Tooth,** view.	3020/920	2.5
5.3	Summit of **Cove Mt.**	3050/930	2.6
3.8	**Hemlock Point.**		4.1
3.7	Descend swiftly.	2600/792	4.2
3.5	Regain crest of Cove Mt.		4.4
1.2	Blue-blazed trail to **Pickle Branch Shelter** (0.5 mi.), stream.	1845/562	6.7
0.4	Cross power line clearing.		7.5
0.0	**End:** Cross wooden footbridge over **Trout Creek** and reach **VA 620,** 19.0 mi. NW of Roanoke. Parking for 2 cars in each of 2 lots.	1500/457	7.9

SOUTH

Catawba Mt.

Map: ATC Va. #3, Central Virginia

Route: From VA 311 over Catawba Mt., through Beckner Gap, and across VA 785 to VA 624

Recommended direction: N to S

Distance: 5.9 mi.

Elevation +/-: 2000 to 2600 to 1790 ft.

Effort: Easy to moderate

Day hike: Yes

Overnight backpacking hike: Can be combined with Hike #17 or #19

Duration: 3 to 4 hr.

Early exit option: At 4.3 mi., VA 785

Natural history features: Sawtooth Ridge; views of Dragon's Tooth

Other features: Groceries, restaurant, and lodgings in Catawba

Trailhead access: *Start:* From Roanoke, follow I-81 S 3.0 mi. to VA 311N, follow for approximately 9 mi. Pass turn for VA 864 on L and look for large parking area (10 – 12 cars) on L. *End:* From northern end, continue on VA 311 for 3.0 mi., through Catawba. Turn L on VA 624 and proceed for 0.3 mi. to trailhead. Limited roadside parking, overnight.

Camping: Several campsites

S et between two extremely strenuous sections of the trail, this easy-to-moderate hike crosses the western end of Catawba Mt. and offers variegated landscapes, from rocky knobs to open fields. One of this section's most unusual features is its unexpected trek through cow pastures. If you begin to feel that someone is watching, don't be surprised to look up and meet the gaze of a large brown or black and white bovine. This hike will give you a moderate workout without forcing you into overdrive. Although its views are more subtle than those experienced from Dragon's Tooth and Cove Mt. (Hike #17) or McAfee Knob (Hike

#19), it still offers plenty of photo opportunities. The transition from rocky ridges to open pastures to thick pine groves give this stretch its own identity. If you plan to spend several days in the Catawba Valley, this is a nice hike for the last day of the trip.

Set on a trail corridor, a strip of land purchased for the trail, this section of the AT is managed by the National Park Service. In 1978, land disputes pushed this part of the trail off Catawba Mt., forcing it to instead pass over North Mt. The National Park Service purchased the disputed land and brought the AT back to its original route.

From the parking lot at VA 311 the hike begins with an immediate, steep ascent through a thick stand of mature oak and maple. The trail's hard clay surface is free of large rocks, a welcome break from the more strenuous hikes to the north and south. However, occasional tree roots jut from this smooth surface, so remain cautious. Approximately 250 yd. into the hike, you will pass a trail registration box and begin a more gradual upward climb. The abundance of oak trees here makes this a good stretch for bird watching. Ruffed grouse, ring-necked pheasants, wild turkeys, blue jays, white-breasted nuthatches, and red-headed woodpeckers are just a few of the creatures that feast on the bounty of acorns.

In spring and summer, the trees and the wildlife nesting in them are the view at the beginning of this hike. However, once the leaves begin to fall, Ft. Lewis Mt. can be seen piercing the horizon to the left of the trail, rising over Catawba Valley below. To the right, Silurian sandstone formations rise 20 to 30 ft. above the trail, blocking further views in any season.

After a ten-minute climb up, the trail reaches a wide clearing with a stone fire pit and room for two or three small tents. The area is heavily wooded, but in the fall and winter months there are views to the north of the trail of farmlands and open pastures blanketing the Catawba Valley nearly 2000 ft. below. Beyond the campsite the trail grows more rocky as it ascends into the rock formations that previously flanked the trail. From the top there are views of the valley to the right and the left. The trail is approximately 2 ft. wide here with steep drop-offs on both sides. At 0.3 mi. a side trail leads 50 ft. to the left for a clear view of Fort Lewis Mt.

The trail continues upward for 50 yd., and the going gets steeper as it climbs. After clearing the crest of the knob (0.4 mi.), the trail dips just as steeply downward over large rocks and exposed roots, then heads upward once again. The trail continues this up-and-down pattern for the next 2.9 mi., crossing over several steep knobs known locally as Sawtooth Ridge. The points of the saw's teeth offer repeating views of Fort Lewis Mt. to the left and Cove and North mountains to the right. From September through November, these mountains form a particularly scenic picture of red, yellow, and orange stripes, a striking contrast to the bright green pastures.

Hiking along the rocky ridge it is hard to believe that this section of the AT was once a swampy mud flat. However, during the Paleozoic period, the area was actually quite flat. Five hundred million years ago, Virginia lay near the equator and Africa was attached to the east. As Africa drifted away, inland seas came and went, covering the landscape. The seas brought sand and silt, which collected into mud flats. Over time, the tremendous weight caused the area to bow over 40,000 ft. (seven times deeper than the Grand

Canyon). Then, 250 million years ago, Africa crashed back into Virginia, cracking and heaving the compacted mud flats that had become thick layers of stone. When Africa left again, and the seas receded, the upheaved rocks formed the base of the mountains that surround the area today.

The climbs through this area can be quite steep, but they are rarely more than 100 ft. long. As the trail zigzags along the ridgeline, sudden, steep drop-offs, bouncing from one side of the trail to the other, are reason enough to remain alert. You will also want to be on the lookout for loose rocks and snagging roots. In spring and summer, thick ferns cover the forest floor, often camouflaging these dangerous ambushes. The trail continues through thick stands of trees as birch, Virginia pine, and hemlock begin to dot the forest of maple and oak. In the fall, pokeweed makes a lush green ground covering, fringed with the white blossoms of Queen Anne's lace. In the spring, buttercups, chickweed, violets, and wintergreen spot the greenery with bright yellows, pinks, and purples.

Nearly 2 mi. into the hike, the trail opens up into a low area with far fewer trees. As you travel over the next 200 yd., keep a sharp lookout for blazes—they are your only guide as the trail is swallowed by pokeweed and other ground cover. Although there are fewer trees immediately lining the trail, thick branches of the oak, maple, and hemlock that grace

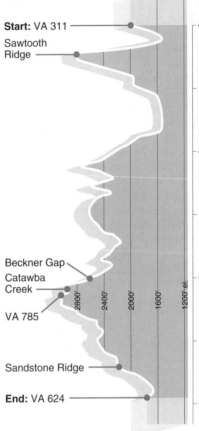

created using Maptech TopoScout ®

the trees on the hills around you provide a cool, shady canopy. Soon, the trail reappears and begins another rocky ascent. At the top of the next knob, there is another small campsite with a fire ring, but no water. For the next 200 yd., ground cover again obscures the trail. It becomes visible

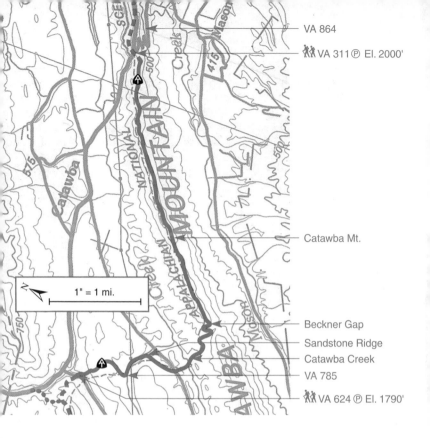

VA 864

🚶🚶 VA 311 Ⓟ El. 2000'

Catawba Mt.

Beckner Gap

Sandstone Ridge

Catawba Creek

VA 785

🚶🚶 VA 624 Ⓟ El. 1790'

1" = 1 mi.

shortly before it travels to the side of the ridge, where it passes more tall Silurian sandstone formations on the left.

The final tooth of the ridge (3.3 mi.) is a rocky area surrounded by old Virginia and white pines. On a breezy day, the wind blowing through their long needles is a soothing whis-per, often blended with the songs of the red-breasted nuthatch and the red crossbill, which feed on the trees' seeds. White-footed mice, chipmunks, and red squirrels also come here to dine. Watching a red squirrel devour a pine cone is an amusing pastime. In two minutes flat, the animal can strip an average-sized cone (approximately 45 seeds), turning the cone as it eats.

Beyond this rocky outcrop, the trail cuts to the left and begins a steep descent over a series of switchbacks. After the second turn, a wooden stile, the first of several stiles you will encounter, carries the trail over a barbed-wire fence. The wooden planks that form the ladders on each side of these 4-ft.-high inverted Vs are much sturdier than they look. Be careful of slippery footing in wet or icy conditions, however.

Beyond the stile, the trail cuts through a small cluster of white pine trees before entering an open field. The yellow, coarse field grass is stiff and crunches under your feet. It can also grow quite high and you will be thankful if you are wearing long pants or at least mid-calf socks as you proceed through this scratchy field. Continue to descend through an open area the size of four football fields. White blazes on the wooden utility poles 150 yd. ahead are your next directional clue. As you cross the field, look above the power lines and to the right for a glimpse of Cove Mt. and Dragon's Tooth (see Hike #17).

As you pass under the power lines (4.0 mi.) and enter Beckner Gap, look to the right to see Crosstrails Bed and Breakfast gracing a high hill. This is the only sign of commerce for miles. The inn sits at the intersection of the Appalachian and the Bikecentennial trails and is surrounded on three sides by National Park Service land. There are two rooms for rent in the

main house and additional accommodations in the nearby carriage house. Perhaps the best feature of this overnight option is the outdoor hot tub, providing a front row seat from which to view Catawba Mt. in the distance and the spectacle of stars that brighten the mountain sky at night. Road access to the inn is from VA 785, 0.3 mi. ahead (an early exit option for this hike).

The trail continues on to a tributary of Catawba Creek and crosses the water on a narrow wooden footbridge. Approximately 100 ft. beyond the stream the trail climbs another stile, then follows the left bank of Catawba Creek itself. Although the creek is narrow (less than 10 ft. across) and not very deep, it once carved out much of the surrounding landscape. The entire Catawba Valley was created by the creek cutting through its soft sandstone layers. Near the stream, look for soft, crumbling, fossil-bearing shale.

Another stile and 100 yd. further, a second wooden bridge, slightly wider than the first, carries the trail over Catawba Creek. Pass through another open field and ascend toward VA 785 (4.3 mi.), which leads to the right 2.0 mi. to VA 311, passing the inn you spotted earlier. VA 311 leads east past the northern end of this hike to I-81. There is a grocery store on VA 311 in Catawba, 0.25 mi. east of the turn from VA 785.

To continue on the AT, you will have to climb over one stile to get to the road and another to reaccess the trail on the other side. Once it crosses VA 785 the trail passes through another open field. It is here that you're apt to feel like the target of a voyeur. As you follow along a fence you may find several sets of eyes following you—this is a prime grazing area for local cattle. They appear only mildly disturbed by human interruptions and rarely stop chewing as hikers pass. Keep a sharp lookout for blazes, which appear along the fence sometimes to the right and sometimes to the left, taking you through this maze of barbed wire and cattle. Also keep a watchful eye on the ground. This is one of the best fertilized sections of the trail.

The blazes along this stretch are somewhat difficult to follow. Once you pass through an opening in the fence, look ahead for a fence supported by green metal posts (the other fence posts are wooden) and follow that to the right. In 50 yd., cross another stile and begin a slight ascent. As you climb, turn and look behind you and to the right for a view of Sawtooth Ridge growing smaller in the distance.

The trail cuts back into the woods and makes a sharp left onto an old road at 4.7 mi. The trail follows the 3-ft.-wide gravel and dirt road along the left side of a small stream. In 0.3 mi., a footbridge carries the trail over the stream. Just before the bridge, a campsite includes a stone fire ring, room for two small tents, and, for the first time in this section, a water source. Beyond the bridge, the trail ascends into a grove of Virginia and white pines.

Continue upward, making an easy climb to the top of Sandstone Ridge, appropriately named for its Silurian sandstone base. The trail crosses one last stile at the top of the ridge, then descends over a series of steep switchbacks. After 0.5 mi. of downward zigzags, the trail crosses a small stream and reaches VA 624.

HIKE #18 Itinerary

Miles N	NORTH	Elev. (ft/m)	Miles S
5.9	**Start:** Ascend from **VA 311.** Parking lot is on S side of road, 9.0 mi. N of I-81, 1.0 mi. E of Catawba.	2000/610	0.0
5.6	Side trail leads L 50 ft. to views of Fort Lewis Mt.		0.3
5.5	Begin 2.9-mi. passage over **Sawtooth Ridge** (on Catawba Mt.) with several short, steep ascents and descents.		0.4
2.6	Begin descent.	2600/792	3.3
1.9	Cross under power lines and enter **Beckner Gap.**		4.0
1.7	Cross **Catawba Creek.**		4.2
1.6	**VA 785,** early exit option.		4.3
1.2	Sharp L onto narrow gravel road.		4.7
0.9	Cross bridge and ascend through pine forest.		5.0
0.5	Cross stile at top of **Sandstone Ridge.**		5.4
0.0	**End:** Limited roadside parking at **VA 624,** 0.3 mi. W of VA 311, 2.5 mi. W of Catawba.	1790/546	5.9

SOUTH

McAfee Knob Loop

Map: ATC Va. #3, Central Virginia

Route: From VA 311 to McAfee Knob and Devil's Kitchen on Catawba Mt. and back

Recommended direction: S to N to S

Distance: 7.2 mi.

Elevation +/-: 2000 to 3200 to 2000 ft.

Effort: Strenuous

Day hike: Yes

Overnight backpacking trip: Optional

Duration: 4 1/2 hr.

Early exit options: None

Natural history features: McAfee Knob; Devil's Kitchen

Other features: Nearby Roanoke is Va.'s largest metropolitan area W of Richmond. See Hike #17.

Trailhead access: *Start:* From Roanoke, follow I-81 S 3.0 mi. to VA 311N, follow for approximately 9 mi. Pass turn for VA 864 on L and look for large parking area (10 – 12 cars) on L. *End:* Same.

Camping: Johns Spring Shelter; Catawba Mt. Shelter; and designated campsites only

One of the most famous points along the southern AT, especially among photography buffs, McAfee Knob (pronounced MAC-a-fee by locals) deserves a day hike of its own. Approaching from the south, the 3.5-mi. ascent of Catawba Mt., gaining 1200 ft., is strenuous, but the views from the knob are worth the effort and are quite possibly the best Virginia has to offer.

From the parking lot, cross VA 311 and pick up the AT at a stone stairwell. This road is a main thoroughfare between Roanoke and Blacksburg. Use extreme caution. The AT begins an immediate, steep ascent, leaving the highway behind as it crosses up a wide old woods road. In early spring, the area is abloom with a variety of wildflowers including violets, dwarf iris, buttercups, and lady's-slipper. In April, the trees are dotted with the bright red blooms of the redbuds. Rhododendron, dogwood, and blueberry bushes also make the area green and colorful.

A series of switchbacks brings the trail to the crest of a narrow ridge. As the AT passes over the top of the ridge, there are steep drop-offs to the left and the right. To the north, Catawba Valley sprawls below, scattered with rustic farmhouses and open green pastures. To the right, mountains rise in the distance.

Continuing its climb through a forest of young Virginia pine and hickory, the trail gets narrower and rockier as it leaves the old woods road and follows the ridge. After 0.25 mi. of steep, uphill hiking, the AT dips slightly, reaching an AT bulletin board and registration post. A scan of some of the comments in the registry from hikers returning from the knob will increase your anticipation of the sights ahead. Beyond this checkpoint, the trail cuts to the right and begins a slight descent. Don't get used to the easy gait—you're in for some mighty steep uphill climbs ahead.

The drooping pink petals of the vetch flower line the trail in early spring as it continues through a rocky area. The several rocky sections here were created 250 million years ago when the African plate crashed into, and then receded from, what is now Virginia. During this process, the land bowed, rippled, heaved, and cracked to form Catawba and Tinker mountains. They sit at the front edge of a giant sandstone rock block known as the Pulaski Fault. The force of the ocean from the south and east created the formation by pushing it up over the neighboring stones.

A series of narrow footbridges carries the AT over the extremely rocky patches that resulted. Although this section of the trail is well cared for, be sure to test the boards for stability and cross with care. An occasional loose plank is inevitable, especially after a harsh winter.

For the next mile, the AT parallels the ridge crest. Although the climb is predominantly uphill, occasional descents offer a slight respite. Ahead and to the left, large sandstone formations wait to be conquered. The trail winds its way over these rocks to the metal Johns Spring Shelter, 1.0 mi. into the hike. Built in 2003, the three-sided shelter looks a little dubious, but despite some sagging, it provides an excellent spot for a water break. The sheet metal structure, which sleeps up to ten, is maintained by the Roanoke AT Club. There are a fire pit, picnic table, and outhouse at the site, and a narrow spring runs near the open side. Be warned: Unless you are hiking after a heavy rain, the spring will probably be dry.

Beyond the shelter, the AT curves to the left and passes over a flat area before beginning another steep, rocky ascent. Small blue flags and violets dot the area. As the trail continues to cut upward through the rocks, Catawba Valley is visible below. The ascent tapers off, and the trail is basically flat once again as it continues to wind over and around massive sandstone formations. The eroded rock forms sandy patches along the trail. Look closely, and you may even find a seashell.

At 1.9 mi., the trail turns right onto an old road and then descends to a junction with a blue-blazed trail leading a few hundred yards to a narrow spring. Treat the water before drinking it. The AT continues ahead, crossing a dry streambed and reaching Catawba Shelter at 2.0 mi., just beyond a narrow footbridge.

Two blue-blazed trails to the right of the AT lead to the shelter. The open side of the shelter faces away

Thru-Hiking Lab Report

Hiking in the spring is glorious, but there is a substantial risk that you will catch whatever seasonal virus it is that drives people to think they should hike all the way from Georgia to Maine. This insidious disease has a long incubation—so long that you may think you have escaped. However, here are some symptoms that may precede the onset:

—The victims (you or a loved one) start collecting maps and guidebooks.

—They ask everyone they meet about tents, Gore-Tex, and water filters.

—They start introducing themselves by a funny new name.

—They insist on knowing the weight, to the nearest gram, of everything they buy.

—They don't like their 100% cotton underwear and socks anymore.

—They develop an obsessive interest in weather, day length, elevation gains and losses, and how far they can hike in one day

The most severe form of this syndrome was first described in 1948, but it was rare until the 1960s. Supreme Court Justice William O. Douglas succumbed in 1958. By 1982 there were 1000 cases on record; that number doubled in only 7 years. In the 1990s it became a major epidemic, with thousands coming down with it each year.

The virus respects neither age, sex, physical handicap, nor nationality. An 86-year-old got it in 1975, and a 6-year-old got it just 5 years later. Some people get it several times, and many victims write books about their struggles. Several dogs and at least one cat have fallen prey to it. More men than women suffer from the disease, but, as with many other conditions, women are catching up. The causative agent has not been identified; there is some evidence of a tiny parasite that burrows through brain tissue, causing major behavorial changes but minor permanent damage.

No remedy has been found; victims harbor the ailment for the rest of their lives and seem to be highly infectious. However, many victims can lead lives that are surprisingly close to normal if they can acknowledge their affliction and get the hiking done, either all at once or in sections. Many self-help books are available, and support groups exist in some communities.

—Doris Gove

from the trail, toward an open, mossy area. The wide patches of moss color the area bright green. The shelter sleeps up to six, but there is plenty of room for two or three small tents in the immediate area. A nearby spring provides a semireliable water source.

The AT bears sharply to the left and ascends through a heavily forested area dominated by redbud, pine, and mountain laurel. Catawba Mt. is renowned for its redbud trees, which color the mountain brightly in early spring. The small tree is actually a member of the pea family and from late summer through early winter dried seedpods hang from its branches. The tree is also known as a Judas tree or flowering Judas; it is believed that Judas Iscariot hanged himself from a Eurasian species of redbud. Although the seedpods are not an important source of nutrition for forest creatures, they and the flowers are edible and are sometimes added to salads.

At 2.3 mi., the trail crosses a wide, rocky road and passes up a log staircase before continuing its steep ascent. The trees diminish for a short stretch as the AT crosses through a sloping meadow and under a power line (2.5 mi.), then makes a sharp right into another thick forest and continues its ascent. At 2.6 mi., a rocky outcrop to the right provides a nice view of Catawba Valley and North Mt. to the left. This preview of the picture-perfect shots waiting just ahead makes a great incentive to forge onward.

The trail dips for approximately 100 yd. beyond the lookout before beginning its final approach to McAfee Knob. Ahead, the trail curves to the left of a 20-ft.-high boulder of brown Silurian sandstone. Although the formation is towering today, it, too, will some day erode to sand. Beyond the

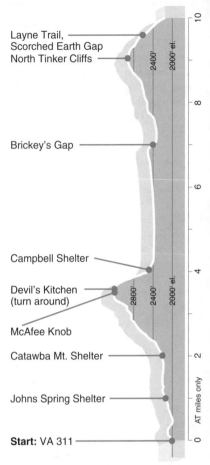

boulder, the trail picks up an old forest road and continues to ascend.

As the AT curves to the right, an unmarked side trail leads to another rocky lookout on the left. The rocky ledge is slick and may be slippery

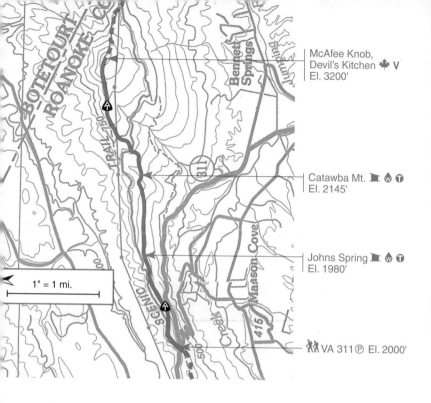

McAfee Knob,
Devil's Kitchen 🍁 V
El. 3200'

Catawba Mt. 🪨 💧 🚽
El. 2145'

Johns Spring 🪨 💧 🚽
El. 1980'

🚶🚶 VA 311 Ⓟ El. 2000'

1" = 1 mi.

after a recent rain or snow melt. If you decide to check out this view, proceed with caution. This is one of several side trails along this stretch. To stay on course, keep a close eye on the white AT blazes and stay on the old road.

At 3.5 mi. you will reach McAfee Knob at a small clearing at the end of the road. Follow the narrow side trail to the left and onto a cliff several hundred feet wide. Giant rock fingers jut out from it to form overhangs that extend more than 20 ft. beyond the supporting rock below. There are also several interesting alcoves to explore. Be careful, especially near the edges. Note that no camping or fires are permitted at the knob.

Appalachian Trail founder Benton MacKaye wrote that one purpose of hiking the trail was to "see what you see." The view from the vantage point of McAfee Knob gives hikers great purpose indeed. There are magnificent views of Tinker Cliffs to the east,

North Mt. to the north and west, and the Catawba and Roanoke valleys below. An estimated five thousand hikers visit this site each year, so it's unlikely you'll have the spot all to yourself. However, the knob is so awe inspiring that it is not unusual to be oblivious to those sharing your roost. October is the peak use period, when the hardwoods are streaked with autumn brilliance, and a cooler breeze rustles the hemlocks and tough clumps of grasses that survive in the rock crevices. Some folks come up here to sketch, others to take photographs. For many, this is a prime backdrop for picnicking, reading, sunbathing, or just sitting and thinking.

Although it will be hard to tear yourself away from McAfee Knob, 0.1 mi. beyond it steep rock steps descend into Devil's Kitchen, an area of 20-to-30-ft.-high sandstone pillars that are also fun to explore. Weather and erosion make the rock pillars appear as several cubes stacked on top of one another. Although the climb down into the pillars, over slick rock steps, can be a bit hellish, no other hints as to why this is the Devil's Kitchen are apparent. Instead, the formations conjure images of Stonehenge.

For a challenging but manageable day hike, turn back here and retrace your steps to VA 311. McAfee Knob will undoubtedly beckon you for one final look as you pass back through. Don't be surprised if an entirely new picture emerges: the view is slightly different from every angle.

Optional Extended Hike: For an overnight trip, continue as the AT descends to the lower ridge of Catawba Mt. and into Catawba Valley, crosses toward North Mt., and traces Tinker Mt. to the east. The 17 mi. between the northern end of Hike #19 and the southern end of Hike #20 are located almost entirely on a National Park Service corridor. These miles have limited views and even fewer water sources or exit options than the adjacent stretches of the AT.

At 0.6 mi. beyond McAfee Knob, the AT reaches Pig Farm campsite, equipped with picnic tables, a fire grate, and views of Roanoke Valley to the right. Beyond the camp area 0.1 mi. is Campbell Shelter, which sleeps up to six. There is water available here from a nearby spring. If you opt for the two-day excursion, the next exit points are 3.1 mi. beyond the Campbell Shelter, where an old road leads left approximately 2 mi. to VA 779, and at Scorched Earth Gap (6.1 mi. from McAfee Knob). Here, the yellow-blazed Andy Layne Trail leads left 3.1 mi. to VA 779 and a small overnight parking area. The water sources throughout this section are scattered and unreliable. Be sure to pack plenty of fluids.

HIKE #19 Itinerary

Miles N	CIRCUIT HIKE	Elev. (ft/m)	Miles S
	Cross under power line.		
	Catawba Mt. Shelter, privy, camping.	2145/654	
	Short trail to spring.		
	Metal **Johns Spring Shelter,** spring, privy.	1980/604	
	Bulletin board and trail register box.		
	Begin descent over several long switchbacks.		
	End: Parking area at **VA 311,** 9.0 mi. N of I-81. Cross VA 311 to AT on old woods road.	2000/610	
	REVERSE DIRECTION. Go South. Read from top down.		
3.6	**Devil's Kitchen;** HIKE TURN-AROUND POINT.	3200/975	
3.5	Lookout cliffs at **McAfee Knob** offer views of Catawba and Roanoke valleys.		
2.5	Cross under power line.		
2.0	**Catawba Mt. Shelter,** privy, camping.	2145/654	
1.9	Short trail to spring.		
1.0	**Johns Spring Shelter,** spring, privy.	1980/604	
0.4	Bulletin board and trail register box.		
0.2	Begin ascent over several long switchbacks.		
0.0	**Start:** Cross **VA 311** to parking area; 9.0 mi. N of I-81	2000/610	

CIRCUIT HIKE

Black Horse Gap to VA 652

Map: ATC Va. #3, Central Virginia

Route: Through Jefferson NF from Black Horse Gap across Wilson and Curry creeks and over Fullhardt Knob to VA 652

Recommended direction: N to S

Distance: 11.5 mi.

Elevation +/-: 2400 to 1500 to 2675 to 1400 ft.

Effort: Moderate

Day hike: Yes

Overnight backpacking hike: Optional

Duration: 5 to 7 hr.

Early exit options: At 5.0 mi., Curry Creek Trail; at 5.8 mi, Salt Pond Rd. (USFS 191); at 7.7 mi., Fullhardt Knob Fire Rd.

Natural history feature: Fullhardt Knob

Other features: Supplies, restaurants, and lodging in Troutville, near S end

Trailhead access: *Start:* From Roanoke, head N on the BRP approximately 23 mi. to BRPMP 97.7 in Black Horse Gap. There is a small parking area at the parkway. Do not block gate. Hikers leaving cars overnight are asked to notify the parkway ranger station, 800-727-5928. From here, gated USFS 186 leads 100 ft. W to trailhead. See Hike #21 for alternate route. *End:* From Roanoke, go N on US 11 for 10.0 mi. to Troutville; head S on VA 652 for 0.5 mi. to trailhead and roadside parking or AT lot at 11 and 652.

Camping: Wilson Creek Shelter; Fullhardt Knob Shelter; and where permitted along trail

---

This section of the AT swings far enough away from the Blue Ridge Parkway (BRP) to escape most traffic sounds. A steep climb to Fullhardt Knob in the middle of the hike, gaining 1000 ft. over 1 mi., is tempered by two long descents, one falling over the first 3 mi. of the hike, and the other covering the final 2 mi. to VA 652. The views of the surrounding peaks from the 2700-ft. knob are worth the effort. As a result, the distance seems shorter than it actually is. Nonetheless, we recommend three early exit options for those who want to shorten the miles in fact.

This hike lies within a stretch of the AT that was displaced by the construction of the BRP. When the AT in Virginia was first blazed, in the late 1920s and early 1930s, it followed the Blue Ridge, as it does in Pennsylvania. However, as development spread throughout the area, trouble started brewing for the trail. In 1935, the National Park Service proposed extending Skyline Drive further down the Blue Ridge, all the way to North Carolina and Tennessee. AT founder Benton MacKaye was adamantly opposed to the extension. But Myron Avery, who headed the ATC at the time and also founded the Potomac and the Maine clubs, thought it was a splendid idea. And Avery was the type of man who made sure things got done.

Despite MacKaye's contention that the highway would degrade the wilderness environment of the ridge, Avery believed the extension of Skyline Drive (which would become the BRP) would enable more hikers to enjoy the trail and make it easier for trail maintainers to reach remote sections of the AT. There was one major obstacle: the proposed highway extension literally traced the AT for 202 mi. If the road was to go in, the trail would have to be moved. In the end, Avery's way of thinking prevailed, and MacKaye withdrew from his involvement with the AT. (Years later, he renewed his involvement. During his hiatus from the AT, MacKaye founded The Wilderness Society.)

Rerouting efforts were also plagued with troubles. Development made new segments problematic before the new routes were completed. Footpaths over which the trail was rerouted turned into roads. Then, in the early 1940s, the U.S. government purchased more land for the Jefferson NF and proposed a new route for the trail. With help from the Roanoke AT Club, the relocation work was completed in 1954.

At several points, the original route of this hike went down the middle of what is now the parkway. Today the hike starts a stone's throw from the BRP, but quickly heads away as it follows its alternate route. The hike begins on the western side of USFS 186, also known as Old Fincastle Rd. In the 1700s, this road was one of the easier routes over the mountains for settlers heading west. In the 1830s, the road became part of the Fincastle and Blue Ridge Tpk., which ran from Fincastle to Buford's. The Mountain Gate Toll House and spring were located southeast of the present trailhead. When settlers passed by this point, the gatekeeper signaled to Buford's in the valley below, and relayed how many people to expect for dinner. Today, the road is used primarily by USFS personnel and trail maintaining clubs.

The AT follows a narrow, well-graded footpath as it cuts away from the parkway and heads west through thick shrubs of deep green Catawba rhododendron. The evergreen colors the area year round, but is especially brilliant in late spring and early summer when its purple flowers are in full bloom. After approximately half an hour of easy, downhill hiking (1.1 mi.), the AT climbs a short hill known as Blue Knob. From here, look to the west for a view of the rocky promontory known as Shirleys Knob. As the trail continues downward it moves further away from the parkway and the surrounding trees close in. A forest of oaks, maples, and hickories grows thick around the trail, creating a cool, shady archway. Although the trees limit the view, the darkness is comforting and the sunlight peeking through the branches reflects interesting shadows on the soft dirt trail. While passing through the wooded area in spring, look for wood-betony, a hairy plant with tubular red or yellow flowers. In areas where the woods open up a bit to let some sunlight in, small white clusters of beetleweed can also be found.

At 2.4 mi. a blue-blazed trail on the right leads 150 ft. to Wilson Creek Shelter. Built by the Roanoke AT Club in the mid-1980s, the shelter can accommodate up to six overnight hikers. There is also plenty of room for tents just below the shelter, and there is a stream. It is peaceful here and a nice place for a rest, although you probably won't need one just yet.

The trail crosses Wilson Creek at 3.1 mi. (1500 ft.) and begins a mild ascent. After half an hour or so of gradual uphill climbing, the trail dips to cross a branch of Little Wilson Creek at 4.3 mi. and then continues upward. Although this isn't exactly a mild climb, it passes quickly. Forest diversions also ease the way. In the fall, expect to see squirrels scurrying about the forest, playfully gathering their winter stash of acorns. In spring, fawns trailing behind their white-tailed mothers are a common sight.

At the top (4.6 mi.), the trail cuts through a wide, wooded gap between Grindstone Knob and an unnamed 2500-ft. peak. Beyond the gap, the trail begins another descent. As you make the easy jaunt down toward Curry Creek, the trail heads

Continued on p. 172

Start: Black Horse Gap, USFS 186, BRPMP 97.7

Wilson Creek Shelter

Wilson Creek

east. Look to the north for passing views of the Curry Creek Valley. From this vantage point, the creek appears as a narrow line cutting through the thick green forest. The AT reaches Curry Creek at 5.0 mi. (1500 ft.) in a thick forest of mature timber. Across

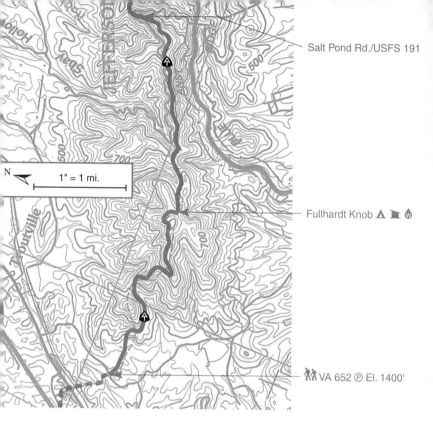

Salt Pond Rd./USFS 191

Fullhardt Knob ▲ 🚩 ⓦ

🏃🏃 VA 652 ⓟ El. 1400'

N ← 1" = 1 mi.

the narrow creek, the Curry Creek Trail leads right approximately 2.5 mi. to roadside parking at VA 640 for a possible early exit option.

The banks of Curry Creek make a nice place to stop and dawdle for a bit. Although the water should be treated before drinking, it is cold and refreshing. Towering oaks keep the area around the creek well shaded in stark contrast to the sunlight that peeks through directly above the creek, reflecting bright beams in the water.

Beyond Curry Creek, get ready for a steep ascent—the toughest stretch of this hike. For the next 0.8 mi., the AT ascends over a series of switchbacks, gaining 1000 ft. as it rises to meet Salt Pond Rd. Once again, the climb is eased by surrounding forest diversions. In spots where the trees are less dense and sunlight creeps through their shady branches, look for wild blueberries, which tolerate the shade fairly well. Their warty twigs bear small, white, bell-shaped flowers in the spring and sweet, purplish berries in summer. A treat for humans and animals alike, the blueberry was once a primary food plant for Native Americans in this region, who dried the berries, then pounded them together with strips of dried venison to make pemmican, a durable winter staple.

At 5.8 mi. the AT crosses the wide, rocky surface of Salt Pond Rd. (USFS 191), most likely named by early European settlers who took their cattle up the hill to this spot for salting. Salt Pond Rd. leads to the left 1.1 mi. to BRPMP 101.5 and is gated at the parkway. Roadside parking on BRP is possible. To the right, Salt Pond Rd. leads approximately 4 mi. to VA 711 (which leads to US 11 via VA 640).

On the west side of Salt Pond Rd., the AT makes a sharp turn to the south as it picks up a grassy narrow footpath. The trail is primarily level as it follows the footpath across the ridge crest for the next 1.9 mi. The woods are less dense here and the added sunlight encourages a variety of wildflowers including mountain lily in the spring and goat's-rue in the summer and fall. The petals of the goat's-rue (also known as devil's

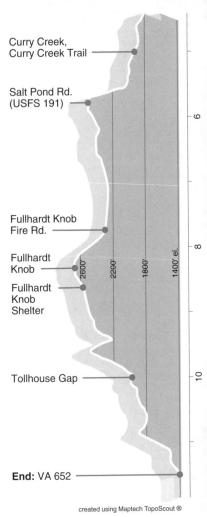

created using Maptech TopoScout ®

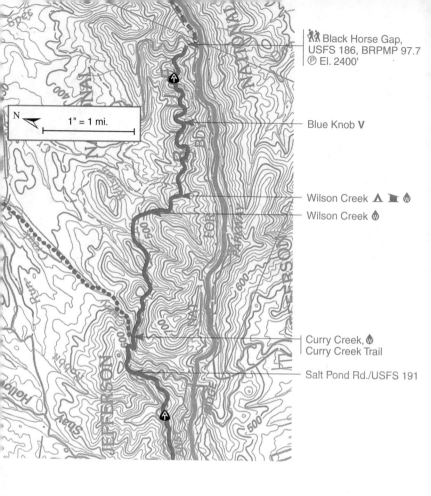

❺❺ Black Horse Gap,
USFS 186, BRPMP 97.7
Ⓟ El. 2400'

Blue Knob V

Wilson Creek ▲ ■ ◍
Wilson Creek ◍

Curry Creek, ◍
Curry Creek Trail

Salt Pond Rd./USFS 191

shoestrings) actually look like pink, floppy goat ears as they hang limply from the hairy one-to-two-foot-high stems. The plant was once fed to goats to increase their milk production. When it was discovered that the plant contained rotenone (used as an insecticide), the practice was dis-

AT sign, north of Troutville

continued. Although you aren't likely to see any goats grazing on the hillside, you do have a good chance of seeing white-tailed deer feeding on the rhododendron, which is still plentiful as you continue to climb.

At 6.4 mi. the trail crosses the high point of the ridge and begins a short descent. As you follow the slight dip along a narrow crest, you will be able to catch glimpses of Fullhardt Knob up ahead. The trail makes a sharp left turn onto Fullhardt Knob Fire Rd. (7.7 mi.). The road leads downhill one-quarter of a mile to Salt Pond Rd. (USFS 191). An early exit option is possible from Salt Pond Rd.; the fire road is closed to private vehicles. Limited roadside parking is available. To continue the hike, follow the fire road to the left and ascend steeply over the next mile as you view Full-

hardt Knob straight ahead. As the trail ascends, it intersects with several unblazed side trails. The AT is well marked and as long as you keep an eye on the white blazes you'll stay on the right path.

At 2675 ft. Fullhardt Knob is the tip of a of a long finger of quartzite that extends to the southwest from the main Blue Ridge. The gray rock was formed over 500 million years ago and layered upon older rocks to form a series of ridges and ledges. When you reach the top of the climb, an unblazed trail to the left leads 60 ft. to one of these quartzite ledges. From here, the BRP appears as a narrow black ribbon streaming through the forest. The best views are in the fall when the Blue Ridge Mountains to the south are ablaze with orange, red, and yellow. Although the view increasingly will become obscured by trees, be on the lookout for additional ledges as you make your way down the western side of the knob.

At 8.6 mi. the AT leaves the fire road and veers to the right to pick up a narrow footpath. The fire road continues up a steep incline, following a blue-blazed trail to reach Fullhardt Knob Shelter in 465 ft. In case you are low on water, there is a cistern behind the shelter that's good for a refill. However, there is not much else up there to make it worth the difficult climb. Constructed in the 1960s, the shelter is a bit more worn than its predecessor at Wilson Creek. However, it is well maintained and is a peaceful spot in which to rest a bit or pitch a tent. The shelter accommodates six people.

The vegetation surrounding you on the descent from Fullhardt Knob is very much like that of the climb up, in reverse order. As the trail falls, the trees grow thicker, and plenty of rhododendron mixes with the oak and maple trees. The rhododendron are at their peak, bursting with lilac-shaded funnels, from May to early June. Their bounty throughout this section makes late spring nearly as colorful as early fall, when the leaves have changed to bright reds and yellows, but haven't yet fallen to the forest floor.

At 9.2 mi. the trail enters a section of long switchbacks that descend toward Tollhouse Gap. The graded trail disappears as the AT enters Tollhouse Gap (10.0 mi.) in a saddle between Fullhardt Knob and the main Blue Ridge. In the gap, follow the white blazes as the trail seems to disappear, swallowed by the tall oak trees. Gnarled and twisted tree limbs are a sign that the trees are quite old. Some of the oak trees in this section could be more than 500 years old.

Beyond the gap, the well-graded surface returns and the descent continues. The next mile is a steep fall, but several switchbacks ease the drop. Just before intersecting with VA 652, the graded section ends as the AT enters an open field. Look to the far west to see Tinker Mt. abutting the horizon. The AT follows an old farm lane for a short distance, then continues through open fields to reach VA 652.

The town of Troutville, located 0.5 mi. north of the southern end of this section, is a popular spot for AT thru-hikers and offers plenty of welcome refreshments after a hard day of hiking. There are several restaurants along the US 11 corridor, ranging from fast food to family dining. There are also several motels for folks planning to spend more than a day in the area. The town of Cloverdale, with more places to refuel yourself and your car, is 4.0 mi. north of Troutville on US 11.

Miles N	NORTH	Elev. (ft/m)	Miles S
11.5	**Start: In Black Horse Gap at USFS 186,** 110 ft. W of BRPMP 97.7. Parking in pull-off on BRP. 23.0 mi. N of Roanoke.	2400/732	0.0
10.4	**Blue Knob** with view of Shirleys Knob.		1.1
9.0	Descend through dense forest.		2.0
8.6	Blue-blazed trail to **Wilson Creek Shelter,** 150 ft.	1830/558	2.4
7.9	Cross **Wilson Creek.**	1500/457	3.1
6.7	Cross branch of **Little Wilson Creek.**		4.3
6.0	Cross **Curry Creek** in mature forest. **Curry Creek Trail** leads R 2.5 mi. to VA 640, early exit option; begin steep ascent.		5.0
5.2	Cross **Salt Pond Rd. (USFS 191).** Road leads S (L) 1.1 mi. to BRPMP 101.5 and R 4 mi. to VA 711. Early exit option.	2500/762	5.8
4.6	Pass over high point of ridge.	2530/771	6.4
3.3	Turn sharply L onto **Fullhardt Knob Fire Rd.** (early exit option) and begin steep ascent.		7.7
3.2	Crest of **Fullhardt Knob.**	2675/815	8.3
2.4	Veer R; blue-blazed trail leads straight ahead 465 ft. to **Fullhardt Knob Shelter,** water.	2670/814	8.6
1.5	**Tollhouse Gap.**		10.0
0.0	**End: VA 652,** 0.5 mi. S of Troutville and US 11; roadside parking.	1400/427	11.5

SOUTH

Black Horse Gap to Bearwallow Gap

Map: ATC Va. #3 & 2, Central Virginia

Route: Through Jefferson NF from Black Horse Gap along the BRP over Harvey's Knob to Bearwallow Gap

Recommended direction: S to N

Distance: 8.0 mi.

Elevation +/-: 2400 to 2530 to 2000 to 2230 ft.

Effort: Easy

Day hike: Yes

Overnight backpacking hike: No

Duration: 2 1/2 hr.

Early exit options: At 2.5mi. and 5.6 mi., BRP crossings; proximity to parkway offers many other opportunities

Natural history feature: Bearwallow Creek

Social history features: Black Horse Gap; Bearwallow Gap

Trailhead access: *Start:* From Buchanan intersection of US 11 and VA 43, go E on VA 43 for 5.0 mi. to BRP at Bearwallow Gap, milepost 90.9. Go S 7.0 mi. to limited trailhead parking in Black Horse Gap. See Hike #20 for alternate route. *End:* From Buchanan intersection of US 11 and VA 43, go E on VA 43 for 5.0 mi. to BRP at Bearwallow Gap, milepost 90.9. Roadside parking on VA 43. The AT is 100 yd. S across BRP on VA 695.

Camping: Bobblet's Gap Shelter, and where permitted along trail

For the few hours it takes to walk this easy, scenic ramble, all hikers can imagine themselves AT surveyors of the late 1920s. Much of the 8.0-mi. stretch coincides with the AT's original route. The surveyors were such skilled route-finders that the builders of the Blue Ridge Parkway, starting after 1935, were hard pressed to find better alternatives. The controversy surrounding a similar situation along Skyline Drive in the 1920s and 1930s had caused the first fracture within the young AT community. At issue was a new kind of road (the parkway) destroying a new kind of recreation facility (the long-distance trail), and it led AT planners to relocate the trail well west of the parkway—south of Black Horse Gap (see Hike #20). From here south there is a distinct and permanent break from the parkway, an escape provided by the western-leading prospect of Tinker Mt. The AT between Black Horse and Bearwallow gaps, however, was not relocated.

For modern hikers, the result on this short walk is a trail rarely out of sight and sound of the parkway. While this makes for an experience that is less than quintessentially AT, it does provide two outstanding benefits. First, its proximity to the parkway

Blue Ridge Parkway: A Road to Yesterday

Connecting the only two national parks traversed by the AT—Shenandoah and Great Smoky Mts.—the 469-mile Blue Ridge Parkway was authorized by Franklin Roosevelt in 1935 and finally completed during Ronald Reagan's presidency in 1987. For nearly 100 miles, the AT and the parkway travel the Blue Ridge within close proximity, with the trail crossing the parkway nine times.

The parkway preserves artifacts of cultural history as well as natural wonders. Along the parkway, from or near the AT, nature trails lead to a reconstructed farmstead near Humpback Rocks; to Whetstone Ridge, from which pioneers obtained sharpening stones; and to Yankee Horse, a ridge that earned its curious name when a Union cavalryman destroyed his horse, injured in a fall from the ledge, there.

Early European settlers of the 18th century occupied themselves much the way the Delaware, Catawba, and Shawnee nations had before them. They gathered berries and nuts and hunted abundant game. Modern hikers can enjoy similar treats. For the knowledgeable trekker there are hickory nuts, morel mushrooms, blueberries, and ramps to enliven trailside dining.

With 40 to 90 inches of annual precipitation, you can't always find sunshine along the parkway, but the woods here seem to come alive when dripping with summer dew or sagging under snow. The famous fog of the Blue Ridge sometimes puts a damper on long-distance viewing from overlooks, but it adds a mystical quality to the forest that can be seen only on foot.

offers unparalleled access to the trail for people just passing through and looking for a manageable AT hike. Also, the parkway was constructed with views in mind; there is a scenic overlook every few miles. This hike offers easy access to several parkway viewing points.

Sights along the way include Sharp Top, which is one of the three Peaks of Otter, the hollows of Goose Creek Valley, and expansive views of the Valley of Virginia (a regional name for the Great Valley of the Appalachians,

which aligns with the Blue Ridge for its entire length [see Hike #7]).

There are two ways to approach this hike. One is to cover your own desired distance on the AT, jumping off virtually at will to a waiting second car. While overnight parking is not recommended, roadside parking is permitted. Or, follow the route north from Black Horse Gap the full 8.0 mi. to Bearwallow Gap. As an incentive for going the whole way, consider that you might stumble onto long-missing buried treasure! Legend has it that in about 1821 Thomas Jefferson Beale, whose existence is a matter of record, buried nearly 3000 pounds of gold, some 5000 pounds of silver, and a large quantity of jewels just east of the ridge near Bearwallow Gap. Beale claimed to have brought the fortune east from lands in the southwestern United States that were then held by Spain.

The hike begins in Black Horse Gap at BRPMP 97.7, where gravel USFS 186 crosses the parkway. Moving north (to the right), the trail crosses two knobs, gaining less than 100 ft., enough to warm up most hikers. Although the parkway is close by, the trail ducks in and out of a forest of oak, maple, hickory, and other deciduous species mixed with white pine and scattered rhododendron.

The trail descends along a ridge to cross the parkway, at 0.7 mi., from the Taylors Mt. Overlook. The open ridge along this hike reveals the quartzite base that is typical along the Blue Ridge here. It contrasts with the lava basalt and greenstone of the Shenandoahs to the north. Looking east and down on the Goose Creek watershed, it is easy to imagine 19th-century travelers making their way over the ridge. Black Horse Gap was a busy east–west turnpike passage through the Blue Ridge; several travelers a week made the crossing. Many stayed a night a the Mountain Gate Toll House, now long gone, which accommodated travelers just south of Black Horse Gap on the Blue Ridge and Fincastle Tpk., now

USFS 186. While the views of the gap and valley are pleasing, you won't see any descendents of the buffalo that reportedly crossed the Blue Ridge at Black Horse Gap until the arrival of European settlers in the 18th century. It was the buffalo path that provided the initial route for the turnpike.

Continuing north, often alongside the parkway's low stone wall, the trail at 1.7 mi. passes a junction with the Spec Mines Trail, a blue-blazed path descending westward from the other side of the parkway. This trail is the AT connector for a 12-mi. circuit hike using several trails in the vicinity. Many such circuits are described in the ATC's *Appalachian Trail Guide to Central Virginia.* Best access over the parkway is from the Montvale Overlook, a quarter mile further on, at BRPMP 95.9, where there is a picnic table and a chance to enjoy the view of the Piedmont to the east.

Wherever your glance may fall, chances are there will be oaks in your field of view. One oak, the chestnut oak, is the most common species of tree in the mid-to-northern Virginia Blue Ridge. Oaks of all varieties bear the unfortunate distinction of being the trees most likely to be obliterated by lightning. The oak's vascular cambium—the bustling network moving water and nutrients through the tree —creates a horizontally etched, rough surface bark that does not channel rainwater efficiently. The smooth bark of a sycamore, for example, or the vertical ridges in a maple, encourage a kind of watery film all the way down the trunk in a shower. This film protects the sycamore, maple, and other species by allowing lightning strikes to ride the water to the ground. An electrical strike to an oak follows the water-bearing vascular system beneath the outer bark rather than outside the tree. The heat of lightning, as much as 50,000 degrees, causes the cambium to expand and explode, literally blowing the tree apart from within. Those lucky oaks that do not succumb to lightning will stand longer than most other trees in the eastern forests; the average oak lives about 450 years.

Heading back into the woods, while you compare tree barks, the AT continues near the parkway until, at 2.5 mi., it makes a crossing to Harvey's Knob Overlook at BRPMP 95.3. From here, Peaks of Otter seem only a stone's throw away. Sharp Top and Flat Top are both popular summer and autumn hikes. Their names make them easy to distinguish, with Sharp Top jutting skyward like a shark fin. There was a movement early in the century to rename Sharp Top for President Jefferson, who ascended the mountain as a septuagenarian while on one of his numerous survey excursions. Instead, an entire national forest, which surrounds the trail's corridor on this hike, now bears his name.

For the next half mile after Harvey's Knob Overlook, hikers can enjoy the fruits of the labors of the early surveyors; the wide trail here precisely follows the original AT route devel-

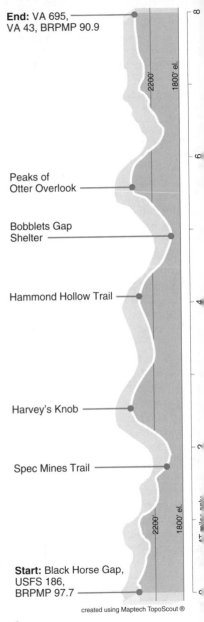

End: VA 695, VA 43, BRPMP 90.9

Peaks of Otter Overlook

Bobblets Gap Shelter

Hammond Hollow Trail

Harvey's Knob

Spec Mines Trail

Start: Black Horse Gap, USFS 186, BRPMP 97.7

created using Maptech TopoScout ®

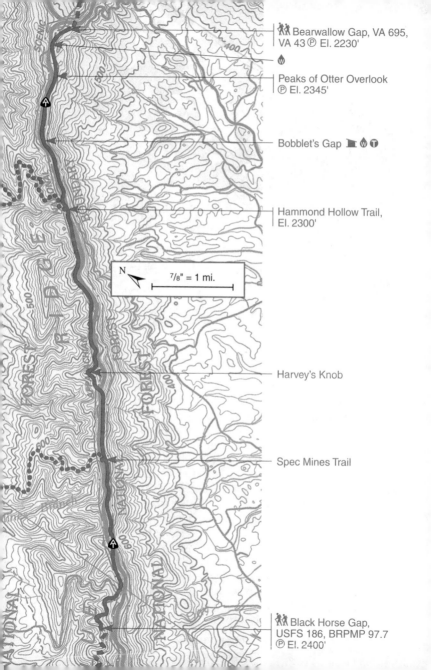

🥾🥾 Bearwallow Gap, VA 695,
VA 43 Ⓟ El. 2230'

Ⓦ

Peaks of Otter Overlook
Ⓟ El. 2345'

Bobblet's Gap ▬ Ⓦ Ⓣ

Hammond Hollow Trail,
El. 2300'

N

⁷⁄₈" = 1 mi.

Harvey's Knob

Spec Mines Trail

🥾🥾 Black Horse Gap,
USFS 186, BRPMP 97.7
Ⓟ El. 2400'

Dogwood in bloom, Humpback Rocks

oped in 1930. Ambling north 0.4 mi. around Harvey's Knob, the AT makes its only break from the parkway on this hike, then descends and rejoins the parkway, continuing close to it on gentle rises and drops until the junction with the blue-blazed Hammond Hollow Trail at 4.1 mi. This 2.0-mi. spur to VA 645 can be combined with USFS dirt roads and the Spec Mines Trail to form several circuit hikes.

At 4.9 mi. a blue-blazed spur trail descends left of the AT 350 yd. to Bobblet's Gap Shelter. The easy access from the parkway to the shelter (less than 0.4 mi.) has made it a pop-

ular overnight spot for youth who enjoy being able to drive so near the place. Hikers in search of solitude likely will find none at this shelter. Thru-hikers, however, sometimes benefit from short-term hikers bearing gifts from the nearby outside world. There is a privy behind the shelter and water is available from an unprotected spring 100 yd. behind the shelter. About 0.1 mi. beyond the shelter trail is a junction with USFS 4008.

The AT crosses the parkway to Peaks of Otter Overlook at 5.6 mi., but you should pause for the view over North Fork Goose Creek Valley, folded like a whipped cream landscape. In contrast to the lava basalt surface rock of the AT north of Rock Fish Gap (see Hike #33), this section of the Blue Ridge was constructed by uplift of pressurized quartzite, folding one fault over another. In the valley below Peaks of Otter Overlook, this process seemingly was halted while in mid-fold, exposing the fault's anterior. It is, technically, a breech.

From the overlook, the trail saunters along another 2.4 mi. of easy, pleasant—albeit almost roadside—walking. In the clearings here and there, especially near the parkway wall, low bindweed and Bowman's-root bloom May through June. A member of the morning-glory family, the low bindweed can be identified by leaves shaped like arrowheads and a whitish-pink flower with five petals. Bowman's-root, a rose, has five white petals, connected only at the center, and in summer evenings they appear to float 3 ft. from the ground against a dark background, like white starfish swimming trailside. The tranquility summoned by the sight of the flowers belies the ancient medicinal use of the leaves: They induce convulsive vomiting.

At 8.0 mi. the trail crosses under the parkway to VA 695, 100 yd. S of BRPMP 90.9—the end of the hike. Roadside parking is just north of the parkway.

Miles N	NORTH	Elev. (ft/m)	Miles S
8.0	**End:** On **VA 695** in **Bearwallow Gap,** 100 yd. S of BRPMP 90.9 and VA 43. 5.0 mi. E of Buchanan. Roadside parking on VA 43.	2230/679	0.0
5.6	**Peaks of Otter Overlook;** cross BRP, early exit option.	2345/714	2.4
4.9	Blue-blazed trail L 350 yd. To **Bobblet's Gap Shelter,** water, privy.	2000/610	3.1
4.1	**Hammond Hollow Trail,** circuit connector.	2300/701	3.9
2.5	**Harvey's Knob Overlook;** cross BRP, early exit option.	2530/771	5.5
1.7	**Spec Mines Trail** across parkway heads W to circuit hikes.		6.3
0.8	Cross BRP from **Taylors Mt. Overlook.**		7.2
0.0	**Start:** In **Black Horse Gap** at **USFS 186,** 110 ft. W of BRPMP 97.7. Parking in pull-off on BRP. 23.0 mi. N of Roanoke.	2400/732	8.0

SOUTH

Cove Mt. to Jennings Creek

Map: ATC Va. #2, Central Virginia
Route: Through Jefferson NF from Bearwallow Gap at the BRP along the crest of Cove Mt. to Jennings Creek
Recommended direction: S to N
Distance: 6.4 mi
Elevation +/-: 2230 to 2720 to 950 ft.
Effort: Strenuous
Day hike: Yes
Overnight backpacking hike: Optional
Duration: 4 1/2 hr.
Early exit option: At 1.8 mi., Little Cove Mt. Trail

Natural history feature: Jennings Creek
Social history feature: Purgatory Creek
Trailhead access: *Start:* From Buchanan intersection of US 11 and VA 43, go E on VA 43 for 5.0 mi. to BRP at Bearwallow Gap, milepost 90.9. Roadside parking on VA 43. *End:* From I-81 take exit 48 onto VA 614E, N of Buchanan. Go 4.5 mi. to trailhead parking lot for 12 cars at Jennings Creek on R.
Camping: Cove Mt. Shelter, and where permitted along trail

This rugged hike offers remarkable rock formations of Erwin quartzite and soft shale, along with a virtual botanical garden of the wildflowers of the southern Blue Ridge in spring and early summer. Rose azalea give the woods a kind of landscaped quality, interspersed with lily-of-the-valley, violets, and irises. There are also yellow and pink lady's-slipper—probably more in one setting you would encounter anywhere else on the AT in Virginia.

The trip is very strenuous and should be attempted only by hikers in good condition. If the prospect of 11 or 12 mi. on flat ground seems manageable, then this up-and-down hike of half that distance will be tolerable. Although Cove Mt. rises only 2270 ft., its northern side presents a total of ten knobs, which make most of the hike an up-down act. What's more, there are no reliable water sources between start and finish, and there are no really viable early exit options, the shortest requiring a total hike of 5.3 mi., only 1.1 mi. less than the main hike. This exit, via the blue-blazed Little Cove Mt. Trail that intersects the AT hike at mi. 1.8, adds several stream crossings and valley vegetation to contrast the ridge walk that begins the main hike. It makes a delightful, 2.8-mi. descent largely along the ridge of Little Cove Mt., the last 0.5 mi. hugging Little Cove Creek. The trail and creek finish in a simultaneous rush at Jennings Creek on VA 614, 0.7 mi. south of the parking area at the northern end of the main hike.

Traveling north from the trailhead parking area at VA 43, the AT begins an immediate, steep ascent of Cove Mt. that will gain 500 ft. in less than 0.5 mi. as it moves along a narrow ridge. The trail offers a brief breather in the sag between the first peak, a false summit at just under 2700 ft., and the forested summit (2720 ft.) at 1.4 mi.

Joining azaleas along the way are Jack-in-the-pulpit, bloodroot, orchids, showy orchis, and lady's-slipper. Orchids are among the most complexly evolved plants. Their pollination ecology was a special curiosity to Charles Darwin and many others who have followed. Of the orchids, the lady's-slipper is perhaps the most studied. Most flowers that rely on insects for pollination give them a little something in return: nectar. Not the lady's-slipper. Its scent attracts insects, but their search within the "slipper" yields no rations. Insects crawl around the interior of the flower, then, giving up, try to escape. The only way out is to climb the length of the stigma, leading to their escape and, in the process, pollinating the flower. Now that's a smart flower!

From the Cove Mt. summit, the AT begins a nearly 5-mi. descent to Jennings Creek, punctuated by repeated short-but-steep ascents over seemingly endless knobs. At the junction with the blue-blazed Little Cove Mt.

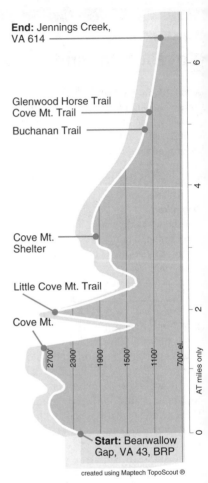

created using Maptech TopoScout ®

Trail, at 1.8 mi., the AT breaks sharply to the northeast (left). If you are already dreaming of level ground, you may want to take this much easier route down the mountain to VA 614 and enjoy Little Cove Creek. But there is much to see along the AT route to Jennings Creek.

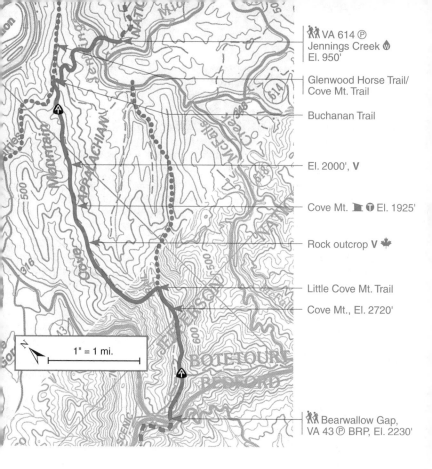

VA 614 Ⓟ
Jennings Creek 🚰
El. 950'

Glenwood Horse Trail/
Cove Mt. Trail

Buchanan Trail

El. 2000', **V**

Cove Mt. 📷 ⦶ El. 1925'

Rock outcrop **V** 🍁

Little Cove Mt. Trail

Cove Mt., El. 2720'

1" = 1 mi.

Bearwallow Gap,
VA 43 Ⓟ BRP, El. 2230'

Proceeding north, the downs and ups and downs continue. Winter hikers probably won't take comfort in the fact that, through the leafless trees, they can actually view the summit whose name evokes their experience on the ridge: Purgatory Mt. The peak derives its name from Purgatory Creek, the headwaters of which lie on the mountain. It seems 19th-century wagoners also found themselves in a never-ending, uphill battle: to free horses and wagons from the deep mud at a creek crossing north of Buchanan. They likened the experience to being in purgatory—it would end sooner or later, but it was hell while you were stuck there. The wagoners, by the way, were contract shippers whose employees hauled goods by driving teams of horses. Called "teamsters," the men who fought the mud at Purgatory Creek were the forebears of truck drivers and freight workers known today by the same name.

At 2.4 mi. a quartzite outcrop offers a rest stop and a view of Bearwallow Creek to the southwest. From this vantage point, the southern peaks of the Blue Ridge can be seen coming together as a topographic puzzle, a so-called main ridge and adjacent companion mountains—an illustration that there are two geologic phenomena known as the Blue Ridge. The first is the nearly unbroken line of ridges that, in relief, appears as a 1000-mi. single mountain with many component peaks and sags. The "second" Blue Ridge is the overall collection of mountains and hollows, spread in varying widths and shapes along the length of the range. These peaks of the Blue Ridge Mts., such as the northern part of Cove Mt., are arms or legs or completely disconnected from the main chain.

Another knob and sag later is the short access trail to Cove Mt. Shelter, at 3.2 mi., and the halfway point in this hike. Like AT hikers, the shelter itself has traveled down the trail, moving some 25 mi. south from Cock Knob in 1981 when the James River Face Wilderness was designated by Congress. Official wildernesses are to remain, as much as possible, free from signs of human impact. Hence, many shelters and structures that predate wilderness designation eventually fall into ruin and rot to the ground. Cove Mt. Shelter was barely 20 years old at the time of the James River Face designation. To protect the investment and meet the growing demand for shelters along the AT, the shelter was dismantled and moved to its current location.

Anyone who has made it to Cove Mt. Shelter, even carrying only a day pack, will marvel at the achievement of getting the materials up the slope. As one backpacker lamented in the Cove Mt. Shelter logbook about traveling north on this ridge: "From the top of Cove Mt. to this shelter, you lose nearly 800 ft., but it feels like you're going uphill the whole time. That's a lot of up just to go down. Every 100 ft. of descent is rewarded with a 50-ft. climb. It ain't no day at the beach." And overnight hikers be warned. Either carry in an evening and morning's supply of water, plus enough for the hike out, or be prepared to bushwhack 0.5 mi. down the steep slope to Cove Creek.

Just beyond the shelter access trail, then again at 3.7 mi., are rest stop opportunities with views. The first, a quartzite crag, overlooks Purgatory Mt. and the town of Buchanan, which is reachable on foot by the Buchanan Trail (3.8-mi. from its junction with the AT). The second, a formation of quartzite and shale, offers views to the northeast over the Jennings Creek Valley. Reaching the Buchanan Trail at 4.9 mi., the AT has topped its final knob in this Cove Mt. crossing, and the descent becomes more deliberate. For hikers exhausted after several down-and-up miles, this rapid descent is no picnic. You've descended nearly 1000 ft. from the summit of Cove Mt., with another 800 to go. Happily, the perfect spot for dipping tired feet awaits at Jennings Creek, just at the bottom of the slope.

Recall the sage of Cove Mt. Shelter, who lamented that the descent of the height was "no day at the beach." In fact, as far as the mountain's mineral composition is concerned, it very nearly is—or was. The upper reaches of Cove Mt. are constructed of quartzite, a rock composed principally of quartz from silica, or sand. The heat and pressure of the mountain-building episode that gave birth to Cove Mt., the Cambrian era of 500 million years ago, metamorphosed the gravelly mixture into the white and gray quartzite visible on the rock formations along the AT here.

The lower reaches, encountered by the AT from about 5.4 mi. to the end of the hike, are shale, a sedimentary rock formed from compacted clay. The dry soils create a near-desert environment that seems somewhat out of place so close to the fertile farmland of the James River, a few short miles away. The sight of prickly-pear, a cactus that blooms in bright

Thru-hiker writing in trail register.

yellow flowers in June and July, only reinforces the feeling that you've hiked up an Appalachian mountain and come down a Rocky. The purplish-red fruit of the prickly-pear is edible; a cultivated variety is a prized ingredient in a soup of haute cuisine.

June near the foot of Cove Mt. offers displays of wild pink, more common in the Carolinas but infrequent along the Blue Ridge this far north. Identify it by its five-pointed, red star formation. A poppy known as bleeding-heart, with deep-red puffs hanging clustered from a red stem, is rarer still. It is also poisonous, a proper inducement to leave-no-trace hiking. At 6.4 mi. the trail bottoms out at VA 614 and Jennings Creek at Panther Ford. Parking is at the trailhead. It's time to cool your feet and find a place to watch the anglers patiently working to coax trout onto a line.

HIKE #22   Itinerary

Miles N	NORTH	Elev. (ft/m)	Miles S
6.4	**End: Jennings Creek at VA 614,** 4.5 mi. E of I-81 Exit 48, just N of Buchanan. Parking for 12 cars in lot.	950/290	0.0
5.2	Cross **Glenwood Horse Trail/Cove Mt. Trail;** W, it joins Buchanan Trail below AT; E, it goes toward Arcadia.		1.2
4.9	**Buchanan Trail** leads L 3.8 mi. to VA 43; spring 300 yd. down trail, then R 100 yd. on Cove Mt. Trail.		
3.7	View of Jennings Creek.		2.7
3.3	View of Purgatory Mt. from rocks.	2000/610	3.3
3.2	70-yd. trail to **Cove Mt. Shelter.**	1925/587	3.2
2.4	View of Bearwallow Creek and southern Blue Ridge from rock.		4.0
1.8	Junction with **Little Cove Mt. Trail** to R, early exit option, 3.5 mi. to VA 614 parking.		4.6
1.4	Summit of **Cove Mt.**	2720/829	5.0
0.0	**Start:** In **Bearwallow Gap;** roadside parking on VA 43 at BRP, 5.0 mi. E of Buchanan.	2230/680	6.4

SOUTH

HIKE #23
Apple Orchard Falls Trail to Jennings Creek

Map: ATC Va. #2, Central Virginia

Route: Through Jefferson NF from Apple Orchard Falls Trail, along Bryant Ridge over Floyd Mt., Button Hill, and Fork Mt. to Jennings Creek

Recommended direction: N to S

Distance: 11.1 mi. total, 10.9 mi. on AT

Access trail name and length: Apple Orchard Falls Trail, 0.2 mi

Elevation +/-: 3420 to 1440 to 2040 to 950 ft.

Effort: Moderate

Day hike: Yes

Overnight backpacking hike: Yes

Duration: 8 hr.

Early exit option: At 2.7 mi., Cornelius Creek Shelter trail

Natural history features: Apple Orchard Falls; Black Rock; Cornelius Creek

Social history features: Panther Ford; Button Hill

Trailhead access: *Start:* From Buchanan intersection of US 11 and VA 43, go E on VA 43 for 5.0 mi., to BRPMP 90.9 at Bearwallow Gap. Go N (L) to BRPMP 78.5, Apple Orchard Falls Trail, roadside parking. To avoid 0.2 mi. on Apple Orchard Falls Trail, go to USFS 812 (Parkers Gap Rd.) at milepost 78.4. Go L; trailhead is in 0.3 mi.; limited roadside parking. *End:* From I-81, take Exit 48 onto VA 614E, N of Buchanan. Go 4.5 mi. to trailhead parking at Jennings Creek on R.

Camping: Cornelius Creek Shelter; Bryant Ridge Shelter; North Creek Campground; Jellystone Park (privately operated); and where permitted along trail

---

This hike travels mostly forested ridge lines and stream valleys, emerging only briefly at Black Rock for views to the north and west. But what it lacks in plentiful vistas, it makes up for in abundant flowers and flowering shrubs in season—Canada mayflowers, orchids, pink lady's-slippers, rhododendrons, and azaleas to delight every hiker—and lush hemlock, sugar maple, and a trout steam not far from the trail. From Apple Orchard Falls Trailhead parking at the Blue Ridge Parkway,

descend Apple Orchard Falls Trail 0.2 mi. to its junction with the AT (limited parking is also available at the AT junction with USFS 812). Hikers who enjoy cascading falls—and who doesn't?—might consider a 2.8-mi. round-trip detour down to Apple Orchard Falls. Hemlocks dripping with moss lean toward the creek over wading pools, as the trail drops as quickly as the cascading water. The walk from the falls back to the AT requires a climb of 1000 ft. in less than 1.5 mi. A spring is located 0.1

mi. from the AT down Apple Orchard Falls Trail on the right.

The AT heads south from Apple Orchard Falls Trail by slabbing the western verge of Rich Mt. In spring, wild leeks, known in Virginia and West Virginia as ramps, abound here. The onion scent of the leaves and its spokes of lilylike white flowers make it easy to spot, but rarely are both present on the plant simultaneously. Unlike in most green plants, which absorb energy and reproduce at the same time, the ramp's flowers and leaves have separate lives. In early spring, the overwhelming, pungent smell of ramp beds alerts the hiker to the presence of ramps nearby. John Eastman, in his natural history of eastern North American plants, *The Book of Forest and Thicket,* writes that one of America's great cities owes its name to the ramp. The Menominee tribe of lower Lake Michigan called a particularly "rampy" shoreline area *shika'ko,* or skunk place, in reference to the pungent onion odors—this is the place we now call The Windy City. Ramp bulbs, crushed to a pulp, were used by Native Americans as a remedy for insect bites.

The bulbs can bring out the best in trailside cooking, especially when tossed with dried tomatoes and basil over pasta. The ramp makes a fine, traditional Blue Ridge soup when boiled with other dried or fresh vegetables carried by hikers. Fortunately for the culinary-minded hiker, the black morel mushroom is a companion that often is found in the rich beech-maple forest humus favored by ramps.

At 1.2 mi. is the junction with Cornelius Creek Trail, which follows a small stream gurgling to life here to its confluence with Cornelius Creek. The AT actually crosses the creek at 2.4 mi., but trail access to the creek begins here. The Cornelius Creek Trail leads into a remote world of trout pools and cascades beneath a hemlock canopy, joining the creek at 1.0 mi. and ending at Apple Orchard Falls Trail at 2.9 mi.

Along the AT here and on other north-facing slopes, the hemlock has a hand in making its own ecosystem. The needle litter generated by these 100-ft. trees makes for a dry, acidic topsoil. Two orchids, the showy orchis and the rattlesnake plantain, thrive here. The tree often germinates on rotting logs and mossy rock, also the habitat of a variety of woodland mushrooms that sprout up in late summer. When not dominating a grove by itself, the hemlock shares the upper story with sugar maple, yellow birch, and beech.

At 1.8 mi. a side trail leads to the right 50 yd. to Black Rock. At 3402 ft., it offers the most expansive views along this hike, with distant vistas westward of the Alleghenies. Closer and to the south (left), the twin Peaks of Otter, Flat Top and Sharp Top, can be seen. Hikers seeking accommodations closer to civilization than those offered by shelters and campgrounds can spend an evening at the Peaks of Otter lodge or campground, where a restaurant and cocktail lounge extend a view of Sharp Top that is a fitting reward for a day of hiking. Short hikes to these two famed peaks begin from the lodge area. In spring, purple rhododendron lend color to the views from Black Rock.

Descending from the Black Rock side trail, the AT follows groves of hemlock, sugar maple, and laurel to crossings of Cornelius Creek, the first at 2.4 mi. and the second at 2.7 mi. The sugar maples along the AT here in the southern Blue Ridge rival their famed brethren of New Enlgand in abundance and vibrant color. Those renowned oranges and yellows derive from the cells of a class of pigments called carotenoids, the same cellular compound that gives corn and carrots their distinctive colors. Each year when the days grow shorter and the green-colored chlorophyll molecules break down to reveal each leaf's natural color, the sugar maple and its relatives—the striped, red, and black maples—begin their show. Carotenoids, our health-conscious culture tells us, are the source of beta-carotene. In spring, when the warm days cause maple sap to run and sugarers to tap, we can anticpate the sweetness of maple syrup with the knowledge that the delectable extract is laced with the compound every nutritionist is demanding we eat.

The blue-blazed side trail at 2.7 mi. leads 0.1 mi. to the Cornelius Creek Shelter, a simple structure accomodating six. Water is available from several springs splashing toward the creek. A trail behind the shelter leads 0.2 mi. to the BRP at milepost 80.4, in an open area known as Floyd Field. Parking is roadside.

From the shelter access trail, the AT ascends nearly 500 ft. in an easy 0.7-mi. climb from Cornelius Creek to the wooded summit of Floyd Mt. at 3.3 mi. As it clings to the southern and eastern ledges ascending Floyd Mt., the trail breaks from the BRP corridor and the main Blue Ridge, entering wild woodlands and leaving any sounds of automobiles behind. This region presents a roadless remoteness rarely experienced again on the AT, heading north, until it reaches New England, except in the James River Face Wilderness 20 mi. north. This landscape is a testament to the recovering powers of the eastern forests of the United States. In the 1930s, when the BRP was under consideration, Bryant Ridge and Fork Mt. were open balds, first harvested for their timber, then grazed for the grasses that grew on the denuded crests.

Humans have played a direct role in the evolution of the Blue Ridge, and one story of deforestation unfolds along the AT here, especially at 4.4 mi., as the trail rises from the sag between Floyd Mt. and Bryant Ridge: chestnut oak blight. Huge, long-decaying trunks of American chestnut tell the story of the eastern hardwood forest. Once prized for its nut and for its hard timber, only saplings awaiting certain infestation remain as the live reminders of the former eastern hardwood forest. The blight, brought to the United States from Asia, changed the fate of this forest.

Today, false foxglove, Deptford pink, and jewelweed combine with wild columbine to create a forest of flowers along Bryant Ridge. One cannot tell the history of the Appalachians and the 2100-mi. trail through them without giving due recognition to the wild columbine. One of the most common wildflowers of the Appalachians, wild columbine is easily identified by its five red, upended spurs atop red tubes: separate petals, each from its own spur. The five unite as a single sepal at the mouth, revealing a yellow inner flower.

The spurs are nectar repositories, deep within the flower. The stamen and pistils create a roadblock to pollination, as though the flower were specifically designed for the long beak of the hummingbird. Columbine thrive on rocky slopes, in open woods, and along the edges of young forest and farmland, which make up the majority of the AT landscape. From early spring to late summer, wild columbine offers AT hikers reason enough to sit, rest, and await the ruby-throated hummingbirds that thrive on its nectar.

Despite their popularity among contemporary wildflower seekers, columbine was no blossoming symbol of love in early mountain culture. Indeed, to send one's lover a bouquet of columbine was a belligerent

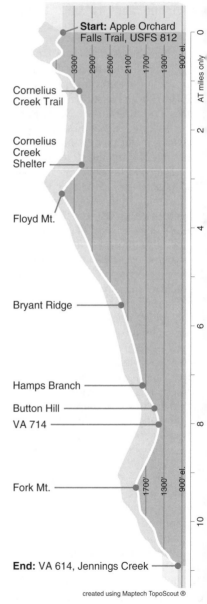

created using Maptech TopoScout ®

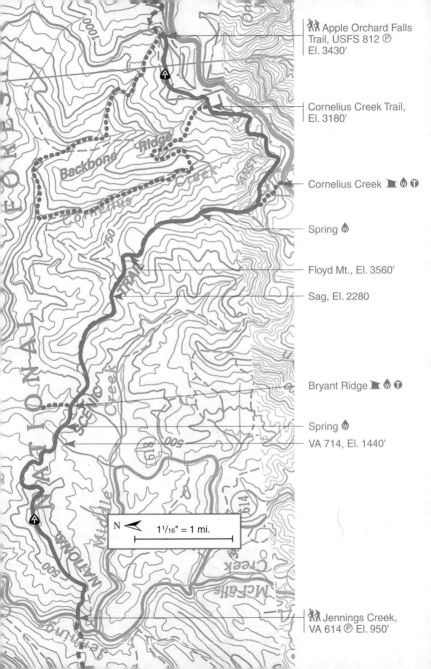

🚶🚶 Apple Orchard Falls
Trail, USFS 812 Ⓟ
El. 3430'

Cornelius Creek Trail,
El. 3180'

Cornelius Creek 🏕️ 💧 🚻

Spring 💧

Floyd Mt., El. 3560'

Sag, El. 2280

Bryant Ridge 🏕️ 💧 🚻

Spring 💧

VA 714, El. 1440'

N ◀ 1¹⁄₁₆" = 1 mi.

🚶🚶 Jennings Creek,
VA 614 Ⓟ El. 950'

signal that the receiver had been cuckolded. In deep-woods society, in which entire lives could be spent within a few square miles of a hollow and a marriage vow was known to mean "until things change," a man returning to an empty cabin and a bunch of columbine knew he would be cooking for himself.

From 4.5 mi., the trail continues its downward trend, slowed only by switchbacks and an easy ascent to slab around a knob of Bryant Ridge at 5.6 mi. Since the crest of Floyd Mt., at 3.3 mi., the trail has dropped more than 1200 ft., to 2280 ft., before moving over two knobs and heading down once again in earnest at 6.2 mi.

Hamps Branch joins the trail at 7.2 mi., and follows it through a grove of hemlock and laurel to a campsite at 7.5 mi. Here a blue-blazed side trail leads 0.2 mi. to Bryant Ridge Shelter. Built in 1992 and accommodating up to sixteen hikers, Bryant is one of the newest, and certainly one of the most spacious, shelters along the AT in Virginia. It was built by the Natural Bridge AT Club, the ATC, and other partners as a memorial to AT hiker Nelson Garnett. The shelter was designed by a fellow student. Water is from a reliable spring; a privy is available. *Note:* A relocation that will take the AT directly past the shelter is planned, but is not expected to be open before the summer of 2000. For further information, contact the ATC.

About a quarter of a mile beyond the shelter cutoff, the trail enters an area known as Button Hill, owing its name to the hundreds, perhaps thousands, of buttons scattered about. At one time, a nearby garment factory used this area as a dumping ground for rejected materials.

The trail reaches VA 714 at 8.0 mi. at the road's end, an early exit option. VA 618 is 0.7 mi. south, at a point 1.5 mi. east of VA 614. In wet or snowy weather, it may be difficult for small cars to travel on the final section of this dirt road. If you plan to end your hike here, it may be necessary to stash your second car at Bryant Cemetery on VA 714, 0.6 mi. south of the AT junction.

Continuing to Jennings Creek, the trail makes a 600-vertical-ft. ascent of Fork Mt. at 9.3 mi., before it loses nearly 1000 ft. en route to Panther Ford at VA 614. The trail crosses a spring at 8.6 mi. Panther Ford, at the end of the hike, is the site of two rather grisly local stories. One legend recalls a young woman and her son who were killed by a mountain lion, hence the enduring, if unofficial, name of Panther Ford. Another tale, this one (mostly) documented, is of George Bannister, a freed slave who grew tobacco in the flats above Panther Ford. Apparently, in a flash flood in 1877, Bannister was swept downstream while seeking shelter in a shed near the creek. His body came to rest along the banks at Panther Ford. Local histories also claim he was carrying more than $300 when he perished, and the money was never found. Whether Bannister met foul play, disguised as foul weather, has never been proven.

HIKE #23   Itinerary

Miles N	**NORTH**	Elev. (ft/m)	Miles S
	**Total: 11.1 mi. with access on Apple Orchard Falls Trail.**		
0.2	Access: Meet **Apple Orchard Falls Trail** at BRPMP 78.5; roadside parking. Take to L.		0.2
10.9	**Start: Apple Orchard Falls Trail** and **USFS 812** (Parkers Gap Rd.) junction with AT; limited parking.	3420/1042	0.0
9.7	Cross **Cornelius Creek Trail;** leads R 1.0 mi. to creek and 2.9 mi. to Apple Orchard Falls Trail.	3180/969	1.2
9.1	Trail to **Black Rock** (50 yd. to R).		1.8
8.5	Cross **Cornelius Creek.**		2.4
8.2	Cross **Cornelius Creek;** trail 0.1 mi. to **Cornelius Creek Shelter,** water, privy; early exit option; ascend.	3100/945	2.7
7.6	Crest of Floyd Mt.	3560/1085	3.3
6.5	Sag.	2930/893	4.4
5.3	Slab around **Bryant Ridge.**	2280/695	5.6
3.7	Meet **Hamps Branch,** follow 0.3 mi.		7.2
3.4	Campsite, trail to **Bryant Ridge Shelter** (0.2 mi.), spring, privy.		7.5
3.2	**Button Hill.**	1500/457	7.7
2.9	**VA 714,** early exit option.	1440/439	8.0
2.3	Spring.		8.6
1.6	Crest of **Fork Mt.**	2040/622	9.3
0.0	**End: VA 614** at **Jennings Creek, Panther Ford;** roadside parking. 4.6 mi. from Arcadia.	950/290	10.9

SOUTH

HIKE #24
Apple Orchard Falls Trail to Petites Gap

Map: ATC Va. #2, Central Virginia

Route: Through Jefferson NF from AT junction with Apple Orchard Falls Trail over Apple Orchard Mt., along Thunder Ridge, into Thunder Ridge Wilderness, and on to Petites Gap

Recommended direction: S to N

Distance: 7.3 mi.

Elevation +/-: 3430 to 4225 to 2370 ft.

Effort: Moderate

Day hike: Yes

Overnight backpacking hike: Optional

Duration: 3.5–4 hr.

Early exit options: At 2.3 mi. and 3.6 mi., BRP

Natural history features: Apple Orchard Mt.; The Guillotine; Thunder Ridge Wilderness

Social history feature: Glenwood Estate

Other feature: Thunder Ridge Overlook

Trailhead access: *Start:* From Buchanan intersection of US 11 and VA 43, go E on VA 43 for 5.0 mi. to BRP at Bearwallow Gap, BRPMP 90.9. Go N (L)11.0 mi. to USFS 812 (Parkers Gap Rd.); go W (L) 0.3 mi. to limited roadside parking at trailhead. Park along BRP if no room at trailhead. See Hike #23 for alternate parking. *End:* From Buchanan intersection of US 11 and VA 43, go E on VA 43 for 5.0 mi. to BRPMP 90.9 at Bearwallow Gap. Go N 20.0 mi. to USFS 35; go L 340 ft. to limited trailhead parking. For alternate approach see Hike #25.

Camping: Thunder Hill Shelter, and where permitted along trail; no camping on Apple Orchard Mt.

H ikers in search of a wildflower ramble need look no further. The nearly 800-ft. climb to the summit of Apple Orchard Mt. might be more demanding were it not for so many occasions to stop and enjoy the rhododendron, azalea, and mountain laurel beneath a canopy of old-growth northern red maple. If that's not enough to make a hiker stop and smell the flowers, then surely the yellow lady's-slipper, showy orchis, and seemingly endless carpet of large-flowered trillium will do the trick. In the first days of spring, blood-root can be seen emerging from the humus, its "veins" showing conspicuously on a single leaf wrapped around the stem.

On Apple Orchard Mt. the AT also visits the highest peak along the AT within 200 mi. to the south and a 1000 mi. to the north. A long-distance hiker heading north wouldn't encounter a summit as tall as Apple Orchard Mt. until the 4802-ft. Mt. Moosilauke in New Hampshire. To the south, the next-highest elevation on the AT is Chestnut Knob, at 4409 ft., in Virginia near the Tennessee line.

Although hikers rue sharing the summit with an air-traffic radar dome, the views from atop Apple Orchard would offer a worthy reward for a much longer, more strenuous climb.

From the trailhead at USFS 812 (Parkers Gap Rd.), the trail begins a steady, steep ascent of Apple Orchard Mt. that lasts more than 0.5 mi., levels to a more moderate ridge walk at about 0.7 mi., and emerges from a wood at 1.4 mi. just at the summit (4225 ft.). Expansive views carry all the way to the village of Lexington 30 mi. north and to the famous Natural Bridge area more than 8 mi. to the northwest. This is the perfect spot for a rest and to do a little exploring of the northern red oak forest that gives Apple Orchard Mt. its misguided moniker. There are no apple trees here. Hundreds of years of deep freezes and ice storms have given the trees a deformed, twisted look, reminiscent of trees in the neglected, overgrown orchards found along the ridges bordering the Great Valley from the southern Appalachians to Virginia and north to Vermont. Whether the trees on this mountain were mistaken for apple trees or merely reminded pioneers of them, no one is sure.

Leaving the summit, descend a downright amazing series of more than a hundred rock steps. The steps help prevent the destructive erosion of the subsoils such intense visitation would otherwise cause. It bears noting that these steps, like the trail itself, are not a naturally occurring phenomena. They are the fruit of back-breaking work performed by AT volunteers, and are solid evidence of how much work the volunteers do.

While the staircase is firmly embedded in the mountain, just beyond it awaits a rock that seems to hang in the air above the trail. This is The Guillotine, at 1.7 mi., a huge granite boulder wedged into the cleft through which the trail passes. Aptly named, the rock appears poised for a purpose, but hikers can pass beneath it assured that it has held this position for millions of years.

Thunder Ridge and Apple Orchard, along with several other peaks stretching south to Sharp Top Mt., are part of the Pedlar Formation, a 50-mi.-long mass of igneous rock of which several area peaks are composed. The Pedlar Formation was constructed during the Grenville orogeny (a mountain-building episode) some 1.1 billion years ago. It was, writes John A. Conners in his natural history, *Shenandoah National Park: An Interpretive Guide,* either part of the massive Canadian Shield that now makes up the middle section of the United States, or formed from the sediment deposited from the shield. If the latter is true, the rock that would become the Pedlar Formation was then buried and pressurized, and emerged millions of years later as its current mass. The formation found its current location by migrating west and coming to rest atop the younger basalt foundation of the Blue Ridge. For the modern hiker, it means a soil well suited for dense vegetation.

After a brief stretch in the Thunder Ridge Wilderness, to which it will return later in this hike, the trail exits the woods and, at 2.3 mi., crosses the parkway at milepost 76.3. A return walk down the parkway from here would make a circuit hike of 4.7 mi., a shorter hike that requires only one car. You can park roadside here, as well; that is not recommended for overnight. Traveling north, the AT bottoms in the sag between Apple Orchard Mt. and Thunder Hill, then ascends toward Thunder Hill Shelter, 0.3 mi. uphill from the parkway crossing.

The walled spring there is a bit more reliable as the setting for a souvenir photograph than for water in the dry season of July and August, but the privy is operational. A more reliable water source requires a quarter-mile detour south on the parkway before ascending Thunder Hill. To reach this spring from the parkway crossing, go south on the BRP 350 yd. to a gated forest road; the road leads 100 yd. to a walled spring.

The AT crosses the forested summit of Thunder Hill at 2.8 mi., descending along the ridge to the junction with Hunting Creek Trail just before crossing the parkway at 3.6 mi. (an exit option for this hike with roadside parking.) The almost continuous rhododendron tunnel of the blue-blazed Hunting Creek Trail is reminiscent of Merck Wood in J. R. R. Tolkien's *The Hobbit*. The path offers

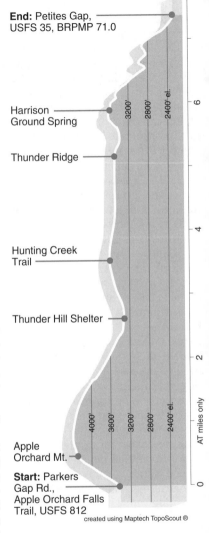

End: Petites Gap, USFS 35, BRPMP 71.0

Harrison Ground Spring

Thunder Ridge

Hunting Creek Trail

Thunder Hill Shelter

Apple Orchard Mt.

Start: Parkers Gap Rd., Apple Orchard Falls Trail, USFS 812

AT miles only

created using Maptech TopoScout ®

Petites Gap, USFS 35℗ BRPMP 71.0, El. 2369'

Harrison Ground Spring 💧

Thunder Ridge, El. 3685'

Thunder Ridge Wilderness

Hunting Creek Trail

Thunder Hill 🏕️💧🚻

Apple Orchard Mt., El. 4225'

USFS 812 ℗ Apple Orchard Falls Trail, BRPMP 78.4, El. 3430'

$1^{1}/_{16}" = 1$ mi.

Painted trillium

an enchanting diversion through the thicket to the babbling creek for which the trail is named. Camping is permitted along the trail; hikers are urged to camp at established sites to avoid further impact on the forest. Near the bottom of this 2-mi. path the rhododendrons give way to imposing hemlocks above the trail.

Continuing near the parkway, the trail crosses below the Thunder Ridge Overlook at 3.9 mi., and at 4.0 mi. reaches a stone lookout that offers long views of the Thunder Ridge and James River Face wildernesses, as well as stop-you-on-the-trail views of the James River and the Allegheny Mts. to the west. It's a perfect spot to rest and admire the sights

before beginning to ascend Thunder Ridge once again.

At 4.3 mi. the AT reenters Thunder Ridge Wilderness. Designated by the U.S. Congress in 1984, the 2450-acre preserve combines with the nearly 9000 acres of adjacent James River Face Wilderness to string together a sizable stretch of protected forest hugging the parkway. Because there were homesites, logging, and coke making in the area into the 20th century, there are still signs of human presence in Thunder Ridge, such as rectangular clearings dotted with young recovery-species trees and grass-and-debris-covered ditches that once housed coke ovens. As the years pass and the forest fully recovers, the area will one day again be a pristine wilderness of "new" old growth. Now, hickory and white oak are doing their best to get reestablished there.

In keeping with wilderness management practices, no viewsheds are opened by cutting stands of trees in front of rock ledges, so there are few places offering open views. One, on the crest at 6.1 mi., provides a nice view north toward Glenwood Furnace, the charcoal operation that would change the face of the landscape by turning more than 20,000 acres of hardwood into charcoal. The Glenwood Estate, 29,000 acres in all, is the nucleus of the Glenwood Ranger District through which the AT travels here.

The wooded summit of Thunder Ridge, at 5.2 mi., is noted only by the flat terrain and a huge boulder to the left of the trail. Camping is permitted on the ridge, but no water is available. The trail finds water at Harrison Ground Spring, at 5.9 mi. At this site once stood the homestead of a hermit—whose name, if accounts are correct, was George Harris, not Harrison. The place provides an unprotected water source and a bit of flat ground for pitching a tent. In June, to camp at Harrison Ground is to sleep among the flowering rhododendrons. The spring, only a trickle here, gains force as it descends, forming several pleasant cascades by the time it reaches Petites Gap. The next water source on the AT is a very unreliable spring just southeast of the trail at 6.4 mi.

From Harrison Ground, the trail continues a 1.0-mi., 1300-ft. descent into Petites Gap down Thunder Ridge, pausing in flats and sags intermittently. Even without extensive views for the descent, the sights and sounds of the forest make this trip through the oak and pine wilds a memorable one. Besides, there is a lot to see underfoot. White Clintonia, also known as speckled wood lily, can be found growing in the shade. A common companion of red maple saplings, the flower is named for a well-known politician—not the forty-fourth President of the United States, but the former governor of New York State, naturalist DeWitt Clinton. The hike ends at USFS 35 (Petites Gap Rd.), 100 yd. west of BRPMP 71.

HIKE #24   Itinerary

Miles N	NORTH	Elev. (ft/m)	Miles S
7.3	**End:** In Petites Gap on **USFS 35 (Petites Gap Rd.)**, 100 yd. from BRPMP 71.0, 23.0 mi. from Buchanan, limited trailhead parking.	2370/722	0.0
6.9	Trail joins old road.		0.4
6.4	Intermittent spring.		0.9
5.9	**Harrison Ground Spring**, then reach old road with good views.		1.4
5.2	Reach wooded summit of **Thunder Ridge.**	3685/1123	2.1
4.6	Begin ascent of **Thunder Ridge.**		2.7
4.3	Enter **Thunder Ridge Wilderness.**		3.0
4.0	Stone overlook with views to James River and the Allegheny Mts.	3500/1067	3.3
3.6	Cross **BRP** at milepost 74.9.		3.7
3.5	Junction with **Hunting Creek Trail,** leads 2.0 mi. to Hunting Creek and USFS 45.	3600/1098	3.8
2.6	**Thunder Hill Shelter,** seasonal spring, privy.	3300/1006	4.7
2.3	Cross **BRP** at milepost 76.3, early exit option.		5.0
1.7	Pass under **The Guillotine.**		5.6
1.4	**Apple Orchard Mt.** summit, descend via rock steps.	4225/1288	5.9
0.0	**Start:** Trailhead parking on **USFS 812 (Parkers Gap Rd.),** at junction with AT and **Apple Orchard Falls Trail,** 0.3 mi. N of BRPMP 78.4, 17.0 mi. from Buchanan.	3430/1045	7.3

SOUTH

Petites Gap to James River

Map: ATC Va. #2, Central Virginia

Route: From Petites Gap at USFS 35 (Petites Gap Rd.) through the James River Face Wilderness in Jefferson NF over Highcock Knob and across Big Cove Branch to the James River and US 501

Recommended direction: S to N

Distance: 9.9 mi.

Elevation +/-: 2400 to 3000 to 700 ft.

Effort: Moderate

Day hike: Yes

Overnight backpacking hike: Optional

Duration: 6 to 8 hr.

Early exit option: None

Natural history features: James River Face Wilderness; Big Cove Branch; Matts Creek; Devils Marbleyard; James River gorge

Social history feature: Hickory Stand

Other features: Several circuit trails intersect AT throughout this section

Trailhead access: *Start:* From Buena Vista, head S on BRP to milepost 71.0; turn R onto USFS 35 (Petites Gap Rd.). Trailhead is 100 yd. W of parkway. Note: Access to USFS 35 may be closed in winter. There is limited parking. For alternate approach, from S, see Hike #24. *End:* From Natural Bridge interchange on I-81, head E 14.0 mi. on VA 130 to Snowden Bridge (after passing through Glasgow, road is also US 501). Follow US 501 as it splits to R and goes over bridge. Trailhead with limited parking area (4 to 5 cars) is on US 501, 145 yd. S of southern end of bridge. From trailhead, US 501 continues 3.0 mi. to intersect with BRP.

Camping: Marble Spring and Grassy Island Ridge campsites; Matts Creek Shelter; but in Petites Gap (BRP land), no camping and campfires

---

This moderately easy trek is one of the most scenic hikes in central Virginia (located generally in Jefferson NF). Pack plenty of film along with your picnic lunch. After conquering the first uphill mile, from Petites Gap Rd. to Highcock Knob, the rest of the hike is smooth sailing as the trail slopes downward, taking you past rocky bluffs and through wooded hollows as you explore Marble Spring, Big Cove Branch, Matts Creek, and other splendid parts of the James River Face Wilderness. Throughout this hike, the James River Gorge is frequently visible in the distance, flanked by the rocky cliffs of Little and Big Rocky Row on the northern side of the river.

Stretching from the Allegheny Mts. to the Chesapeake Bay, the 450-mi. James River is Virginia's largest water-

Virginia's Treasure Trove of Wildlands

The movement to set aside large tracts of land in the United States as wilderness areas was started in 1924 by Aldo Leopold. A U.S. Forest Service employee at the time, Leopold would later gain notoriety as the father of the wilderness movement in the United States and one of the greatest conservationists of all time. As support for wilderness areas grew, spawning groups such as The Sierra Club and The Wilderness Society, Congress took notice and, in 1949, legislation to create a national wilderness system was introduced. Fifteen years later, President Lyndon Johnson created the National Wilderness Preservation System and signed the Wilderness Act into law.

Today there are nearly 109.5 million acres of wilderness on federal lands, 140,000 of which are located within Virginia's George Washington and Jefferson national forests. Although there is some wilderness within Shenandoah National Park, the bulk of Virginia's twenty-five wilderness lands are under U.S. Forest Service jurisdiction and make up 5 percent of the total national forest base of 1.8 million acres.

The act defines wilderness as "an area where the earth and its community of life are untrammeled by man, where man himself is a visitor who does not remain" and, more concretely, "an area of undeveloped Federal land retaining its primeval character and influence, without permanent improvements of human habitation, which is protected and managed so as to preserve its natural conditions."

In the urban sprawl that dominates much of the East, finding areas that are big enough and are not only unpopulated but also roadless has been quite a challenge, and Virginia is unique among Eastern states in having so many wilderness areas. Remarkably, the first eleven areas in Virginia were not created until 1984; the other four were added in 1988. They range in size from the 2500 acres of Thunder Ridge to the 11,000-acre Mountain Lake Wilderness. For the U.S. Forest Service rangers who manage these wildlands, the biggest challenge is minimizing human impact on them while ensuring that recreationists are able to enjoy the pristine landscape. Although rules vary from one wilder-

way. Its gorge is a geologic anticline composed of Precambrian and Paleozoic rock formations, cut through the Blue Ridge between the Maury River near Glasgow and the Blue Ridge Parkway crossing at Otter Creek. Nearly 1000 plant species grace the watershed, a number unmatched anywhere else in the central Virginia Blue Ridge. Wildflowers abound in spring and summer, counting gaywings, trailing arbutus, galax, wintergreen, and columbine among the bounty. In the fall, purple asters, blazing-stars and Maryland Golden-asters blend with brightly

ness area to the next, they all heed leave-no-trace ethics, including camping at least 100 ft. from trails and water, packing out all garbage and food, and sticking to existing trails. In all Virginia wilderness areas, group size is minimized to ten and travel is restricted to foot or horseback. (Only foot travel is permitted on the AT.) No motorized or mechanical equipment, including chainsaws and bicycles, is permitted in a wilderness area.

The AT cuts through several of Virginia's wilderness areas. Two of the most frequently visited are Lewis Fork and Little Wilson Creek (see Hike #3). Both areas are located within Mt. Rogers National Recreation Area, which includes the highest point in Virginia. The AT here is often crowded. However, additional trails offer a chance for solitude. Further north, a 3328-acre wilderness area lies on the eastern slope of Peters Mt., from which it takes its name. Upland willow oak are scattered over the high mountain as it rises up to 3956 ft. The AT crosses the area through Pine Swamp Branch and follows Peters Mt. along the wilderness boundary (see Hike #14). Another popular wilderness destination for AT hikers is the James River Face Wilderness (see Hike #25). Located in the Jefferson National Forest, the 8900-acre area is known to locals as "The Face." With elevations ranging from 650 ft. at the banks of the James River to 3073 ft. at Highcock Knob, James River Face has a wide variety of vegetation and unique geological features including the gigantic stone blocks known as Devil's Marbleyard. The AT is one of several hiking trails that pass through the area. The 11,113-acre Mountain Lake Wilderness is the largest wilderness area in the Jefferson National Forest. Named for the only natural lake in western Virginia, the area straddles the Eastern Continental Divide and offers rich stands of virgin spruce and hemlock and diverse flora and fauna (see Hike #15). Currently, the U.S. Forest Service is reviewing thirty-eight roadless areas in the George Washington and Jefferson national forests for possible wilderness designation in the future. This is part of a continuing planning effort to maintain the remote wilderness experience in Virginia.

speckled strawberry bushes to keep the area colorful. There are also plenty of water sources along this stretch. The longest distance without water is the 3.6 mi. between Marble Spring and Big Cove Branch.

From USFS 35 (Petites Gap Rd.,) the AT passes a James River Face Wilderness information station and begins its steep, steady ascent of Highcock Knob. As it approaches the 704-ft. climb, the trail leaves parkway land and enters the Jefferson NF and the James River Face Wilderness. The 8903-acre wilderness, designated by Congress in 1975, was one of the first to be established in the eastern United States.

Passing through a thick stand of white pine and lush hemlock, the trail is wide and smooth, compensating for the steep incline. Throughout this section, be extremely watchful for blazes, which are less frequent here than elsewhere. At 0.5 mi. the trail dips into a shallow sag, then continues its steady ascent, growing rockier as it climbs. Don't be fooled by the false summit at 0.8 mi.; you haven't reached the top yet. You do get a slight respite, however, as the AT cuts into another, much sharper sag, referred to by locals as Archie's Notch.

The sag is named for Archibald "Bear" Tolley, a bear hunter who preyed throughout these parts in the mid-1800s. The legendary predator kept a cabin on the lower east side of Petites Gap. According to legend, Tolley had two pet roosters that often perched high on a big oak tree on the side of the nearby promontory, thus the name High Cock Knob. The name was changed to Highcock in 1940. The trail reaches the knob's rocky, 3073-ft. summit at 1.2 mi., and almost immediately begins the 773-ft. descent to Marble Spring.

As you head downward over the rocky trail, beware of loose rocks, but try to look up occasionally for views of Rocky Row and Bluff Mt. in the distant north. The site of "Bear" Tolley's cabin is also believed to be in this vicinity. At 1.8 mi. the AT takes a sharp right onto a wide, graded trail and

gradually tapers its descent. For nearly a mile, the trail follows the route originally designed in 1930.

At 2.2 mi. the trail passes a campsite. The wide area is open and inviting with plenty of room for tents around a large fire ring. A path leads 110 yd. downhill to Marble Spring, a narrow, unprotected stream. This campsite is a good spot to stop and rest, but if you can hold out a little longer before digging into your lunch sack, there are better dining spots not far ahead. From the campsite, an unmarked trail on the right leads 0.8 mi. to the BRP. This is not recommended as an alternative route, however, as the trail is hard to find from the parkway.

From the campsite, the wide, mossy trail cuts into a thick stand of pine before passing an open view of East Fork of Elk Creek Valley and Thunder Ridge to the left. Beyond this clearing, the trail narrows again as it circles the deep gorge ahead. At 2.7 mi. you will reach a level clearing as the AT crosses the Sulphur Springs Trail. Beyond this intersection, the AT leads left and follows a ridge around Hickory Stand, offering views of Highcock Knob and Thunder Ridge to the west. The 6.6-mi. Sulphur Springs Trail begins at USFS 35 (Petites Gap Rd.), 2.6 mi. beyond the southern end of this section. The circuit trail follows an old roadbed as it climbs past the unprotected Sulphur Spring and up Sulphur Spring Hollow before crossing the AT. Along the way, the trail passes several large rocks that offer fine views of the James River. Sulphur Springs Trail crosses the AT again 5.0 mi. from the southern end and ends at the Balcony Falls Trail, just beyond Hickory Stand.

For more than a century, Hickory Stand was a focal point for hiking in what was first the Glenwood Estate and later the Jefferson NF. Five trails converge near the top of the stand, but none actually cross it. In the late 1800s, the knoll of Hickory Stand's southeast shoulder was also referred to as Lovers Retreat—whether hiking in fall foliage or springtime bloom, the colors here are fancifully romantic. In addition to the Sulphur Springs Trail, the Balcony Falls Trail, Piney Ridge Trail, Belfast Trail, and Gunter Ridge Trail also cross near this site and create a variety of possible circuit hikes.

As the AT continues through a thick forest of oak, hickory, and pine, be on the lookout for white-tailed deer, which are extremely populous here. In the fall and winter, when other areas have turned brown, you may be surprised by the lush greenness of this section. Mountain laurel, rhododendron, and other evergreen and deciduous understory species flourish in this area year round, keeping the area bright and colorful.

At 3.4 mi. keep an eye on the white blazes as the trail curves to the right, then, in 150 yd., makes a sharp left, avoiding an old trail straight ahead. After the turn, the trail begins a steep, rocky descent as it makes a pass around Lovers Retreat. A half mile

further on, the trail reaches a low point as it skirts a saddle on the right, then begins a rocky, winding ascent through a flurry of magnolia bushes and hemlock. At 4.5 mi. you will reach a 2650-ft. crest on the western spur of Hickory Stand. Here, the AT intersects with the Belfast Trail.

The 2.8-mi. Gunter Ridge Trail leads west to a junction with the Belfast Trail in 0.4 mi. Beyond the junction, the trail continues 1.0 mi. further to Devils Marbleyard. Also called Belfast Slide, Devils Marbleyard consists of 8 acres of Antietam quartzite. According to geologists, the river of rocks formed when ice froze in the cracks of the quartzite and forced the rocks to separate. Locals tell a more interesting tale. According to a 17th-century legend, an elderly missionary and a young woman came to the valley to teach Christianity to the Native Americans. Prior to their arrival, the indigenous people worshipped The Great Spirit while standing under a pinnacle on a high ledge. Soon after the missionary arrived, an intense drought ruined crops and dispersed game. The inhabitants blamed the missionary and planned to sacrifice him and his companion. Just as they began to burn the intruders, a ferocious storm smashed the pinnacle and ledge, leaving behind the field of boulders. Today, it is one of the most popular hiking destinations within the James River Face Wilderness. Beyond Devils Marbleyard, the Belfast Trail continues 1.4 mi. to USFS 35/VA 781. After passing the Belfast Trail's eastern end, the AT takes a sharp right as it dips to 2588 ft. Here the trail makes another hard right and continues the 1820-ft. descent to Matts Creek. As you wind down the rocky pathway, get ready to use some of that film as you catch the first of many great views of the James River gorge to the distant left.

As the trail continues downward to meet Matts Creek, it makes two sharp switchbacks, then passes another open view of the gorge at 5.4 mi. From this vantage point, you can also see Big Rocky Row and Bluff Mt. Look out for a few scattered rocks as the trail enters a series of nine steep switchbacks. As you zigzag your way down the mountain, take time to inspect the collection of Erwin quartzite strewn about the trail. You will be able to compare it to the Hampton shale found near Big Cove Branch just ahead. Unlike the quartzite, which appears as a solid mass, shale is a layered rock that, formed primarily of clay, can often break apart in your hand.

The trail meets Big Cove Branch at 1853 ft., 5.8 mi. from the start of this section of the AT. On the opposite side of the stream, several wide, flat rocks provide good benches, making this a nice place to stop for lunch. Beyond Big Cove Branch the trail skirts the northern side of the ridge, offering more views of the bright blue roaring river below. From here, the next mile is an easy, gently sloping descent. As you continue to catch glimpses of the James River to the

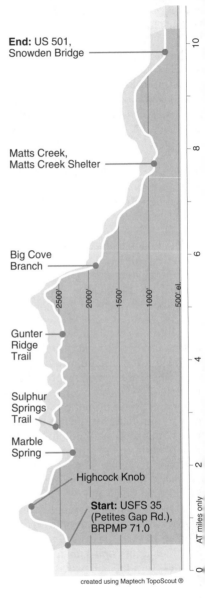

End: US 501, Snowden Bridge

Matts Creek, Matts Creek Shelter

Big Cove Branch

Gunter Ridge Trail

Sulphur Springs Trail

Marble Spring

Highcock Knob

Start: USFS 35 (Petites Gap Rd.), BRPMP 71.0

AT miles only

created using Maptech TopoScout ®

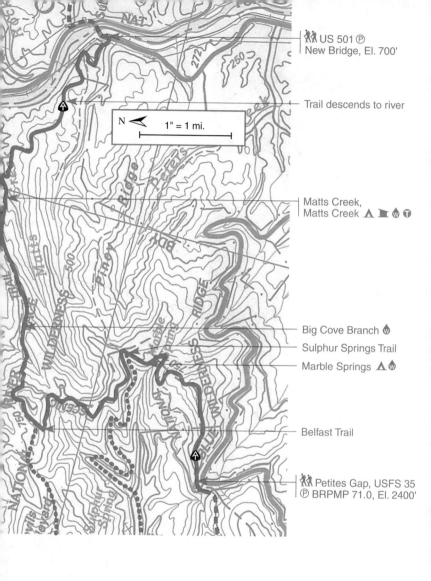

US 501 Ⓟ
New Bridge, El. 700'

Trail descends to river

N ◄ 1" = 1 mi.

Matts Creek,
Matts Creek ▲ ◼ ◗ ⓣ

Big Cove Branch ◗

Sulphur Springs Trail

Marble Springs ▲ ◗

Belfast Trail

Petites Gap, USFS 35
Ⓟ BRPMP 71.0, El. 2400'

Footbridge to Matts Creek Shelter

descent as the faint rumbling of Matts Creek grows increasingly louder. Soon the rapidly flowing stream appears to the right of the trail, as the ridge you have just abandoned rises higher to the left.

When the trail intersects with Matts Creek at 7.7 mi., a sturdy wooden bridge provides easy crossing. The bridge is dedicated to Henry Lanum, a former trail-work supervisor for the Natural Bridge AT Club. The Matts Creek Shelter is nestled just beyond the bridge. This is another excellent spot to stop and take a breather. While you're here, take a little time to check out your surroundings. With room to sleep up to six, the shelter is a three-sided structure with the open side facing the river. The nearby area includes a picnic table, a large fire ring, and even an outhouse out back —a rarity for these parts. Look for Carolina hemlock along the creek and rocks that have broken from the Hampton formation, a Cambrian shale deposit more than 500 million years old.

Just beyond Matt's Creek Shelter a reroute leads down to the James River and follows the river's edge for approximately 1 mi. It then crosses the river on the James River Footbridge, which at 625 feet is the longest pedestrian-only bridge on the Appalachian Trail, according to the Appalachian Trail Conservancy. Just beyond, walk beneath the railroad bridge to reach the end of the hike on US 501, 145 yd. south of Snowden Bridge.

left, you're also apt to see a freight train tracing its far edge.

At 6.4 mi. the trail joins Grassy Island Ridge and follows it for the next half mile. The ridge literally forms an island of green as the grassy path winds around formations of Unicoi quartzite. The rocks were created when the African and North American plates collided. Before the trail leaves Grassy Island Ridge it enters a flat, mossy area. The spot is large enough for a tent, but has no immediate water source.

Beyond this viable but less than ideal campsite, the trail cuts to the right of the ridge and enters a steady

If the hiking has made you hungry and you're looking for some quick grub, head right on US 501 and proceed 4.0 mi. to Big Island. With a population of 325, there's not a lot here. But you will find a food market, gas station, and short-order restaurant. The town of Glasgow, 7.0 mi. west on VA 130, is a bit larger (pop. 1250) but the selection of amenities is about the same.

HIKE #25   Itinerary

Miles N	NORTH	Elev. (ft/m)	Miles S
9.9	**End:** Small parking area 145 yd. S of Snowden Bridge on **US 501**, 4.0 mi. from Big Island.	700/213	0.0
9.7	Crest of ridge. Descend through hemlocks and pines.	1350/411	0.02
7.7	Cross **Matts Creek** on rocks; **Matts Creek Shelter,** privy, and several small swimming holes.	835/255	2.2
6.4	**Grassy Island Ridge;** campsite, no water.		2.9
5.8	Cross **Big Cove Branch** and ascend 9 switchbacks.	1850/564	4.1
5.0	Ridge crest.	2590/789	4.9
4.5	**Belfast Trail** leads W to Gunter Ridge Trail (0.4 mi.) and Devils Marbleyard (0.5 mi.).		5.4
4.0	Rocky descent to low saddle.		5.9
2.7	Intersect **Sulphur Springs Trail** (leads sharply R 2.9 mi. to USFS 35/VA 781).		7.2
2.2	Campsite at site of former Marble Spring Shelter in sag. Path leads 110 yd. downhill to Marble Spring.	2300/701	7.7
1.2	Rocky, wooded summit of **Highcock Knob.**	3000/914	8.7
0.8	**Archie's Notch.**		9.1
0.0	**Start:** Trailhead parking on **USFS 35 (Petites Gap Rd.)** 100 yd. W of BRPMP 71.0. Head past James River Face Wilderness information station. 23.0 mi. from Buchanan.	2400/731	9.9

SOUTH

Punchbowl Mt. to James River

Map: ATC Va. #2, Central Virginia

Route: From BRPMP 51.7, through Washington NF over Punchbowl and Bluff mountains, through Saltlog and Saddle gaps to Little Rocky Row, over Johns Creek to USFS 36 (Hercules [Amlite] Rd.)

Recommended direction: N to S

Distance: 9.8 mi.

Elevation +/-: 2170 to 3370 to 800 ft.

Effort: Moderate

Day hike: Yes

Overnight backpacking hike: Optional

Duration: 5 to 7 hr.

Early exit option: At 5.1 mi., blue-blazed trail

Natural history features: Bluff Mt.; Big Rocky Row; Fullers Rocks; Little Rocky Row; James River

Social history feature: Ottie Cline Powell memorial

Other features: Several circuit hikes cross the AT throughout this section

Trailhead access: *Start:* At BRPMP 51.7, 6.1 mi. S of US 60 near Buena Vista and 12.2 mi. N of US 501 near Big Island. There is room for 10 to 12 cars in lot across from trailhead. Hikers parking overnight are asked to contact BRP ranger station at (800) 727-5928. *End:* From Glasgow, follow VA 130/US 501 E 6.0 mi. to USFS 36 (Hercules [Amlite] Rd.); bear L, and follow 0.9 mi. to AT crossing; roadside parking. More AT parking is available back toward VA 130. If you come to US 501 crossing of Snowden Bridge you have missed turn for USFS 36.

Camping: Punchbowl Shelter; Johns Hollow Shelter; and where permitted along trail; on BRP land, camp only in designated areas.

This hike follows the crest of the main Blue Ridge, taking you over the summits of Punchbowl Mt., Bluff Mt., Big Rocky Row, and Little Rocky Row while offering several excellent views of the James River gorge to the south and of the surrounding Amherst and Rockbridge counties. (The entire hike is in Washington NF except for 0.1 mi. in the BRP boundary at the N end.) After the first 2 mi. of uphill climbing, southbound hikers will enjoy a gen- erally downward slope, although several series of steep switchbacks do call for caution. A variety of ferns, mountain laurel, rhododendron, and other evergreen and deciduous understory species keep sections of this hike painted bright green year round. Bluff Mt. is also known for its orchid varieties, including pink lady's-slipper, whorled pogonia, and southern rein. Nodding ladies' tresses, another orchid variety, have also been spotted near the Punch-

Punchbowl Shelter

bowl Shelter. A few stretches of this section are rather desolate, the result of a 1963 fire that scorched the forest from the James River gorge to the summit of Rocky Row.

The small monument to Ottie Cline Powell you will pass on this hike is one of the most poignant sights along the AT. In November 1891, just five days before his fifth birthday, Ottie Powell set out with a group of other boys to gather wood for their Tower Hill schoolhouse. When the other boys returned with the fuel, Ottie was not with them. A scouting party discovered the imprint of a dragged stick in the path and guessed the boy had turned the wrong way. Hundreds of area residents joined the boy's father in searching the countryside,

but the little boy was not found. Five months later, on April 5, 1892, four men crossing the summit of Bluff Mt. discovered the body of Ottie Cline, his hat on his head, 7 mi. away from where he'd started.

To begin the hike, cross diagonally to the right (west) from the parkway parking area and begin an immediate ascent of the western bank through a thickly wooded area. As you make a sharp left and continue upward, the climb is steep, but the winding trail is smooth and easy to maneuver on. As the trail enters a short series of steep switchbacks, fall and winter hikers will have views of Bluff Mt. to the left. At 0.4 mi. the AT meets an old road that is now hidden by fallen tree branches and low-lying brush and full of deep, rocky ruts. A side trail leads 0.2 mi. to the right to Punchbowl Shelter. An unprotected stream runs in front of the wooden structure, 50 ft. downstream from its pond outlet. The shelter sleeps six, with plenty of tent space nearby.

From the junction with the old road, the AT makes a sharp left. Look for blazes as you continue to ascend the moss-covered trail, which is flanked by berry bushes and grows rockier as it climbs. At 0.6 mi. the trail cuts to the left as an old road enters from right. As you pass through scattered stands of red spruce, the trail begins to level out and soon crosses the wooded summit of Punchbowl Mt. at 2870 ft.

From the summit to Little Rocky Row, the AT zigzags over the Amherst-Rockbridge county line, tracing the border whenever the trail reaches a ridgeline. As you continue across the crest, you can see mountains to the left and right of the trail. The AT slopes slightly into a shallow sag before resuming a steep, upward climb, this time to the summit of Bluff Mt. at 2.0 mi.

But first, at 1.5 mi., the trail bears left and joins an old road to ascend seven switchbacks. As the trail cuts back and forth through a pine-covered area, the mountainous view to the east jumps between the left and the right of the trail. As you near the top, the climb grows steeper and rockier. Moss-covered rocks rise above to the right, and fall and winter hikers enjoy a view of the valley below on the left. The rocky trail is carpeted with pine needles from the thick surrounding stands of Norway spruce, which blend with hemlock and magnolia bushes to keep the area green. At 2.0 mi. your hard effort is rewarded as you reach the 3370-ft. summit of Bluff Mt., once known as Thunder Hill.

Large cement blocks, remnants of a fire tower that was built in the 1920s and remained active until 1976, are scattered over the wide, grassy peak. These blocks now provide fine benches, on which to stop, catch your breath, and enjoy the panoramic view of sprawling countryside to the west and green hills and mountains in the east. From this vantage point, Buena Vista, Lexington, and the Shenandoah Valley with the Allegheny Mts. beyond are visible to the northwest, while Tobacco Row Mt.'s High Peak rises to the southeast. One of the peaks visible to the southwest is Target Hill where, in the late 1850s, Stonewall Jackson field-tested the Parrott rifle. In 1864, a Union general named Hunter fired a cannon from the summit toward the Virginia Military Institute (VMI) in Lexington, giving the peak the local nickname "Hunter Hill." During very dry seasons you are apt to be joined by USFS rangers armed with binoculars and a radio as they search for signs of fire.

On the opposite side of the clearing and to the left, the memorial to Ottie Cline Powell remains a well-kept tribute. The site is adorned by small Tonka trucks and other toys, and bunches of fresh-cut flowers left by passing AT hikers. Engraved on the flat, gray stone are the lines

> *This is the exact spot Little Ottie Cline Powell's*
> *Body was found April 5, 1891,*
> *After Straying from Tower Hill School House Nov. 9,*
> *A distance of 7 miles.*
> *Age 4 years, 11 months.*

The events actually happened one year later than noted.

Just beyond the memorial, look for blazes and a trail marker as the AT takes a sharp left off an old road and begins a 777-ft. descent into Salt Log Gap. Although the climb down is not as lush as the climb up, Norway spruce again dominate the area, their needles forming a soft carpet on the swiftly dropping trail. As you descend, look for passing glimpses of Little Apple Mt. to the east and Silas Knob, Rocky Row, and Apple Orchard Mt. ahead. When hiking in the fall or winter, beware of large rocks scattered about; they are easy to step over if spotted, but easy to stumble over when obscured by fallen leaves or snow.

After passing through a small, cleared sag, the trail crosses a small knoll. For a feeling of accomplishment, stop and turn around to see the conquered Bluff Mt. rising behind you. Continue along a level corridor for 200 yd., then bear left through a tight saddle. The trail reaches Saltlog

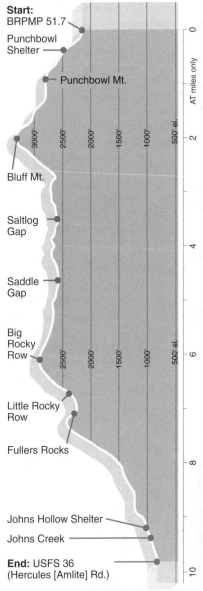

created using Maptech TopoScout ®

XX BRPMP 51.7 Ⓟ
El. 2170'

Punchbowl ▲ ◾ ⓦ
El. 2500'

Bluff Mt., El. 3370' **V**

Saltlog Gap,
Belle Cove Trail,
White Oak Flats Trail

Saddle Gap, El. 2590'

Big Rocky Row,
El. 2990' **V**

Fullers Rocks, El. 2470'

Rocky Row Trail

Johns Hollow ▲ ◾ ⓦ ⊤

Johns Creek ⓦ

XX USFS 36
(Hercules [Amlite] Rd.) Ⓟ
El. 800'

VA 130/US 501,
James River

Gap at 3.5 mi., where it intersects with several circuit trails, including the blue-blazed Belle Cove Trail to the right, which leads 5.0 mi. to US 501, and the unblazed White Oak Flats Trail to the left, leading 4.0 mi. to the parkway at mi. 55.2. Following directional signs, continue along AT, passing a rock overhang on the left and continuing downward.

Look for spleenwort fern and moss over the next mile as the narrow trail continues to descend. To the left, large slabs of quartzite rise high above you, while a precariously sharp drop-off borders on the right. At 4.6 mi. listen for echoing footsteps and voices as the trail skirts a natural amphitheater on the west side of Silas Knob, named for an early surveyor briefly lost on the knob. Maury River valley and the Allegheny Mts. can be seen to the west. To the southwest, look for Three Sisters Knobs, an 8150-acre roadless area now managed by the USFS as a remote highland. Approximately 0.5 mi. ahead is Saddle Gap at 2590 ft.

In the gap, a blue-blazed trail leads 2.5 mi. to the left to USFS 36 (Hercules [Amlite] Rd.), where there is roadside parking. The "horn of the saddle," a cluster of rough, gray quartzite boulders, sits at the northern end of the sag. The trail continues through a rocky area, then begins a gradual ascent as it winds through a thickly wooded area. There are more views of the Allegheny Mts. to the right, and magnolia bushes, pine, fern, and low shrubs return.

At 6.0 mi. a narrow side path leads 40 ft. to the left for excellent views of a distant slate quarry, and, from left to right, a panoramic view of Peavine Mt., High Peak of Tobacco Row Mt., the James River, Terrapin Mt., Highcock Knob, and Apple Orchard Mt. This is also a good spot for lunch or a lengthy water break.

Until 1880, slate could be picked up or pried out of the ground by anyone who happened along. Then the Virginia Slate Mining Co. opened a quarry in the area of Buckingham County, now known as Slate Quarry Hollow. Over the past thirty years, the quarry, also known as "blue hole," was expanded to the Hercules, then Amlite, mines, which are also seen from this viewing point. The vein produces a deep-black roofing slate on which much of Buckingham County thrives today. The Virginia Slate Mining Co. ended operations in 1915 and reopened its quarry in 1995. It is known for producing some of the highest quality roofing slate in the world.

The AT continues across the summit of Big Rocky Row (elev. 2990 ft.) then enters a steep, rocky descent. As the trail passes a rock slide ahead and above you to the right, look to the west to see Lees Carpet, a division of Burlington Industries. From a distance the 34-acre complex looks like a large farm. As you get closer, you'll get a better view of what is really the largest carpet manufacturing facility under one roof in the world.

The trail continues winding downward and becomes increasingly rocky, calling for extra-careful footwork in several spots. As you descend, look for passing views of the James River gorge below and to the left. In early spring, this stretch of the trail is carpeted with the pale pink creeping phlox.

The Trail winds its way through a series of sharp switchbacks, crosses a flat, wooded area, and drops into a sharp sag. Then, at 6.7 mi., it begins its ascent of Little Rocky Row (2430 ft.), over terrain similar to that of Big Rocky Row. As you make the climb to Little Rocky Row, along a steep, moss-covered trail, you will continue to catch occasional glimpses of the James River to the left and mountains behind you to the right. At the top of Little Rocky Row, there are more clear views of the wide, winding blue river below. Following the Trail along the ridge of Little Rocky Row, you will pass a path on the left that leads 3 yd. to Fullers Rocks (2470 ft.). A popular destination of area day hikers, Fullers Rocks offer views to the north, east, and south of Peavine Mt., High Peak on Tobacco Row, the James River, and, beyond the river, the steep, forested bluffs of the James River Face Wilderness.

The junction with Rocky Row Trail follows another viewing area. The blue-blazed trail leads 2.7 mi. to VA 130/US 501, 3.0 mi. from Glasgow. In 1894, fire swept over the entire Rocky Row area and over Bluff Mt. A second fire roared through the area in 1918, destroying everything from the James River to the Pedlar River. And in 1963 a 2300-acre fire moved from the James River gorge up to the summit of Little Rocky Row, where it stopped near this point of the AT.

Head to the left and begin a steep, rocky descent over a series of twenty-one switchbacks at 7.2 mi. The 1963 fire left this section far less wooded than previous stretches of this hike, allowing an almost continuous view of the James River to the east. The lack of trees has allowed more shrubs and other sun-loving greenery to grow here. In spring and summer, look for the rose-purple blooms of wild geranium along the trail. At the sixteenth switchback an old road cuts to the left as the trail winds to the right.

The switchbacks end at 8.5 mi. and the AT follows an old road for a short distance before turning to the left. The pine trees prevalent in the earlier part of the hike are again scattered about the area. The trail passes between two 2-ft.-high posts and crosses an old logging road in a slight sag before continuing downward. The forest continues to grow thicker as old oak and hickory hardwoods mix with young pine. Although you can no longer see the James River, you can now hear Johns Creek gurgling ahead.

Flat areas now predominate as the trail continues through the heavily forested area. The occasional up or downhill climbs are extremely gradual and a wide, smooth surface makes this an easy stretch. As the trail cuts down a steep bank, look for Johns Hollow Shelter below and to the left. Although the trail remains flat, it is also narrow and is bordered by a steep drop-off on the left; proceed with caution.

At 9.2 mi. the AT passes a blue-blazed trail on the left, leading 135 yd. to Johns Hollow Shelter, located between a creek and an unprotected spring. Several maps refer to this area as the John S. Tyler Hollow. This shelter sleeps up to six and offers ample nearby tent space. There is also a privy. If you pass through this area in the spring, be prepared to stop and examine a variety of wildflowers, including trailing arbutus, birdfoot violet, bleeding-heart, and wild geranium. Later in the year, blazing-star, cardinal-flower, and false foxglove are also prevalent.

Beyond the shelter, the AT makes a sharp turn as it crosses over a flood runoff area. The trail is very narrow and quite slick; be extremely careful. As you continue toward Johns Creek, watch closely for blazes, which are less frequent and hard to see throughout this stretch. The AT cuts to the left and down a few rock steps to intersect at 9.4 mi. with Johns Creek, a shallow, gently rolling stream. Cross the creek on wide flat rocks. Watch your step; they're slippery. Beyond the creek, the trail cuts up a minor crest. As you reach the top, the climb becomes more gradual and the forest opens up to allow more sunlight. Continue along a mostly flat trail through a forest of pine, hemlock, and fern. At 9.8 mi. the AT intersects with USFS 36 (Hercules [Amlite] Rd.), and the end of this hike.

HIKE #26   Itinerary

Miles N	NORTH	Elev. (ft/m)	Miles S
9.8	**Start:** At parking lot on E side of **BRPMP 51.7.** Ascend bank on W side of road.	2170/661	0.0
9.4	Side trail 0.2 mi. R to **Punchbowl Shelter,** camping, water.	2500/762	0.4
8.9	Wooded summit of **Punchbowl Mt.**	2870/875	0.9
7.8	Summit of **Bluff Mt.,** views; Ottie Cline Powell Memorial.	3370/1027	2.0
6.3	**Saltlog Gap; Belle Cove Trail** to R; **White Oak Flats Trail** to L.	2570/783	3.5
5.2	Natural amphitheater; **Saddle Gap.**	2590/789	4.6
5.1	Blue-blazed trail to L 2.5 mi. to USFS 36, early exit option.		4.7
3.8	Path to L 40 ft. for excellent view.	2900/884	6.0
3.7	Summit of **Big Rocky Row.**	2990/911	6.1
3.1	Begin ascent to **Little Rocky Row.**	2430/741	6.7
2.7	Path to L leads 3 yd. to **Fullers Rocks.**	2470/753	7.1
2.6	Begin 1.3-mi. descent on **21 switchbacks. Rocky Row Trail** leads R 2.7 mi. to VA 130/US501.		7.2
0.6	**Johns Hollow Shelter.**	1020/311	9.2
0.4	Cross **Johns Creek.**		9.4
0.0	**End:** Roadside parking at **USFS 36 (Hercules [Amlite] Rd.),** 0.9 mi. N of VA 130/US 501 and the James River and 6.0 mi. E of Glasgow.	800/244	9.8

SOUTH

Long Mt. Wayside to Little Irish Creek

Map: ATC Va. #1 & 2, Central Virginia

Route: Through Washington NF from US 60 along Brown Mt. Creek to Pedlar Lake

Recommended direction: N to S

Distance: 6.3 mi.

Elevation +/-: 2065 to 1400 to 1050 ft.

Effort: Easy

Duration: 3 to 3 1/2 hr.

Day hike: Yes

Overnight backpacking hike: Optional

Early exit option: At 3.8 mi., USFS 38 (Pedlar Lake Rd.)

Natural history features: Brown Mt. Creek; Swapping Camp Creek; Little Irish Creek

Social history features: Brown Mt. Creek settlement ruins; Brown Mt. Creek

Bridge; Swapping Camp Creek; Pedlar Lake

Trailhead access: *Start:* From Buena Vista, go 9.0 mi. E on US 60; pass under BRP at 4.0 mi. Overnight parking in lot at Long Mt. Wayside, on L. *End:* From Buena Vista, go 4.0 mi. E to intersection with BRP. Just past BRP, go R onto USFS 315. Go about 6 mi. to junction with USFS 311. Go L and, at the road's end in 0.5 mi., go R onto USFS 39. Overnight parking available in pull-off at junction with AT, 0.2 mi. after turning onto USFS 39.

Camping: Brown Mt. Creek Trail Shelter, and where permitted along trail

S uitors in search of the perfect setting for a marriage proposal need look no further! The valley of Brown Mt. Creek is an enchanting place of old stone ruins, a waterfall, and sparkling pools concealed behind curious rock formations. Beyond the creek, the trail visits woodland full of secret hollows hidden by flowering shrubs and ferns. Almost always there is water within sight or sound. This is a memorable hike.

It is also one that hikers of any ability can manage. There is very little climbing, and most of the descent is

gradual. Near Pedlar Lake (also known as Lynchburg Reservoir) there are a few brief sections along narrow ledges where small children should be coached to go slowly, but even over these 100 or so yards they will likely be able to travel on their own two feet.

With some 3 hours of walking on this trip, there is plenty of time to amble among the ruins or sit by tumbling water. This is a "thermos hike," easy enough to carry a container of hot coffee or tea, and with many places to enjoy it. With so much to explore, the real challenge is getting oneself to move along. Luckily, Brown Mt. Creek valley is also a splendid spot for camping, whether at the shelter 1.8 mi. from the trailhead or at other sites along the stream.

From the Long Mt. Wayside trailhead on US 60, cross the road heading diagonally to the right (west) to find the AT entrance. The gentle slope of the trail, actually the remnant of one of several old roads through the valley, makes for easy going on the steady, 1100-vertical-ft. descent to Pedlar Lake.

At about 0.3 mi., an unnamed, unmapped branch of Brown Mt. Creek appears about 50 yd. to the left of the trail, barely visible through the thicket, then is lost from view. Continue descending; at 0.5 mi. the stream reemerges in full view as a tumbling, junior-sized waterfall. Only 10 minutes into the hike and it's time for a coffee break. The forest floor is open and stable, which makes crossing off-trail 60 yd. to the creek safe for both hiker and landscape. Once there, lounging on the rocks, viewing the densely wooded valley, it is difficult to imagine that from the early 1900s until early in the 20th century most of the land below was open farmland.

The idea of farming the valley becomes even more remarkable further into the hike, where in many places the slopes are steep and the bottomlands stretch barely 100 yd. from the base of Long Mt. to the foot of Brown Mt. Purchased by a former slave after the Civil War, the valley

was home to tenant farmers, former slaves who rented the cabins, now remembered only by the ruins that dot the valley floor. The stone walls that intermittently hug the stream bank illustrate the precarious situation faced by 19th-century settlers scraping out an existence in the narrow bottom between two mountains. It took only a good summer rain, let alone the melting snow of spring, to raise Brown Mt. Creek over its banks and into the front yards of valley residents. The still-standing stone flood walls offered protection from flash floods and helped keep the creek in check during the thaw.

The trail descends another 0.4 mi. and crosses the small branch. Brown Mt. Creek itself makes an abrupt entrance from the right at 0.9 mi., then leads the way past chimneys, foundations, property-line walls, and other remnants of civilization. Just beyond the crossing of a second side branch, at 1.2 mi., a double chimney can be seen across the creek. Downstream another quarter of a mile, a spring surrounded by a stone wall still provides water. The spring, like others in the valley, is unprotected. Chemical treatment or adequate filtration is recommended before drinking.

Hiking among the ruins, which resemble a ghost town, it is easy to imagine that all the inhabitants took their leave simultaneously. This is nearly true. With the start of construction of Pedlar Dam, another 4 mi. downstream, in 1904, and the eventual evacuation by the Forest Service of all valley inhabitants, by 1908 the last settlers had been relocated off the federally appropriated lands.

The 0.1 mi. side trail east to Brown Mt. Creek Shelter is at 1.8 mi. Overnight hikers who find the shelter filled to capacity by AT backpackers can continue 150 yd. on the AT downstream to a tent camping area just across a narrow footbridge. Water is available from two unprotected springs near the shelter.

After crossing the creek at the footbridge at 1.9 mi., the trail hugs the western bank of the creek and meanders over rolling abandoned dirt roads, now merely wide footpaths. Primarily used for foot traffic even when the valley was settled, the roads nonetheless were the sole horse and wagon routes through the narrow dale. While the roads close to the stream offered a gentler grade, they also presented the distinct possibility of losing horse and goods over the bank and into the creek. For the modern hiker, in many stretches the wide paths grant a chance to walk side by side. Over the next mile, the trail's passage on the west bank affords an elevated view of stone walls and other ruins on the opposite side.

At 2.2 mi. a stone flood wall more than 200 yd. long begins. This wall and the immediately surrounding area are troves of relics. Pieces from glass jars, nails, bits of plates and saucers, and other artifacts can be unearthed by poking around in the leaves for half an hour or so.

From 2.2 mi. until the Brown Mt. Creek Bridge crossing (2.8 mi.), the stream offers several wading pools near campsites; a few of the larger pools can legitimately be called swimming holes. The camping areas at 2.7 mi. create a perfect spot to stop, if not to camp, then at least to sit a while and dip your feet. On a hot day, even in summer, the pool is freezing cold, and a short dip is just enough to cool a hiker down to a perfect napping temperature. And this is the place for a nap, under a canopy of hickory and oak that drape over the stream like elms over small-town Main Streets. The sun peeks through boughs, a leaf drops into the pool and glides downstream, and suddenly an hour has passed.

Perhaps the ultimate swimming pool on the creek, although one that's much more exposed, is just above the Brown Mt. Creek Bridge. The bridge itself might be the ideal spot for that marriage proposal. The water comes cascading full force into a pool here and sprays mist as it strikes the east bank. The glen is at its narrowest, bringing the two mountains almost to the touch. A giant straddling the 15-ft.-wide stream would have one foot on Brown Mt. and the other on Long Mt. The trees bend as if at their knees to the stream. It's a magical spot.

The AT leaves the last old road and the stream after the bridge. The road continues south 0.3 mi. to a tent camping area at the confluence of

Coyote Calling Cards

Few sights are more captivating than watching a coyote trot along an open ridge, then thrust into overdrive on the hunt. With a bushy tail, erect ears, and scraggly mutt look, the coyote is downright cute, even at its maximum speed of about 40 m.p.h. Along the AT in the Virginias, coyote favor open woods not too far from the edge.

Reviled by farmers for preying on livestock, the coyote is as likely to chow on rodents, foxes, and other predators as lamb and chicken. Actually, coyotes are omnivores; they'll munch on just about any available entree, animal or vegetable. When they do hunt, it is with a surgeon's efficiency. They select their prey carefully, usually finding a weak member of the flock or injured wild animal. Instead of recklessly "wolfing" a carcass like a dog at a garbage can, coyotes make an incision at the abdomen and carefully extract their victuals innards first. Humans need not worry about such treatment because coyotes shy away from humans.

They generally hunt at night or dusk, most often alone or with a mate. However, they socialize in packs, often yapping together before going off to hunt alone. They mate for life and show remarkable loyalty to their mates; they are known to bring food to sick or injured, even trapped, mates or other coyotes.

Because coyotes are shy around humans, you're more likely to spy the evidence of one than the animal itself. As with most animals in the wild, the presence of coyotes can be readily recognized by their scat and tracks. Their footprints resemble dogs', but are more oval and leave only two claw prints. Coyote feces also resemble those of a dog, but are more of an elongated jumble of undigested feathers, leaves, fur, and bones. The color of eastern coyote ranges from strawberry blonde to cinnamon, although black coyotes are not uncommon.

Brown Mt. Creek and Shady Mt. Creek at USFS 39, north of Pedlar Lake.

Continuing across the Brown Mt. Creek footbridge, the AT ascends to afford a view to the western side of the stream of the massive Scare Rock. According to legend, a slave-owning farmer named Jesse Richeson was returning home on horseback after savagely beating a slave who worked

for him in the valley. The beating, not the first such abuse doled out by Richeson to slaves, had left the slave near death. Richeson rode homeward down the river as night fell.

As he passed the huge outcrop next to the road, some unseen creature lept from the rock onto Richeson's horse and held him tight around the waist from behind.

Although Richeson could not see his attacker, he could not free himself of it. Apparently the horse sensed it, too, and was so frightened it broke into a gallop. Upon his return home, Richeson told the story of the dreadful assailant. Frightened and quite beside himself, he went to bed. Neither Richeson nor the horse lived to see the next morning.

At 2.9 mi. the trail ascends and traverses a knob covered in hickory and hemlock, trees that are larger and older than those in the valley just behind. At 3.2 mi., after crossing an unmarked path (a remnant of an old road) the hike is on level ground until coming to a stone-wall-enclosed spring. A faintly visible deer path, 150 yd. from the spring, leads 175 yd. west from the AT to a giant yellow-poplar. With a diameter of more than 5 ft., it is one of the largest poplars in the Pedlar District. A regular Rip Van Winkle sort of tree, it's a worthy distraction for any hiker who passed up a nap opportunity back on the creek.

Continuing south on the AT, the trail emerges from the woods onto USFS 38 (Pedlar Lake Rd.) at 3.8 mi. For a 7.5-mi. circuit hike back to Long Mt. Wayside, a left turn onto the road provides a pleasant, but paved, walk to the trailhead. It is also possible to leave a car here for day use and an early exit option. The road marks the end of the hike beside Long Mt. and begins the journey over and along the knobs and ledges of Piney Mt. Continuing south, the AT crosses

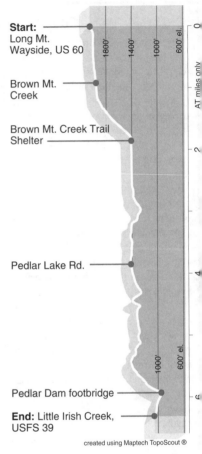

Start: Long Mt. Wayside, US 60

Brown Mt. Creek

Brown Mt. Creek Trail Shelter

Pedlar Lake Rd.

Pedlar Dam footbridge

End: Little Irish Creek, USFS 39

created using Maptech TopoScout ®

USFS 38 and descends into the woods and to a single-log bridge at Swapping Camp Creek at 4.0 mi.

In the days when goods and people moved slowly through the valley, the camp served as a bartering and trading center. In the early days of valley settlement, when there were few towns nearby in which to spend

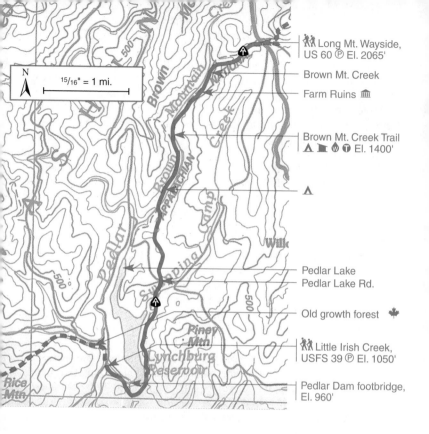

	Long Mt. Wayside, US 60 ⓟ El. 2065'
	Brown Mt. Creek
	Farm Ruins 🏛
	Brown Mt. Creek Trail △ 🏕 💧 🚻 El. 1400'
	△
	Pedlar Lake
	Pedlar Lake Rd.
	Old growth forest 🍁
	Little Irish Creek, USFS 39 ⓟ El. 1050'
	Pedlar Dam footbridge, El. 960'

coin or currency, bartering for tools, farm implements, and stock formed the basis of the valley economy.

The first look at the lake and the mountains beyond is perhaps the most expansive one from the trail above the dam, so hikers of a mind to get a closer look should take it here. The best vantage point is from the middle of Swapping Camp Creek 250 yd. below the log bridge at 4.0 mi. A point of no-trace hiking bears noting. To avoid damaging streamside vegetation and riparian habitat when following this narrow stream, walk either well away from its bank or right in the middle of the stream.

The next 0.5 mi. takes you over a small knob that is a veritable garden of rhododendron, laurel, ferns, and marsh marigolds. When the knob bottoms out abruptly at a spring that bubbles from the mountainside, and the trail seems momentarily to end at a sharp turn just beyond the spring at a moss-covered stone face, one couldn't be blamed for imagining a tall bunny wearing a derby hat dashing past.

The spring, at 4.3 mi., emerges in the first of nine gullied hollows the trail encounters over the next 1.3 mi. Soon Pedlar Lake comes into view as the trail skirts a ledge a couple of hundred feet above, and a hundred yards or so from, the lake. The trail is circling the lake in a dance that reveals a new perspective on the water at every turn, then moves briefly away into narrow hollows where the drop from the trail can be a steep 15 or 20 ft. The gullies sometimes run with water in spring, leaving the rocks on which the trail crosses very slippery. All the better reason to go slowly enough to enjoy the sights.

Much of the land in the immediate vicinity of the lake is managed by the city of Lynchburg. The reservoir of Pedlar Lake is the town's water supply. Hikers are permitted close-up visits to the water, and thanks to the beaver who call the lake home, getting close is easy, for the water-dwelling rodents have cleared parts of the shoreline. Otters also are known to inhabit the Pedlar Lake environs. Hikers will have to leave swimming and camping to the wildlife because these activities are not permitted to us at the lake.

The lake is nearly as popular with birds as with hikers. Blue heron, swans, loons, hooded mergansers, and other species are known to visit the lake, as are bald eagles. Mallards are regular migratory visitors. The luckiest of hikers might catch sight of an elusive coyote trotting along the shoreline.

At 5.8 mi. the trail leaves Forest Service land and crosses Lynchburg-managed lands, then descends steep steps to the base of Pedlar Dam, where a footbridge crosses the Pedlar River at 5.9 mi., as it makes its first appearance from the spillway. There is no trace of the town that once inhabited the valley below the dam's 138-acre lake, where Brown Mt. Creek and Swapping Camp Creek form the Pedlar River at their confluence. Residents of Waya were relocated to make use of a basin so well designed to hold water that few engineers could build it better.

Following the paved road beneath the dam at 6.0 mi., the trail then joins gravel USFS 39 at 6.2 mi., then reenters national forest lands at the Irish Creek AT trailhead. This is the finish line for the day hike, but all hikers are encouraged to add 0.3 mi. and a little time to visit the old-growth Canadian hemlock and white pine in a 4.5-acre study area, just up trail as the AT begins its 1200-ft. ascent of Rice Mt.

These few acres are an eastern rarity; they have never been harvested for lumber. The northern-native Canadian hemlock, which migrated south during the last two Ice Ages, seem quite at home here. Whereas much of the southern Appalachian forest is dense in understory shrubs and small flowering trees, an indication of a relatively young forest, this stand is inhabited by giant trees and open ground beneath. The forest floor is inhabited by ferns and flowering herbs.

Optional Extended Hike: For a longer day hike or an overnight trip, hikers can continue on the AT, ascending Rice Mt. to the BRP at milepost 51.7. The longer hike offers views of Coleman, Shady, and Piney mountains, the kinds of grand views that are not found in the shorter jaunt through the creek valley. Hikers opting for this extended 10.5-mi. hike should bear in mind that beyond the vicinity of Pedlar Lake and Little Irish Creek there are no exit opportunities until the trail has ascended all seven high points of Rice Mt. to arrive at the parkway. For even the ablest of hikers, it's at least a 3-hour uphill hike to cover the extra 4 miles.

HIKE #27   Itinerary

Miles N	NORTH	Elev. (ft/m)	Miles S
6.3	**Start:** Parking lot at **Long Mt. Wayside** on **US 60,** 4.0 mi. E of BRPMP 45.6 and 9.0 mi. E of Buena Vista.	2065/629	0.0
5.4	Trail joins **Brown Mt. Creek**		0.9
5.1	Pass ruins of tenant farms.		1.2
4.5	**Brown Mt. Creek Trail Shelter** trail (0.1 mi. E), privy, water, campsites.	1400/427	1.8
4.4	**Footbridge** crossing.		1.9
3.6	**Campsites,** pools in creek.		2.7
3.5	**Brown Mt. Creek Bridge** crossing.		2.8
2.9	Pass second stone-wall-enclosed spring.		3.4
2.5	Cross **Pedlar Lake Rd.,** begin walk of Piney Mt.		3.8
2.3	Cross log bridge over **Swapping Camp Creek;** view from midstream.		4.0
0.4	Cross footbridge at base of **Pedlar Dam.**	960/293	5.9
0.0	**End:** At **Little Irish Creek,** on **USFS 39;** roadside parking. Approximately 10.5 mi. SE of Buena Vista.	1050/320	6.3

SOUTH

Tar Jacket Ridge to Cold Mt.

Map: ATC Va. #1, Central Virginia

Route: From USFS 63 over Tar Jacket Ridge, through Hog Camp and Cow Camp gaps, and over Bald Knob to Salt Log Gap at US 60

Recommended direction: N to S

Distance: 8.2 mi.

Elevation +/-: 3250 to 4060 to 2100 ft.

Effort: Moderate

Duration: 5 hr.

Day hike: Yes

Overnight backpacking hike: Optional

Early exit options: At 2.2 mi., USFS 48; at 4.3 mi., Old Hotel Trail

Natural history features: Little Cove Creek; South Fork Piney River

Social history features: Hog Camp Gap; Cow Camp Gap; 12 mi. of stone walls; balds of Tar Jacket Ridge and Cold Mt.; wreckage of fighter plane

Other features: Junction with Old Hotel Trail, which can be used for optional circuit hike

Trailhead access: *Start:* From I-81 take exit for Buena Vista, heading E on US 60. Cross under BRP at 4.0 mi. Approximately 3.0 mi. beyond BRP, turn L onto VA 634. When road appears to end (approx. 3 mi.) veer R to continue on VA 634, which becomes USFS 63. Continue 4.1 mi. more to parking area at trail crossing. (Note: Trailhead is in Salt Log Gap North. Do not confuse with Salt Log Gap South, 22 mi. S on AT.) To park on USFS 48 at Cow Camp Gap (early exit option), from VA 634 turn R onto VA 755 which becomes USFS 48. *End:* From Buena Vista, go 9.0 mi. E on US 60; pass under BRP at 4.0 mi. Overnight parking in lot at Long Mt. Wayside, on L.

Camping: Hog Camp Gap campsite; Cow Camp Shelter; primitive campsite on USFS 507

Forget that long flight to Scotland to walk the Highlands' open ridges. The panoramic views from the grassy knolls of Tar Jacket Ridge and Cold Mt. are waiting. They are easy to ascend for hikers of any ability and they are just a short drive from the quaint Virginia village of Lexington, a combination that makes for a fine European-style ramble.

This hike's two expansive miles of upland open grasses and shrubs offer more than views of nearby valleys and distant mountains. Blossoms of stiff gentian and lady's-slipper provide an up-close lesson in the evolution of these open ridges from cleared pasture back to forest. In fact, were it not for the ongoing mowing and controlled burning by the USFS and the Natural Bridge AT Club

(NBATC), which maintains this section of the AT, prickly coralberry shrubs would begin that process by completely overtaking the grassy summit of Cold Mt. Efforts to keep the pastures open demonstrate the delicate balance between natural ecosystems and the human history preserved along the AT corridor.

One safety precaution bears noting before you head for the trailhead. The open walking that makes Tar Jacket Ridge and Cold Mt. such treats creates a serious threat to hikers in the event of an electrical storm. In summer's thunderstorm season, consult local weather forecasts and don't be fooled by sunny skies that contradict the forecasts. Conditions can change quickly. On the other hand, a surprise autumn snow shower atop these ridges can be a storybook come alive if you have good soles on your boots and a walking stick to steady the descent. In a word, dress for surprises. This hike can reasonably be handled traveling in either direction. It is described here north to south so that hikers who prefer to avoid the steep climb up Bald Knob can enjoy it on the way down instead.

From Salt Log Gap at the USFS 63 trailhead the AT heads south, ascending Tar Jacket Ridge through a series of switchbacks. It is a quick ascent, but never too challenging, thanks to the excellent trail planning of the NBATC—and the payoff will come quickly. In spring, scattered saplings, offspring of the few remaining apple trees along the way up, provide a colorful floor show of blossoms before serving as snacks for white-tailed deer. In autumn, when the decrepit ancient apple tree to the right of the trail has dropped its fruit, early evening hikers who go quietly might come upon spotted fawns and their mother enjoying supper.

The switchbacks continue, a bit sharper and steeper all the while, until 1.3 mi., when suddenly it seems that all of Virginia appears below the open summit of Tar Jacket Ridge. The summits to the left are The Priest, Little Priest, The Cardinal, The Friar, and Little Friar. A stone wall, through which the trail passes, is a reminder of the region's former days as high-elevation grazing land.

The stone wall will reappear in several places over some 12 mi. The persistence of the structure over so many miles suggests a different class of farmer than inhabited much of the Blue Ridge to the north in what is now Shenandoah National Park, where subsistence farmers held token livestock to augment the game they hunted and the berries and mushrooms they gathered in the forest. Here in the southern Blue Ridge the 12-mi. stone wall indicates a wealthy farmer with both land to enclose and hands available to do it. Local histories about this wall conflict over whether the structure was built by slave labor or by the hired hands of an early ridge baron.

The AT dips, then, at 1.6 mi., regains 100 ft. to the second crest, where the commanding view demands a rest stop atop Tar Jacket Ridge. As with the names of many of the mountains of the Blue Ridge, Tar Jacket's has changed over time to suit the fancy of locals or the function of the hillside. According to the ATC guidebook to the region, the tale passed down by an early president of the NBATC is that the dense, thorny thicket that dominated the ridge after its grazing days ended would literally t'ar your jacket, as pronounced in the vernacular.

At 1.8 mi. the trail begins a casual 300-ft. descent through what remains of the chestnut forest. Once the dominant hardwood species of the Appalachians, but destroyed by blight in the early 20th century, now only dispersed saplings push their way up beneath the oaks and black walnuts. Once so plentiful that cows and sheep grazed the ridge upon the nuts that covered the ground, the saplings of today survive just briefly before succumbing to the blight.

At 2.2 mi. the trail emerges from the woods and enters the narrow valley of Hog Camp Gap. If the name Hog Camp Gap sounds too authentic to be made up, it should. The open pasture here, like the balds of Tar Jacket and Cold Mt., was cleared for warm weather grazing in the early 19th century. In another stroke of utilitarian place naming, the gap on the other side of Cold Mt., to be visited on this hike, is known as Cow Camp Gap.

Camping is permitted in the meadow of Hog Camp Gap, which is also accessible by car on gravel USFS 48. At times this accessibility gives the meadow the atmosphere of a festival of campers, but finding solitude in the meadow or in the surrounding forest is easy enough. From a tent nestled among the tall grasses, the meadow is a terrific spot for stargazing, not to mention watching the superb sunsets and sunrises the spot affords. Unprotected but reliable springs are located 150 yd. along a marked side trail. A more vigorous spring, albeit requiring a hike in itself to get to, lies 0.4 mi. west on USFS 48. This road makes an early exit possible if you have arranged to have a car here (see "Trailhead access").

Crossing USFS 48 and passing through a wooden gate, the AT begins a steady, but gradual, 525-ft. ascent of Cold Mt. Once again, remains of the stone wall appear; the climb continues through shagbark hickory. Glimpses through the trees of Elk Pond Mt. and Spy Rock, followed by a curious, overhanging chunk of granite and, in season, the yellow lady's-slipper nearly underfoot all combine to take the attention away from the climb.

At 2.7 mi., after a nearly half-mile ascent, the trail finds level ground and a grassy road, which leads 300 yd. to the awesome openness of Cold Mt.—but not before stopping for another view of Spy Rock, The Priest, The Cardinal, Little Priest, and the Friar, plus Rocky Mt. There is also an open view of Tar Jacket Ridge from the kind of vantage point that always makes a hiker ask: Did I really just hike over that mountain? Continue ascending for the next 0.8 mi. until reaching the summit at 3.5 mi., where the trail crosses open, grassy knolls at the top of the world, or so it seems. Cattle that grazed atop Cold Mt. in the 19th century arguably enjoyed the most expansive views of any bovines before or since. From the summit, literally dozens of peaks lie in view, most prominently the ones mentioned above. On a clear day, McAfee Knob, nearly a hundred hiking miles down the AT (see Hike #19), can be seen. From this vantage point on the right day, it seems close enough for a day hike.

Any such thoughts vanish upon closer examination of the more immediate landscape. Coralberry dominates the open crest, its dull red lending the appearance of the heather of the Scottish Highlands. Clouds form and disappear, then form again from the winds that clash from the west and northeast. It can all seem a bit unnatural. Considering that the bald summit is itself artificially induced, human-powered clouds don't seem extraordinary. The summit remains bald through regular mowing and burning, without which the coralberry and other shrubs would soon overtake the crest, followed by locusts and scrub pines and then, in several generations, a fully recovered forest. But conserving the grasslands and farming landscape atop Cold Mt. are as important to the efforts to protect the AT corri-

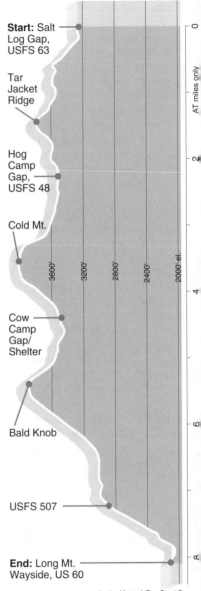

created using Maptech TopoScout ®

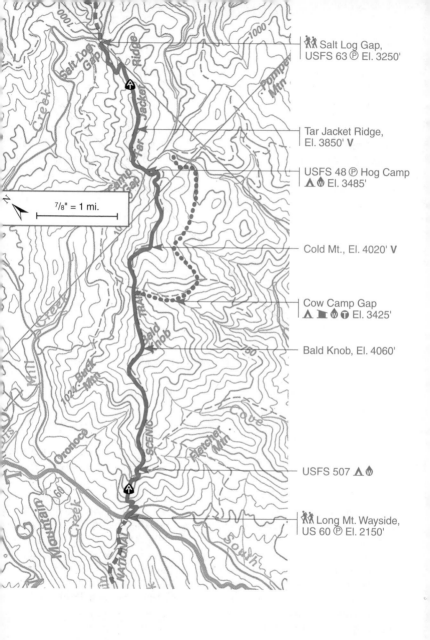

XX Salt Log Gap,
USFS 63 Ⓟ El. 3250'

Tar Jacket Ridge,
El. 3850' **V**

USFS 48 Ⓟ Hog Camp
▲ ⓦ El. 3485'

Cold Mt., El. 4020' **V**

Cow Camp Gap
▲ ▬ ⓦ Ⓣ El. 3425'

Bald Knob, El. 4060'

USFS 507 ▲ ⓦ

XX Long Mt. Wayside,
US 60 Ⓟ El. 2150'

dor as the scenery below—both are part of the story.

Leaving the open ridge at 3.5 mi., the trail descends into woods, steadily falling toward Cow Camp Gap through shag hickory and oak. Just after passing through more remnants of the stone wall, the trail passes a prominent outcropping to the right, which provides yet another view of the surrounding summits.

Descending more steeply, Dutchman's-breeches, flapping in spring breezes, share the trailside understory with the occasional bloodroot. At 4.3 mi. the trail bottoms out and crosses a grassy road at Cow Camp Gap. To the right, the blue-blazed Old Hotel Trail leads 0.7 mi. to an early exit for this hike at USFS 520 0.5 mi. south of USFS 48, on which parking is allowed.

To the left, the blue-blazed trail descends 0.5 mi., to Cow Camp Gap shelter, a delightful spot nestled into the hillside, complete with a babbling spring and the sound of the wind rushing through Cow Camp Gap above. In addition to the shelter, which rarely sees a vacancy on a summer weekend, there are campsites near the creek. Water can be taken from two nearby springs.

A detour from the AT here along the Old Hotel Trail turns this hike into a splendid, easy day-long circuit hike that wraps back around Cold Mt. and Tar Jacket Ridge. Hog Camp Gap is 2.8 mi. beyond the shelter; Salt Log Gap is another 3.2 mi. Because the final 3.8 mi. of this AT hike consists of a steady climb of Bald Knob and a

steep descent that only once pokes from the trees for a view, the Old Hotel option is for some the preferred route. The ATC's guidebook to the AT in central Virginia describes this and other fine circuits in the area.

From Cow Camp Gap, the trail starts a 600-ft.-plus, 1-mi. climb of Bald Knob. Its days as a grazing haven long gone, the mountain is now misnamed because the crest and summit have recovered to forest. By 4.8 mi. it's time for a break, and one is provided by the odd appearance of the wreckage of a navy fighter plane that went down near the trail in 1978, killing two aviators. Since then, a tale circulating among hikers recounts seeing one of the aviators peacefully walking the trail in the mists of bald Cold Mt. If the ghost story is nothing but a tall tale, facts recorded at the wreckage may have given rise to it: The only items aboard the plane to escape the inferno were a pilot's log book and a helmet, both lying beside the trail, unharmed, as if left by a hiker setting out on a walk. The wreckage lies about 45 yd. below the trail, and is best explored after autumn has taken the leaves from the trees. Back on the trail, another 150 yd. along the ascent, an overlook offers views back to Cold Mt. and the rolling farmland in the distant east. Don't be surprised to see the misty image of a navy pilot admiring the view!

For the final half-mile ascent to the forested summit of Bald Knob, the trail moves under cover of hickory and scattered mountain ash. With few opportunities to peek through the trees, Jack-in-the-pulpit and columbine attract attention to the forest floor. At 5.3 mi. a slab of granite marks the summit at 4060 ft. before the trail, almost immediately, begins a nearly 2000-ft. descent punctuated by several knobs and, as veteran AT thru-hikers would say, many PUDs—pointless ups and downs.

Along the next mile, there are a few grassy knolls that make for fine napping in the afternoon sun. Where the grasses meet the forest, called the "edge," chokecherries grow in small colonies. As appetizing as the berries appear, the name of the fruit is to be taken as warning. They are not poisonous, but these things taste awful. Still, chokecherry jam can be found in local pantries and the occasional country store. Enough sugar can cure most anything.

The trail crosses USFS 507 at 7.2 mi., just before a final, steep descent. A reliable, but unprotected, spring lies 0.4 mi. east. Hikers traveling south to north won't have another opportunity for water until the detour to Cow Camp Gap Shelter, so a full charge for the 2000-ft. climb of Bald Knob is advised. Also, 0.3 mi. east down gravel USFS 507 is a primitive campsite for a few tents. Long Mt. Wayside, called by some hikers "The Final Resting Place," referring to how strenuous they find the descent of Bald Knob, awaits at US 60 and the end of the hike.

Miles N		Elev. (ft/m)	Miles S
	NORTH		
8.1	**Start:** In **Salt Log Gap** on USFS 63; 7.1 mi. from US 60 at a point 4.0 mi. E of BRPMP 45.6; parking.	3250/990	0.0
6.8	Crest of **Tar Jacket Ridge.**	3850/1173	1.3
5.9	**Hog Camp Gap,** camping, water; cross USFS 48, parking, early exit option.	3485/1062	2.2
4.6	Summit of **Cold Mt.,** view.	4020/1226	3.5
3.8	**Cow Camp Gap:** blue-blazed Old Hotel Trail leads L (E) 0.5 mi. to **Cow Camp Gap Shelter,** campsites, springs, privy; continue E for circuit hike; to R, trail leads 0.7 mi. to USFS 520, which leads R 0.5 mi. to USFS 48 for early exit option. Begin ascent of **Bald Knob.**	3425/1044	4.3
3.3	Airplane wreckage.		4.8
3.2	View to east from ledge.		4.9
2.8	Wooded summit of **Bald Knob.**	4060/1237	5.3
0.9	Cross **USFS 507;** to L are camping, 0.3 mi., and spring, 0.4 mi.		7.2
0.0	**End:** Parking lot at **Long Mt. Wayside** on US 60, 4.0 mi. E of BRPMP 45.6 and 9.0 mi. E of Buena Vista.	2150/655	8.1
	SOUTH		

Salt Log Gap North to Fish Hatchery Rd.

Map: ATC Va. #1, Central Virginia

Route: From USFS 63 at Salt Log Gap North, over Wolfs Rocks and Porters Ridge to Fish Hatchery Rd.

Recommended direction: S to N

Distance: 8.7 mi. total; 7.7 mi. on AT

Access trail name & length: Dirt road (no name), 1.0 mi.

Elevation +/-: 3300 to 3900 to 3500 ft.

Effort: Easy

Day hike: Yes

Overnight backpacking hike: Optional

Duration: 4 to 5 hr.

Early exit option: At 1.7 mi., Greasy Spring Rd. (USFS 1176A)

Natural history feature: Wolf Rocks

Social history features: Old logging roads and railroad beds follow route of 1740s expedition

Other features: Lace Falls (Statons Creek Falls), 4.7 mi. W of S end; Montebello State Fish Hatchery (see Hike #30); groceries available in Montebello

Trailhead access: *Start:* From I-81 take exit for Buena Vista, heading E on US 60. Cross under BRP at 4.0 mi. Approximately 3.0 mi. beyond BRP, turn L onto VA 634. When road appears to end (approx. 3 mi.) veer R to continue on VA 634, which becomes USFS 63. Continue 4.1 mi. more to parking area at trail crossing. (Note: Trailhead is in Salt Log Gap North. Do not confuse with Salt Log Gap South, 22 mi. S on AT.) *End:* From Montebello, head E on VA 56 for 1.2 mi. to VA 690 and sign for Montebello State Fish Hatchery. Turn R onto VA 690 toward hatchery; VA 690 becomes dirt USFS road; proceed to large parking area on L. On foot, continue on road past gate and up steep hill 1.0 mi. to AT.

Camping: Piney River (North Fork) and Porters Field campsites; Seeley-Woodworth Shelter; Montebello Camping and Fishing Resort (see Hike #30)

Although some parts of this hike are rocky and call for extra caution, this is, overall, a relatively easy hike, with short, gradual inclines and frequent downward dips. The hike starts in Salt Log Gap North at USFS 63 and, as it heads toward Wolf Rocks, at 3900 ft. the highest point on this hike, the AT touches upon a bit of Virginia's early commerce. The term "Salt Log" refers to fallen logs in which notches were cut and filled with salt for livestock. Raising livestock was one of the main trades of the area in the early 1900s.

Another profitable trade was the lumber business. The forests of the surrounding area were largely stripped of their timber before World War II. From 1916 to 1938 the South River Lumber Co. set up shop in the area, laying down 57 mi. of railroad track.

Timberlands of profitable trees were estimated to contain 60 percent chestnut and 10 percent yellow-poplar, with the remainder coming from oak and various softwoods. The company brought 100 million board feet from the area before the chestnut blight and the Great Depression, coupled with enough heavy floods to wipe out all the bridges, put it out of business.

Leftwich Timber, later known as the Woodson Lumber Co., also took advantage of the rich area forests and rivaled the South River business. The Piney River-area company built many miles of track and enjoyed great success until the blight and the depression forced it to fold as well. Eventually, the cut-over timberlands were sold to the USFS. Now, all that remains of this early industrial boom are old railroad beds, which the AT crosses and follows frequently throughout this section.

As a result of the early commerce that took place along this section of the AT, the surrounding forest is a mix of knotty, old oaks and hickory trees towering over younger offspring. The newer growth paints the forest bright green in spring and summer. With just a smattering of evergreens, the forest is dominated by deciduous trees that turn a delightful spectrum of red, orange, and yellow in early fall.

Beginning at USFS 63 in Salt Log Gap, head north and ascend through a thick forest of pine and oak. In spring, look for a stray white apple blossom or two, signs of an old apple orchard that once thrived in the area but is now overshadowed by hardwoods. The dirt and gravel surface of the trail and extremely gradual incline make for an easy start.

The climb lasts a mere 0.3 mi. and soon you are descending as the AT bears left around a sloping ridge crest and passes down a series of wide, flat rock steps. The rocks may be slippery after a recent rain, but are securely embedded in the surrounding soil and are otherwise easy to cross. As the trail continues to make a gradual descent, it becomes dotted with moss-covered rocks that make it slippery in some spots but passage overall remains quite manageable.

A 1.0 mi. the trail levels and also narrows to barely more than 2 ft. wide. Thick hardwoods drop off to the right of the trail as it follows the crest of Rocky Mt. approximately 250 ft. above you on the left. Paralleling the overshadowing crestline, the trail continues to fall and rise, never climbing more than 50 yd. at a time. In late fall, dried oak leaves crunch below your feet. The oak's flat, saucer-like acorns, a signature of the tree, dot the trail. However, most of the nuts are quickly retrieved by gray squirrels, a noisy bunch throughout this stretch.

At 1.2 mi. the AT dips into a low saddle and crosses USFS 246, a wide dirt road. On the far side of USFS 246 climb up a log staircase and begin another short ascent into another thick stand of oak and hickory trees. If you are able to find a few nuts that haven't been shuffled away by squirrels or other forest rodents, notice the differences between the acorn and the hickory nut, which, besides lacking a cap, is longer and lighter brown and may be more difficult to spot than acorns. Hickory nuts are a forest delicacy. You may even see a wild turkey feasting on them.

Make a switchback to the right and cross another old road (1.3 mi.), much narrower and rockier than the first. In the next 0.4 mi. the AT crosses an abandoned logging railroad bed and two old woods roads before reaching the intersection with Greasy Spring Rd. (USFS 1176A) at 1.7 mi. Greasy Spring Rd. is believed to have gotten its name from dishwater thrown into a nearby spring branch by logging company cooks. To reach the spring, go right on the road for 285 yd., then follow faint former AT blazes. Turn right at a double blaze and go 130 yd. to an unprotected, unmarked spring. Although the water should be treated, no signs of cooking grease are apparent today.

To exit the AT at this point, follow Greasy Spring Rd. to the left 0.2 mi. to a fork. To the left is USFS 246, where there is limited parking. The fork to the right continues on USFS 1176 for less than one mile to southern trailhead parking. *Note:* Parking on USFS 246 is not recommended after recent rains, floods, or snowmelts. Wet conditions make this route extremely muddy and difficult to pass. Cars can easily become stuck.

Beyond Greasy Spring Rd. the AT climbs another set of log stairs. In spring and early summer look for drooping red blooms of columbine, identified by the bright yellow stamens peeking from the blossom. Flypoison is also populous here in June and July. Its leafless stem juts above the other plants to display a cluster of tiny white flowers.

As the trail continues upward, the climb steepens. Several loose rocks require cautious footwork, especially in the fall and winter months when they are camouflaged by fallen leaves or snow. Pass an unmarked spring at 1.9 mi. and continue the upward climb. As the trail ascends through the heavy woods, yellow birch trees join the mix. The tree is identified by its shiny, yellowish bark, which curls away from the tree in narrow strips.

Just beyond the 2.0 mi. mark the trail gives way to large, loose rocks for a short but unsteady stint. These 2-to-3-ft. granite boulders are spotted with patches of moss. This 25-yd. section is difficult to cross, but, once you make it through, a smooth trail and secure footing resumes.

At 2.6 mi. the AT reaches the high point of the hike on the crest of a ridge. Granite boulders, some over 200 ft. high, are strewn throughout the wooded area. With some careful maneuvering, and the help of a few fallen trees, you can hoist yourself up to the tops of these boulders for a look out over the Piney River valley below. If you'd rather not work that hard for a photo opportunity, continue 0.1 mi. ahead to Wolf Rocks. At

3900 ft., Wolf Rocks sets the stage for a panoramic view of Rocky Mt., Elk Pond Mt., Main Top, Spy Rock, Three Ridges, and The Priest (see Hikes #30 and #31). This view is particularly photogenic in early fall when the shot is enhanced by vibrant shades of red, orange, and yellow. Also, the area surrounding Wolf Rocks differs from the lower forest. Thickets of rhododendron and a few hemlock trees keep the spot green throughout the seasons.

Beyond Wolf Rocks, the trail descends toward the North Fork of Piney River. In spring, look for bright pink, star-shaped flowers that burst from the surrounding laurel trees. Although you might see a white-tailed deer munching on the lush green foliage, don't be tempted to join the salad bar. Mountain laurel's foliage is toxic to humans. Even its flower's nectar, while harmless to bees, can be fatal to humans. As a result, honey found in these parts is to be avoided.

At 3.2 mi. make a wide swing to the left and continue downward, away from the ridge. Keep an eye on the blazes as the trail begins following an old road, then takes a left at a fork. Just beyond the fork, there is a campsite to the right of the trail. The flat, open area is wide enough for two to three tents and includes a fire pit. On the AT 60 yd. beyond the campsite is a water source, a branch of the North Fork of the Piney River. Crossing over the river, the trail cuts through a thick

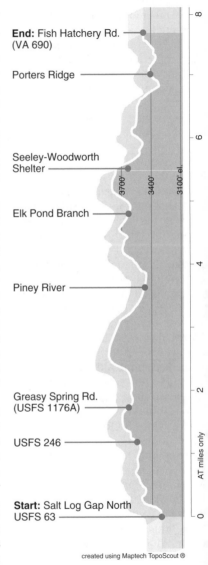

created using Maptech TopoScout ®

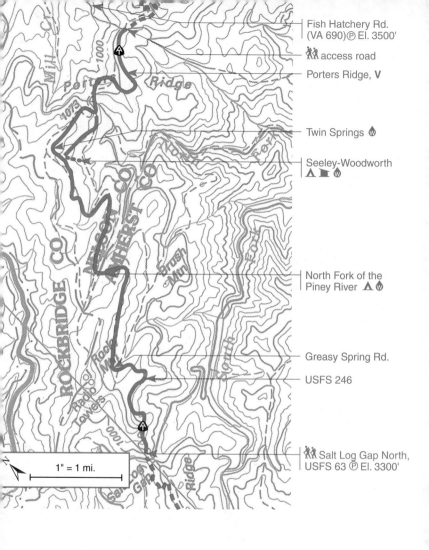

Fish Hatchery Rd.
(VA 690) Ⓟ El. 3500'

🚶🚶 access road

Porters Ridge, **V**

Twin Springs 💧

Seeley-Woodworth
▲ 🏕 💧

North Fork of the
Piney River ▲ 💧

Greasy Spring Rd.

USFS 246

🚶🚶 Salt Log Gap North,
USFS 63 Ⓟ El. 3300'

1" = 1 mi.

grove of hemlock and beech, then, 50 yd. further on, reaches a second branch of the river.

According to local tales, Parson Robert Rose owned 33,000 acres in this area in the 1740s, and, in 1747, built his house, "Bear Garden," at the intersection of the Tye and Piney rivers. On December 6, 1749, Rose, accompanied by John Blyre, a nearby neighbor, and Henry Bunch, a surveyor, set out on a three-day exploration of the area. They followed the north bank of the North Fork of Piney River to Elk Pond Branch, ascended along Elk Pond Branch, passing through the gap between Porters Ridge and Elk Pond Mt. that is now known as Porters Field and camped at the head of Mill Creek. Backtracking the next day they reached the North Fork of Piney River and followed it to its source and Lovingston Spring. The AT picks up part of these explorers' path as it intersects the North Fork of the Piney River at this point.

Another 50 yd. beyond the second Piney River branch, the AT crosses an old road and an old logging railroad bed. As you pass these points, you will cross from Amherst County to Nelson County. For the next mile, the trail makes an easy climb upward toward Elk Pond Mt., passing through more dense stands of shagbark hickory and oak. This type of hickory gets its name from the long strips of bark that flake away like feathers from the tall trees.

After cresting the ridge at 4.4 mi., make a sharp left and cross over the top of Elk Pond Mt. At 5.1 mi. the trail swings left again as you make your way across the shoulder of this 3750-ft. peak. The trail continues to follow a slight upward grade for the next 0.4 mi., then reaches a blue-blazed trail at 5.5 mi. The blue-blazed trail leads 120 yd. to the right to the Seeley-Woodworth Shelter. A gushing spring behind the lean-to makes a refreshing (although unprotected) water source. If you haven't dipped into your lunch sack yet, this is a fine place to do so. Old hardwoods keep the area well shaded in spring and summer. In fall, try your luck again with another search for hickory nuts and acorns.

Still making a gradual ascent, the AT enters a hemlock and rhododendron grove at 5.8 mi. where it passes Twin Springs. One spring is 66 yd. to the left of the trail. Its twin runs 25 ft. to your right. Less than 200 yd. further, pass another spring on the right. All three springs are unprotected. From the springs, ascend slightly before making a steep descent toward Porters Field. As the trail begins to level (6.7 mi.), turn left onto an old logging road that follows the path of Rose and his comrades to Porters Field (formerly Porters Ridge).

The low, open area is an excellent camping site, popular among AT thru-hikers. An unprotected spring cuts through the area, providing a convenient water source. The absence of trees permits some shade-intolerant plants to flourish near the field. Look for hawthorn bushes, a thorny shrub that bursts with white or light pink blossoms in late spring. Don't get too close; its sharp thorns provide a thick coat of armor around the plant that can be quite painful if touched. Wild crabapple trees also grow along the edge of the field and produce pretty pink blossoms in spring.

Leaving Porters Field keep one eye on the blazes as the trail follows a road to the right, then turns left, and, in 100 ft., bears left again, leaving the road and beginning a steep ascent. The second of two roads to the left leads to a small campsite and unprotected spring. The other road was a logging railroad bed in the early 1900s. At 7.0 mi., after a steep and rocky climb, the trail reaches the crest of Porters Ridge and provides a view of the 4040-ft. wooded summit of Maintop Mt., its rocky outcrops abutting the northeast horizon.

As you begin a steep descent through a shagbark hickory grove, in winter the leafless trees permit views of Spy Rock, The Priest, and Little Priest straight ahead as well as continuing glimpses of Maintop. Although most of this view will be obscured by leaves during the spring and summer seasons, occasional peeks at Maintop are a year-round treat. The AT continues to cut steeply downward over loose, rocky terrain. At 7.7 mi. turn left onto the dirt road; it leads downhill 1.0 mi. to Fish Hatchery Rd. and the northern end of this hike.

If you are retrieving a car from Salt Log Gap North, a detour to Statons Creek Falls is recommended. Turn left out of the parking area and continue along USFS 63, which becomes VA 634, then turns right onto VA 633. Reach Statons Creek Falls 4.7 mi. west of the trailhead. Also known as Lace (pronounced Lay-cee) Falls, the cascading waters of Statons Creek are worth taking the long way home. For a better look, follow the steep path toward the stream gorge. As the water tumbles over the rocky creekbed, its delicate splashing is mesmerizing. Don't be lulled into a false sense of security; use extreme caution near the falls. Wet rocks make the area very dangerous. Enjoy the view, but do watch your step.

Between the northern end of this hike and the southern end of Hike #30, the AT covers 3.7 mi. of rugged terrain, climbing nearly 900 ft. to the top of Maintop Mt., then dropping over 700 ft. to reach the beginning of the next hike. There are some scenic views of the surrounding mountainsides from Maintop and those planning to spend a few days in the area may wish to check it out. However, these miles have been omitted from this book in order to make conquering the 3100-ft. climb to the top of The Priest (see Hike #30) an enjoyable one-day excursion.

HIKE #29   Itinerary

Miles N		NORTH	Elev. (ft/m)	Miles S
Total: 8.7 mi. with access on dirt road.				
1.0	**Access:** Go downhill on dirt road (becomes VA 690) to parking lot at State Fish Hatchery, 1.7 mi. S of Montebello.		3500/1066	1.0
7.7	**End:** Turn L onto dirt road.			0.0
7.0	Crest of **Porters Ridge,** view.			0.7
6.7	**Porters Field,** camping, water; begin ascent of Elk Pond Mt.			1.0
5.8	**Twin Springs.**			1.9
5.5	Blue-blazed trail to R leads 120 yd. to **Seeley-Woodworth Shelter,** camping, water.		3770/1149	2.2
4.8	Top of **Elk Pond Mt.**			2.9
3.6	**Campsite;** in 60 yd., cross two branches of the **North Fork of the Piney River.**			4.1
2.7	**Wolf Rocks;** view.		3900/1189	5.0
1.7	Cross **Greasy Spring Rd. (USFS 1176A);** spring 415 yd. to R.			6.0
1.2	Cross **USFS 246.**			6.5
0.0	**Start:** At parking lot in **Salt Log Gap North** on **USFS 63;** 15.2 mi. NE of Buena Vista.		3300/1006	7.7

SOUTH

Cash Hollow to Tye River

Maps: ATC Va. #1, Central Virginia
Route: Through Washington NF from VA 826 over The Priest and across Cripple Creek to Tye River
Recommended direction: S to N
Distance: 6.2 mi. total; 5.7 mi. on AT
Access trail name & length: VA 826, 0.5 mi.
Elevation +/-: 3320 to 4060 to 970 ft.
Effort: Strenuous
Day hike: Yes
Overnight backpacking hike: Optional
Duration: 3 to 5 hr.
Early exit option: None
Natural history features: The Priest; Cripple Creek
Social history features: Lesene SF, 5.0 mi. from the largest chestnut planting and research program in the U.S.; Montebello State Fish Hatchery, 3.7 mi. from S end

Other features: Views from The Priest, Little Priest, and Tye River overlook
Trailhead access: *Start:* From Montebello, head E on VA 56 to VA 826; turn R and proceed 4.2 mi. to parking area at Crabtree Meadows primitive camping area. *Note:* VA 826 forks at 3.7 mi.; make sharp L. From campground, continue on foot along VA 826 for 0.5 mi. to AT. *End:* From Montebello, head E on VA 56 8.2 mi. to trailhead parking lot on R at Tye River. There is room for approximately 20 cars. Overnight parking is permitted. For alternate route, see Hike #31.
Camping: Primitive camping at Crabtree Meadows (no camping or campfires within 500 ft. of the Crabtree Falls Trail and parking areas); The Priest Shelter and where permitted along trail

T his rough section of the AT takes you over The Priest, at 4063 ft. the highest point of the Religious Range, which also includes Little Priest, The Cardinal, and The Friar. The Priest to the south and Three Ridges to the north form the portal of the Tye River valley, which lies between the Blue Ridge and Piedmont mountains. On the northern edge of The Priest, the trail drops 3100 ft. in 4 mi. to reach the Tye River. In the crystalline rock that lies below

the plants and trees of the area, geologists have discovered traces of the mineral zircon dating back more than 1.8 billion years, making it much older than the rock of this area. Scientists believe the Religious Range must have begun forming during an ancient mountain-building time, and the zircon crystals eroded and washed away, blending with the sand on the beach. Later, when the African plate collided with what is now Virginia, the beach, with the zircon crystals, was thrust up into the mountains you will pass over today.

There is a bounty of wildflowers throughout this hike. In the spring, look for trillium, fire pink, rock twist, wild geranium, cut-leaved toothwort, and a variety of violets. If you look extra closely, you might also spot a Turk's-cap lily near the top of The Priest. The long, orange-and-brown-spotted petals of this tall, graceful lily bend backward far enough to touch one another behind the blossom, thus resembling a Turkish headpiece.

VA 826 meets the AT in a sag called Shoe Creek Hill (3320 ft.) There's no warm-up time in this section; once you turn left onto the AT The Priest greets you with an immediate ascent. The trail climbs swiftly through a forest dominated by chestnut oaks and a smattering of pure chestnuts. If your great-grandparents happened to hike through this section, they saw a different forest, one bursting with hardy, towering chestnuts. However, in the last century, the American chestnut has all but disappeared, wiped away by an imported blight that has left only a few stands. Today, the rare chestnuts that do grace the trail barely reach 20 ft. and usually live only long enough to produce one or two seed crops before they are also overcome by the blight. In 1983 a group at West Virginia University organized the American Chestnut Foundation, which is working to restore what was once one of America's favorite trees.

Oaks, however, are plentiful here, providing you with several shady spots in which to escape hot summer sun as you continue to climb. In fall and winter, when most of the leaves have fallen, you can see The Priest in the distance, beckoning—or taunting —you. The Priest has been an area landmark since the early 1700s. Some say it got its name from the DuPriest family, who lived in the region and may have owned the mountain. Others believe a prominent 18th-century pastor, Robert Rose (see Hike #29), named the entire Religious Range. Still others claim a small monastery was once located nearby, and the peak is named for a solitary priest who lived on the mountain.

At 0.7 mi. an unmarked trail to the right leads to the 3733-ft. summit of Little Priest. The side trail takes a 200-yd. dip before making a 1.5-mi. rise to the summit. According to legend, British Maj. Thomas Massie, a colony sympathizer, built a fortified residence in the saddle between Big and Little Priest mountains, which he planned to occupy in the event of British victory.

Beyond the Little Priest side trail, the AT passes a tall chunk of granite on the right before making a sharp left and heading northward. A blue-blazed side trail at 0.9 mi. leads straight ahead 0.1 mi. to The Priest Shelter. Built in 1960 by the USFS, the shelter is now jointly maintained by USFS and the Natural Bridge AT Club. The shelter sleeps six and is flanked by several tent sites.

If you've already worked up a thirst, and you probably have, the shelter offers a real treat. On the left side of the shelter (as you stand facing it) there is a deliciously cold (though unprotected) spring. Indulge! But do save plenty of water for later—your workout has hardly begun. In the spring, wildflowers are plentiful near the shelter. Look for bursts of white trillium, blending with purple and yellow violets.

Beyond the shelter the trail crosses three side paths to the left as it leads through a series of twisted oak trees and an occasional wild cherry tree. Although all of the paths offer some viewing opportunities, the best views are from the fourth side trail (1.3 mi.), which leads 50 yd. to the left to large sandstone formations. If you hoist yourself up onto the boulders, you will get a panoramic view of Elk Pond and Maintop mountains to the left, Big Spy Mt. straight ahead, and Devils Knob, Black Rock Mt., and Humpback Mt. to the right. In the immediate foreground a prominent ridge, Pinnacle Ridge, stretches before you. When the construction of the BRP forced several miles of the AT to be relocated (see Hike #20), mostly onto USFS land, the narrow, rocky ridge was considered as an alternative route.

As you continue toward the wooded summit of The Priest, look for Turk's-cap. The blossoms are at their peak from June to August. Thick carpets of moss are also prevalent on The Priest, and it is dotted in early spring with pink phlox.

At 1.4 mi. a narrow ridge leads to a small clearing and another dry campsite. Beyond the site, the trail crosses over the top of The Priest (no views from here) and begins an immediate descent, dropping nearly 3100 ft. over 37 long switchbacks.

Although water is scarce on the mountain, there are plenty of prime dry campsites. The oak, cherry, and remaining chestnut trees keep the area well shaded and the high ridges boast frequent cool breezes. Pass another campsite at 1.6 mi. and bear left, descending a steep, narrow ridge. Watch your step. The drop-off to the east is straight down. Take it slow and enjoy the peaceful setting. In spots where the trees are less dense and bits of sunlight shine through the leaves, try to spot an elderberry bush. Its small, bright red fruit gives away its identity. A gray catbird or brown thrasher might help you locate the shrub. There aren't enough elderberry to create a vital food source, but the birds relish the few berries they can find.

Continuing down the razor-edged ridgeline, you will catch your first glimpse of the Tye River valley through the trees at 2.0 mi. In 1969 Hurricane Camille unleashed devastating floods through the valley, causing more than one hundred deaths in the surrounding Nelson County. More than a mile of the AT was completely washed away. Today, views of the valley include large Cambrian sandstone and quartzite formations. Hidden for 350 million years, the rocks were uncovered by the floods. The gorge area offers splendid views, but the waters can be extremely rough, especially after a heavy rain.

The trail levels off as it passes through a narrow saddle (2.1 mi.), and then continues a much more gradual descent. A mile further on, the trail descends a 30-ft.-long set of steps and then begins another series of switchbacks. Passing glimpses of two of the Three Ridges come into view.

At the 3.0 mi. mark, the trail reaches a rocky outlook on the right. Offering a spectacular view of the Tye River and Silver Creek valleys, over 2000 ft. below, this is a good spot for lunch. Rested and ready to press onward, continue downward to the banks of Cripple Creek. As you make another steep descent over sharp, narrow switchbacks, the energy you spend trying to avoid tumbling over the edge will make the earlier climb seem like a cakewalk. In autumn, a coating of oak leaves adds color to the forest floor, but it also makes the trek down even trickier.

Your efforts pay off at 4.4 mi. when, with the major switchbacks behind you, Cripple Creek rolls gently ahead. A log bridge takes you over, and rocks near the creek's edge seem as through they were designed to be a resting area. You'll be thankful for waterproof boots as you forge onward, crossing two more branches of the creek without the luxury of a footbridge. The area is quite damp, especially after recent rains. In early

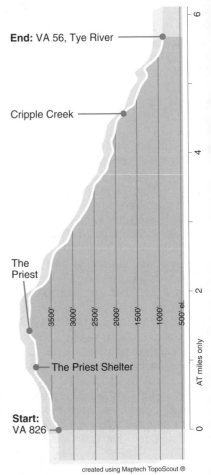

created using Maptech TopoScout ®

spring, look for toothwort. The moisture-loving plant sports dainty white blossoms, but is best identified by its wide leaves with toothlike lobes.

Bear left onto an old road (4.7 mi.) and then, in 25 yd., cut to the right to

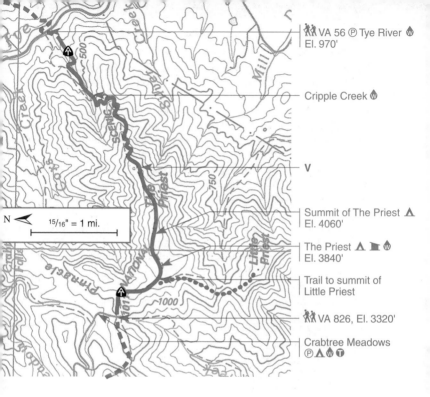

N ← ¹⁵/₁₆" = 1 mi.

🚶🚶 VA 56 Ⓟ Tye River ⍵
El. 970'

Cripple Creek ⍵

V

Summit of The Priest ▲
El. 4060'

The Priest ▲ ◼ ⍵
El. 3840'

Trail to summit of
Little Priest

🚶🚶 VA 826, El. 3320'

Crabtree Meadows
Ⓟ▲⍵Ⓣ

continue downward over a narrow trail. Continue to watch for white blazes as you turn onto another old road 0.1 mi. further, then make a sharp turn to the right onto yet another former roadbed. The trail moves from old roads to narrow pathways to well-worn trail that might have once been roads, and the entire final stretch of this hike can get a bit confusing. The AT is well marked. If you go a few feet without seeing a white blaze, retrace your steps.

You are apt to get so tuned in to keeping up with the trail that you will hardly notice civilization creeping up on you. Just as you begin to feel confident that you have missed a turn, Tye River and VA 56, with the trailhead parking lot on the right, stretch out before you. (For more on Tye River, see Hike #31).

After conquering The Priest you deserve a treat. Turn right out of parking area and head east on VA 56 to the town of Tyro (1.4 mi.), where Ben & Jerry's awaits you. For a less caloric appeasement, check out Crabtree Falls, one of the most popular destinations of day hikers throughout the Blue Ridge. From the parking area at Crabtree Meadows camping area, pick up Crabtree Falls Trail to left. The 2.9-mi. blue-blazed trail traces Crabtree Creek as it connects the camping area to the Crabtree Falls parking area on VA 56. Along the way, the well-graded trail passes five scenic overlooks, each allowing an impressive view of deep blue water cascading over high rock formations. These major cascades, combined with several smaller ones, have a total fall of over 1200 ft. The trailside view from one cascade to the next is also worth

the trip. In spring, the area is overflowing with wildflowers as pink lady's-slipper, Jack-in-the-pulpit, Indian-pipe, and various other blossoms brighten your way. Rhododendron and azalea bushes also add color to the area in spring and continue to keep the area green and scenic throughout the season.

If you plan to spend a few days in the area you may be able to enjoy the Montebello Camping and Fishing Resort's variety of recreational diversions. Located 8.2 mi. west of the northern end of this hike, the site includes a 4-acre lake for fishing and swimming. There is also a smaller lake stocked with rainbow trout. Accommodations include pull-through sites with full hookups, bathing facilities, and a cabin that can sleep up to twelve. The crowds gathered around the smaller, stocked lake are mostly families with young children. The lake is so fully stocked that fishing in it may be more of a carnival game than a sport, but the excitement on the children's faces says the enjoyment of a family outing is the most important thing. The country store at the site exudes small-town charm.

Miles N	**NORTH**	Elev. (ft/m)	Miles S
Total: 6.2 mi. with access on VA 826.			
5.7	**End:** Parking area on **VA 56 at Tye River,** 8.2 mi. E of Montebello, 1.4 mi. W of Tyro.	970/296	0.0
4.6	Branch of **Cripple Creek.**		1.1
4.4	Log bridge over **Cripple Creek.**		1.3
3.0	Rocky outlook with view of Tye River.		2.7
1.6	Dry campsite.		4.1
1.4	Summit of **The Priest,** campsite.	4060/1237	4.3
1.3	Side trail to view, 50 yd. to L.		4.4
0.9	Side trail straight ahead 0.1 mi. to **The Priest Shelter,** water, camping.	3840/1170	4.8
0.7	Unmarked trail to R (1.5 mi.) to summit of Little Priest.		5.0
0.0	**Start:** VA 826 meets AT at Shoe Creek Hill.	3320/1012	5.7
0.5	**Access:** From parking area at Crabtree Meadows primitive camping area, follow VA 826 (foot traffic only) to AT. Approximately 5.6 mi. SE of Montebello.		0.5

SOUTH

Reeds Gap to Tye River

Map: ATC Va. #1, Central Virginia

Route: Through Washington NF from Reeds Gap, over Bee Mt. and Three Ridges, to Tye River

Recommended direction: N to S

Distance: 10.5 mi.

Elevation +/-: 2650 to 3970 to 1000 ft.

Effort: Moderately strenuous

Day hike: Yes

Overnight backpacking hike: Optional

Duration: 5 1/2 to 7 1/2 hr.

Early exit option: None

Natural history features: Hanging Rock; Chimney Rock; Harpers Creek

Other features: Views from Hanging Rock and Chimney Rock; junction with Mau-Har Trail; grocery store just before southern trailhead on VA 56, detour to Campbell Creek waterfall on Mau-Har Trail

Trailhead access: *Start:* From Rockfish Gap at intersection of I-64 and BRP, head S on parkway for 13.6 mi. At BRPMP 13.6, turn R and head E on VA 664 for 100 yd. to trailhead. There is ample roadside parking. Please notify ranger if you plan to park overnight. (See Hike #20.) Look for trail sign near fence on E side of cleared field. *End:* On BRP, continue S to mile 27.0, then head E on VA 56. Pass through Montebello (see Hike #30) and continue 8.2 mi. to trailhead parking lot on R (S) side of road. The town of Tyro is 1.5 mi. further E on VA 56.

Camping: Maupin Field and Harpers Creek shelters, and where permitted along trail; no camping in Reeds Gap (BRP property)

This hike guarantees a workout as it takes you up over 1300 ft. from Reeds Gap to the northernmost ridge of Three Ridges, then down even further, dropping 3000 ft. to meet Tye River. (Most of the hike is in Washington NF.) Several rock slides make the section even more strenuous. However, your efforts will not go unrewarded. As you stop to catch your breath, and you often will, you'll be treated to panoramic views of towering mountains like The Priest, and deep, rolling valleys including

those of Harpers Creek and Tye River. There is also a variety of wildflowers throughout this section, most blooming from late April to early May. Look for trillium, wild geraniums, and several types of violets, casting purple, lavender, and yellow blossoms along the trail. A camera, extra film, and plenty of water are musts. Binoculars will also be appreciated. Be sure to save a few frames of film to capture Tye River's foaming ripples and cascades at the southern end of the hike.

From the AT signs at VA 664, head southwest through an open field, then cut into a forest dominated by oak and maple trees. This hike lets you know what you are in for from the start. As you enter the woods, the AT begins a steep ascent of Meadow Mt., crossing over the first of several rock slides waiting ahead.

The rock slides were left in the wake of Hurricane Camille, a record-breaking rainstorm that tore through the area in August of 1969, dowsing some places with up to 3 ft. of rain in less than 6 hours. The rocks are loose in some spots and often quite slick, creating a tricky obstacle course even for the most surefooted. Although Camille makes most other rainstorms look like spring showers, use extra caution in all wet weather; the rocks will be slippery as well as wobbly.

Less than a mile into the hike (at 0.8 mi.), the trail crests Meadow Mt. Although the oaks and their deciduous relatives are thick around the trail, an overlook to the right offers a great view to the west. In winter, you can see the Blue Ridge Parkway carving a thin black line through the valley below. Peer hard to the south to see Meadow Mt. Campground and Torry Ridge rising in the distance. At the crest, there is a small clearing. The shady trees, nearby view, and peaceful atmosphere make a nice, although dry, campsite.

Once you've caught your breath, descend through a more sparsely wooded area. Thick undergrowth including pachysandra and a variety of ferns cover the trail in spring and summer. Keep an eye on the white blazes.

At 1.7 mi., the trail joins a wide, well-graded fire road and begins one of the few easy sections of this hike. A blue-blazed trail to the right leads 100 yd. to the Maupin Field Shelter and the Mau-Har Trail. The shelter is maintained by the Tidewater AT Club and the USFS and accommodates up to six overnight visitors. There are also several tent sites near the shelter. For a tasty, cold treat, be sure to visit the spring in back of the building. This is the last chance you'll get to fill up your water bottles until Harpers Creek Shelter on the southern side of the ridge at 7.9 mi.; the summit is dry. This water should be treated. In late spring and early summer, don't be surprised to find a caretaker at the site, tending to the shelter or pruning the nearby grounds. AT traffic and Mau-Har users combine to make this a heavily traveled area.

From the shelter, the Mau-Har trail leads 3.0 mi. to the south, tracing the narrow Campbells Creek. The route takes hikers past a 40-ft. waterfall before rejoining the AT at mi. 8.8 on this hike. Many day hikers use this side trail to shave a few miles (almost 4) off this section. Those looking for an easier day may consider this alternative route, but be warned: there's only one waterfall on the side trail and there are several great views waiting on the AT.

Beyond this blue-blazed diversion, the AT veers off the road and to the left as it begins another steep, but mercifully short, climb, to the top of Bee Mt. The hardy stands of oak trees throughout the area make this a prime area for bird watching. As you climb, look for northern bobwhites, tufted titmice, brown thrashers, and white-breasted nuthatches searching for acorns on the trees in spring and summer. If it sounds like something is whistling through a long, metal tube, you are probably hearing the call of the veery bird. A member of the thrush family, veery project a resonant sound that is very distinct from those of other forest chirpers. The light brown and white bird is approximately 7 in. long and feeds on the ground rather than on trees. It's quite populous in these parts, but is rarely seen or heard north of Maryland.

At 2.1 mi. the AT reaches the 3300-ft. peak of Bee Mt. and a limited view to the east. Contrary to the name, bees are not any more prevalent here than at other points along the trail, although a variety of wildflowers helps ensure that the insects frequent their namesake in spring. Wild geranium is one of several plants you may find here in spring. Its purplish petals are lined with nectar guides. The dark purple veins direct bees to a white, fuzzy petal base. You'll be able to tell if the bees have already been there. After pollination, the petals drop off and the pistil lengthens.

From Bee Mt., the trail begins a steady, 2.0-mi. ascent toward the north ridge of Three Ridges. A few minor dips give you a moment to

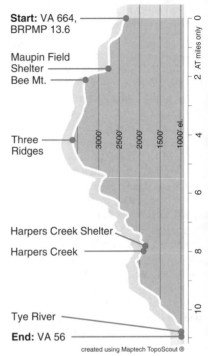

created using Maptech TopoScout ®

catch your breath, but a rocky trail and another deep rock slide keep you on your toes—and possibly on your hands and knees in some spots. There are no points for form; just do what it takes to keep your balance.

At the 3.7-mi. mark, less than half a mile before the top, the trail passes over the rocky crest of Hanging Rock, offering views to the west of Harpers Creek, Three Ridges, and The Priest. This is a good spot for a water break and a chance to break out some high-carbohydrate snacks that will give you an energy boost. This is

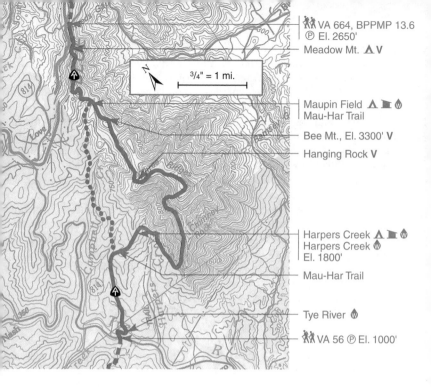

🚶🚶 VA 664, BPPMP 13.6
Ⓟ El. 2650'
Meadow Mt. ▲ V

Maupin Field ▲ ▰ ⬤
Mau-Har Trail

Bee Mt., El. 3300' V

Hanging Rock V

Harpers Creek ▲ ▰ ⬤
Harpers Creek ⬤
El. 1800'

Mau-Har Trail

Tye River ⬤

🚶🚶 VA 56 Ⓟ El. 1000'

also the time to take out the camera and snap a few photographs of The Priest, towering in the southwest. This is a much better view than you'll get at the top.

Once you've stopped panting and taken some time to enjoy the view and the steady, light breeze, continue half a mile beyond Hanging Rock to the north peak of Three Ridges. At 3970 ft. this flat, wooded dome trends north and south to form the northern wall of the Tye River valley. You'll be glad the climb is over, but the ensu-

ing descent is the only reward you'll get. Thick stands of oak and maple trees obstruct the view in spring, summer, and early fall. You can look into Harpers Creek valley in winter, but the view from Hanging Rock is much better.

The trail crosses rocky switchbacks ahead as it begins a long, steep descent. There are more overlooks along the way as you make your way across the second ridge of Three Ridges. In fall, the red, yellow, and orange foliage in Tye River valley create more photo opportunities. This area is currently being considered for national wilderness designation.

Just past the second ridge (5.9 mi.), Chimney Rocks on the right create another interesting diversion. The projecting granite formations get their name from their long, rectangular, blocklike appearance. On a foggy day, especially after a good fall rainstorm, the rocks look like smokestacks. You may want to pause for a few photos here, but if you can hold out for a short while longer, don't break out the lunch sacks just yet— there's a better spot a little further ahead. From Chimney Rocks, follow a rocky trail over the third ridge of Three Ridges and come to a massive, flat, rock overlook on the right. The area is the size of a small living room and offers a panoramic view of The Priest and Harpers Creek valley that's better than anything on television. This is *the* spot for lunch, or just to sit in awe for a while as you look out into deep, winding valley.

For the next 1.6 mi. the trail descends, steeply at times, over extremely rocky terrain. During this downward trek, the AT crosses at least four more rock slides. Whether it's an illusion caused by fatigue, or a function of being on the less sunny side of the ridge, the rocks on the downward slope are wetter and even more wobbly than those the trail covered on the earlier part of this hike. As you make this rocky descent, the valley below is frequently visible; switchbacks toss it back and forth from right to left. Near the beginning of the descent, the narrow ridge actually allows views on both sides of the trail for a short distance. Further down, the trail grows quite narrow, revealing steep drop-offs to the left.

At 7.9 mi. the trail turns to the left and joins an old road as it continues its gradual descent. A road to the right leads 130 yd. to Harpers Creek Shelter (1800 ft.). The shelter was built by the USFS and can accommodate six overnighters. There are also plenty of tent sites on the flat, open grounds that surround the structure. The forest is far enough from the shelter to provide room for tents and a fire ring, but close enough to keep the area cool in spring and summer. Water is available from Harpers Creek, which crosses 75 ft. in front of the shelter. Head up creek a few feet and look for a spring on the left. Although the water should be treated, this is a good place to refill. It's the first source of water since Maupin Field Shelter.

Beyond the shelter the trail passes by the low remains of a stone wall outlining a square area. The area inside the square is clear, except for a few small trees, and has a fire ring, a rocky mound, and plenty of room for tents. Harpers Creek, just ahead, provides a close enough water source to make this a good spot in which to camp.

Although the water levels of Harpers Creek can be high and the current is known to be swift, this is another favorite spot on the hike. The creek trips over large rocks, creating a small waterfall effect. Up creek, large rocks provide a podium from which to view the water tumbling over smaller rocks below. The storybook setting makes climbing over all those other slippery rocks worth the trip.

After a wet and wobbly trek across the creek, the AT trends upward for approximately 1 mi. The well-graded dirt trail makes this gradual climb so easy you'll hardly notice the slight ascent. Look for bright white trillium blossoms as you climb through the area in spring. The plant, with its broad leaves and three showy petals, thrives in moist, wooded areas.

At 8.8 mi. the AT meets the southern end of the blue-blazed Mau-Har Trail, which enters from the right. A few feet further on the AT reaches a ridge. The trees are thicker here than they were near the creek, making the area much darker. Beyond the short peak, the AT slopes downward again.

The descent is moderate in the beginning, but becomes steeper as it sets into another series of switchbacks. Logs built into the trail to slow erosion also help slow momentum and keep you from tumbling down the hill.

The steepness of the trail over the next mile forces you into a galloplike gait. Although you'll be concentrating on keeping your footing, be on the lookout for white blazes, especially double blazes, which indicate a sharp turn ahead. If you miss the double blaze near the 9.8-mi. mark, you are apt to gallop right over a barbed-wire fence to the left of the trail. Beyond the fence lie a wide pasture and, in the distance, a silo, barn, farmhouse, and several cows. This isn't typical wildlife viewing, but it is a picturesque setting.

Beyond the farm, the trail narrows significantly as it continues to descend. Just as you start to feel sure that the end of the hike is near and all the hard parts are behind you, the trail makes an abrupt ascent. The climb is just enough to command your attention, but not enough to cause concern. In less than 50 ft. the steep descent continues, as the trail passes over a series of wide steps built by conscientious AT maintainers.

You'll know the end is near when the trees start to thin, allowing glimpses of Tye River rumbling below. The only way across the river at this point is a high, 148-ft.-long suspension bridge. The view from the bridge is an exquisite topping to an already scenic stretch of trail. This is when you'll be glad you saved a few frames of film. As you cross the bridge and look out on the wide, blue waterway, you'll forget any aches you may have felt along the trail.

Tent sites at both ends of the bridge and several deep swimming holes make this area a popular spot for local residents. Don't expect to have this peaceful moment all to yourself. Instead, expect to see groups of people picnicking on nearby rocks, students, possibly from nearby Southern Virginia College, collecting water samples, and artists sketching in their pads or painting easel-held canvases. Beyond the bridge, the AT crosses VA 56, and brings you back to your second car.

Note: Approximately 2 mi. west of the northern end of this hike, Sherando Lake Campground provides an alternative to wilderness camping for hikers who want to spend a few days exploring the area, but also relish the thought of a hot shower. Located within Washington NF, the facilities feature drive-up campsites, each with a fire ring, tent platform, and picnic table. A bath house is located near the park entrance. Opportunities for swimming, fishing, and boating are available in the summer months. To access, head west on VA 664 to its end. Turn right onto VA 814; the entrance is on your right in less than a mile.

HIKE #31   Itinerary

Miles N	NORTH	Elev. (ft/m)	Miles S
10.5	**Start:** Roadside parking on VA 664, 100 yd. E of BRPMP 13.6, 16.4 mi. S of Rockfish Gap.	2650/808	0.0
9.7	Crest of **Meadow Mt.,** view, campsite.		0.8
8.8	Trail to R (100 yd.) to **Maupin Field Shelter,** water, camping, and N terminus of Mau-Har Trail.	2720/838	1.7
8.4	Top of **Bee Mt.,** limited view to E.	3300/1006	2.1
6.8	View from **Hanging Rock.**		3.7
6.3	Top of **Three Ridges** in thick woods.	3970/1210	4.2
4.6	Second ridge of **Three Ridges,** views to E and S; Chimney Rocks are just beyond.		5.9
4.3	Third of **Three Ridges;** flat rock overlook offers views of The Priest and Harpers Creek valley.		6.2
2.6	Road to R leads 130 yd. to **Harpers Creek Shelter,** water.	1800/549	7.9
2.5	**Harpers Creek.**		8.0
1.7	S terminus of Mau-Har Trail.		8.8
0.7	Descend series of switchbacks.		9.8
0.1	Suspension bridge over **Tye River,** view, camping.		10.4
0.0	**End:** Parking area for 20 cars at **VA 56,** 11.3 mi. E of BRPMP 27.0, 8.2 mi. E of Montebello, 1.5 mi. W of Tyro.	1000/305	10.5

SOUTH

Reeds Gap to Cedar Cliff

Map: ATC Va. #1, Central Virginia
Route: From Reeds Gap at BRP past Three Ridges Overlook to Cedar Cliffs and Dripping Rock at BRP
Recommended direction: S to N
Distance: 4.8 mi.
Elevation +/-: 2650 to 2800 ft.
Effort: Easy
Overnight backpacking hike: Optional
Duration: 2 1/2 to 3 1/2 hr.
Early exit option: None
Natural history features: Three Ridges Overlook; Cedar Cliffs
Social history feature: Big Meadows Wildlife Management Area

Other features: Picnic tables at 0.5 mi.; views from Cedar Rock and Three Ridges Overlook
Trailhead access: *Start:* From Rockfish Gap at intersection of I-64 and BRP, head S on BRP for 13.6 mi., then E on VA 664. Trailhead is 100 yd. beyond parkway. There is ample roadside parking. Please notify ranger if you plan to leave car overnight. (See Hike #20.) Look for trail sign near fence on E side of cleared field. *End:* From Rockfish Gap at intersection of BRP and I-64, head S on parkway for 9.6 mi. to Dripping Rock parking area.
Camping: Permitted except within sight of parkway or picnic areas.

This is a nice, short hike with which to begin, or end, a weekend camping trip. However, the views from Three Ridges Overlook and Cedar Cliffs make it worth venturing out for an easy day trip as well. This is a particularly good hike to take in early spring, when the flowers are just beginning to bloom and the area is covered with brilliant shades of red, purple, and yellow. Practice identifying different varieties of violets. This hike is also a visual treat in early fall, when the oak leaves are bright red and the maples display brilliant orange and yellow hues.

Picking up along a small fence, the hike begins with a slight ascent into a lightly wooded area. Paralleling the fence, the AT climbs through a thin oak forest. The branches are no numerous enough to form a shady canopy, making this stretch of trail quite hot under July and August's blazing sun. Take your mind off the heat by searching for wild geraniums identifiable by their hairy leaves and rose-purple petals. In fall and winter scan the ground for acorns, or squirrels stashing away a treat.

Before you know it, the trail make a downward approach to the Three

Ridges Overlook (0.5 mi.), with picnic tables and a parking area at the southern end. This is a popular spot along the Blue Ridge Parkway. On a clear day, expect to see many cars parked along the roadside and their occupants out enjoying the view. Don't be discouraged by the lack of solitude. There's plenty of trail ahead and the view is worth a few more moments of civilization.

Although most of this hike is still ahead of you, if you're enjoying it as a relaxing afternoon trip, this is a great spot for lunch. Or, if you're an early riser, this would be a great place to enjoy a morning cup of coffee before finishing your trek. At the very least, shutterbugs should plan to stop long enough to take a few photographs. From this vantage point, you can see the 4063-ft. peak of The Priest rising in the southwest, trimmed by the Tye River valley. Sherando Lake is visible straight ahead in fall and winter, with Torry Ridge reaching into the sky behind it.

Beyond the picnic area, the AT crosses the BRP at the 13.1-mi. mark and descends into the woods, heading westward. The oak and maple trees grow thicker. Expect to see white-tailed deer, squirrels, and rabbits as you continue across a fairly level, well-graded trail. Less than half a mile further, the trail crosses a large rock slide. Beware: There is some tricky footwork involved here. Several of the rocks are loose, and thick moss leaves some spots quite slick, especially after a recent rain. As you make your way through this obstacle course, don't put your hands down anywhere you can't see them—the rocks are prime snake housing.

The most common varieties of snakes along the Blue Ridge are copperheads and timber rattlers. These pit vipers, identified by their triangular heads and elliptical pupils, have hinged fangs that can plant a poisonous bite. To avoid being bitten, avoid reaching into dark areas (including in between rocks or fallen trees) and use a stick to move suspicious-looking objects.

The AT climbs a steep rock staircase built by the Old Dominion AT Club to help ease the ascent, and continues upward, making a slight dip before crossing a small stream at 2.7 mi. This is a good spot to refill water bottles, especially if you've decided to make this an extended trip by connecting it to Hike #31. The stream is unprotected and water must be treated or filtered.

After ascending a steep side hill, you'll be indebted to the Old Dominion AT Club once again as you climb another set of their handiwork, this time made of logs and taking you downhill. Beyond the log staircase, a blue-blazed trail to the left leads 135 yd. to a rocky, open area (3.6 mi.). There are great views to the north and to the west of the wide valley below. Sherando Lake Campground (see Hike #31) is on the far side of the valley, and the Big Meadows

Wildlife Management Area rises above it. In summer, the fresh mountain air delivers the sweet scent of the thimbleberry. If your sense of smell fails you, look for the small, white, roselike petals, which reach their peak in mid-July. The shrubby plant has bristly hairs and heart-shaped leaves and bears small, red berries that resemble miniature raspberries.

The AT leaves the woods and crosses over the grassy top of Cedar Cliffs (4.2 mi.). From here, there are more stellar views to the north and west, including another photo opportunity of Sherando Lake. This is an especially beautiful site when fall foliage is at its peak. It's also a wonderful place to watch the sun set. The trail winds to the right and reenters the woods as it begins a gradual ascent. This easy uphill climb continues 0.6 mi. to cross the parkway once again, bringing you to the Dripping Rock parking area.

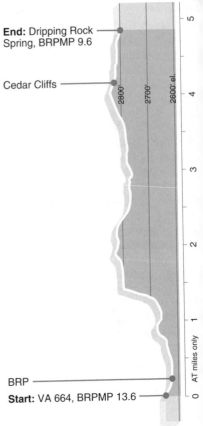

created using Maptech TopoScout ®

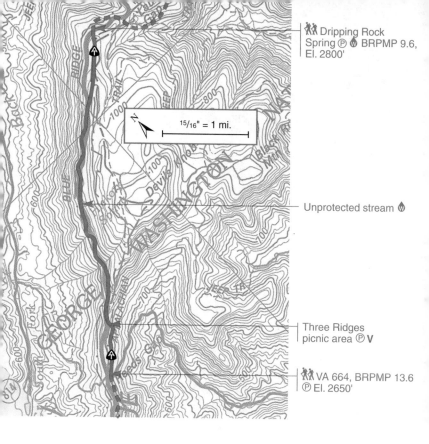

人人 Dripping Rock
Spring Ⓟ 🔥 BRPMP 9.6,
El. 2800'

Unprotected stream 🔥

Three Ridges
picnic area Ⓟ V

人人 VA 664, BRPMP 13.6
Ⓟ El. 2650'

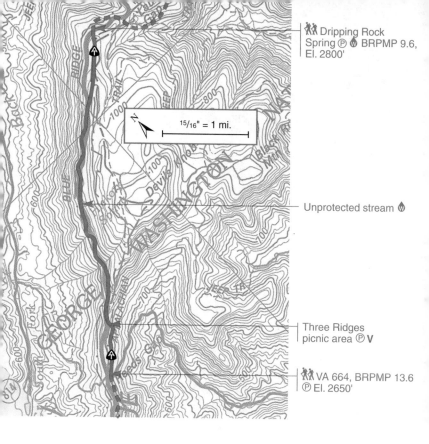

^15/16^" = 1 mi.

HIKE #32 Itinerary

Miles N	NORTH	Elev. (ft/m)	Miles S
4.8	**End: Dripping Rock Spring** and parking area at BRPMP 9.6, 9.6 mi. S of Rockfish Gap.	approx. 2800/853	0.0
4.2	Grassy ledge of **Cedar Cliffs,** view.		0.6
3.3	Descend log steps.		1.5
2.7	Cross small stream on steep hillside.		2.1
1.3	Descend rock steps.		3.5
1.2	Blue-blazed trail leads 135 yd. L to view.		3.6
0.9	Begin gradual ascent.		3.9
0.5	Cross **BRP** at Three Ridges parking and picnic area (view) and enter woods.		4.3
0.0	**Start:** Roadside parking at **VA 664,** 100 yd. E of BRPMP 13.6, 13.6 mi. S of Rockfish Gap.	2650/808	4.8

SOUTH

HIKE #33
Humpback Rocks

Map: ATC Va. #1, Central Virginia

Route: From Dripping Rocks trailhead parking on the BRP over Humpback Mt. and Humpback Rocks to Humpback Rocks parking near BRP

Recommended direction: S to N

Distance: 4.8 mi.

Elevation +/-: 2800 to 3600 to 2400 ft.

Effort: Moderate

Day hike: Yes

Overnight backpacking hike: Optional

Duration: 2 to 3 hr.

Early exit option: At 1.3 mi., trail to BRP

Natural history feature: Humpback Rocks

Social history feature: Farmstead at BRP Humpback Rocks Visitors Center

Other features: Views from Humpback Mt. and Humpback Rocks

Trailhead access: *Start:* From Rockfish Gap intersection of BRP and I-64, head S on BRP for 9.6 mi. to Dripping Rock parking area. *End:* From Rockfish Gap intersection of I-64 and BRP, head S on parkway 6.0 mi. to Humpback Rocks parking area.

Camping: Permitted except within sight of parkway or picnic areas.

This short hike is designed especially for Blue Ridge Parkway travelers who want to experience a bit of the 493-mi. parkway corridor on foot. Just as museums and living history exhibits bring the nation's longest national park to life, this easy hike shows the Blue Ridge landscape as history in the making. Along the way, you will visit old stone walls built by hardscrabble mountaineers, a "deadened" meadow where trees were killed while still standing to encourage meadow grasses, views of historic Waynesboro, and, after the hike, an historic farmstead with preserved cabin and outbuildings. Of course, there are also the unforgettable Humpback Rocks.

The ramble is manageable by anyone wearing sturdy walking shoes and whose physical conditions allow them to take a vigorous 2- to 3-hr. hike. Along the way are the views south and north from Humpback Mt. and the extended views west from Humpback Rocks. Backpackers seeking a night out can continue on to Rockfish Gap for a total trip of 10.7 mi. But first, Dripping Rock Spring, at the southern end of the hike, is the perfect place to charge yourself and your water bottles with clear spring water.

From the Dripping Rock trailhead parking area, at BRPMP 9.6, the AT begins a steady but gradual ascent of Humpback Mt. After passing Laurel Springs, east of the trail, the ascent becomes slightly steeper. In spring and early summer, Laurel Springs is more reliable than in drier months. But at any time of year, the mountain laurel and azaleas welcome hikers—especially in May and June, when their blooms dominate the picture.

At about 0.9 mi., the trail finds level ground. Although the ascent will resume and continue for another 2.0 mi., it is quite gradual and even, at times, unnoticeable. Still, any hikers wishing for a chance to return to the parkway and the "civilized" world can take the cutoff trail to the Humpback Rocks picnic area at 1.3 mi. Just 0.3 mi. down the blue-blazed trail, the picnic area has rest rooms and water in season, generally May through November. It's worth a brief, 250-yd. detour down this path to see a fine example of the stone walls still found in the area. This one incorporates a rocky outcropping from the mountain as part of its barrier for wandering livestock.

On the AT at 1.3 mi. is another stone hog wall. Farmers in the region let their razorback pigs roam about the hillside to fatten on acorns, hickory nuts, and, until the species was devastated by blight, chestnuts. To keep the pigs from wandering completely off the mountain, over time they collectively constructed miles of these fences with the most plentiful material at hand—stone.

An open greenstone cliff announces the ridge of Humpback Mt. at 1.9 mi., offering long views east toward the Piedmont and south along the Blue Ridge. The famous Wintergreen ski and golf resorts are in the near foreground. There are hikers who curse the existence of ski slopes and a golf course within view of the AT and other primitive hiking trails. Then again, there are stories of AT thru-hikers pausing for several days of rest and relaxation in the posh, elegant spas of Wintergreen, some of them getting so pampered that the spot spelled the end of their journey altogether.

Once attaining the ridge, the trail will follow it for more than a mile of moderate walking. About half way along, at 3.0 mi., the trail finds the northern summit which, at 3600 ft., reveals views worthy of a rest stop, possibly even a nap. The Shenandoah Valley opens below and to the west, Rockfish Gap to the north, and the Rockfish River valley to the east, along with the Piedmont and its farms.

With such expansive views east over the horizon, Humpback has a bit of a following among sunrise hikers. Reserved for the truly adventurous—and experienced, we hasten to add—sunrise hiking begins in the fading light of a moon just past full. The moonlight and a flashlight provide enough glow for the surefooted to make the 3-mi. trek from Dripping Rock to the summit of Humpback. As the first light of day emerges over the Piedmont, the hikers are there to greet it. Less experienced or less daring hikers can await the sunrise from an east-facing overlook along the parkway, then start an early morning hike. It will still be a memorable day.

Following the ridge of Humpback, the trail begins its descent, at times steeply. It can be challenging on the knees and feet through here, the toll of descending from the splendid ridge. At 3.1 mi. another stone wall offers a rest spot where the trail passes through a gap in it, as does the occasion to investigate a greenstone talus, a huge pile of rock cascading down the slope. Geologists speculate that at one time the mountain was composed of a much taller cliff. When erosion made it too top heavy, it tumbled to the side to create this magnificent assemblage.

At 3.9 mi. a blue-blazed side trail leads left 250 yd. to Humpback Rocks, a massive greenstone outcropping. Just as the stone walls and other artifacts of the Blue Ridge point to its human history, this giant rock formation tells the tale of the mountain's natural history. Greenstone is a metamorphosed rock, which means it was transformed underground through intense pressure from above. It was transformed to greenstone from basalt (cooled lava). The story goes this way: Volcanic activity produced lava, which cooled to basalt. Ages of sedimentary rock and tectonic activity buried the basalt. Further ages of heat and pressure metamorphosed the rock, which moved to the surface in later mountain-building episodes.

The rock offers more historical views: of the colonial city of Waynesboro to the north (see Hike #34); to

the west of George Washington NF, in an area once completely denuded of forest but now a sea of green; and just below, west of the parkway, of a pioneer farm exhibit, which recreates 19th-century life on the Blue Ridge. After the hike, a visit there is in order. The cabin, smokehouse, springhouse, and other outbuildings are all constructed of the ubiquitous stone and wood, the other natural resource plentiful in settlement days. These, along with barns, corncribs, butter churns, and assorted other artifacts remind us that life on the ridge back then was nearly totally consumed with the tasks of survival.

Back on the AT, the trail continues its descent, steeply dropping through a series of rocky switchbacks, past the base of Humpback Rocks, and under the shade of an immense double oak tree. At 4.3 mi. the trail descends wooden steps and leaves the ridge.

For a finale, stop at the wooden bench in an open meadow at 4.7 mi., where common evening primrose and soapwort bloom in the fall. Just beyond the meadow the trail reaches Humpback Rocks parking and the end of the hike at 4.8 mi. The paved road from the parking area leads 200 yd. to the parkway.

Optional Extended Hike: Backpackers (and ambitious day hikers) may continue northward, over Dobie Mt., down through the Mill Creek valley, and on to Rockfish Gap at the end of the parkway. With the exception of a 700-ft. ascent from Mill Creek to the ridge of Elk Mt., the terrain on the 5.9 mi. of this extended hike is rather even.

Mill Creek valley is a magical place. Your car may be parked only a couple of miles away, and other autos may be passing by only a mile west on the parkway, but the modern world is a distant memory along Mill Creek. There are several pools, a few small cascades, and always the sound of water and the creatures drawn to it —birds in the trees, and the deer, raccoon, and other denizens of the evening traipsing through the leaves for a drink.

The Paul C. Wolfe Shelter, built and maintained by the Old Dominion AT Club, accommodates ten people. However, hikers out just for the night should come prepared for tent camping because AT backpackers have few other shelter choices in the area. There are several exceptional places for camping along Mill Creek, and the water supply there, though unprotected, is plentiful.

At Rockfish Gap, 20.5 mi. west of Charlottesville, plenty of parking is available on the parkway at its junction with I-64/US 250.

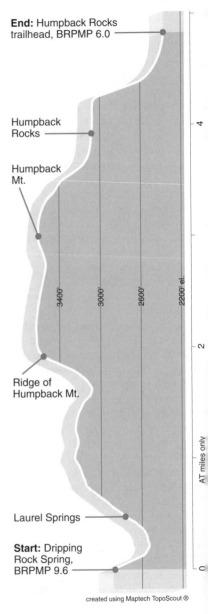

End: Humpback Rocks trailhead, BRPMP 6.0

Humpback Rocks

Humpback Mt.

3400' 3000' 2600' 2200' el.

Ridge of Humpback Mt.

AT miles only

Laurel Springs

Start: Dripping Rock Spring, BRPMP 9.6

created using Maptech TopoScout ®

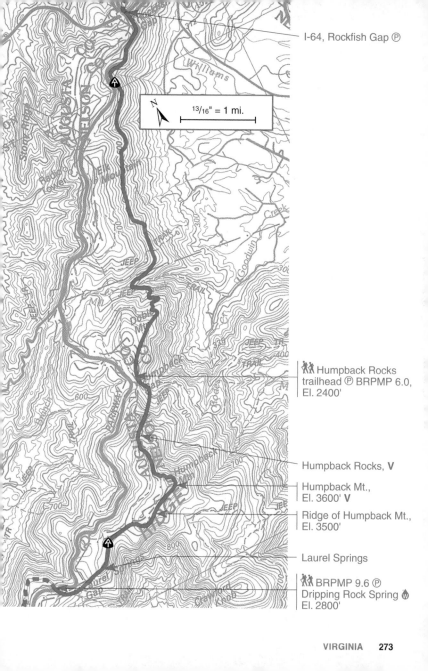

I-64, Rockfish Gap ℗

¹³/₁₆" = 1 mi.

🚶🚶 Humpback Rocks
trailhead ℗ BRPMP 6.0,
El. 2400'

Humpback Rocks, **V**

Humpback Mt.,
El. 3600' **V**

Ridge of Humpback Mt.,
El. 3500'

Laurel Springs

🚶🚶 BRPMP 9.6 ℗
Dripping Rock Spring 💧
El. 2800'

HIKE #33 Itinerary

Miles N	**NORTH**	Elev. (ft/m)	Miles S
4.8	**End: Humpback Rocks parking area;** take paved road to L 200 yd. to BRPMP 6.0, 0.2 mi. S of Humpback Rocks Visitors Center and 6.0 mi. S of I-64 in Rockfish Gap.	2400/732	0.0
4.0	Begin steep descent.		0.8
3.9	Trail to L 250 yd. to **Humpback Rocks,** views.		0.9
3.0	**N summit of Humpback Mt.,** view.	3600/1097	1.8
1.9	**Ridge of Humpback Mt.,** views.	3500/1067	2.9
1.3	On L, 0.3-mi. trail to **Humpback Rocks picnic area** on BRP, seasonal rest rooms and water, early exit option.		3.5
0.4	**Laurel Springs,** to R.		4.4
0.0	**Start: Dripping Rock Spring** at BRP trailhead, milepost 9.6; parking area. I-64 at Rockfish Gap is 9.6 mi. N.	2800/853	4.8

SOUTH

McCormick Gap to Turk Gap

Map: PATC Va. #11, Shenandoah NP, S Dist.

Route: From McCormick Gap at SDMP 102.1 over Bear Den Mt. and Calf Mt. to Jarman Gap, and through SNP over Sawmill Ridge and Turk Mt. to Turk Gap at SDMP 94.2

Recommended direction: S to N

Distance: 7.8 mi.

Elevation +/-: 2435 to 2975 to 2175 to 2625 ft.

Effort: Moderate

Day hike: Yes

Overnight backpacking hike: Optional

Duration: 4 1/2 hr.

Early exit options: At 1.8 mi. and 6.2 mi., Skyline Dr.; at 4.3 mi., Bucks Elbow Mt. Fire Rd.

Natural history features: McCormick Gap; Beagle Gap; South Fork Moormans River

Social history features: Calf Mt.; Waynesboro

Other features: Junctions with Turk Branch Trail and Turk Mt. Trail; McCormick Gap and Sawmill Run overlooks

Trailhead access: *Start:* From the I-64/US 250 junction with Skyline Dr. in Rockfish Gap (SDMP 105.0), travel N on the Drive to parking area at SDMP 102.1. *End:* From SDMP 102.1, continue 8.0 mi. N on Skyline Dr. to parking in Turk Gap.

Camping: Calf Mt. Shelter, and see "Camping" in Introduction.

On this southernmost hike in Shenandoah National Park the proximity of the AT to a modern highway, Skyline Dr., belies the wildness of surrounding landscape. Once entering the park, at Jarman Gap (4.3 mi.), the trail wends between the borders of the largest congressionally designated wilderness in the park. To get there the AT mostly follows a narrow protected corridor purchased by the National Park Service specifically for the trail. For that initial section, the landscape you will see to the east and west of the trail is privately owned. The Calf Mt. traverse lies entirely on private land, but the views from Bear Den Mt. and Calf Mt. are no less splendid for being of privately owned land. Bear Den and Calf mountains are the northernmost balds along the Virginia and West Virginia stretches of the AT. Hikers need not leave the trail to capture expansive views on both sides, although the opportunities for a ledge-side rest stop are worth taking. Those seeking an extended hike or wishing to cover all the AT miles along Skyline Dr. can start out from Rockfish Gap, 0.2 mi. north of the Skyline Dr. bridge over US 64, at the northern terminus of the Blue Ridge Parkway.

From the McCormick Gap parking area, the AT crosses to the west of Skyline Dr. and begins a steady, mile-long, 400-ft. ascent of Bear Den Mt. through locusts and white pines. It's a steep start and the first of four similar ascents on the hike, but none is so relentless that an active adult could not handle them all with enough energy to spare to really enjoy the trip.

After 200 yd. the pine thicket takes over, as the trail climbs through a copse that is dark and dense, giving a sense of night in the middle of the day. Quiet hikers in early morning may come upon deer slumbering only 10 yd. off the trail. And they call this ridge Bear Den for a reason; the chokecherries at the edge of the thicket sometimes attract black bears to the cool underbrush.

At 0.7 mi. the trail emerges into the open grassland of the Bear Den ridgeline, offering views to the north of Bucks Elbow Mt. and to the southwest of Waynesboro, a city of some 20,000 that has served as a regional industrial center since the first days of the Industrial Revolution. First settled in the 1730s when Joseph Tease opened a tavern there, and first named Teaseville, the city's location along the South River and near the Rockfish Gap passage of the Blue Ridge was its greatest attraction. Produce moved east from the valley while goods from Richmond and other eastern cities moved west to the frontier. Incorpo-

rated as Waynesboro in 1834, the name changed in honor of Revolutionary War hero Gen. Mad Anthony Wayne, the city became an iron-and-steel-producing center when the railroad arrived. The area also earned a reputation for the manufacture of railroad cars. Today, the quiet city still has a solid industrial base and still serves throngs of travelers making their way through Rockfish Gap.

At the summit of Bear Den Mt., at 1.2 mi., a police signal tower and the faint sounds of planes overhead break the spell of nature only briefly. Of the three most common mechanical intrusions along the AT, automobile sounds being the third, radio towers and airplanes cause the greatest infringement, but quickly pass from memory after the trail passes them. Just before the signal tower, a post marks an otherwise unmarked (no blazes, no signs) path through the grasses to a green shale outcropping, a perfect spot for a rest stop and a long view north of the Blue Ridge.

Descending Bear Den, the trail moves amidst wild strawberry bushes, luscious in June, then joins a dirt road bordering open fields at 1.5 mi. From here, the trail offers open views to the north and east of Calf Mt. and Little Yellow Mt.; to the northwest is Ramsey Mt. At 1.8 mi. the trail crosses Skyline Dr. at milepost 99.5 in Beagle Gap. For hikers planning only a short jaunt over Bear Den, or an early exit from this hike, there is parking for a dozen cars in a lot at Beagle Gap, with more parking available on

Shenandoah National Park

For hikers on the Appalachian Trail in Shenandoah National Park, there are countless opportunities to view the pristine, forested slopes and valleys. These are the kinds of scenes that one would expect to inspire the creation of a national park. But when Congress authorized SNP in 1926, much of the Blue Ridge was a hardscrabble landscape, left nearly barren by erosion, bad farming techniques, mining, and timber harvesting. The chestnut forest was dead or dying, victim of the chestnut blight that was changing the treescape of the eastern United States. Thousands of acres of trees were left standing without a leaf.

In its favor were the steep stream valleys and enchanting hollows, waterfalls, and, from the ridges, the endless views of the Allegheny Mts. to the west and the Piedmont to the east. The Blue Ridge also had George Freeman Pollock, since the 1890s the flamboyant owner of the Skyland resort high atop the ridge. Pollock's 6000 acres encompassed the famed Stony Man Mt. and Whiteoak Canyon, home of the last stand of virgin hemlock on the Blue Ridge—trees Pollock had saved from the logger's axe by purchasing one tree at a time.

Pollock and Virginia U.S. Senator Harry Flood Byrd are remembered as the principal advocates who won the park's designation. Eager for tourism revenue, the Virginia Commonwealth purchased 160,000 acres for the park, which it donated to the initiative. The park was dedicated by President Franklin D. Roosevelt in 1936.

Today, SNP is testament to the rejuvenating powers of nature. Its 194,000 acres present a world-renowned picture, dominated by chestnut oak forests, cove hardwoods, and yellow poplars. The flowers of dogwood, rhododendron, and mountain laurel grace the understory in spring. SNP visitors can see the views from the park's 500 miles of trails or from Skyline Drive's 75 scenic overlooks, eat lunch at one of 300 picnic sites or 4 major picnic areas, or spend a night at one of 700 campsites, 4 campgrounds, or 2 lodges. All of the hiking trails in SNP except the AT are blazed with blue; the yellow blazes signify equestrian trails.

the roadside. In the broad saddle between Calf and Bear Den mountains, the pastures of Beagle Gap look eastward and below to stream valleys with such whimsical names as Lickinghole Creek, Tuckedaway Branch, and one no Appalachian area could be without—Beaver Creek.

For the modern hiker, the grasslands of Beagle Gap are easily accessible by Skyline Dr., but for 19th-century farmers and their cattle, the 2000-ft. spring ascent up Beagle Gap Rd. from Jarman Gap to summer pasture was an arduous journey of a few days. Still, hikers making the final climb up Calf Mt. from the Beagle Gap meadow might wish for the herder's life after catching a glimpse of Turk Mt. from the summit pastures.

Leaving Beagle Gap the trail makes quick work of a 400-ft. climb through oak and scattered red cedar to the first height of Calf Mt., a knob rising 2900 ft. and also known as Little Calf, at 2.1 mi. Along the ridge over the next half mile are several huge oaks, survivors of the days when most of the woodland here was cleared for grazing. Two stone walls mark the divisions between the domains of early farmers. At 2.4 mi., as the trail passes through open woods, an unmarked but clearly visible trail leads west 0.1 mi. to a splendid lookout over Mike's Knob to the South River valley and the Alleghenies beyond. The cliffs of Calf Mt., like those of Bear Den Mt., are of green shale, a sedimentary rock formed by the pressurized breakdown of minerals beneath the earth's surface. Its soft, claylike quality differs from that of the more common greenstone, a hard metamorphosed remnant of basalt lava evident along much of the Blue Ridge.

The open summit of Calf Mt. (2975 ft.) comes almost as a surprise at 2.7 mi. The woods open like a curtain to reveal long views to both sides of the trail. Ramsey Mt. and the slightly higher Turk Mt. rise to the west, almost within arm's length. Buck's Elbow (3100 ft.) stands over its little sibling, Beaver Creek Mt. (1400 ft.) to the east. The steep ridge drops dramatically to the valley floor more than 2000 ft. below. This moving setting is favored by hikers for watching the seasonal migration of hawks in mid-to-late September.

Leaving the views of Calf Mt. (it's not easy!), the trail descends steadily

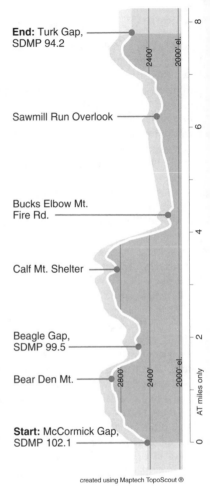

created using Maptech TopoScout ®

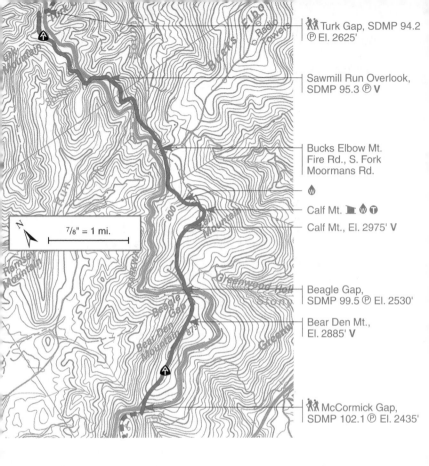

ᛘᛘ Turk Gap, SDMP 94.2
Ⓟ El. 2625'

Sawmill Run Overlook,
SDMP 95.3 Ⓟ **V**

Bucks Elbow Mt.
Fire Rd., S. Fork
Moormans Rd.

🚰

Calf Mt. 🏕 💧 👕
Calf Mt., El. 2975' **V**

Beagle Gap,
SDMP 99.5 Ⓟ El. 2530'

Bear Den Mt.,
El. 2885' **V**

ᛘᛘ McCormick Gap,
SDMP 102.1 Ⓟ El. 2435'

N
⁷/₈" = 1 mi.

on the steep northwest slope, first through more older growth oaks, then under a dense canopy of young forest of mixed locust, black walnut, and maple along an old road. Indicative of the immature woods, the understory is largely composed of azalea and blackberries. At 3.0 mi. the trail veers west onto a narrow footpath in a nascent beech grove under the shade of maple, and descends more steeply still.

At 3.3 mi. a blue-blazed trail leads 0.3 mi. to Calf Mt. Shelter. The shelter is owned and maintained by the PATC and may be used overnight (despite the fact that some publications state that the shelter is for day use only). The shelter sits 500 ft. above Skyline Dr., which is about half a mile away. To the northwest lies the wilderness containing Sawmill Ridge and Turk Mt.—it is a very quiet place, indeed. A reliable spring is down the same path, 175 yd. before the cabin, but another water source is available just 0.6 mi. farther on the AT.

From the cutoff trail it is a steep, half-mile descent nearly to Skyline Dr., then skirting east of the road to a spring at 3.9 mi. On the level trail over the next 0.4 mi., you're as likely to hear the cars buzzing along Skyline Dr. as the call of the wild. At 4.3 mi. the trail reaches Bucks Elbow Mt. Fire Rd. in Jarman Gap, 175 yd. east of Skyline Dr., completing a descent of nearly 800 ft. from the open summit of Calf Mt. The fire road serves as an exit option for this hike. Limited parking is available here, and 100 ft. west on the road is milepost 96.8 of Skyline Dr. Jarman Gap marks the southern boundary of SNP. The PATC maintains the AT for the entire length of the park.

The small stream to the right of the trail marks the headwaters of the South Fork Moormans River. The river gains steam quickly when the three tributaries of Turk Branch empty into it, then descends along a fire road to the Charlottesville Reservoir. The fire roads along the north and south branches formed the original route of the AT here, and many hikers prefer it to the new route. The 9-mi. route north from here to the junction with the present-day AT at Blackrock Gap never strays far from the sight and sound of rushing water. And a series of cascades on Big Branch provides a waterfall experience rarely seen walking the ridge the AT now follows.

An alternate route to the endpoint of today's hike that will let you sample some of the river experience is to hike 2.0 mi. along the yellow-blazed South Fork Moormans River Rd., which the AT crosses 300 yd. beyond the Elbow Mt. road. The route then ascends 2.1 mi. back to the ridge following the Turk Branch Trail. The walk along the river and ascent along Turk Branch, with the sounds of the squirrels and birds darting about in the wilderness through which Turk Branch travels, as well as the several stream crossings, make it the perfect complement to the ramble over the higher elevations of Calf and Bear Den mountains. But be warned, the Turk Branch Trail ascends more than 1000 ft. in its 2.1 mi. to the AT at Turk Gap, and the total trip from McCormick Gap is 8.4 mi. instead of 7.8.

Continuing from Jarman Gap past the Moormans River Rd., the AT begins a steady ascent of a high knob between Bucks Elbow and Turk mountains, reaching the summit at 5.6 mi., 500 ft. above Jarman Gap. From the knob there are views to the north of Waynesboro and Sawmill Ridge, while back to the east lies

Bucks Elbow Mt. The surrounding oak and pine forest demonstrates the role of fire and dryness on these steep slopes. The sandstone slopes offer poor absorption, hence dry soil. The dryness promotes fire, which inhibits the development of a complex oak and hickory or maple and beech climax forest, which one finds on the moist slopes of the region. The oak here rarely mature to fullness before being stifled by dryness.

Descending more casually than it rose, the trail drops 250 ft. over half a mile of pine and oak, then at 6.2 mi. crosses to the west of Skyline Dr. at Sawmill Run Overlook, at milepost 95.3 and an elevation of 2315 ft. From the south end of the overlook, you can look straight down a deep, steep canyon, sliced by the east branch of Sawmill Run through Erwin quartzite. A half-mile walk south to Sawmill Ridge Overlook will reveal a spectacular view through the water gap Sawmill Run cut between Sawmill Ridge and Ramsey Mt.

From Sawmill Run Overlook, the trail ascends once again, now climbing the final peak of this hike, Turk Mt., a sandstone and quartzite ridge surrounded in places by massive talus, piles of rock blocks that accumulate as a mountain slowly collapses from the top. This final climb is a moderate one, moving only a few hundred feet west of Skyline Dr., the hiker's seemingly ever present companion through SNP.

At 7.6 mi., just as the trail crests the eastern knob of Turk Mt., a blue-blazed trail to the left leads 0.9 mi. west to the summit of Turk Mt. With only another 350 yd. to go, hikers with energy and daylight to spare should take the detour to the top. It requires a 500-ft. climb in under a mile, but the sights on the horizon and underfoot make it a worthwhile diversion. The sandstone surface on the summit abounds with fossilized wormholes. These tubular holes may seem unremarkable, but they are deserving of contemplation considering they were dug in the sand a million years ago or more by prehistoric worms.

Also underfoot in June are lilies, while at eye level in August and September are the flowers of the wafer-ash, a shrub or small tree with long-stalked leaves. Its flowers are clusters of paper-thin white disks. An elderly hiker we met on a hike of Turk Mt. described the shrub as a "communion tree," owing to the flowers' resemblance to the host used in Roman Catholic ritual. The views from the rocky ledges of Turk Mt. open from west to east, offering the South River and Great Valley west of the Blue Ridge as well as the many folds and layers of the ridge moving northeast.

From the junction with Turk Mt. Trail, the AT descends toward Skyline Dr. into Turk Gap at 7.8 mi. and an elevation of 2625 ft. The parking area is directly across the Drive at milepost 94.2.

Miles N	**NORTH**	Elev. (ft/m)	Miles S
7.8	**End: Turk Gap, SDMP 94.2,** 11.0 mi. N of I-64 intersection with Skyline Dr. in Rockfish Gap.	2625/800	0.0
7.6	Crest **E knob of Turk Mt.** Blue-blazed trail leads W 0.9 mi. to summit of Turk Mt., view.		0.2
6.2	Cross **Skyline Dr. to Sawmill Run Overlook,** at SDMP 95.3, early exit option.	2315/706	1.6
5.6	Knoll with view of **Bucks Elbow Mt.**	2455/748	2.2
4.4	Yellow-blazed **S Fork Moorman's River Rd.** heads E; starting point for 4.1-mi. alternative route to Turks Gap.		3.4
4.3	**Jarman Gap;** enter SNP. Junction with **Bucks Elbow Mt. Fire Rd.,** leads 100 ft. W to SDMP 96.8, early exit option.	2175/663	3.5
3.9	Spring.		3.9
3.3	Trail to **Calf Mt. Shelter,** spring, privy (0.3 mi.).		4.5
2.7	Summit of **Calf Mt.**	2975/906	5.1
2.4	Trail to W (0.1 mi.) to **Calf Mt. Overlook,** views.		5.5
1.8	**Beagle Gap, SDMP 99.5,** early exit option; begin ascent of Calf Mt.	2530/772	6.0
1.2	Summit of **Bear Den Mt.**	2885/879	6.6
0.7	Emerge into open grassy area on **Bear Den Ridge,** view.		7.1
0.0	**Start: In McCormick Gap,** at SDMP 102.1, 3.2 mi. N of I-64 intersection with Skyline Dr. in Rockfish Gap.	2435/742	7.8

SOUTH

Blackrock and Wildcat Ridge

Map: PATC Va. #11, SNP, S Dist.

Route: Through SNP from Jones Run Trail over Blackrock, past Calvary Rocks to Wildcat Ridge Trail at SMDP 92.1

Recommended direction: N to S

Distance: 8.1 mi.

Elevation +/-: 2700 to 3090 to 2300 to 3050 ft.

Effort: Moderate

Day hike: Yes

Overnight backpacking hike: Optional

Duration: 4 hr.

Early exit options: At 0.9 mi., Trayfoot Trail; at 2.5 mi. and at 4.3 mi., Skyline Dr.; at 5.4 mi., blue-blazed trail to SDMP 90.0

Natural history features: Blackrock Gap; Blackrock

Other feature: Horsehead Mt. and Riprap overlooks

Trailhead access: *Start:* From the I-64/US 250 junction with Skyline Dr. in Rockfish Gap, travel N on the Drive to Jones Run parking for 12 cars at SDMP 84.1. For an alternate route, see Hike #36. *End:* From Rockfish Gap drive N on Skyline Dr. to Wildcat Ridge parking, milepost 92.1; parking for 12 cars.

Camping: Blackrock Hut, and see "Camping" in Introduction.

There are several spots along the AT that stop hikers in their tracks, so surprising, immediate, almost overwhelming is the view. Blackrock is such a place. A massive, 1000-ft. pile of quartzite blocks, Blackrock was once a towering cliff more than twice its current size, until the softer sedimentary shale beneath it eroded to the point at which it could no longer serve as a foundation to the cliffs. Although much of this hike meanders close to—practically alongside—Skyline Dr., the trail's short dips away from the road and its quick jaunts over several knolls offer plenty of time in the woods.

Hikers may choose to approach this jaunt from south to north, thereby saving Blackrock for the near-finish of the hike—despite a challenging climb of nearly 800 ft. in little more than a mile. The hike is described here from north to south to allow you a chance to experience Blackrock after a gentle climb of the western ledge of Pinestead Mt. If you're out to cover all of the AT in Shenandoah, add 2 mi. to this hike to end at Turk Gap, the northern terminus of the previous hike.

From Jones Run parking area, follow Jones Run Trail 100 ft. east to its junction with the AT and head south (right). The trail passes through a stand of trees remaining from a former apple orchard. The trees offer nothing in the way of food for hikers, but white-tailed deer and an occasional black bear visit to sample the scrawny apples that several of the trees still manage to produce.

At 0.2 mi. the trail crosses to the west of Skyline Dr. at milepost 84.2 and enters the Blackrock area, beginning a steady but lazy ascent. Chestnut oaks tower over the trail and a midstory of maple. Still further below, mountain laurel and scattered azalea dot the rocky understory. To the west, Luck Hollow and the twin forks of White Oak Run, 1000 ft. below, create a wind draft that races up the slopes to rustle leaves on an otherwise calm day.

At 0.9 mi. the AT and Trayfoot Mt. Trail nearly intersect at a signpost marker. A 10-ft. path separates the trails. Due to careless crossings by hikers between the two trails there are many places along the ascent to Blackrock marred by the blurring of the two trails' boundaries. Don't add to the problem here. Stay on the trail. To the left, the blue-blazed Trayfoot Mt. Trail descends from this point for a quarter of a mile to the Blackrock parking area on Skyline Dr.; to the right, it ascends to Blackrock. Hikers out for a quick jaunt to Blackrock can park at the Blackrock parking area, take Trayfoot Mt. Trail to the summit, and return on the AT to this spot (it's okay to cross between the two trails here). Trayfoot Mt. Trail also forms part of an easy, 2.5-mi. circuit hike from the Blackrock parking area to Blackrock Hut with a return via the AT.

Along the final 0.3 mi. to Blackrock, the trail reveals views west of Austin Mt. and Dundo hollows, especially in winter, when there are also views of the Allegheny Mts. across the Great Valley of the Appalachians. These long, open views are the hallmark of the southern SNP section of the AT. Scarcely half a mile west of Skyline Dr. and 5 mi. east of US 340, a busy north – south highway, the landscape below appears as wild as any within the AT corridor. The western summits of the Blue Ridge here— Trayfoot, Hall, Austin, and Furnace— do a great service by forming a wall of green between the AT and civilization in the valley.

The AT holds out many such surprises, and at times seems to reveal them just for dramatic effect. As you emerge from beneath the oaks onto Blackrock, at 1.2 mi., Trayfoot Mt. appears so suddenly to the west, and is so steeply sloped, it seems to be in motion toward the AT. The second-tallest summit in the southern section of the park, its slopes are like a patchwork quilt of giant rock screes, which are massive fields of quartzite pressed into the slopes.

Because it's nearly impossible to take one's eyes from the north slope of Trayfoot, about half a mile across an open chasm, you may not be aware that you've wandered onto the open ledges of Blackrock until you

Hiking with a Hand Lens

Some of the best views on the AT require no blue sky: the hairy underside of a lousewort leaf, the downy silencer of a discarded owl feather, the bloodsucking gear of a mosquito.

I always carry a 10X hand lens in my pack. It weighs less than my compass and has a string so that I can hang it around my neck. Most nature centers and college bookstores sell hand lenses.

Make sure you get one that magnifies at least ten times. Plastic 3X or 5X lenses don't help much, though they are easier for small children to use. A glass lens that slides into a protective case will last the longest. You can also buy 16X lenses that might require more light and a bit of practice or compact field microscopes with about 30X magnification and their own light source.

To use a 10X hand lens, place the lens close to your eye, almost touching your eyebrow, and bring, say, the owl feather closer and closer until it's in focus—usually within a few inches. If you want to look at flowers or mosses, get down to their level; don't pick them just to get a good look at them.

Look at *everything.* For example, whether a flower is new to you or you're reacquainting yourself with a familiar one, look at its stamens and pistil. Look at each plant part to find out why botanists need so many words for "hairy."

Hand lenses are cheaper and lighter than binoculars, and you will get views you never knew were there.

—Doris Gove

find yourself standing amidst the rubble of lichen-covered blocks the size of pick-up trucks. These square boulders of Hampton quartzite are stacked above the trail as well as dropping some 500 ft. toward the headwaters of White Oak Run. Although the total diameter of the Blackrock area is a mere 200 ft., every boulder in the pile offers a different perspective on the landscape. It's the perfect spot at which to lose some time.

The typically light-colored quartzite appears blackened by black tripe, a lichen that covers every inch, hence the name Blackrock. The collapse of the wall that composed these cliffs, some hundred million years ago, has been kind to hikers. The odd marvel of the big blocks, the open nearness of Hall Mt. and Trayfoot Mt.'s 3121-ft. mass, and the long views west of Furnace Mt. and Austin Mt. in Shenandoah's wilderness are almost too much for the senses. One hardly knows where to look! The only remedy is to take a look from many angles.

From atop Blackrock there are three trail junctions of note to hikers planning to venture into the Trayfoot

Mt. wilderness. The first is the Black-rock Spur Trail, leading due west from open ledges of Blackrock. This blue-blazed spur leads 0.1 mi. to a junction with the Trayfoot Mt. Trail and, at that junction, becomes Furnace Mt. Trail. The spur is used largely by southbound hikers as a shortcut to the interior. Following the AT around Blackrock another hundred feet, to 1.3 mi., there is a junction with Trayfoot Mt. Trail, which has paralleled the AT. To the left (north) is the return to Blackrock parking. To the right (south) Trayfoot Mt. Trail will loop westward to the junction with Blackrock Spur. The third junction of note is at the point where Trayfoot Mt. Trail begins its westward loop, with an unblazed dirt road that bears left (south) and descends 0.5 mi. to another junction with the AT.

Descending to the southeast, the AT runs parallel to the dirt road from which Trayfoot Mt. Trail splits. The ridge is narrow here, with hollows opening from sharp drops on either side. At 1.8 mi. a blue-blazed trail drops steeply to the west 0.2 mi. to Blackrock Hut (in SNP, three-sided shelters are called huts), situated in a quiet ravine. Hikers arriving early in the morning or just before dark might be treated to the sight of a black bear investigating the smells of the previous night's campers. Bobcat are known to explore the steep ravine for rodents and other delicacies, but you are more likely to spy their scat than the animals themselves.

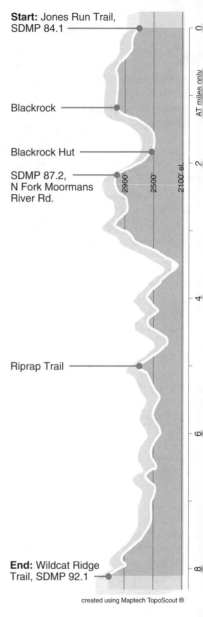

Start: Jones Run Trail, SDMP 84.1

Blackrock

Blackrock Hut

SDMP 87.2, N Fork Moormans River Rd.

Riprap Trail

End: Wildcat Ridge Trail, SDMP 92.1

AT miles only

2900'   2500'   2100' el.

created using Maptech TopoScout ®

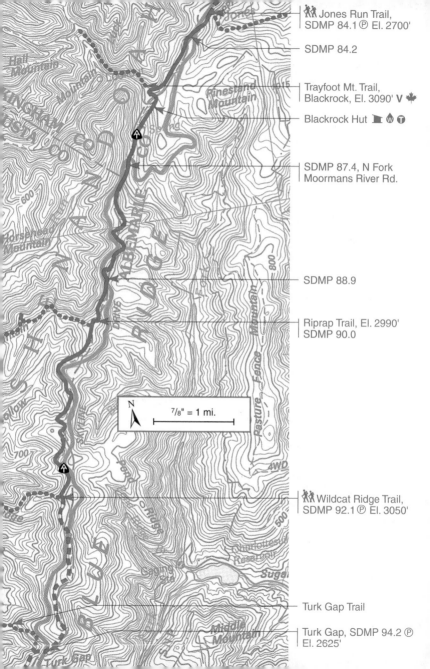

Jones Run Trail, SDMP 84.1 Ⓟ El. 2700'

SDMP 84.2

Trayfoot Mt. Trail, Blackrock, El. 3090' V 🍁

Blackrock Hut 🔥 💧 🚻

SDMP 87.4, N Fork Moormans River Rd.

SDMP 88.9

Riprap Trail, El. 2990' SDMP 90.0

N
⅞" = 1 mi.

Wildcat Ridge Trail, SDMP 92.1 Ⓟ El. 3050'

Turk Gap Trail

Turk Gap, SDMP 94.2 Ⓟ El. 2625'

The spring at the shelter, emerging from a pipe, is regarded as very reliable, and even when checked on a late August hike was found to be positively surging. The spring forms the western headwaters of North Branch Moormans River. It is also the only water source on this hike, so it is worth a trip down into the ravine to charge your water bottles.

It is a steep climb out of the Blackrock Hut ravine, but the remote stillness interrupted only by the gurgle of the spring, just 15 ft. from the hut, makes this a preferred place for a night in the park. It always bears noting that the huts and shelters along the AT are intended primarily for backpackers spending several nights out. Presumably, hikers out for just one evening can more easily strap a tent onto their packs and find a cozy spot elsewhere in the park. Certainly, in late May and June, thru-hikers traveling north from Georgia will be found here frequently.

Back on the AT heading south, 100 ft. beyond the shelter access trail, the trail once again meets the old road which split from Trayfoot Mt. Trail, then follows the road to a junction, at 2.2 mi., with Skyline Dr. at milepost 87.2. The trail crosses to the east of the Drive and follows closely beside it for 0.2 mi., to 2.5 mi., where the AT nears Skyline Dr. at the north end of the North Fork Moormans River Fire Rd., which follows the river 9.5 mi. to a junction with the AT at Bucks Elbow Mt. Fire Rd. Adjacent to the Drive and the AT is the trailhead

parking area for Paine Run Trail and the fire road, which is also open to horseback riding. Paine Run Trail descends 3.7 mi. to a junction with Trayfoot Mt. Trail.

The North Fork and South Fork Moormans River roads comprise a former route of the AT down one stream valley and up the other, joining the present day AT again in Jarman Gap (see Hike #34). This 9.4-mi., yellow-blazed system from Blackrock Gap to Jarman Gap offers a wonderful circuit hike utilizing the fire roads and the present day AT. For this and other circuits in the park, consult the ATC's *Appalachian Trail Guide to Shenandoah National Park* and the PATC's *Circuit Hikes in Shenandoah National Park*.

From a small knob at 2.9 mi. there are limited western views of the Paine Run gorge between Horsehead (to the right) and Rocks (to the left) mountains. The top, or caps, of Rocks Mt. appears to be folding down, almost melting into the gap. The Erwin quartz caps are relatively young surface rock compared with the quartz and sandstone of the valley and substrata, formed during the Hampton formation.

The trail continues to follow the Drive, then leaves it to ascend a knob above the Horsehead Mt. Overlook. Descending once more, the trail crosses to the west of Skyline Dr. at 4.3 mi., just south of Horsehead Mt. Overlook. A five-minute detour to the overlook offers a bird's-eye view of pitch pine forests that tell a story of the Blue Ridge. These scrub trees cling to the rocky, thin soils of the western slopes, often growing where no other vegetation can gain a foothold. Pitch pines sometimes mark the locations of forest fires, acting as the hearty harbingers of future forests that will recover as the soils and conditions do.

From the Drive, the trail ascends along a dry ridge through pine and oak forest to the junction with the Riprap Trail at 5.0 mi., one of the busiest intersections in the southern SNP. The 6.3-mi. hike you can begin here to Calvary Rocks, Chimney Rock, and Cold Spring Hollow returns on the Wildcat Ridge Trail to mi. 8.1 of this hike. It is popular for its abundant views and beautiful forest undercover of Catawba rhododendron and pink azalea. Calvary Rocks are the points of an uplifted spine of quartzite carved into teeth by ice floes, really a single ridge more than a collection of rocks. Chimney Rock, a cliff of quartzite that drops more than 30 ft., stands like a skyscraper beyond Calvary Rocks. The "rocks" are a worthwhile diversion, but caution is advised. It's not hard to get lost playing on the rocks when venturing from Riprap Trail.

At 5.4 mi., a blue-blazed trail leads 0.1 mi. east to parking at the Riprap trailhead. From here, the AT hugs the ridgeline and Skyline Dr., never venturing far from the road and out of earshot of it for only a short stretch. The trail and the road pause at Riprap Overlook at 7.4 mi., and so should the hiker. To the north (right) the massive, barren talus of Calvary Rocks can be seen. These flat surface rocks cover an area the size of a soccer field, and are remnants of earlier geologic upheavals that froze, cracked, and tumbled what had been sheets of rock into the hollows below. The talus rock actually shifts slightly with extreme changes of temperature, and while experts say they are not about to drop from the side of the mountain, they prove too inhospitable for all but the simplest plant life. At 8.1 mi. the AT intersects with the Wildcat Ridge Trail. Parking at SDMP 92.1, and the end of this hike, is 0.1 mi. east.

Optional Extended Hike: If you just haven't had your fill for the day of Blue Ridge walking, continue another 2.3 mi. to Turk Gap, the northern terminus of Hike #34. The AT will cross Skyline Dr. at 8.4 mi. and ascend over 0.5 mi. to a wooded summit of 3100 ft. It's a fine stretch in winter, when there are views east of Goat Hollow and Goat Ridge from a few openings about 100 ft. east of the trail. The trail descends into Turk Gap parking area at 10.4 mi. and milepost 94.2 of Skyline Dr.

Miles N	**NORTH**	Elev. (ft/m)	Miles S
8.1	**Start: Jones Run Trail** parking at SDMP 84.1, 19.0 mi. N of I-64 in Rockfish Gap.	2700/823	0.0
7.9	Cross to W of **Skyline Dr.** at SDMP 84.2.		0.2
7.2	10-ft. path to **Trayfoot Mt. Trail,** which leads 0.3 mi. to Blackrock parking area; early exit option, alternate route to Blackrock.		0.9
6.9	**Blackrock,** views W; junction with **Blackrock Spur Trail,** leads 0.1 mi. W to Trayfoot Mt. Trail and Furnace Mt. Trail.	3090/942	1.2
6.8	Cross **Trayfoot Mt. Trail.**		1.3
6.3	Blue-blazed trail leads 0.2 mi. W to **Blackrock Hut,** spring, privy. AT joins old road.		1.8
5.9	Cross **Skyline Dr.** at SDMP 87.2.		2.2
5.6	Junction with **Moormans River Rd., SDMP 87.4; Paine Run Trail.**	2300/701	2.5
3.8	Cross **Skyline Dr.** at SDMP 88.9, early exit option.		4.3
3.1	Junction with **Riprap Trail,** start of 6.3-mi. circuit hike to Cold Spring Hollow and back to AT via Wildcat Ridge Trail.	2990/912	5.0
2.7	Blue-blazed trail leads 0.1 mi. L to **Skyline Dr.** at SDMP 90.0, parking, early exit option.		5.4
0.7	**Riprap Overlook.**		7.4
0.0	**End:** Junction with **Wildcat Ridge Trail;** to L, trail leads 0.1 mi. to SDMP 92.1, parking; 10.9 mi. N of I-64/US 250 in Rockfish Gap.	3050/930	8.1

SOUTH

Jones Run Trail to Pinefield Gap

Map: PATC Va. #11, SNP, S Dist.

Route: Through SNP from Jones Run Trail over Big Flat Mt. and Loft Mt. to Pinefield Gap

Recommended direction: S to N

Distance: 11.3 mi.

Elevation +/-: 2700 to approx. 3300 to 2500 ft.

Effort: Easy

Day hike: Yes

Overnight backpacking hike: Yes

Duration: 6 1/2 hr.

Early exit options: At 2.1 mi., 2.5 mi., and 9.7 mi., Skyline Dr.; at 3.4 mi., Doyles River Trail; at 6.7 mi., Frazier Discovery Trail

Natural history features: Deadened forests

Trailhead access: *Start:* From the Swift Run Gap entrance to SNP at US 33, go S on Skyline Dr. approximately 18.5 mi. to Jones Run Trail parking at SDMP 84.1. The AT is 100 yd. E on Jones Run Trail. For alternate route, see Hike #35. *End:* From the Swift Run Gap entrance to SNP at US 33, go S on Skyline Dr. approximately 9.5 mi. to Pinefield Gap parking, SDMP 75.3. The access trail to Pinefield Hut leads from the back of the parking lot 150 yd. to the AT.

Camping: PATC Doyle River cabin (reservations required); Loft Mt. Campground (open April to October); Pinefield Hut; and see "Camping" in Introduction

---

D on't let the mileage scare you: This is an easy hike. With its ready access to Loft Mt. Campground providing early exits, it is also a perfect hike for introducing a friend or child to the AT. The scenic rewards are as plentiful and effortless to reach as they are varied and expansive. The terrain is gentle, with no sharp ascent of more than a hundred yards, and soft underfoot—almost always on soil and grasses free from rocks. The trail runs close enough to Skyline Dr. and Loft Mt. Campground that one never feels totally out in the wilds.

To reach the AT from the Jones Run Trail parking, follow the blue-blazed trail east 50 yd. to the AT. Jones Run Trail descends straight ahead into a gorge and along waterfalls for 2.5 mi. to its junction with the Doyles River Trail, which leads 2.2 mi. up the Doyles River past more waterfalls to a junction with the AT 3.4 mi. north of this point. This waterfall ramble offers a scenic side trip from the AT, but requires a 1300-ft. descent and a 1500-ft. ascent back to the trail.

Traveling north (left) on the AT from the junction with Jones Run Trail, the trail follows level terrain

White-tailed deer

0.4 mi. into Dundo Group Camp-ground, which is open only to orga-nized group outings (call SNP headquarters, 703-999-2229, for reser-vations). The water spigot and privy, however, are open to all visitors and are readily visible from the trail.

The casual walk continues amidst chestnut oak and maple with Skyline Dr. above to your left and the Doyles River valley visible through the trees below to your right. Past an aban-doned footpath on the left at 0.9 mi., the trail moves to the right of a small knoll, then descends gently to meet gravel Madison Run Rd. and Browns Gap Rd. just as they and the AT meet Skyline Dr. at milepost 82.9. Crossing to the left of the Drive, the AT turns north as Madison Run Rd. descends to the west and Browns Gap Rd. descends to the east. Gen. Stonewall Jackson used these two roads through Browns Gap to con-duct his famed Valley Campaign during the Civil War. Modern hikers ascending north along the AT will enjoy long views of farmland and Massanutten Mt. to the west.

At 1.8 mi. the Big Run Loop Trail opens up a world of circuit hikes on the Blue Ridge's western slope and in its valley, including a popular jaunt that takes the Big Run Loop north-ward 4.2 mi. to rejoin the AT at Big Run Overlook. Big Run Loop con-nects with the Rockytop and Big Run Portal trails, which in turn form the trunk lines of a nearly hundred-mile wilderness trail system. Only half a mile or so from Skyline Dr., the crowds thin and the opportunities for quiet camping abound.

The AT crosses to the east of Sky-line Dr. at 2.1 mi., at SDMP 82.2, and ascends lazily along an eastern ledge until passing through the Doyles River Overlook at 2.5 mi., where there is parking for fourteen cars. Situated at the western end of the gorge carved by the Doyles River, this is a fine spot for rest stop. The view from left to right is of Gibson, Martins, and, at the end of the gorge, High Top mountains. Almost as striking as the view is the windlike sound of water echoing from below, a sound that will travel with you as you move north along the ledge under a para-sol of oak.

The AT crosses Doyles River Trail at 3.4 mi. Doyles River parking on Sky-line Dr., offering an exit option for a short hike, is 200 yd. up the hill to the left. Downhill are the scenic falls of Doyles River and the splendid seclusion of Doyles River Cabin. The cabin, which sleeps twelve and may be reserved through the PATC, is perched atop a cliff, offering arresting views of Cedar Mt. It is, without exaggeration, a picture-perfect place to watch a colorful sunset and spend an evening—but the precipitous roost is not recommended for small children.

From Doyles River Trail, the AT begins a casual ascent of Big Flat Mt. Never challenging, the climb is just enough to get the blood moving after time in the car. The trail is generous with level rest spots; they come every 50 yd. in case hikers need them. Most won't, as it's only 0.3 mi. to the ridge of Big Flat, a walk even toddlers can handle.

Alongside the trail the blackberry thicket and bramble provide ample cover for deer and fox, but not so much cover to hide them from your view. Deer, at least, will be hard to avoid. The thicket here illustrates the stunted rejuvenation of farm field to forest. Cleared beginning in the 1850s for grazing, this patch of level ground above the gorge was grassland until the park's designation permitted recovery to forest. The woodlands recovered and hardwood species such as oak and hickory returned in the 1950s, but a gypsy moth outbreak in the 1980s has devastated the foliage. This phenomenon can be viewed from many overlooks of the southern section of SNP, where acres of denuded forest struggle to outlast the insects. Robbed of leaves devoured by moths, the trees have no means to photosynthesize their food. Many have withered, but the power of the forest to overcome such adversity can be seen in the oak saplings emerging from the bramble. The forest will outlast even the moths.

At 3.7 mi., the flat top for which this mountain is named is reached after an easy ascent. A huge, open, flat slab of limestone provides one of several outstanding views along this saunter. To the west is the easily identifiable Rockytop, a mass of quartzite and basalt. To the north, or right of Rockytop, are Brown Mt., Rocky Mt., and Loft Mt.

The treeless slopes and hollows of Brown Mt. and Rocky Top are not victims of the moths that plagued other nearby forested slopes. In 1985, a hiker attempting to light a cookstove set off a blaze that consumed 4000 acres of the Big Run valley between the two mountains. Because the fire was caused by human activity, the Park Service contained it before it caused even more damage. Fires caused by lightning or other natural occurrences are sometimes left to burn as nature intended. Decisions about whether to contain a fire within a national park also depend upon its proximity to human habitation. With people living closer to the park each year, naturally occurring blazes could be subject to control in order to protect people outside the park.

Almost as remarkable as the vastness of the burnout on Brown and

Rocky mountains is the speed with which the forest is recovering. Ten years after the fire, there are places on the hillside above Big Run that resemble a tree nursery. Climbing from among the new grasses are pines and locusts, and already the deer are munching on the leaves of small trees. The recovery of the forest has been good news for Big Run, the watershed that drains 22 square mi. to the east of Rocky Top and Brown mountains. The largest watershed in SNP, it had been muddied by erosion from the treeless slopes of Rocky Mt. and other peaks, robbing the Big Run of oxygen and threatening the health of the stream. Now they are running cleaner than at any time since the fire.

Traveling north from the Big Flat overlook, the terrain remains level for 300 yd. along the ridge. From the deer prints visible in wet weather along the trail, this section of the AT might appear to have more four-legged hikers than human ones. It is likely that the proximity to Loft Mt. Campground draws deer in search of snacks. After summer campers have abandoned the area for the winter, evidence of bears coming to clean the brush of berries, mainly paw prints around puddle edges and scat on the rocks, can also be seen. There are plenty of blackberries along Big Flat for summer hikers to live the bear's life for a while.

The AT begins an easy ascent of Loft Mt., reaching the first junction with Loft Mt. Campground trail at 4.2

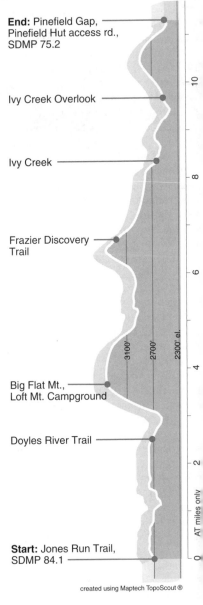

End: Pinefield Gap, Pinefield Hut access rd., SDMP 75.2

Ivy Creek Overlook

Ivy Creek

Frazier Discovery Trail

Big Flat Mt., Loft Mt. Campground

Doyles River Trail

Start: Jones Run Trail, SDMP 84.1

3100' 2700' 2300' el.

AT miles only

created using Maptech TopoScout ®

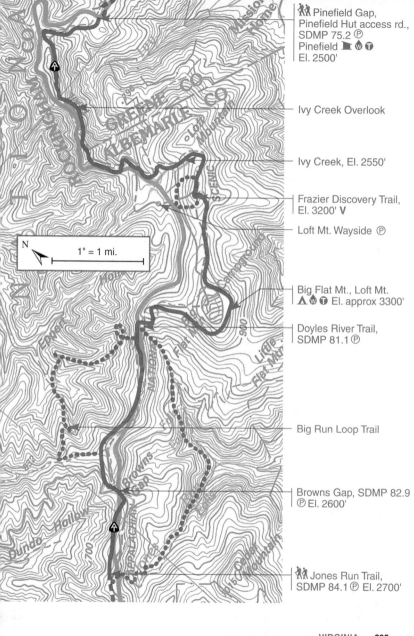

Pinefield Gap, Pinefield Hut access rd., SDMP 75.2 ℗
Pinefield 🏕 🅦 🚻
El. 2500'

Ivy Creek Overlook

Ivy Creek, El. 2550'

Frazier Discovery Trail, El. 3200' **V**

Loft Mt. Wayside ℗

Big Flat Mt., Loft Mt. ▲ 🅦 🚻 El. approx 3300'

Doyles River Trail, SDMP 81.1 ℗

Big Run Loop Trail

Browns Gap, SDMP 82.9 ℗ El. 2600'

Jones Run Trail, SDMP 84.1 ℗ El. 2700'

N 1" = 1 mi.

mi. Concrete posts mark each of the three side trails to the campground. There are showers, laundry, toilets, picnic areas, and a camp store (accessible from the AT at 5.5 mi.). A wayside exhibit area and restaurant are at SDMP 79.5. From the first side trail junction, the AT starts a 1-mi. trip around the edge of the campground, all the while hugging the ridge and offering plentiful views to the east and south.

The first of these views, at the junction of the second access trail to the campground, opens south over Doyles River valley to Cedar Mt. and Pond Ridge, offering a telling scene from the Blue Ridge story. From here, the ridge is revealed as a crooked line of mountains and hollows sandwiched between the "Foothill Zone" of the Piedmont and the valleys of the Shenandoah and South rivers. The Blue Ridge Mts. are constructed largely of a resistant, metamorphosed sedimentary and volcanic rock, appearing in many places along the trail as the darkly speckled basalt known as greenstone. The craggy hollows between the slopes and, to the east, the rugged inner Piedmont are the eroded remains of the same formation that created the ridge, an uplift known as the Blue Ridge Anticlinorium.

As the trail skirts the campground picnic area, it is possible to enjoy lunch at a table a mere 25 yd. from the trail as it opens a view eastward toward the Piedmont. The trail follows the ridge and reveals views to the east also of Fox Mt. and to the northeast of the jumbled mass of, left to right, Wyatt, Brokenback, and Countyline mountains (in the foreground). Basalt boulders, remnants of lava flows, dot the picnic grove as if placed by design, while the trail traverses a vein of white quartzite that glistens in the morning sun.

With so many overlooks along the trail here, a point of leave-no-trace hiking bears noting. Where once strategically placed access paths led to overlooks every 100 yd. or so, there are now multiple pathways leading from the AT. Each new path degrades the surrounding vegetation; eventually, the entire rim will be open to the trail. Hikers should follow only established pathways to the ledges then return to the trail along the same pathway. Although unmarked the established paths to the rim are easy to spot.

The AT continues past the trail to the camp store (only 70 yd. from the trail) at 5.5 mi. and enters an area formerly known as Patterson Field. The former pasture, which lies in the sag between Big Flat and Loft mountains, is a living, changing natural history museum. The trail tread is matted green grass, not dissimilar to the kind found in many backyards but here it is a remnant of pasture. Berries and low brush push up to the trail; black locusts and other regenerative species form a low cover; and young, new oaks emerge below the locusts. The older, giant oaks, 3 to 5 ft in diameter, were present long before

19th-century farmers cleared the flat acres of the northern Blue Ridge for pasture. Together, the old oaks, the remnant apple trees and grasses, the locusts that sprouted after the park's designation, and now the new oaks and maples trace the natural history from colonial days to modern times.

At 6.0 mi. the trail begins its ascent of Loft Mt., casually traipsing 0.3 mi. up through a stand of cedar and locust. Then the trail enters a series of sharp switchbacks, and ascends especially steeply for a final 75-yd. climb before leveling off at 6.6 mi. on a crest. The Deadening Nature Trail enters from the left and follows the AT to a spectacular overlook. High above Skyline Dr., the view is open to the southwest and the northwest, revealing Massanutten Mt. across the Shenandoah Valley and the Allegheny Mts. on the horizon. On a clear day, the South Fork Shenandoah River shines to the northeast.

The Frazier Discovery Trail follows the AT another 150 yd. north, then leaves the AT at 6.7 mi., beginning its 0.6-mi. descent to Skyline Dr. at the entrance to Loft Mt. Campground, directly across from Loft Mt. Wayside, parking, and the Loft Mt. Restaurant, open Memorial Day through Labor Day. The still-standing deadened oaks and hickories along the trail are hundreds of years older than the locust, maple, and chestnut oak that now make up the forest. To clear the steep hillside for pasture, the mature trees were stripped of their bark, a process known as deadening, so that they would die in place. Without a canopy of leaves, sunlight reached the ground and encouraged grasses, which fed cattle. The trail, and a shortened version of this hike, ends at SDMP 79.5.

Moving north from the Frazier Discovery Trail, the AT follows a gentle descent along the Loft Mt. ridgeline under a low canopy for 0.2 mi., then descends sharply below the summit, which rises to the right. At 7.6 mi. a path leads left 180 yd. to a spring near a park maintenance building. The trail continues its descent, reaching the bank of Ivy Creek at 8.0 mi. The next 0.3 mi. are a pleasant stroll along the stream among tall hemlocks that litter a bed of soft needles. Below the hemlocks is an understory of mountain laurel, while rising above are ledges of Weaverton quartzite. Skyline Dr., only 350 yd. to the west, is a world away; if you didn't see its proximity on the map, you wouldn't believe it. Here in the darkened wood, where the trail crosses Ivy Creek at 8.3 mi., is a fine place to find a rest spot among the soft needles.

From the creek the trail ascends, then switches back to climb more steeply, coming to within 100 ft. of Skyline Dr. and continuing a steady rise with the road falling to the left. The hemlocks of the Ivy Creek glen give way to chestnut oak and gray maple; then the trail breaks through the trees at 9.0 mi. atop a level plateau to reveal long views west of Rockytop and Trayfoot mountains. The construction of Skyline Dr., snaking northward, has exposed Hampton strata, formed from sand and mud sediments some 250 million years ago. From this perch on the AT, the mica minerals exposed in road cuts can sparkle in the sun like diamonds, on some days making the Drive from here look more like a river than a road.

Staying close to the Drive, the trail descends to Ivy Creek Overlook, passing through the southern end at 9.7 mi. at SDMP 77.5. Take a moment here to enjoy the view to the east, back down the trail, into Ivy Creek valley beneath Loft Mt. on the right and Big Flat on the left.

Leaving the overlook, the trail makes a casual ascent to a wooded summit, only to descend again toward Skyline Dr. A side trail at 10.7 mi. leads 180 yd. left to SDMP 77.5, and the trail breaks to the right and continues a descent to a point about 30 yd. from the Drive at 11.1 mi., before tumbling into the dirt access road to Pinefield Hut at 11.3 mi. Pinefield Hut is 170 yd. to the right down the road. On the way, the trail passes a seasonal spring 75 ft. down the road; another spring and privy are behind the shelter. To the left, the trail leads 150 yd. to Pinefield Hut parking at SDMP 75.2 and the end of the hike.

Optional Extended Hike: Still have more hiking in mind? You can hike 1.9 mi. further to Simmons Gap. From the access road, the AT ascends through a meager stand of black locust and walnut amidst scattered remnant apple trees. The thickets growing in the occasional clearings 20 yd. to the east are lush with black berries. As Skyline Dr. breaks east ward, below, and the trail starts a sharper ascent north of Weaver Mt. all is quiet. Here the trail is far from the Drive and the campers of Loft Mt. At 12.3 mi. the trail finds the wooded summit of Weaver Mt. at 2864 ft. Fol lowing its eastern ledge, then slab bing to the northwest, the best view is a winter one, to the west through the trees and straight down the valley of Twomile Run. The South Fork Shenandoah River can be seen 5 mi to the northwest and 1800 ft. below

The 611-ft. drop into Simmons Gap is covered in just over a mile of more locust and scattered hemlock and eastern cedar. Descending, it's hard not to notice the roar of the wind whipping through the gap as loud as a waterfall. The seemingly ever present wind is part of the life cycle of Simmons Gap, one of the many wind gaps the AT passes through in the Blue Ridge. While some gaps along the Appalachians were formed by water—the most famous along the AT in the Virginias being Harper Ferry Gap where the Potomac meets the Shenandoah—Simmons Gap was formed by the erosion brought about by ceaseless breezes. In the floor of the gap, at 13.4 mi., the trail meets Fork Hollow Fire Rd. at Skyline Dr., milepost 73.2. The AT crosses to the northeast where roadside park ing is available.

HIKE #36 Itinerary

Miles N	NORTH	Elev. (ft/m)	Miles S
11.3	**End: Dirt access road.** To R 170 yd. is **Pinefield Hut,** spring, privy; to L 150 yd. is Pinefield Hut parking at Pinefield Gap, SDMP 75.2, approximately 9.5 mi. S of US 33 entrance to park.	2500/762	0.0
10.3	**Wooded summit,** no views.	3080/939	1.0
9.7	**Ivy Creek Overlook,** SDMP 77.5, early exit option.		1.6
8.3	**Ivy Creek,** hemlock grove.	2550/777	3.0
6.7	**Frazier Discovery Trail** leads 0.6 mi. to SDMP 79.5, early exit option.	3200/975	4.6
6.6	Views from **Loft Mt.**	3315/1011	4.7
5.5	Pass trail to **camp store** (70 yd.).		5.8
4.2	Post marks first side trail to **Loft Mt. Campground.**		7.1
3.7	Views from **Big Flat Mt.**	approx. 3300/1033	7.6
3.4	Cross **Doyles River Trail,** trail L 200 yd. to parking at SDMP 81.1 (early exit option), R to Doyles River cabin; Big Run Loop Trail rejoins AT.		7.9
2.5	Pass through **Doyles River Overlook** at SDMP 81.9; views of river gorge and mountains; early exit option.		8.8
2.1	Cross to E of **Skyline Dr.** at SDMP 82.2.		9.2
1.8	Junction with **Big Run Loop Trail;** loop rejoins AT 4.2 mi. N.		9.5
1.2	**Browns Gap** at SDMP 82.9; junction with Madison Run Rd. and Browns Gap Rd.; cross Drive.	2600/792	10.1
0.4	**Dundo Group Campground** (reservations required), water, privy.		
0.0	**Start: Jones Run Trail,** parking at SDMP 84.1, approximately 18.5 mi. S of US 33 entrance to park.	2700/823	11.3

SOUTH

HIKE #37

Simmons Gap to South River Falls

Maps: PATC Va. #11, SNP, S Dist., & #10, SNP, Central Dist.

Route: Through SNP from Simmons Gap at SDMP 73.0 over Flattop Mt. to Powell Gap, over W slope of Little Roundtop Mt. to Smith Roach Gap, over Hightop Mt. to Swift Run Gap and South River Picnic Area, SDMP 63

Recommended direction: S to N

Distance: 12.7 mi. total; 12.6 mi. on AT

Access trail name & length: South River Falls Trail, 0.1 mi.

Elevation +/-: 2250 to 3590 to 2800 ft.

Effort: Moderate to strenuous

Day hike: Yes

Overnight backpacking: No

Duration: 6 1/2 to 8 hr.

Early exit options: At 3.3 mi., 4.9 mi., 8.3 mi., and 9.5 mi., Skyline Dr.

Natural history features: At 3587 ft., Hightop Mt. is the highest point in the S Dist. of SNP. Much of the section has wilderness status.

Social history features: John Lederer's explorations; Gov. Spottswood's explorations

Trailhead access: *Start:* From Harrisonburg, proceed E on US 33 for approximately 22 mi. to Skyline Dr., entering SNP 7.0 mi. E of Elkton and US 340. Head S on Skyline Dr. for 7.7 mi. to Simmons Gap at SDMP 73.2. Trailhead is at intersection of Skyline Dr. and Simmons Gap Fire Rd. There is roadside parking for 6 to 8 cars. *End:* From US 340 in Elkton, head E on US 33 for 7.0 mi. to Skyline Dr. Head N on the Drive for 3.0 mi. to South River Picnic Area. Side trail in SE corner of picnic area leads 0.1 mi. to AT. There is ample parking in picnic area lot. Rest rooms and water are also available at picnic area.

Camping: No public camping areas or shelters (Hightop Hut is for long-distance hikers only); permit required for backcountry camping, see "Camping" in Introduction

I f you're looking for a good workout in a peaceful setting, this is the hike for you. Located in the wildest, least developed area of Shenandoah National Park, this section of the AT is riddled with steep, winding climbs and sloping downward trends. Its appeal comes from the satisfaction of climbing Hightop, the highest peak in the southern end of the park. There are also several smaller personal triumphs along the way as the trail crests a series of peaks that make up Roundtop and Hightop mountains. Although the steep climbs make this hike moderately strenuous, the surface of the trail is well maintained and easy to pass in most sections. There are few water sources along this section so

The Legend of John Lederer

The few traces of Native American habitation found in Shenandoah National Park, including arrowheads, spear points, and stone tools, show that humans lived in the area at least 11,500 years ago. Historians believe that the first Europeans to climb into the Blue Ridge Mts. and look out at the view of the frontier wilderness did not arrive until a little more than 300 years ago. These early explorers were likely hunters, trappers, traders, and missionaries; there are no written records of these visits.

The earliest known account of European exploration in the Shenandoah region is chronicled by John Lederer, a German medical practitioner. On March 18, 1669, Lederer wrote in his journal that he climbed the Blue Ridge Mts. to begin a six-day adventure over the snow-covered peaks in search of passage through the mountains and into the Shenandoah Valley. Lederer encountered some Sioux-speaking natives living east of the Blue Ridge crest. He wrote that their leaders were eloquent in speaking and skilled in governing. How-ever, resident Native Americans had disappeared from the Shenandoah Valley west of the Blue Ridge by the time Lederer arrived. The last traces of Native Americans in the Shenandoah Valley date back to the 1500s. It is believed that the French and Dutch traders, who paid guns and ammunition in exchange for furs, gave the Iroquois of the north the power they needed to drive other Native inhabitants out. By the time Lederer arrived, the valley was a fur plantation and a warpath for Native Americans battling tribes further south.

Today, US 33, just east of Swift Run Gap, is thought to approximately trace the route Lederer followed. Many historians also agree that the peak Lederer climbed to begin his trek is the summit of what is now known as Hightop Mt. The Hightop Summit hike starts at SDMP 66.7 and leads through 1.5 mi. of hardwoods to reach an outcropping of Catoctin greenstone where, on a clear day, hikers can view the entire southern third of the park. Could Lederer have enjoyed the same view over 300 years ago?

---

be sure to fill your canteen before you start. This hike isn't graced by the scenic views afforded to many other stretches, making it a particularly good hike to take on a cloudy day when you won't be able to see much anyway!

This section begins in Simmons Gap, a 600-ft.-deep wind gap carved in the Catoctin formation of the Blue Ridge crest. Catoctin rocks are characterized by underlying greenstone that was once flowing lava. As the lava cooled and then was altered by heat, pressure, and hot water, the rock's color changed from black to green. Notice the craggy appearance of the greenstone and compare it to the squarish edges of the quartzite stones further north.

From the intersection of Simmons Gap Fire Rd. and Skyline Dr. at SDMP 73.2, the trail follows Simmons Gap Rd. east of Skyline Dr. for less than 40 ft. before turning left onto a grassy path. The road leads south to a ranger's office and Park Service maintenance facilities. Water is available from a faucet at the ranger station, in case you need to fill up before you hit the trail. The hike starts with a steep ascent, as the trail passes under a series of power lines before making its way to the top of Flattop Mt. As the trail climbs, it intersects a thick forest dominated by towering chestnut oaks, the most populous tree in the park. Among the chestnuts, look for red oaks, hickories, and an occasional pine tree. This area of SNP is home to trees that are older than those elsewhere in the park.

After enough of a climb to get your heart pumping, the ascent tapers to a gradual climb, then, at 0.4 mi., the trail dips to descend over wide rock steps. Don't be lured into thinking the climb is over—the trail bends to the left beyond the stone stepladder and continues its sharp uphill climb. The trail is wide and grassy and the few rocks that do break the surface are firmly embedded in the surrounding soil. As you climb, be on the lookout for white-tailed deer and black bear. Bobcats are also common to the area, although they are rarely seen by hikers. If the soil is moist or covered

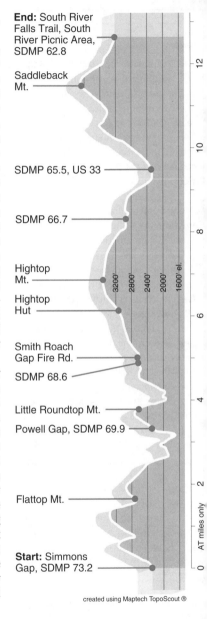

End: South River Falls Trail, South River Picnic Area, SDMP 62.8

Saddleback Mt.

SDMP 65.5, US 33

SDMP 66.7

Hightop Mt.

Hightop Hut

Smith Roach Gap Fire Rd.

SDMP 68.6

Little Roundtop Mt.

Powell Gap, SDMP 69.9

Flattop Mt.

Start: Simmons Gap, SDMP 73.2

AT miles only

created using Maptech TopoScout ®

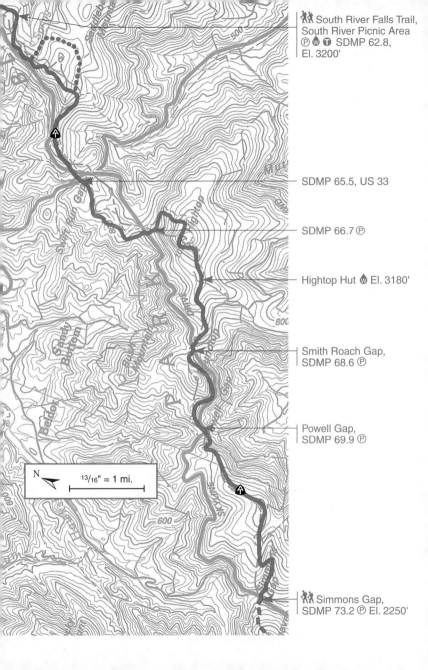

🚶 South River Falls Trail,
South River Picnic Area
Ⓟ 💧 ⊤ SDMP 62.8,
El. 3200'

SDMP 65.5, US 33

SDMP 66.7 Ⓟ

Hightop Hut 💧 El. 3180'

Smith Roach Gap,
SDMP 68.6 Ⓟ

Powell Gap,
SDMP 69.9 Ⓟ

N

¹³/₁₆" = 1 mi.

🚶 Simmons Gap,
SDMP 73.2 Ⓟ El. 2250'

by recent snow, check for the bobcat's tracks, which resemble those of an extremely oversized house cat.

The trail reaches the summit of the shoulder of Flattop Mt. 1.6 mi. into the hike. The mountain lives up to its name and the trail runs evenly along the northern ridge crest. Thick woods in spring, summer, and early fall confine the view to the trail's immediate surroundings. In early spring, before the leaves have fully developed into a thick, shady canopy, look for bloodroot and columbine, just starting to bloom. Later in the season, under the shelter of thick leaves, dogwoods thrive and flower in the understory of the forest.

After following the ridgeline for 1.2 mi. the trail reaches a rocky ledge. Stepping out onto the massive greenstone that juts from the side of the mountain, look to the east over Roach River valley. In mid-October, when colors in the park are at their peak, this view makes up for the limited number of overlooks throughout this section. From this vantage point, you can see vibrant reds, yellows, oranges, and greens forming a patchwork pattern across the rolling pastures for which Virginia is renowned.

Beyond the overlook, the trail crosses to the left of the ridge, then back to the right as it begins its descent into Powell Gap. Soon Skyline Dr. appears in flashing glances through the trees, running parallel below and to the right of the trail. As the trail continues downward, the thick stand of trees that characterized the earlier section of the hike begins to thin and the surface of the trail becomes much rockier. When you hit a double-blazed post (3.0 mi.), prepare to make a sharp right onto a former road. The trail's rocky surface here makes this a tricky turn.

After the turn the descent gets much steeper as Skyline Dr. becomes a constant fixture to the left. Continue swiftly downward through a series of twists and turns, as though descending a spiral staircase. At 3.7 mi. the trail enters a grassy, open area in Powell Gap (2295 ft.) at SDMP 69.9. There is roadside parking here, making this an early exit option on this hike.

In Powell Gap, the trail's underlying rock changes from greenstone to that of the Pedlar formation, a thick, part quartz rock that formed deep inside the earth's crust while the mountain was still in its earliest stages. The Precambrian surface was buried by Catoctin lavas and is now visible in only a few areas of the park.

From Powell Gap the AT crosses to the west side of Skyline Dr. and cuts through a grassy area before ascending into the woods. Approximately 100 yd. beyond Skyline Dr., the next challenge abuts the awaiting horizon. As chestnut oaks, red oaks, and hickories thicken around the trail, prepare to conquer Little Roundtop Mt. Fortunately, the trail is wide and grassy and the upward slope begins as a gentle climb. Look over the right side of the trail to see Skyline Dr. running a parallel course several feet below you. The ascent grows steeper as you proceed (you didn't think you could crest a mountain without a little work did you?) but the climb is short. As the trail reaches higher land, Virginia and white pines begin to mix with the hickory and oak. The higher you go, the more prevalent the pines become, eventually dominating the hardwoods. In 0.5 mi., the trail reaches the summit of Little Roundtop (3.8 mi.) and follows a wide, even trail across its wooded crest. Look for blueberry bushes along the ridge.

As the trail swings to the east side of the mountain, the pines disappear as quickly as they came and oak and hickory dominate the surrounding forest once more. In the winter you can catch glimpses of Powell Gap and Flattop Mt. disappearing behind you. The trail remains wide but gets rockier as it continues along the eastern ridgeline. The trail tests your aerobic endurance with a few steep dips before descending into Smith Roach Gap. As you near Skyline Dr., pine trees return. A thick blanket of fern covers the surrounding ground.

At 4.9 mi. (SDMP 68.6) the trail reaches Smith Roach Gap (2622 ft.) and crosses back to the east side of Skyline Dr. A small parking area makes this a second early exit option. The AT crosses an old fire road and ascends. The fire road leads east 1.0 mi. to the park's boundary. The climb grows steeper as the trail

winds through more old stands of oak and hickory. In fall and winter you can see traces of Skyline Dr. behind you as you continue upward. Standing at the base of a high oak, look for an accumulation of broken branches, a sign that bears have recently been feeding there.

After over a mile of steep uphill climbing, the trail crosses a wide, well-maintained, grass-covered road (6.1 mi.). This is the Hightop Hut service road. The hut itself is located 0.1 mi. to the left and is only available to long-distance AT hikers. However, there is water at the site for endurance and day hikers alike. From the hut a graded trail leads down a small hill to a nearby spring.

Beyond Hightop Hut the trail makes a sharp right and heads up another steep hill. Large rock formations rise up to flank the trail on the east and the west as the AT crosses back onto greenstone. The trail winds through these large mounds of craggy green rock and continues its upward climb. Steps cut into the trail give you a slight boost.

A half mile further on, the trail crosses a damp area, then reaches a yellow marker indicating a nearby spring. The spring is actually a slow trickle spurting from a small pipe into a rocky cubicle. The encasement is approximately 2 ft. square, with water spilling over the sides. Coarse animal hairs sticking out between the stones reveal this as a popular watering hole for local inhabitants. It also provides a refreshing break for weary hikers; the water is cold and deliciously fresh. Fill up your water bottle here and get ready for another climb.

At 6.9 mi. the AT reaches the 3587-ft. summit of Hightop Mt., which offers views to the west of Sandy Bottom Valley and the beginning of Swift Run Gap. Again, these views are at their best when colored with the bright, rusty shades of autumn. On a particularly clear fall or winter day it is possible to see many of the peaks in the southern end of the park.

The earliest record of European exploration in the Shenandoah region recounts the travels of John Lederer, a German doctor who headed to the new frontier in search of timber and furs. On March 18, 1669, he climbed the Blue Ridge Mts. and began a six-day search for a route through them. Many believe it was from Highpoint Mt. that Lederer first viewed the Shenandoah Valley.

After crossing the summit, the trail begins sloping downward. The descent gets steeper as it cuts to the east, passing over a series of stone steps, then switchbacks down the northern side of the mountain. As it continues downward, the trail passes through a forest of dead trees before it is rejoined by the large rock boulders. Forest fires are common in the dry southwestern part of the park, often occurring three to four times annually. Most fires occur in March or April when humidity typically is low. Fires are also prevalent in autumn.

Most fires are sparked by human activity, such as trash burning or careless cooking, but lightning is also a source.

At 8.3 mi. (SDMP 66.7) the trail leaves the forest and rocks behind and enters a low sag carpeted with thick, tall grass. Approximately 100 ft. further the trail crosses Skyline Dr. at a small parking area, offering yet another early exit option. On the western side of Skyline Dr., reenter the woods and immediately begin a steep upward climb. Don't be disheartened. This is a short and easy climb. The trail quickly flattens out as it passes through an old apple orchard, then descends steeply to Swift Run Gap (SDMP 65.5).

At 9.5 mi. the trail picks up Skyline Dr. at the US 33 overpass. Now a major thruway, US 33 is called The Spotswood Trail in memory of Gov. Alexander Spotswood, Virginia's royal governor from 1710 to 1722. Anxious to see some of the frontier settled before the French moved in and established their own colonies, Spotswood set off for the Shenandoah wilderness in 1716 with an entourage of sixty-three men. The group brought horses, hunting dogs, food, liquor, and other supplies. Heading west from Williamsburg, Spotswood crossed the Blue Ridge and entered the Shenandoah Valley, annexing it in the name of King George I of England. Later Spotswood continued to encourage colonization of the Shenandoah Valley with a land-grant program that exempted frontier settlers from taxes. He also negotiated an agreement with the Iroquois in which they agreed to remain north of the Potomac River. By the mid-1720s Spotswood began to see results, as a steadily increasing number of British settlers arrived in areas east and west of the Blue Ridge.

A narrow pedestrian walkway carries the AT along the edge of the Skyline Dr. bridge to the east side of Swift Run Gap (9.6 mi.). Stonewall Jackson's army once camped about 7 mi. west of the gap, in Elkton. Today the town is booming with industry, including Merck & Co. (the pharmaceutical people) and a Coors brewery. The village of Standardsville lies approximately 8 mi. to the east. The closest parking area is at SDMP 64.9.

The gap is underlain by the granite rock of the 1.1-billion-year-old Pedlar formation (see above), producing a rocky climb as the trail reenters the woods and begins a steep, uphill journey. For the next 2.0 mi. the trail cuts upward through a thick, wooded area, to the crest of Saddleback Mt. (11.5 mi.). At 3296 ft., even the peak of Saddleback offers few viewing opportunities, but cresting it is a satisfying achievement and there are several rocks at the top for taking a well-deserved break. In early spring thick patches of trillium seem to race throughout the area.

Beyond Saddleback Mt. the trail makes its final descent, heading through a thick pine and oak-pine forest before intersecting with the well-graded South River Falls Trail at 12.6 mi. This blue-blazed side trail leads 0.1 mi. to the South River Picnic Area and the end of this hike.

Even the final approach to the picnic area is a gentle upward slope, culminating a day of challenging but rewardingly attainable climbs that make this hike a satisfying way to explore what scientists believe is one of the oldest sections of SNP.

HIKE #37   Itinerary

Miles N	**NORTH**	Elev. (ft/m)	Miles S
	**Total: 12.7 mi. with access on South River Falls Trail.**		
0.1	Access: South River Picnic Area parking lot, SDMP 62.8, 3.0 mi. N of Swift Run Gap SNP entrance.		0.1
12.6	**End:** Turn L onto **South River Falls Trail.**	3200/975	0.0
12.3	Join old road entering from R for 0.2 mi.		0.3
12.1	**Saddleback Trail** leads R 0.3 mi. to maintenance building (locked).		0.5
11.5	Reach top of rise on W side of **Saddleback Mt.**		1.1
9.5	Cross **US 33** on Skyline Dr. bridge (0.1 mi.) to Swift Run Gap; early exit option.	2370/722	3.1
8.3	Cross Skyline Dr. at **SDMP 66.7** (early exit option) and begin ascending steep switchbacks.		4.3
6.9	Summit of **Hightop Mt.**	3590/1094	5.7
6.6	Spring.		6.0
6.1	Hightop Hut service road goes L 0.1 mi. to spring, long-distance hikers' shelter.	3180/969	6.5
5.0	Cross **Smith Roach Gap Fire Rd.**		7.6
4.9	**Smith Roach Gap;** SDMP 68.6, early exit option.	2620/799	7.7
3.8	Summit of **Little Roundtop Mt.** and view of Powell Gap.		8.8
3.3	**Powell Gap** at SDMP 69.9; early exit option.	2300/701	9.3
1.6	Summit of shoulder of **Flattop Mt.**		11.0
0.0	**Start: Simmons Gap Fire Rd.** at SDMP 73.2; roadside parking. 7.7 mi. S of Swift Run Gap entrance to SNP.	2250/686	12.6

SOUTH

South River Falls to Bearfence Mt.

Map: PATC Va. #10, SNP, Central Dist.

Route: Through SNP from South River Picnic Area past Lewis Mt. and over Bearfence Mt.

Recommended direction: S to N

Distance: 7.3 mi. total; 7.2 mi. on AT

Access trail name & length: South River Falls Trail, 0.1 mi.

Elevation +/-: 2900 to 3600 to 3300 ft.

Effort: Easy

Day hike: Yes

Overnight backpacking hike: Optional

Duration: 4 hr.

Early exit option: At 3.4 mi., Skyline Dr.; at 5.2 mi., Lewis Mt. picnic area

Natural history features: South River Falls; disease-caused deforestation; 5.0 mi. of intermittent blowdowns; Bearfence Mt. Rock Scramble

Social history feature: Lewis Mt. Campground

Other feature: Camp store at Lewis Mt. Campground

Trailhead access: *Start:* From US 340 in Elkton, head E on US 33 for 7.0 mi. to Skyline Dr. Head N on Drive for 3.0 mi. to South River Picnic Area. Side trail in SE corner of picnic area leads 0.1 mi. to AT. There is ample parking in picnic area lot. Rest rooms and water are also available at picnic area. *End:* From the intersection of US 33 and Skyline Dr., travel N on Drive to Bearfence Mt. parking, mile 56.4.

Camping: PATC Pocosin Cabin; Lewis Mt. Campground; Bearfence Mt. Hut; and see "Camping" in Introduction

---

Although the views are not abundant and the water is scarce, this hike is full of history. Where else could a few hours reveal so much about forest regeneration, the American Civil Rights movement, the birth of the Appalachians and the role of the northeastern winds in the natural selection of tree species? There are gems to be found on this hike, but only the curious will discover them. And it is not as though there are no vistas along the way. Bearfence Mt., near the northern end of the hike,

offers long views and a chance to scramble over rocks high above the Piedmont.

The hike is best approached from the south, to better enjoy the steady rise through mountain laurel and rhododendron along a stone retaining wall built by the Civilian Conservation Corps. For views of valleys and hollows through the trees, take this hike after mid-October has removed the leaves from the trees in the higher elevations. If you time it right, you will be able to see easily through the naked trees to the colorful trees of the lower elevations, which lose their leaves about two weeks later.

The hike begins at the South River Picnic Area, where you will find water for your bottles and public rest rooms. Reach the AT via the 0.1-mi. blue-blazed South River Falls Trail, and turn left to head north. A side trip 1.5 mi. down the South River Falls Trail leads to the 83-ft. falls, third highest in the park. The South River cuts a deep gorge through greenstone rock along the way, making the trip to the falls as scenic as the destination. If accepting this diversion before setting out on the hike to Bearfence, be warned that the elevation loss of 1000 ft. to the falls must be regained!

Traveling north on the AT from the South River Falls Trail, the trail crosses the South River Fire Rd. at 0.5 mi., 350 yd. east of Skyline Dr. For the next mile ascend Baldface Mt. steadily but gently. Much of the hike repeats that theme: There are no outright steep stretches of any length, but over the long haul there is a lot of up.

Still to be seen lying in decay, and standing in places, now longer dead than alive, are American chestnut trees. Once the most valuable and abundant hardwood in the Appalachians, the chestnut was destroyed by the chestnut blight fungus imported from Asia early in the 20th century. With a trunk of 3 to 4 ft. in diameter, and heights up to 90 ft., the chestnut once was the dominant species along the dry ridges the AT follows here. Now they can be seen among the living only in saplings and small trees, most of which grow from the roots of dead chestnuts. In *Shenandoah National Park: An Interpretive Guide,* John A. Conners reports that a few dozen mature trees survive in Michigan, having been taken there by early settlers.

Continuing its steady, gentle rise, and after crossing an old road that served as access to an abandoned quarry below, at 1.4 mi. the trail makes its final push toward the crest. At 1.8 mi. the reward for your casual climb to this point on Baldface is a rock terrace to the left of the trail from which to enjoy the view westward of, left to right, Huckleberry Mt., Abrams Mt., and Piney Mt.

Moving along the ridge, past the summit at 2.1 mi. (elev. 3600 ft.), then descending Baldface, the AT moves under maple and hickory with a dense understory of sumac, chokecherry, and various briar species. In summer, near the several clearings along the way that allow sun to reach the floor, there are blackberry bushes—one of the great joys of hiking provided, oddly, by the intrusion of forest cuts for roads and power lines.

At about 2.8 mi. the trail travels through a gently graded young forest, a former pasture known as Kites Deadening where locusts and black walnuts make a crowd beneath several maples. Like the several other "deadenings" along the AT, Kites Deadening takes its name from the technique used to clear forests for pasture. Because cutting trees and clearing timber is so labor intensive, and because the real aim in clearing a pasture is to allow sunlight to reach the grasses below, settlers often girdled trees. Removing the bark completely around the tree in a swath about a foot tall causes a tree to die over the course of a couple of seasons by blocking nutrients from the leaves.

When the leaves don't grow, photosynthesis is halted, literally starving the tree. Also, without the leaves, sunlight can make its way to the grasses below, allowing the growth of plant life suitable for stock animals. Often, the trees would be felled as needed for firewood over the following years. Evidence of deadening can be seen in many places throughout Shenandoah, both in the girdled trees still rotting on the ground and in the eerie stands of huge, dead oaks and maples surrounded by young black walnut trees that are taking advantage of the fallow grasslands.

At 3.0 mi. the view to the northeast is of Jones Mt., accessible by the Laurel Prong and Jones Mt. trails. In 1996 the topography of Jones Mt. was completely altered by a thousand-year storm and flood. What were once tiny springs crossing the trail are now creeks within deep gorges. The entire course of the Staunton River was moved half a mile north, leaving a gully in place of a scenic trout stream below the Staunton River Trail. Gentle slopes of hickory and maple are now rocky cliffs. Mud slides half a mile wide changed the face of Jones Mt. and opened watercourses that allowed a two-story wall of water to destroy the town of Graves Mill. It is little consolation to the people of Graves Mill, many of whose families have lived in the valley for more than a century, that the storm has provided scientists a rare opportunity to study a once-a-millenium event.

Just beyond a spring to the left of the trail at 3.2 mi., a blue-blazed trail at 3.3 mi. leads 80 yd. east to Pocosin Cabin, managed by the PATC. The cabin is available for a fee by reservation and accommodates up to twelve people in three double-width double bunks—basically, six double beds with foam mattresses. No camping is permitted near this or other cabins within the park. There is a spring just south of the trail, which provides not only water but a fine view of the Conway River valley below.

Moving north on the AT, at 3.4 mi. cross Pocosin Fire Rd. To the left, it leads 150 yd. to SDMP 59.5. To the right, it leads past the cabin and 0.7 mi. further to the site of an early 20th-century mission organized to bring religion and education to the mountaineers who inhabited the hills and hollows of the Blue Ridge. Not long before the establishment of the park in the 1930s, there were dozens of mountain families scratching out a living by hunting, gathering berries and nuts, and grazing their stock on the nuts in the woods. In the lower hollows there was fishing. Many of the mountaineers were described by visitors to the Skyland resort (now a part of the park) as going about their business in winter snows without shoes or coats. The attention to tourism in the Blue Ridge at the turn of the century also brought attention to the conditions of mountain people—many of whom would have preferred to have been left alone.

At 3.6 mi., and for half a mile after, it's impossible to hike without noticing several hundred downed trees. The locusts and other small species in the blowdowns illustrate nature's delicate balancing act in rejuvenating the forest. They are recovery species that dominate the years after farming has ceased and the forest is young. The hardwood hickories and oak, still standing after the storm, are the natural "kings" of this wood, and their presence demonstrates that the forest's climax species are beginning to dominate.

A blue-blazed trail at 5.2 mi. is the spur to Lewis Mt. Campground, 100 ft. west. The camp store, just inside the campground, offers a refreshing rest stop and water May through October. The campground was developed in a misguided attempt at allowing all Americans access to national park facilities. In the separate-but-equal days of the 1930s, Lewis Mt. Campground was SNP's "colored campground." Development of the campground created a stormy controversy. National Park Service personnel favored opening all of Shenandoah's campgrounds to all Americans. They were overruled by

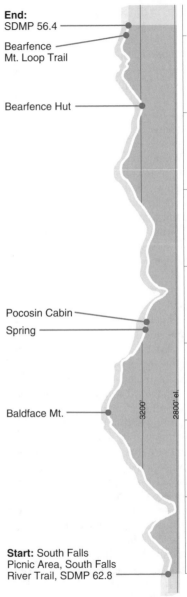

created using Maptech TopoScout ®

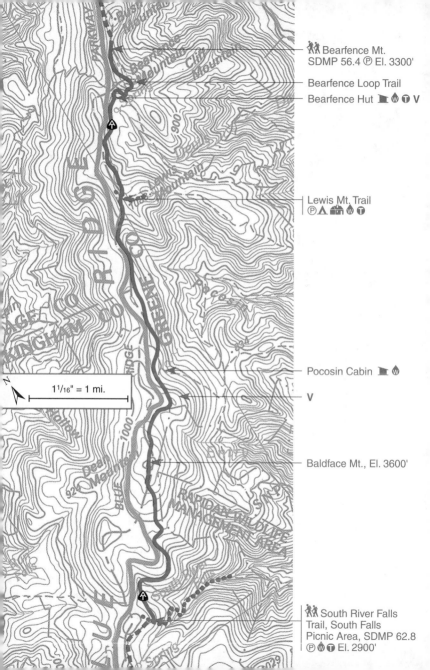

🥾 Bearfence Mt.
SDMP 56.4 Ⓟ El. 3300'

Bearfence Loop Trail

Bearfence Hut 🏕️ 🚰 🚻 V

Lewis Mt. Trail
Ⓟ ⛺ 🏚️ 🚰 🚻

Pocosin Cabin 🏕️ 🚰

V

Baldface Mt., El. 3600'

$1\frac{1}{16}$" = 1 mi.

🥾 South River Falls
Trail, South Falls
Picnic Area, SDMP 62.8
Ⓟ 🚰 🚻 El. 2900'

Mountain laurel

political appointees within the Department of Interior, which administers the NPS. Lewis Mt. Campground provides an exit option for this hike. The campground is reachable by car, just off Skyline Dr. at milepost 57.5. Signs lead to the store and parking.

Beyond the spur trail the AT descends gently, skirting the perimeter of the campground. There are many narrow, unblazed paths through the brush to the campground. Leaving the camp and continuing to descend for a time, at 5.6 mi. the trail finds level ground and keeps it for 0.5 mi. until, at 6.1 mi., it crosses the unblazed spur trail leading downhill to the east 0.1 mi. to Bearfence Mt. Hut.

Like all the three-sided huts (also known as shelters outside the park), Bearfence Mt. Hut is generally intended for use by backpackers out for several days or more, because others can carry tents (see "Camping" section in the Introduction). Many hikers out for only a night or two will carry a tent in case in the event there is no room at a hut. *Note:* Contrary to what some thru-hikers will claim, the huts and shelters along the AT are not meant for the exclusive use of thru-hikers.

At 6.2 mi. the trail crosses the yellow-blazed Slaughter Trail before beginning a gradual ascent of Bearfence Mt. The path rambles through laurel and a tunnel of rhododendron that conjures images of J. R. R. Tolkien's Merck Woods. One almost expects to see a hobbit come trotting down the trail. The AT winds around Bearfence in a steady ascent, offering a rest stop with views west before finishing the climb to the Bearfence Mt. Loop Trail at 6.8 mi. The Bearfence loop adds fewer than 200 yd. to the hike, and is well worth the diversion. The 0.3-mi., blue-blazed trail offers views to the west of Grindstone Ridge and Long Ridge.

A second loop trail, actually a fairly difficult rock scramble, leaves from midway through the lower loop and leads to Bearfence Mt. Rock Scramble, a massive jumble of basalt rocks that looks as though it was tossed there by a single hand. Some hand-over-hand scrambling is required to reach the upper rocks, but with care on a dry day it's manageable for most hikers able enough to have made the hike there. This trail descends the ridge northward and will cross the AT just before Bearfence Mt. parking (see below).

Back on the AT, the trail descends steadily and, at 7.0 mi., meets the Bearfence loop as it descends from the cliffs. Descending further, then leveling, the AT reaches the junction with the Bearfence Mt. Rock Scramble trail at 7.2 mi., 100 ft. east of SDMP 56.4, parking, and the end of the hike.

Optional Extended Hike: For a hike of 11.4 mi. into Milam Gap, continue north over Hazeltop Mt. The highest point on the AT within SNP, it is, nonetheless, wooded, offering few opportunities for views. En route, at 8.6 mi., the trail passes through Bootens Gap at milepost 55.1 of the Drive, where there is parking for eight cars, then begins its ascent of Hazeltop. Although there are spare views, there are several northern red spruce thriving atop the cold, high mountain so far south, and a handful of balsam.

The trail travels the ridge for more than a mile of "green tunnel" walking, then descends into Milam Gap. After a junction with the Mill Prong Trail, which joins the AT to cross Skyline Dr. at milepost 52.8 in Milam Gap, the trail enters the parking area, where there is room enough for twenty cars.

HIKE #38 Itinerary

Miles N	NORTH	Elev. (ft/m)	Miles S
Total: 7.3 mi., with access on South River Falls Trail.			
7.2	**End:** Bearfence Mt. parking at SDMP 56.4.	3300/1006	0.0
7.0	N junction **Bearfence Mt. Loop Trail.**		0.2
6.8	S junction **Bearfence Mt. Loop Trail,** views.	3500/1067	0.4
6.1	0.1-mi. trail to R to **Bearfence Hut,** spring; trail to L leads 0.2 mi. to SDMP 56.8.		1.1
5.2	Short trail to **Lewis Mt. Campground,** store, camping, water, SDMP 57.5, early exit option.		2.0
3.4	**Pocosin Fire Rd.** leads L 150 yd. to SDMP 59.5, parking for 6 cars.		3.8
3.3	Trail to **Pocosin Cabin,** spring, 80 yd. E (R).	3120/951	3.9
3.2	Spring just W (L) of trail.		4.0
3.0	View.		4.2
2.1	Summit of **Baldface Mt.**	3600/1097	5.1
1.8	View from rock ledge.		5.4
0.5	Cross **South River Fire Rd.**		6.7
0.0	**Start: Turn L** onto AT.	2900/884	7.2
0.1	Access: SDMP 62.8, South River Picnic Area, rest rooms, parking lot, water fountain. 3.0 mi. N of Swift Run Gap entrance to SNP. Take **South River Falls Trail** at E side of picnic area.	2900/884	0.1

SOUTH

Big Meadows and Hawksbill

Map: PATC Va. #10, SNP, Central Dist.

Route: Through SNP from Milam Gap at Mill Prong Trail parking through Big Meadows, along Franklin Cliffs, to Hawksbill Gap

Recommended direction: S to N

Distance: 7.4 mi.

Elevation +/-: 3270 to 3600 to 3360 ft.

Effort: Easy

Day hike: Yes

Overnight backpacking hike: Optional

Duration: 5 hr.

Early exit options: At 4.2 mi., 4.4 mi., 4.7 mi., and 5.5 mi., Skyline Dr.

Natural history features: Big Meadows; Franklin Cliffs; Hawksbill Mt.

Social history features: Tanners Ridge Cemetery; Big Meadows; Redgate Fire Rd.

Trailhead access: *Start:* From US 211, head S on Skyline Dr. into SNP's Central District. Go 21 mi. to trailhead parking at Milam Gap, SDMP 52.5. *End:* From US 211, go S on Skyline Dr. 14.1 mi. to trailhead parking at SDMP 45.6 in Hawksbill Gap.

Camping: Big Meadows Campground; Rock Spring Hut; PATC Rock Spring Cabin; see "Camping" in Introduction

There is much to see on this hike, but it is sound you may remember most. The ever present winds circling through the Franklin Cliffs sing in multiple tones. They construct chords, even progressions of chords, that at times sound downright rehearsed. It is the unique exposure of the rocky ledges and their position above two hollows that give the effect.

In Shenandoah National Park, perhaps more than any other place along the AT, there is a blending, almost a blurring, of natural history with the history of people in the place. Nowhere is this more apparent than in Big Meadows, near the beginning of this hike. From the trailhead at Milam Gap, follow a meadow briefly and enter the woods. Still to be seen, but not bearing fruit, are many Milam apple trees, the most common variety grown by mountaineers who settled the Blue Ridge.

Also along the way, just west of the trail, is a small stand of old hickory and oak interspersed with flowering grasses and ferns. This open stand contrasts with most other, younger sections of the Blue Ridge forest. This tiny patch of old woodlands, spared by the loggers and charcoal kilns of the 19th century, show what much of the rest of SNP could look like in another hundred years. The pines and cedar saplings still visible throughout much of northern SNP will one day be largely replaced by the hardwoods that provide autumn color.

Unfortunately, one species that once dominated the Blue Ridge, the American chestnut, will never recover. Victim of a blight caused by an Asian fungus, the tree that once was the very identifier of Blue Ridge forests is now seen only occasionally as a sapling—one that will succumb to its adversary before it reaches maturity. See them while you can!

At about 1 mi., emerge from the woods and cross the road at Tanners Ridge Cemetery. A small settlement once stood nearby; its residents gathered bark for sale to the leather tanning industry. The road leads right 0.2 mi. to Skyline Dr. at Tanners Ridge Overlook, but vehicle access is prohibited. The trail enters the woods again and follows the nearly level plateau that characterizes the Big Meadows area.

At 1.7 mi. begin a gradual ascent as the trail passes over Lewis Spring where it forms Lewis Run, the headwaters of Hawksbill Creek. From its modest beginnings underfoot at the AT, the stream builds and drops 400 ft. over 0.5 mi. as it rushes toward Lewis Falls. At 81 ft., this is the fourth-highest waterfall in the park. This is as close as the AT comes to any falls in SNP, so take the time to wander down the Lewis Falls Trail (here a dirt road, but below a footpath) for a detour and a bit more to admire the view.

If you'd rather not retrace your steps back to the AT from the falls, follow the blue-blazed Lewis Falls Trail 1.1 mi. to rejoin the AT just below Big Meadows lodge and amphitheater. Although it is a bit longer, many AT hikers prefer this route because it takes them a couple of hundred yards away from the activity and bustle of Big Meadows.

From Lewis Spring, above the falls, the AT climbs steadily but moderately, reaching a side trail to Black Rock Viewpoint at 2.1 mi. The trail leads to the right 0.1 mi. to an overlook with views west to the Allegheny, then 0.2 mi. to the lodge at Big Meadows, and, beyond the lodge, the campground. But there's no need to leave the AT to get a view as stunning as the one from Black Rock. (Many ridges and other places along the AT share this name. This Black Rock is not the same as the one visited in Hike #33.)

Just 20 yd. beyond the spur trail the view opens from a ledge, elev. 3600 ft., to reveal Massanutten Mt. to the west—all 52 mi. of it running north to south across the Great Valley. On a clear day, the ridges of the Allegheny Mts. are visible in the distance. At 2.6 mi., a post marks the northern junction with Lewis Falls Trail, which leads left 1.1 mi. back to the waterfall. The blue-blazed trail leads right 0.5 mi. via a connecting nature trail to the open bogs and brush of the main attraction in the area: the meadows.

Some of the plants living in the bogs and mosses of Big Meadows, such as Canadian burnet, are typically found no further south than New England. Like the hemlock and gray birch described later in this hike, they are thought to be remnants of the two most recent ice ages. Although the mile-thick glaciers of the north did not make their ways to Virginia, their southern reaches into New York and Pennsylvania precipitated a climate in Virginia's Blue Ridge more like that of the modern-day northern forest of New York and New England.

They survive here today partly because of the elevation in the Central District of the park. Just as the average temperature drops as one moves north, so it does with every thousand feet or so of elevation gain, anywhere from 1.5 to 2.5 degrees. Through the millennia since the last ice age, this vegetation has migrated up the mountainsides to cooler heights and is slowly being replaced by vegetation more typically associated with the region.

But it is the meadows that bring social history into direct contact with the natural history of SNP. Their very existence amidst the otherwise forested mountains seems out of place to even the casual observer. The fact is, no one knows precisely how the meadows came to be, but the prominent theory begins with lightning and fire. After a storm denuded the forested flatland, a fairly common occurrence, grasses and small shrubs bloomed as part of the natural cycle of forest regeneration.

Native Americans of the Monatack nation, who hunted and gathered berries and nuts along the ridge, realized that game animals enjoyed the bounty of berries in the meadows as much as they did.

This made for fine hunting; so fine, in fact, that archeological evidence suggests the Native Americans made the meadows even larger by burning more woodland, then maintained them through periodic controlled burns. The abundance of arrowheads and other primitive equipment found in Big Meadows indicates that the place may indeed have served as the earthly happy hunting ground of the Blue Ridge.

Due to disease brought through trading with Piedmont white men, Native populations had all but disappeared by the time European settlers moved up the ridge from the Shenandoah Valley and Piedmont. For them, Big Meadows offered prime grazing land for livestock. With the creation of the park in 1936 and the subsequent relocation of the remaining inhabitants of the ridge, the meadows, left to their own devices, should in time revert to forest. However, because Big Meadows is such an important part of the history of the ridge, the National Park Service now maintains 200 acres of the meadows as a living history of both nature and humankind.

Moving north, the AT now closely follows the perimeter of Big Meadows Campground. The campground has tent and trailer sites, as well as a full-service lodge and dining room. While the tent sites won't provide the quietest night one could spend on the AT, Big Meadows makes for convenient camping. There are showers, firewood, and ice for sale, and a laundry. In summer there are programs for children such as bonfires, sing-alongs, and nature hikes. For reservations call 800-999-4714.

At 2.9 mi. the AT crosses Monkey Head, a small knoll that offers views west of Massanutten and Signal Knob at its north end. Over the next 0.4 mi., as the trail circles the campground, there are intermittent footpaths to the right leading to campsites, and occasional views to the northwest of Hawksbill and Stony Man.

Nearly as enjoyable as watching the abundant deer that feed on camp scraps near Big Meadows, and certainly as much a part of the AT experience there, are the curious, whispering children eyeing deer from only steps away. Accustomed to crowds of family campers, the deer often seem as intrigued by the children as the kids by them. Without a legal hunting season within the park, the principle threats to deer are the snacks they receive from unwitting visitors. Yearlings can get hooked on handouts from the summer crowds, and may then be unable to survive the winter.

At 3.2 mi. the trail breaks west to descend into Kite Hollow along and over Little Hawksbill Creek, crossing the stream as both fall steeply. Here

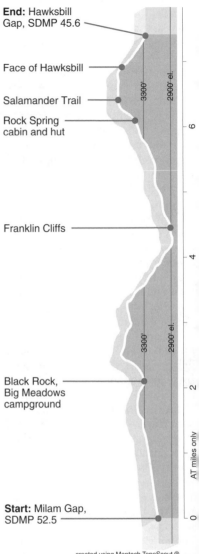

created using Maptech TopoScout ®

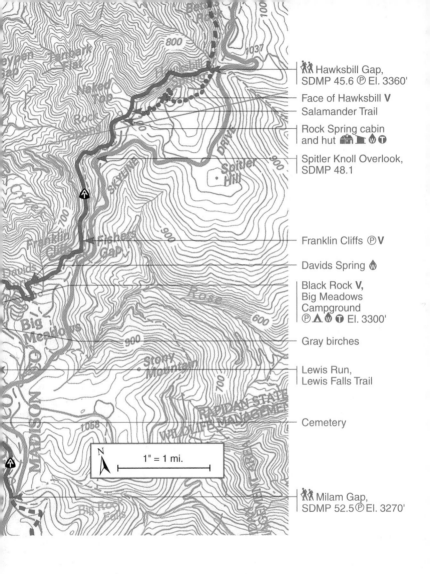

Hawksbill Gap,
SDMP 45.6 Ⓟ El. 3360'

Face of Hawksbill **V**

Salamander Trail

Rock Spring cabin
and hut 🏠🛏️Ⓦ🚻

Spitler Knoll Overlook,
SDMP 48.1

Franklin Cliffs Ⓟ**V**

Davids Spring 💧

Black Rock **V**,
Big Meadows
Campground
Ⓟ🛆Ⓦ🚻 El. 3300'

Gray birches

Lewis Run,
Lewis Falls Trail

Cemetery

N
1" = 1 mi.

Milam Gap,
SDMP 52.5 Ⓟ El. 3270'

are several clumps of gray birch, displaced northerners hanging on unusually far south; it is the southernmost stand in the trail corridor. The trail crosses the stream twice and passes through a small stand of hemlock, then finds gentler terrain as it nears the paved Redgate Fire Rd. beneath Fishers Gap Overlook at 4.2 mi. Overlook parking, 120 yd. east, uphill, facilitates an exit option for this hike. Once known as the Gordonsville Tpk., the road was used by Gen. Stonewall Jackson to move 20,000 troops from the Page Valley over the ridge at Fishers Gap and on to Fredericksburg where they pushed back the Union Army.

Crossing the road, the trail reenters the woods and begins a moderate ascent, all the while hugging the ledge below Franklin Cliffs. A 100-ft. spur trail leading up to Franklin Cliffs Overlook breaks from southern end of the ledge at 4.4 mi. and rejoins the AT at 4.7 mi. (parking for 8 cars). For those seeing the ridge by car, the overlook is grand, but from this ledge the view is better. The hiker is a part of the landscape here, among the cliffs with a vast view to the west.

This is a place where many a long-distance backpacker has seen mileage-per-day goals shattered, captivated by the continuous viewshed like sailors by the songs of the Sirens. It is easy to see why. Every 25 yd. another scene is unveiled. There is Stony Man to the north, identified by its crude, columnar jointing. Another few steps and you notice the village of Stanley, also to the north. A few more steps and it's the talus rocks below that catch the eye.

The tumbled rocks of Franklin Cliffs appear to be tumbling still. A closer look reveals two distinct cliffs formed from separate lava flows. One is of dark, fine-grained basalt, the rock seen almost continuously along the AT in SNP; the other is a coarse, pinkish granite created deep within the earth and pushed upward in earlier volcanic activity.

All the while the wind songs sing, reverberating against the rocks seemingly positioned for the purpose. The distant tumbling waters of Little Hawksbill Creek create a kind of tenor and alto melody, while the wind whipping up the mountain from Kite Hollow carries a soprano overtone, as the basso is provided courtesy of thousands of leaves rustling in the competing winds of from Kite and Mink Hollows. The irregular mantling of the cliffs sends the sounds in all directions. It would be almost impolite not to sit and enjoy nature's concert, so a long, restful recital is advised.

Continuing along the ledge beyond Franklin Cliffs, at 5.2 mi. the trail climbs steeply through two switchbacks, ascending 300 ft. in less than a quarter of a mile. At the cutoff trail to Spitler Knoll Overlook parking area, at 5.5 mi., the trail rests—and so should the hiker after that brief but abrupt climb. An SNP trail post points the way 50 yd. uphill to the lot at SDMP 48.1, which accommodates ten cars. This is another exit option for this hike.

The trail pursues a continual but gradual ascent into the flat between Nakedtop and Hawksbill. Here tall grasses and flowering shrubs provide an ongoing feast for deer. This short stretch between the Spitler Knoll Overlook parking and Hawksbill access trails is one of the surprisingly quiet places along the AT. Given such close proximity to Hawksbill, the highest summit in the park as well as one of the most visited, one would expect throngs marching side by side. But most hikers approach Hawksbill from the other side. There are two access trails and a fire road leading day hikers to the peak directly from Skyline Dr. Backpackers form the majority of traffic here.

Patient hikers who plant themselves in the grass here will be rewarded with the sightings of deer, butterflies in season, grouse and other birds foraging in the grasses, or at sunset perhaps a gray fox or barred owl emerging from the woods.

At 6.1 mi. an SNP trail post marks the junction with a 0.2-mi. spur leading to the Rock Spring Hut and Rock Spring Cabin, managed by the PATC. The cabin can be reserved through the club headquarters. The view from the porch extends across the Shenandoah Valley to the Massanutten ridge, while in the valley foreground the town of Stanley is visible. With such fine views to the west, the porch just might be the ultimate spot to watch a sunset, then linger to see the stars appear above. This perch comes with a caution to hikers traveling with children: The rock on which the cabin roosts drops steeply from the front of the cabin.

Rock Spring Hut, like other three-sided shelters in the park, are available on a first-come basis, but preference is granted to backpackers. After all, campers out in the woods for a night or two can more easily carry their tents. A spring 175 ft. north of the cabin provides water for the cabin and the hut.

Just beyond the cabin cutoff trail, a grassy road veers east over the crest. Continuing north, the AT passes through an overgrown orchard, where aged apple and peach trees are giving way to recovery species such as sumac and pine. Then, at 6.4 mi., a post points the way up the Salamander Trail (also known as Nakedtop Trail) to the summit of Hawksbill. Here hikers who plan to visit the Hawksbill summit have two options: ascend Hawksbill and descend via the well-marked Lower Hawksbill Trail to Hawksbill Gap parking, a steep 0.8-mi. descent, or, return to the AT by retracing your steps on the Salamander Trail. From here, the AT continues north by slabbing around the cliffs of Hawksbill to Hawksbill Gap parking.

The sweeping views from the summit of Hawksbill defy description. On any fogless day the view from the observation platform takes in the Allegheny Mts. to the west, the Blue Ridge snaking north, the Piedmont to the east, Timber Hollow to the north —it's mountains, mountains everywhere.

On their hikes to the Hawksbill summit, early 1900s visitors to Skyland regularly reported seeing the Washington Monument and the Capitol building on clear days. Today, ever present smog has diminished the discernable viewshed to about 20 to 30 mi. except on the clearest of days, when the skyline of Washington, D.C., can be seen.

Before heading down, Byrds Nest #2 or another spot among the rocks is an inviting place for lunch. Byrds Nest #2 is a shelter for day use only; no fires are permitted and the closest water is back at Rock Spring. It primarily provides refuge from sudden storms and a place out of the wind for lunch. (See Hike #40 for more on the Byrds Nest shelters.)

The descent to the Hawksbill Gap trailhead is via the Lower Hawksbill Trail to the north. This 0.9-mi. trail passes among native spruce and balsam. To return to the AT, retrace your steps on the Salamander Trail and to the AT, and continue northward through a thinning canopy until, at 6.9 mi., you cross onto the open face of Hawksbill nearly 500 ft. below the summit. The trail makes a scamper across this craggy ledge. You can delight yourself for hours by climbing among the giant basalt blocks spilling down from the summit. Here among the rocks, the luckiest hikers may catch a glimpse of the rare Shenandoah salamander. There are also views of Luray, home of the famous Luray Caverns, and Ida Valley.

Clearing the rocky face of Hawksbill, the trail enters woodland on level terrain, then, at 7.4 mi., a post points to Hawksbill Gap parking at SDMP 45.6, 10 yd. up the marked path, and the end of this hike.

Optional Extended Hike: If you want to continue another 3.3 mi. to the horse stables at Skyland, Stony Man Nature Trail parking, and the start of Hike #40, here is a glimpse of what is in store. At 7.8 mi. the trail passes beneath Crescent Rock, a cliff of basalt lava flow. At 7.9 mi. a blue-blazed trail leads 0.1 mi. to Crescent Rock Overlook and another 0.3 mi. to a viewpoint from the ledge at Bettys Rock. In spring, Bettys Rock shows moss, phlox, mountain laurel, and the small, three-toothed cinquefoil common in the northern cold climates but quite rare in SNP and points south.

At about 9 mi. Pollock Knob, named for the founder of the Skyland resort, has open views back to Hawksbill and west into the valley. There is another view of Hawksbill, this one from the western ridge of Pollock Knob, at 9.2 mi. The final 0.7 mi. follow the rocky western ledge of the knob, then meander along the corral fence leading to the Skyland stables. Just beyond a dirt horse path leading east, the trail crosses a paved pathway at 9.9 mi. The dirt path leads to the Limberlost trailhead, and the paved path bearing left leads 0.1 mi. to Whiteoak Canyon parking at SDMP 42.5. The Limberlost Trail, also accessible from SDMP 43.0, is a gently graded trail through the hemlock forest. It is the only trail in the park accessible to people with disabilities.

If you have extra time, consider a side trip into Whiteoak Canyon. Its six waterfalls, laurel, and hemlocks were in large part what motivated George Freeman Pollock to establish Skyland in 1896, before the AT or Skyline Dr. were conceived. Most any time of year, Whiteoak Canyon Trail attracts a crowd, to the point of giving rise to jokes that it's the only trail in the park that needs a traffic cop. Even at the busiest of times, it's usually possible to find a spot to watch and listen to a cascading waterfall.

Once you're in the canyon, you can understand the attraction. The place is home to a stand of virgin hemlock, purchased by Pollock on a per-tree basis in order to preserve the old-growth forest. The enchantment of the forest, whose trees today are some 450 years old, moved Pollock to name the spot Limberlost because it painted for him a picture from the novel *Girl of the Limberlost.* From Skyline Dr., Whiteoak Canyon Trail descends more than 2300 ft. over 5.1 mi. to terminate at VA 600.

The AT continues through Skyland between the Drive and Skyland's access road, past the water tank, and on to Skyland's entrance road. Parking for Stony Man Nature Trail and the AT is across the road to the right; the trailhead is at the back of the lot.

Miles N	**NORTH**	Elev. (ft/m)	Miles S
7.4	**End:** In **Hawksbill Gap,** at N end of Lower Hawksbill Trail, and SDMP 45.6, 14.1 mi. S of US 211 entrance to park.	3360/1024	0.0
6.9	Slabbing N face of **Hawksbill,** home of Shenandoah salamanders.	3500/1067	0.5
6.4	Junction with 0.9-mi. **Salamander Trail to Hawksbill** summit (views) and **Byrds Nest #2** (no camping). Lower Hawksbill Trail goes from summit to Hawksbill Gap.		1.0
6.1	0.2-mi. spur trail to **Rock Spring Hut and Cabin;** spring, privy.		1.3
5.5	To R, 50-yd. spur trail to **Spitler Knoll Overlook,** parking at SDMP 48.1, early exit option.		1.9
4.7	Second side trail R to **Franklin Cliffs Overlook.**		2.7
4.4	Side trail R to **Franklin Cliffs Overlook** at SDMP 49.0 mi.; early exit option.	3400/1036	3.0
4.2	**Fishers Gap Overlook** parking, 120 yd. uphill to R; early exit option.		3.2
3.2	N end **Big Meadows,** stand of gray birch, creek.		4.2
2.6	N junction **Lewis Falls Trail,** leads R 0.5 mi. to **Big Meadows.**		4.8
2.2	View of **Massanutten Mt.**	3600/1097	5.2
2.1	To R, trail 0.1 mi. to **Black Rock Viewpoint,** 0.2 mi. to **Big Meadows lodge and campground;** camping, water, and public rest room.	3300/1006	5.3
1.7	To L, pass S junction with **Lewis Falls Trail;** L of trail begins **Lewis Run,** headwaters of **Hawksbill Creek.**		5.4
1.1	**Tanners Ridge Rd.,** cemetery; road leads R 0.2 mi. to Skyline Dr.		6.3
0.9	Spring.		6.5
0.0	**Start:** In **Milam Gap,** at SDMP 52.5, 21.0 mi. S of US 211 entrance to park; parking.	3270/996	7.4

SOUTH

Stony Man Mt. and Marys Rock

Map: PATC Va. #10, SNP, Central Dist.

Route: Through SNP from Stony Man Nature Trail parking in Skyland, over Stony Man Mt. and Marys Rock to the Panorama Restaurant

Recommended direction: S to N

Distance: 9.2 mi.

Elevation +/-: 3700 to 3860 to 3000 to 3730 to 2300 ft.

Effort: Moderate

Day hike: Yes

Overnight backpacking hike: Optional

Duration: 5 hr.

Early exit options: At 1.6 mi., 2.3 mi., 3.0 mi., 4.3 mi., Skyline Dr.; at 6.4 mi., Byrds Nest access road

Natural history features: Marys Rock; Little Stony Man cliffs

Social history features: Stone retaining walls that create terraced ledge for trail; Skyland; Passamaquoddy Trail (former route of AT)

Other features: Junctions with Passamaquoddy, Corbin Cabin Cutoff, Nicholson Hollow, Crusher Ridge, Leading Ridge, and Meadow Spring trails, Byrds Nest #3 day-use shelter

Trailhead access: *Start:* From the US 211 entrance to SNP, go S on Skyline Dr. 7.6 mi. to Skyland resort N entrance, take immediate R into Stony Man Nature Trail parking. *End:* From the US 211 entrance to SNP, go S on Skyline Dr. 0.1 mi. to Panorama Restaurant parking on R. To park a second car here without paying two entrance fees (that's only fair!), use alternate Panorama parking lot on US 211. The two lots are connected by a walkway.

Camping: PATC Corbin Cabin; family cabins at Skyland (contact SNP headquarters); and see "Camping" in Introduction

---

You may want to save this hike for the Appalachian autumn's colors, but it's scenic any time of year. The rugged cliffs of Stony Man and the panoramic views from Marys Rock are two of the most favored spots along the AT in Shenandoah National Park.

The hike starts at the Stony Man Nature Trail parking area at the north end of Skyland, the park's popular family resort. Stony Man Nature Trail is one of several wooded paths that join its network of cabins with the Skyland lodge, amphitheater, and other amenities. The resort is generally open March through November.

Some of the hardiest of backpackers rue the existence of Skyland and the Panorama Restaurant further north, complaining these don't belong on the "pathway through the wilderness." But even the most maverick of backpackers will stop for a stack of pancakes at the Panorama at north end of this hike.

From the trailhead, the Stony Man Nature Trail and the AT share the white blazes as the path begins a gradual, almost easygoing ascent of Stony Man Mt., the second-highest peak in the park at 4010 ft. The trail glides among balsam fir, normally found much further north, and gnarled oaks left deformed by ice storms.

At 0.4 mi., after an ascent of 250 ft., is a junction at which the Stony Man Nature Trail proceeds straight ahead to make a 0.4-mi. loop around the summit. The AT bears right. The trail to the left returns to the Skyland road 150 yd. west of the parking area.

A minor detour to the cliffs is well worth it. The blue-blazed Stony Man Trail opens in 0.2 mi. to views of Page Valley and Massanutten Mt., a 50-mi.-long manodnock dividing the north and south branches of the Shenandoah River.

On the cliffs of Stony Man, the history of humans and nature clash and blur. The stone of Stony Man and Little Stony Man are remnants of lava flow. Upon closer examination behind trees and vegetation, deep depressions and chiseled rocks in the landscape reveal evidence of some 60 years of copper mining atop Stony Man that ended in the 1880s. It was the mountain's poor reserve of copper that encouraged George Pollock's father, the mountain's part-owner, to embrace his son's idea of

Skyland. If there would be no profits from mining, perhaps tourism would make a buck. It was with such resigned blessing that George Freeman Pollock founded the Blue Ridge Park Association in 1889, the precursor to the Skyland resort in 1893.

The cliffs of Stony Man have become ever more popular since Pollock's days, particularly in autumn. Because the hike to the top is an easy stroll, on Sundays there are leaf peekers in oxfords and pumps, not bothering to change from church attire to hiking shoes. Hikers are discouraged from trying this.

Just below the peak is the Passamaquoddy Trail, a former route of the AT. The name Passamaquoddy was appropriated by the never modest Pollack from a New England Native American nation of that name, which means "place of abundant pollock," a North Atlantic fish. The trail follows a route parallel to that of the AT, albeit about a hundred feet lower, and rejoins the AT just north of the Little Stony Man Overlook.

Return to the AT from Stony Man and head north, descending. Here the AT is aligned with the Little Stony Man Trail. At 1.0 mi. the trail reaches the cliffs of Little Stony Man, at 3600 ft. There is a commanding view of Strasburg and its surrounding farmland in the Page Valley to the west. The huge basalt cliffs, remnants of lava flow, form sheets, or cleavage planes, of rock, stacked like cards and tilting to the southeast.

The Pinnacles

From this vantage point on Little Stony Man, you can see the object of Union Gen. Phil Sheridan's rabble-rousing campaign in the valley below. In 1864 a Union division led by Sheridan raced through the 20-mi.-wide valley like a flood, burning barns, stealing chickens, and generally making a nuisance. The general distracted Southern armies by harassing one confederate valley town after another, riding out of these very woods to terrorize the isolated villages below. All this is easy to imagine from the ledge of Little Stony Man, where the most mild-mannered hiker cannot help but feel tall in the saddle.

Leaving the cliffs of Little Stony Man, the trail descends on steep switchbacks and reaches a junction with Passamaquoddy Trail, appearing from the left, at 1.3 mi. The grade slopes gently along terraced stone walls built by the Civilian Conservation Corps during the Roosevelt years.

At 1.6 mi. a post marks a spur trail leading right 100 ft. to the Little Stony Man parking area, an early exit option for the hike at SDMP 39.1. There is parking for twelve cars, with overflow utilizing the roadside.

Continuing north from Little Stony Man parking area, the AT follows

Skyline Dr. to the west, at times closely. A short trail at 2.0 mi. leads right 30 yd. to the Stony Man Overlook. Two more trail junctions, the blue-blazed Nicholson Hollow Trail at 2.3 mi. and Crusher Ridge Trail (to the left) at 2.5 mi., lead to diverting day hikes in the hollows of the Blue Ridge. Nicholson Hollow is also known as Free State Hollow. It seems the families that inhabited the area below recognized no authority or land ownership in the mountains other than their own, a fact that meant ongoing challenges to Pollock's administration of Skyland. Nicholson Hollow Trail leads right 1.8 mi. to Corbin Cabin, nestled in the woods near the Hughes River. The cabin accommodates twelve and may be reserved through the PATC.

The AT descends into a bowl at 2.7 mi. marking the low elevation point of this hike at 3000 ft., then ascends. At 3.0 mi. the trail passes a parking area for the Corbin Cabin Cutoff Trail, another route to the cabin, then, at about 3.1 mi., an unblazed trail leads 0.3 mi. down a steep decline to a spring near the former site of an AT hut. Climbing, the AT crests a knob and, at 3.2 mi., offers long views of the Hughes River drainage, Free State Hollow, and Old Rag, perhaps the most famous, most visited summit in the park. From this prospect, we can see how the granite cliffs of Old Rag, and its compatriot summits Doubletop and Fork, are separated from the main Blue Ridge by a geologic depression known as the Elkton Fault.

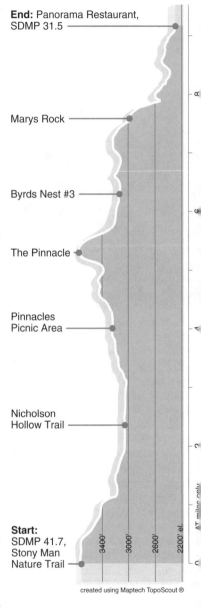

End: Panorama Restaurant, SDMP 31.5

Marys Rock

Byrds Nest #3

The Pinnacle

Pinnacles Picnic Area

Nicholson Hollow Trail

Start: SDMP 41.7, Stony Man Nature Trail

3400' 3000' 2600' 2200' el.

AT miles only

created using Maptech TopoScout ®

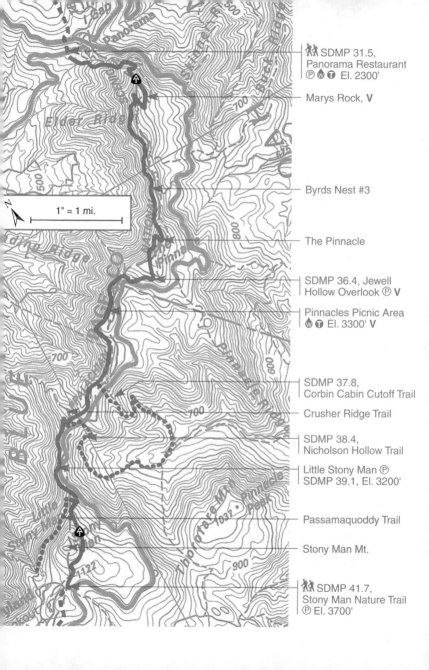

1" = 1 mi.

XX SDMP 31.5,
Panorama Restaurant
Ⓟ Ⓦ Ⓣ El. 2300'

Marys Rock, **V**

Byrds Nest #3

The Pinnacle

SDMP 36.4, Jewell
Hollow Overlook Ⓟ **V**

Pinnacles Picnic Area
Ⓦ Ⓣ El. 3300' **V**

SDMP 37.8,
Corbin Cabin Cutoff Trail

Crusher Ridge Trail

SDMP 38.4,
Nicholson Hollow Trail

Little Stony Man Ⓟ
SDMP 39.1, El. 3200'

Passamaquoddy Trail

Stony Man Mt.

XX SDMP 41.7,
Stony Man Nature Trail
Ⓟ El. 3700'

Descending from the knob, the trail finds an open, level plain known as the Pinnacles Picnic Area, at 3.6 mi. Not as broad or long as Big Meadows, the other major flat atop the ridge (see Hike #39), the Pinnacles is home to blueberries, blackberries, and chokecherries. With these kinds of victuals, there are also deer, raccoon, and other visitors. As the largest picnic area in the park, the Pinnacles draws out other usually wild creatures, such as black bear who come after dark to see what was left behind. Lucky hikers exploring the woods near the Pinnacles in winter snows may catch a glimpse of the elusive bobcat, who finds the open fields prime for hunting in the quiet winter.

At 4.0 mi., still passing through the Pinnacles, the trail passes a sheltered picnic site, toilets, and a water fountain, then travels under a canopy of mountain laurel as it leaves the picnic area but remains on the flat plain. As you follow a narrow ridge of the plain, the woods open to reveal a view of Jewell Hollow and Neighbor Mt. to the northeast. After crossing Leading Ridge Trail, at 4.6 mi., the AT again finds the open flats of the northern Pinnacles, punctuated by irregular rocks and serrated basalt columns. Beyond the high spot of the Pinnacles (known as The Pinnacle; elev. 3730 ft., at 5.3 mi.) there are views northeastward to Thorofare Gap and Hazel Mt., to the north of Thornton Gap.

The trail descends steeply into a saddle as it reenters the woods, moving north for half a mile before finding a level ridge. At 6.3 mi. the trail emerges into a fairy tale clearing, and you are facing an unlikely stone cabin and an unlikelier modern water fountain. You've arrived at Byrds Nest #3. One of five three-sided shelters intended for day use within SNP, Byrds Nest #3 is a fine place to rest and, especially when hiking with children, break for lunch. A picnic table, fireplace, and the seasonally tapped water fountain make for an uncomplicated place to spread a picnic lunch. Byrds Nest #3 doesn't offer lunchtime views, as would a snack eaten while perched atop an overlook, but parents won't have to worry about cups and wrappers and food going overboard to the rocks below.

Much to the disappointment of many a backpacker, the Byrds Nest shelters are not open to camping, except as necessary relief from mountain storms. Reading the hikers' register entries at Byrds Nest, you can sense among them a certain dismay that such a sturdy, strategically located structure can be used only for daytime stops. The park's five shelters were, in fact, once open to backpackers, but were closed to overnight use in the 1960s. Sadly, the "no camping" rule for these shelters is a response to squatters taking up residence in them. It's a real loss for this section of the AT because there are so few camping areas with easy access to the trail, and the narrow ridges provide scant camping opportunities at the required distance from the trail.

Leaving Byrds Nest, at 6.4 mi. pass on the right the access road that leads to SDMP 33.9 0.5 mi. below, an exit option. Some older maps depict a water source at the bottom, but no water can be obtained. Ascend gently through rolling woods of white pine and laurel for 0.5 mi. to the junction with Meadow Spring Trail, which descends right 0.3 mi. to Meadow Spring and Skyline Dr. For backpackers planning to spend the night on the ridge, Meadow Spring is the only choice for water in the vicinity when the fountain at Byrds Nest is inoperable. For day hikers, it's quite a scamper just to fill a water bottle, but you'll want to consider it if you're out of drink and planning to spend a couple of hours relaxing at Marys Rock.

Continuing, the ridgeline reveals views of the valley, reaching a towering granite outcropping, the southern tip of Marys Rock. Passing to the right of the rocks, the AT intersects with the overlook access trail, which leads left for an easy, 0.1-mi. ascent to the northern, exposed tip of the rock: a hiker's Valhalla.

Francis Thornton, for whom the gap below separating the north and central sections of the park is named, owned a large holding from the ridge to the Piedmont. In the early 1800s Thornton brought his wife, Mary, to the ridge on a camping trip. It was on this first trip that Thornton presented to his new bride the gift of the mountain. The couple returned often to camp here, drawing their water from Marys Spring and enjoying romantic, lazy afternoons surveying the scenery from above. Alas, while we still have Marys Rock, the location of the spring is unknown.

Mary Thornton so loved the mountain that when her husband died she moved to a cabin in Thornton Gap. Mary and Francis's love affair with the mountain and each other has inspired many a suitor, even in modern times, to bend a knee on Marys Rock to propose marriage. One shouldn't doubt the enduring qualities of Marys Rock, considering its geologic history. The granite rock, the subsurface mineral left after the erosion of what many suspect had been 5 mi. of lava greenstone, is considered by scientists to be more than a billion years old.

To the west is the Page Valley of the Shenandoah River's south fork, with Massanutten Mt. and the Alleghenies beyond. To the north, the Blue Ridge and the park stretch to the horizon. To the east, Buck Ridge and Skinner Ridge reach for the Piedmont in the distance. The best views are from the rock scramble on the south side, but beware of slick footing in wet weather.

While Mary lived in virtual wilderness in this windy gap, here now sits one of SNP's most customer-friendly establishments: the Panorama, also visible from Marys Rock. Milkshakes, sweets, and other snacks a cardiologist would protest await. From the access trail junction, the AT begins a 1.6-mi. descent toward the Panorama. Along the way, it hugs the eastern ledge, once again revealing remarkable CCC stonework, along with views to the east of Oventop Mt. On a fine afternoon, the most common naturally occurring phenomenon as you head north on the trail will be the throngs of people heading south from Thornton Gap to see the sights from Marys Rock.

At 9.2 mi. a short spur trail to the right leads 50 yd. to the Panorama parking, restaurant, and store, which offers a selection of books and maps on the park and the region. There are also rest rooms and public telephones. The Panorama is generally open from May through October.

HIKE #40 Itinerary

Miles N	NORTH	Elev. (ft/m)	Miles S
9.2	**End: Turn R onto spur trail to Panorama Restaurant** (50 yd.), parking, rest rooms, water, refreshments. 0.1 mi. S of US 211 entrance to SNP.	2300/701	0.0
7.6	0.1-mi. access trail L to **Marys Rock.**	approx. 3450/1051	1.6
6.9	Junction with **Meadow Spring Trail;** spring is 0.3 mi. downhill to R.		2.3
6.4	Byrds Nest access road to SDMP 33.9 (0.5 mi.), early exit option.		2.8
6.3	**Byrds Nest #3** (no camping), water in summer.		2.9
5.3	**The Pinnacle.**	3730/1137	3.9
4.6	Junction with **Leading Ridge Trail,** heading L from AT. Halfway point of hike.		4.6
4.3	**Jewell Hollow Overlook,** SDMP 36.4, early exit option.		4.9
4.0	**Pinnacles Picnic Area;** water fountain, picnic tables, rest rooms.	3300/1006	5.2
3.2	Crest of a knob, view of Old Rag Mt.		6.0
3.0	To R, Corbin Cabin parking, **Corbin Cabin Cutoff Trail,** and SDMP 37.8, early exit option.		6.2
2.7	Trail bottoms in bowl between knolls.	3000/914	6.5
2.5	Junction with **Crusher Ridge Trail,** descending L.		6.7
2.3	Junction with **Nicholson Hollow Trail,** which leads E 1.8 mi. to Corbin Cabin. SDMP 38.4 is 0.1 mi. E, early exit option.		6.9
1.6	100 ft. spur trail to **Little Stony Man** parking, SDMP 39.1, early exit option.	3200/975	7.6
1.3	Junction with **Passamaquoddy Trail,** on L.		7.9
0.4	AT bears R; **Stony Man Nature Trail** goes straight (views from top of Stony Man, 0.2 mi.); to L, trail returns to Skyland road 150 yd. W of parking area.	3860/1177	8.8
0.0	**Start: Stony Man Nature Trail** parking, 100 ft. W of SDMP 41.7; 7.6 mi. S of US 211 entrance to SNP. AT and nature trail co-align for 0.4 mi.	3700/1128	9.2

SOUTH

Thornton Gap to Hogback Overlook

Map: PATC Va. #9, SNP, N Dist.

Route: Through SNP from Thornton Gap over Pass Mt., Sugarloaf Mt., and Hogback Mt. to SDMP 21.1

Recommended direction: S to N

Distance: 11.2 mi.

Elevation +/-: 2300 to 3050 to 2480 to 3440 to 3330 ft.

Effort: Moderate

Day hike: Yes

Overnight backpacking hike: Optional

Duration: 6 to 8 hr.

Early exit options: At 3.2 mi., 3.4 mi., 4.8 mi., and 10.2 mi., Skyline Dr.; at 6.0 mi., Thornton River Trail

Natural history features: Thornton Gap; Beahms Gap; Elkwallow Gap

Other features: Junctions with several side trails for extended hikes or multi-day excursions; the entire hike is located within SNP.

Trailhead access: *Start:* From Luray, head approximately 7 mi. NE on US 211 to intersection with Skyline Dr. at SDMP 31.5. Turn R (S) onto Skyline Dr., then immediately turn R onto access road to Panorama Restaurant and AT visitor center. Parking is available at the restaurant. There is an AT information board in the back left corner of the parking lot. Follow short path uphill to AT. *End:* From S end, continue N on Skyline Dr. to paved parking area on W side of road at SDMP 21.1. For an alternate route, see Hike #42.

Camping: See "Camping" in Introduction; Pass Mt. Hut, reserved for long-distance hikers, backcountry permit required, $1 fee; PATC Range View Cabin, reserved for PATC members; Matthews Arm Campground, 1.9 mi. W of AT, accessible by Elkwallow Trail or road at SDMP 22.2 (4.4 mi. S of Gravel Springs Gap)

T his stretch of the AT makes a pleasant hike through the varied forests of Shenandoah National Park. The south-to-north route provides a leisurely stroll dominated by gentle downward slopes with only a few steep ascents. As the trail crosses over the low peaks, it passes through thickly wooded areas of large old oaks, crowded by slender young oaks and maples. The AT intersects with Skyline Dr. at several points throughout this section, so shortening the hike is a viable option.

If you are getting an early start on the day or are hoping to grab lunch before you head out, note that Panorama Restaurant at Thornton Gap starts serving at 9 a.m. The glass walls of the quaint but casual dining room provide excellent views of the Shenandoah Valley. There is also a gift shop at the site that sells area maps as well as bottled juices, water, and snacks in case you forgot to pack your own.

When you're ready to start hiking, head out of the Panorama and across the parking lot to the AT bulletin board. Follow the path here 50 ft. uphill to meet the AT, and turn left.

The hike starts with a gradual uphill climb through a forest of old oak. The AT crosses to the right of Skyline Dr. and follows a wide service road for a few feet before making a left and hopping up a short bank and back into the woods. Continue to follow the blazes as the trail turns left onto another service road at 0.5 mi. and follows it for approximately 50 yd., before turning left to resume its wooded climb.

Once you're on your way, the trail ascends gradually toward the wooded summit of Pass Mt. Although there are a few steep sections, the climb to the 3052-ft. peak evens out at several points, making it an easy one. The trail passes through a wide, open area shaded by large old oak trees with sweeping lower branches. Before the park was established, this stretch was part of a wide, open field, which allowed the trees to grow to maturity. These tall trees appear even larger next to the young trees that crowd the area today. At 1.3 mi. Pass Mt. Trail leads right 3.0 mi. to US 211, passing Pass Mt. Hut 0.2 mi. from the AT. The hut is reserved for long-distance hikers, but there is a spring behind the hut, and if you need a fill-up now is the chance—the summit of the mountain is dry.

The AT reaches the summit at 2.1 mi. and after a few hundred feet you find yourself heading back downward. Descending Pass Mt., the trail winds through a rocky area (2.5 mi.), as glimpses of Kemp Hollow, Neighbor Mt., and Knob Mt. jump from the right to the left of the trail. As you descend, listen for the low, croaking sound of ravens swooping overhead. Although a raven may appear to resemble a crow at first glance, the sleek black bird is really much larger, with a wingspan of up to 4 ft. In the field the common raven can be recognized by its large size (it commonly weighs about four times as much as the American crow), its pointed wings (as opposed to the relatively blunt and splayed wings of crows), and its long, wedge-shaped tail (most crows have relatively square tails). Any remaining doubts are appeased by the rattling, deep croak of the raven, compared to the crow's nasal caw. Both birds are prevalent in the park, though the raven prefers more remote haunts.

The AT crosses the 3.2-mi., yellow-blazed Rocky Branch Trail at 3.1 mi., then crosses Skyline Dr. in Beahms Gap just ahead. A spur trail to the right at 3.4 mi. leads to the Beahms Gap Overlook and parking area at SDMP 28.5 for one of Skyline Dr.'s many breathtaking views. This is also an early exit option. If you're up for a longer hike and are not into drive-by views, large rocks further up the trail and to the left offer a more natural

Black Bears in Shendandoah National Park

Since their days of virtual elimination, black bears have made an extraordinary comeback in the eastern United States. Native bears were hunted nearly to extinction in the 1800s, but with the restoration of forest habitat they have returned, migrating south from Pennsylvania's Pocono Mts. and east from the Alleghenies. Today approximately 300 of these animals make their homes in the Shenandoah National Park's densely thicketed forest lands. The park has a higher concentration of bears, about one per square mile, than anywhere east of the Mississippi. When you hike the AT here through oak and hemlock forests or mountain laurel thickets or near rhododendron or falling streams, you're in prime bear country.

Contrary to popular belief, black bears do not hibernate. They den for the winter, taking cover in hollow trees, rock cavities, or holes in the ground. While their metabolisms slow by over 50 percent, they don't fall into a sound sleep, and can be awakened easily. During denning, the animals eat and drink nothing, nor do they relieve themselves. Their bodies have the unique ability to reabsorb the toxic by-products of metabolism, a fact that has spurred intense interest among researchers studying human kidney disease.

Shenandoah bears have adapted well to living near people. They are shy, elusive creatures, and would really rather not meet humans. Their diet is mostly vegetarian: nuts, berries, roots, tubers, and grasses, with meat coming from

setting for a peek at the colorful horizon.

The most common mammal in Shenandoah is the white-tailed deer. In 1935 the park was restocked with fifteen deer. They have multiplied to a stable population of several thousand today. These large, graceful animals are extremely populous in the Beahms Gap area and are a frequent sighting for hikers. As you continue down the trail, you're apt to assume the role of the unexpected dinner guest as you pass multiple groups of deer. The animals will silence their munching sounds momentarily as sets of wide brown eyes watch you pass. Their calmness makes it evident that the hiker has become a regular, unalarming interruption. Once you have passed, listen for the chomping to resume.

Do not offer the animals an additional course. Feeding any of the park wildlife is unsafe and illegal. Despite their docile nature, they are wild and can bite, kick, and spread diseases. If fed, deer become easy targets for hunters (although hunting is illegal). Be kind to yourself, and the deer, and resist the temptation.

The trail leads through another brushy, spacious area, then crosses an old road trace at 3.6 mi. Opportuni-

insects and carrion. They are rarely aggressive, though they are opportunists, and will grab a free meal when offered.

Backpacks filled with food and left unattended or stowed in a shelter or tent overnight are top targets, as are garbage cans.

If you come face to face with a bear, use common sense. Treat these large animals with the same respect you would a sumo wrestler. Always yield the right-of-way to bears. Most will flee from you. If a bear doesn't flee, take a nonaggressive stance. Do not make eye contact. Talk in a quiet voice. If the animal continues to approach, talk louder, bang pots, whistle, wave your arms, or shoot the flash of a camera. Never run. A bear can hit speeds of up to 35 mph, and can easily overtake the fastest human sprinter. Most of all, never come between a mother bear and her cubs.

When camping, neatness counts. Never cook or eat where you will be sleeping. Avoid spilling food. Never pour grease drippings into a firepit; that attracts wildlife. Finally, no matter how unlikely a bear visit seems, always hang your food from a rope high in a tree or store it in a bear-proof metal box (available at outdoor supply stores). Hang anything that has a strong scent, such as food, greasy cooking utensils, and toiletries, including toothpaste and soap.

Regard these magnificent animals with healthy respect. View them from a distance with the awe and wonder they deserve.

—Glenn Scherer and David Lillard

---

ties for a water refill exist here on both sides of the trail. A trail to the left, marked by a concrete signpost, leads 100 ft. to an unprotected spring. If you refill here, be sure to use a filter. A few feet further on, a blue-blazed trail to the right will take you 0.5 mi. to Byrds Nest #4. This is one of five three-sided trail shelters located within the park. The shelters are available for picnics and temporary refuge, but overnight stays are not permitted. Piped-in water is available at the site from May to October.

Leaving this area behind, be careful not to trip over the pipe that juts above the trail. As the AT cuts to the southwest side of the ridge, large rocks to the left of the trail provide a great spot to stop for lunch (or a drink of your replenished water supply). As you take a seat, compare your bench to rock formations on other parts of the trail. Much of this section is dominated by greenstone, a heavy, gray-green rock altered from cooled lava flows by heat and pressure. Once a deep black, the surface got its present green tint from the formation of new minerals.

The AT follows a band of greenstone from Thornton Gap to Byrds Nest #4. Here, the trail switches to a band of quartzite, a light gray rock formed over 500 million years ago when much of this area was covered by sea. Streams washed down from the center of North America and dropped loads of sediment on the sea floor. The deposits, mostly sand, gradually turned to rock, and, as they lifted out of the sea over time, became the quartzite cliffs here today. The AT traces this band of quartzite to Elkwallow Gap, where it crosses back onto greenstone. The best way to distinguish the rocks is by the craggy nature of the greenstone, compared to the squarish edges that give quartzite ledges a blocky appearance. The quartzite may still have a greenish hue in some parts, but it is much grayer than greenstone. Both rocks are extremely resistant to erosion.

After a nice rest, the climb ahead will appear only moderately strenuous. This ascent is quite gradual in the beginning. By the time the trail steepens, you're almost to the top. Once there, a yellow-blazed trail to the left (4.4 mi.) leads to the peak of The Neighbor. The 5.6-mi. Neighbor Mt. Trail follows a narrow spur to the tip of The Neighbor (2740 ft.), then leads steeply down to Jeremys Run, a deep canyon intersected by Jeremys Run River. Jeremys Run Trail leads right from Neighbor Mt. Trail for approximately 5 mi. to rejoin the AT at 8.1 mi., near Elkwallow picnic area (8.4 mi.). Views from The Neighbor include a look into Jeremys Run to the north and west with Knob Mt. rising in the distance.

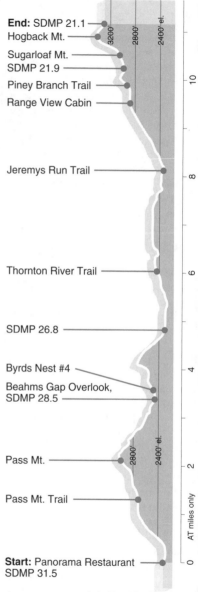

End: SDMP 21.1
Hogback Mt.
Sugarloaf Mt.
SDMP 21.9
Piney Branch Trail
Range View Cabin

Jeremys Run Trail

Thornton River Trail

SDMP 26.8

Byrds Nest #4
Beahms Gap Overlook, SDMP 28.5

Pass Mt.

Pass Mt. Trail

Start: Panorama Restaurant SDMP 31.5

AT miles only

created using Maptech TopoScout ®

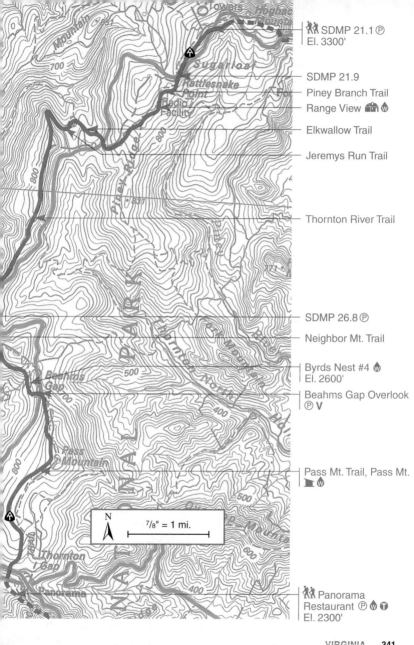

🥾🥾 SDMP 21.1 Ⓟ
El. 3300'

SDMP 21.9

Piney Branch Trail

Range View 🏠 💧

Elkwallow Trail

Jeremys Run Trail

Thornton River Trail

SDMP 26.8 Ⓟ

Neighbor Mt. Trail

Byrds Nest #4 💧
El. 2600'

Beahms Gap Overlook
Ⓟ V

Pass Mt. Trail, Pass Mt.
🏕 💧

N
↑ ⁷⁄₈" = 1 mi.

🥾🥾 Panorama
Restaurant Ⓟ 💧 ☎
El. 2300'

At 4.8 mi. a spur trail to the right leads 0.1 mi. to a parking area at SDMP 26.8, providing another early exit option. For the next 2 mi. the trail cuts across a long, narrow, wooded ridge. It's fairly easy hiking, but watch out for the ambushes of pricker bushes waiting to grab your ankles and slow your trip. With a good eye and some careful maneuvering, you will make it through this stretch and be rewarded with another sloping descent.

Just as you reach the 6.0-mi. point, the trail intersects with the blue-blazed Thornton River Trail. The trail leads to the right 0.3 mi. to SDMP 25.4 where roadside parking makes this a possible early exit spot. From Skyline Dr., the trail continues, following a branch of Thornton River 4.9 mi. to the park boundary. The trail passes through small hemlock stands and is colored in early spring by redbud blooms. There is a parking area at the park boundary.

To press on, continue along the AT for 2 mi., passing over mostly level ground and easy terrain. At 8.1 mi. the AT crosses a creek, then continues through an area scattered with hemlock trees and mature oaks. In spring, the thick covering of oak leaves forms a canopy across the trail as wood fern and pachysandra form a green carpet over the surrounding forest ground.

Just beyond the creek the AT intersects with Jeremys Run Trail, which leads to the left 6.2 mi. to the SNP boundary. An unnamed side trail at 8.4 mi. leads 200 ft. to the Elkwallow Picnic Area. Several picnic tables grace the clearing, which is shaded by the arms of the surrounding oaks. This is a popular picnic spot for motorists touring Skyline Dr. But humans aren't the only creatures prone to dining in the area.

The scraps of leftovers overflowing from the trash cans at the site are also an easy snack for black bears, which roam the park in high numbers—more than one per square mile. Bears in the park are not true hibernators and are a frequent sighting year round. The animals can weigh over 400 pounds and although they are usually unassertive, their astonishing strength calls for respect and caution (see "Black Bears in Shendandoah National Park").

Just ahead, the AT intersects Elkwallow Trail, then crosses Skyline Dr. once again. Elkwallow Trail leads 1.9 mi. west to Matthews Arm Campground. No reservations are accepted here, but there is an ample number of tent sites—more than 150. There are also rest room facilities, a nature trail, equestrian trails, and a picnic area.

At 9.5 mi. a partially obscured service road leads 0.1 mi. to the right to Range View Cabin, a one-room stone cabin built in 1933. The scene recalls the story of Goldilocks and the three bears, which is appropriate for this area. The cabin is equipped with four sets of bunk beds and a stove. An outside fireplace stands under the eaves. The cabin was built and is managed by the PATC and advance reservations are required. There is an unprotected spring just beyond the cabin. From the AT, the service road leads to the left 0.6 mi. to the Piney River Ranger Station and SDMP 22.1.

Beyond the service road, the AT continues to ascend, but as it steepens it also appeases with glimpses of inviting mountain scenery to the west. The trail intersects with an access road at 9.9 mi., and turns right to follow the road for a few feet. When the road cuts to the left, the AT continues straight ahead to intersect with the blue-blazed Piney Branch Trail. The 6.5-mi. side trail follows the Piney River as it cuts through a thick hemlock forest to USFS 600, outside the eastern boundary of the park. Bear sightings are common along the side trail.

At 10.2 mi. the AT crosses Skyline Dr. at SDMP 21.9. For another great view, take a few minutes to wander over to Rattlesnake Point Overlook, 50 yd. to the right. From the 3105-ft. elevation at this spot you can look to the east over Piney River.

Although the large black rat snake is the most common snake in the park, there is still a fairly large population of timber rattlers. Rattlers vary considerably in color and banding—some are almost black, others are various shades of greenish brown. The snakes can be identified by their triangular heads and their rattles.

Snakes generally avoid humans and usually strike only when threatened. The best way to avoid them is to watch where you step and, when climbing in rocks, always be sure you can see where you are putting your hands. The snakes don't always give warning rattle sounds, so use reasonable caution whenever you're hiking through rocky terrain.

Back on the AT, the final mile is an easy ascent. A spur trail at 10.5 mi. leads left 50 ft. to the summit of Sugarloaf Mt. A quarter of a mile further on, the Tuscarora Trail, a 220-mi. loop that rejoins the AT near Carlisle, Pennsylvania, comes in from the left. Just beyond the Tuscarora, another side trail leads 30 ft. to the right, reaching the summit of the fourth peak of Hogback Mt. at 3440 ft. With a bit of stretching and craning, there is a nice view to the south.

Leaving the summit and tracing the ridge, the AT descends to a paved parking lot at SDMP 21.1 at the northern end of this section. From here you can exit the park by driving south to Skyline Dr.'s intersection with US 211. Just beyond the park boundary to the east, a 3-mi. stretch of the highway is lined with seasonal fruit and vegetable stands for replenishing weary hikers. There are also several antiques stores. Don't worry about carrying everything home; basket outlets are plentiful.

HIKE #41   Itinerary

Miles N	NORTH	Elev. (ft/m)	Miles S
11.2	**End:** Paved parking area at SDMP 21.1 approximately 17.5 mi. NE of Luray.	approx. 3300/1006	0.0
10.9	Summit of fourth peak of **Hogback Mt.** 30 ft. to R on spur trail.	3440/1048	0.3
10.5	Summit of **Sugarloaf Mt.** 50 ft. to L on spur trail.		0.7
10.2	Cross **Skyline Dr.** at SDMP 21.9	3100/945	1.0
9.9	Junction with **Piney Branch Trail;** leads 6.5 mi. R to **USFS 600.**		1.3
9.5	Service road leads 0.1 mi. R to Range View Cabin (by reservation), spring. Road leads L 0.6 mi. to SDMP 22.1 and Piney River Ranger Station.		1.7
8.6	**Elkwallow Trail** leads L 1.9 mi. to Matthews Arm Campground with water and rest rooms.		2.6
8.4	Side trail to **Elkwallow Picnic Area** (200 ft.).		2.8
8.1	Junction with **Jeremys Run Trail;** leads L 6.2 mi. to SNP boundary.		3.1
6.0	Blue-blazed **Thornton River Trail** leads R 0.3 mi. to parking area at SDMP 25.4, early exit option.		5.2
4.8	0.1-mi. trail to R to Neighbor Mt. parking area at SDMP 26.8, early exit option.		6.4
4.4	Meet **Neighbor Mt. Trail,** 5.6-mi. yellow-blazed trail to L to peak and Jeremys Run.		6.8
3.6	To L, 100-ft. trail to spring; in a few feet, to R, 0.5-mi. trail to **Byrds Nest #4** (day use only), water May to October.	2600/792	7.6
3.4	To R, short trail to **Beahms Gap Overlook** and parking area at SDMP 28.5; early exit option.		7.8
3.2	Cross **Skyline Dr.** at SDMP 28.6, early exit option.		8.0
2.5	Rocky area with winter views of Kemp Hollow, The Neighbor, and Knob Mt.		8.7
2.1	Summit of **Pass Mt.**	3050/930	9.1
1.3	**Pass Mt. Trail** leads R 0.2 mi. to Pass Mt. Hut.		9.9
0.0	**Start:** Parking area of **Panorama Restaurant** at SDMP 31.5 in Thornton Gap, approximately 7 mi. NE of Luray. Take path leading uphill from AT bulletin board in parking lot 50 ft., turn L.	2300/701	11.2

Hogback Overlook to Jenkins Gap

Map: PATC Va. #9, SNP, N Dist.

Route: Through SNP over Hogback Mt. and Mt. Marshall to Jenkins Gap

Recommended direction: S to N

Distance: 8.5 mi.

Elevation +/-: 3300 to 3475 to 2400 ft.

Effort: Moderate

Day hike: Yes

Overnight backpacking hike: Optional

Duration: 4 to 5 hr.

Early exit options: At 3.1 mi., 4.7 mi., and 6.6 mi., Skyline Dr.

Natural history features: Gravel Springs Gap; Hogwallow Flats; Jenkins Gap

Social history feature: Mt. Marshall

Other feature: Junction with Browntown Trail

Trailhead access: *Start:* From Front Royal, take US 340 S to entrance to SNP, then go S on Skyline Dr. to parking at Hogback Overlook, SDMP 20.8. For an alternate route, see Hike #41. *End:* From Front Royal, take US 340 S to entrance to SNP, then go S on Skyline Dr. to parking at Jenkins Gap, SDMP 12.4.

Camping: Gravel Springs Hut, and see "Camping" in Introduction

---

The hike begins with an easy ascent of Hogback's second peak. At 3475 ft., Hogback is the highest point in the North District of Shenandoah National Park. Unfortunately, the summit is also home to a radio transmission tower and service buildings. The intrusion of contemporary civilization into the hike, however, is soon forgotten in this ramble over the land holdings of a man who greatly shaped the U.S. system of justice.

Traveling close to Skyline Dr., the trail climbs Hogback, pausing at 0.2 mi. to view the dozen hollows that meet in the village of Browntown below. The northern ridge, spilling into the valley, is Gimlet Ridge. To the west of Gimlet is Matthews Arm. Hog-

back is a mountain that blends the old with the new, geologically speaking. Its base was constructed of granite in the Pedlar formation, which was then covered by Catoctin greenstone. The high ridges of Hogback are remnant granite exposed by the erosion of the Catoctin layer.

The AT moves through young woodlands over steady ground to the first peak of Hogback, then drops gently to a sag, where an access trail at 1.2 mi. leads east 100 yd. to Skyline Dr. and Little Hogback Overlook. The overlook, in addition to providing a striking view 2000 ft. down the slope into Browntown Valley, shows the seamless confrontation between the Catoctin formation, which Skyline Dr. follows north from the overlook, and

Fog, from North Marshall Mt.

the Pedlar, which it follows south from here. You can see the difference if you look closely at the road cuts. The Pedlar shows a purplish red along the cracks, or fissures. The Catoctin, geologists surmise, once covered 100 ft. or more above the top of Hogback, but eroded to reveal the Pedlar purples.

A series of switchbacks takes the trail down the east face to Little Hogback at 1.3 mi., where an open view to the northwest of the Browntown Valley below and the town of Front Royal in the distance unfolds from a rock ledge just west of the trail. In winter, the North Fork Shenandoah River can be seen glimmering on its way to its confluence with the South Fork, also seen closer to the ridge,

gliding north 10 mi. northeast on this side of Massanutten Mt.

At 1.6 mi. the trail crosses to the east of Skyline Dr. (SDMP 18.9), just after crossing the Keyser Run Fire Rd., which appears on very old maps as Jinney Gray Rd.—changed, according to John Conners in *Shenandoah National Park: An Interpretive Guide,* because no records could place the name. Now, not even the old road recalls this forgotten person. The road follows the run downstream to a trail through a boulder stream known as Little Devil Stairs. The relatively youthful streams of the Blue Ridge have dumped and strewn boulders down the stream rushes; the large ones near the top of the ridge much too large to be moved downstream except in the largest of storms, once in a generation. Little Devil Stairs is a magnificent hike through the wild, steep canyon of Keyser Run. The *Appalachian Trail Guide to Shenandoah National Park* provides access information on the Little Devil Stairs Trail and other hikes into the canyon.

At 2.9 mi. the yellow-blazed Bluff Trail leads 0.2 mi. to Gravel Springs Hut (and the spring), then to the Harris Hollow Trail, which follows the road bed of the former Browntown-Harris Hollow Rd. for a ways before ditching sharply into the hollow. The road once crossed the Blue Ridge in Gravel Springs Gap. To the east it led into the hollow, then through the Racer Run watergap between Wolf and Keyser mountains. The Gravel Springs Hut, with its dependable Gravel Springs, is the last shelter within SNP for northbound hikers. This spring was once a watering hole of a different sort. During the early prohibition years it was a gathering place for purchasing and sipping bootleg hooch.

Also at 2.9 mi., the Browntown Trail joins the AT for a short stretch. Just beyond, at 3.1 mi., the trail crosses Skyline Dr. at the point where the old road breached Gravel Springs Gap; the AT breaks right to the north, and Browntown Trail heads west into Browntown Valley. There is parking for a dozen cars here (SDMP 17.7).

Ascending, the modern hiker probably won't have the history of American jurisprudence on the mind, but there is a connection. South Marshall and North Marshall were once the property of renowned U.S. Supreme Court Chief Justice John Marshall, who served in the early days of the republic, from 1801 to 1835. Then, the mountain, for it is actually one with north and south summits, was known as Bluff Mt., as recalled by the trail just crossed near Gravel Springs.

The greenstone shelf at 3.9 mi., near the summit of South Marshall, announces views west, perhaps most notably of the ridge construction of Mt. Marshall. The Catoctin lava flows atop a granite decline to the southeast. Erosion has carved a series of hillside depressions and left resistant greenstone in place, forming long steps in the slope, like bleacher seats above an imagined arena down in Browntown Valley. There are places where the rock breaks through to form jagged outcrops, begging exploration. But advance with warning! Our own investigation was cut short when we spied our third rattlesnake and we became, admittedly, more occupied with where we were stepping than what we had come to see.

Passing over the forested summit of South Marshall, the AT makes a lazy descent into the saddle between the north and south summits, losing 125 ft. over half a mile, then, at 4.7 mi., crossing Skyline Dr. near mi. 16.0. There is parking here for a dozen cars, providing an exit option for this hike.

The ascent of North Marshall is made through switchbacks on the lava benches, amid the often-present rhododendron and mountain laurel. Near the summit, at about 5 mi., the uppermost erosion-resistant bench gives a long view to the south and west. Your eyes can follow Skyline Dr. below as it follows the Blue Ridge, appearing as a collection of peaks and ridges arranged so that at times its seems almost arbitrary where one ends and the next begins. You can see that the ridge is the result of several mountain-building episodes, with new rock piled or molded atop older rock. After millennia of erosion of surrounding surface rock, the summits are left standing like snowmen in spring.

On the casual descent of North Marshall in Hogwallow Flats, the trail passes Hogwallow Spring, found about 25 ft. from the trail on an unmarked, easy-to-miss spur to the right, at 6.1 mi. The spring's offering is predictable, but not the approach. Even when you know it's there you can walk right past the spur.

In broad Hogwallow Flats, the trail crosses Skyline Dr. (SDMP 14.2) at 6.6 mi., 300 yd. south of Hogwallow Flats Overlook. The flats are a terraced series of steps in the hillside formed by the varying degrees of resistance of the underlying Catoctin rock. A short detour to the overlook reveals long views east of the Piedmont and the village of Flint Hill below. Nestled into the hills, Flint Hill was a resettlement community, one of several

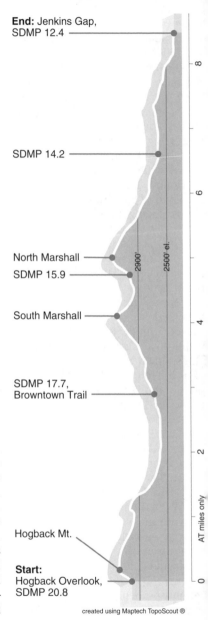

End: Jenkins Gap, SDMP 12.4

SDMP 14.2

North Marshall

SDMP 15.9

South Marshall

SDMP 17.7, Browntown Trail

Hogback Mt.

Start: Hogback Overlook, SDMP 20.8

2900'

2500' el.

AT miles only

created using Maptech TopoScout ®

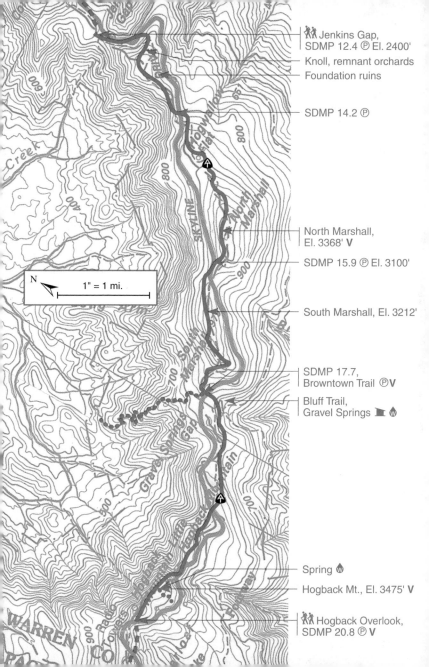

Jenkins Gap,
SDMP 12.4 Ⓟ El. 2400'

Knoll, remnant orchards

Foundation ruins

SDMP 14.2 Ⓟ

North Marshall,
El. 3368' **V**

SDMP 15.9 Ⓟ El. 3100'

South Marshall, El. 3212'

SDMP 17.7,
Browntown Trail Ⓟ**V**

Bluff Trail,
Gravel Springs ◼ ⓦ

Spring ⓦ

Hogback Mt., El. 3475' **V**

Hogback Overlook,
SDMP 20.8 Ⓟ **V**

N

1" = 1 mi.

created as new homes for people displaced by the establishment of SNP. Only a dozen miles from the ridge, it was a world apart for people accustomed to spending most of their lives among a handful of neighbors, scraping out an existence in the hollows—a life they were loathe to leave. Flint Hill is a tony, picturesque town now, with a country inn and horse stables for the gentry.

Back on the AT, the trail meanders away from the Drive, passes the foundations of two old farm buildings at 6.8 mi., and ascends. A knoll at 7.1 mi. hosts abandoned orchards. Some of the trees continue to drop apples, tasty enough for local wildlife but pale in comparison to the apples available each fall in the surrounding countryside. The Shenandoah Valley is one of America's largest apple-producing regions, adding to the colorful delights of autumn hiking in the park.

Descending steeply at times, the trail slides along the eastern slope for nearly 0.5 mi., then follows Skyline Dr. from just above it for a final half mile. The trail crosses an old road at 8.4 mi., then reaches the yellow-blazed Jenkins Gap Trail and Jenkins Gap and the end of the hike at 8.5 mi. There is parking for about a dozen cars in the lot, which also serves the Jenkins Gap Overlook. From the overlook, once again we see Flint Hill, the unwanted home of more than fifteen Jenkins families who were relocated to the valley by the park project. Timothy Jenkins settled in this area of the ridge in the mid-1700s, and his name has been given to the gap and two mountains, Jenkins and Little Jenkins. The land vacated by descendants of Jenkins and hundreds of other mountain families has given the rest of us the Blue Ridge to enjoy.

HIKE #42 Itinerary

Miles N	NORTH	Elev. (ft/m)	Miles S
8.5	**End: Jenkins Gap** trailhead parking at SDMP 12.4, 19 mi. N of US 211/Thornton Gap entrance and 12.4 mi. S of US 340 entrance to park in Front Royal.	2400/732	0.0
7.1	Remnant orchards.		1.4
6.8	Foundations of 2 farm storage buildings.		1.7
6.6	Cross **Skyline Dr.** at SDMP 14.2, early exit option.		1.9
6.1	**Hogwallow Spring,** water.		2.4
5.0	Summit of **North Marshall;** cliffs.	3368/1027	3.5
4.7	Cross **Skyline Dr.** at mi. 15.9, early exit option.	3100/945	3.8
4.1	Summit of **South Marshall.**	3212/979	4.4
3.1	Cross **Skyline Dr.** at SDMP 17.7 (early exit option). Then Browntown Trail heads W, away from AT, and down the mountain. The AT turns N (R).		5.4
2.9	Junction with **Bluff Trail to Gravel Springs Hut** and spring (0.2 mi.). AT follows Browntown Trail for next 0.3 mi.		5.6
1.6	Cross **Skyline Dr.** at SDMP 19.4.		6.9
1.3	Summit of **Little Hogback Mt.;** views.		7.2
1.2	Trail (100 yd. E) to **Little Hogback Overlook** at SDMP 19.7.		7.3
0.3	0.2-mi. trail R to spring.		8.2
0.2	Summit of **Hogback Mt.,** second peak, highest point of trail in North District of SNP.	3475/1059	8.3
0.0	**Start: Hogback Overlook** parking at SDMP 20.8, 11 mi. N of US 211 entrance to park in Thornton Gap.	3000/914	8.5

SOUTH

Jenkins Gap to Chester Gap

Map: PATC Va. #9, SNP, N Dist.

Route: From Jenkins Gap to Compton Peak and Compton Gap, and descending to US 522

Recommended direction: S to N

Distance: 7.7 mi.

Elevation +/-: 2400 to approx. 2875 to 940 ft.

Effort: Easy

Day hike: Yes

Overnight backpacking hike: Optional

Duration: 4 1/2 hr.

Early exit options: At 2.0 mi., Skyline Dr.; at 5.5 mi., VA 601

Natural history features: Jenkins Gap; Possum Rest; Moore Run; Sloan Creek

Social history feature: Tom Floyd Wayside

Other features: Junctions with Dickey Ridge and Compton Gap trails

Trailhead access: *Start:* From Front Royal, take US 340S just outside of town to the entrance to SNP and Skyline Dr. Go S on Skyline Dr. to trailhead parking at SDMP 12.4 *End:* From Front Royal, at the intersection of US 340 and US 522, go S on US 522 approximately 5 mi. Look on R for white blazes and limited roadside parking just beyond Natl. Zoological Park. Not recommended for overnight parking.

Camping: Tom Floyd Wayside Campground and Shelter, and see "Camping" in Introduction.

This easy hike, which begins only a few minutes' drive from the north entrance to Shenandoah National Park, offers a fine opportunity to enjoy nearly the full breadth of experience that is the AT in the Virginias. It begins with a classic Blue Ridge view of Jenkins Gap and ends with a stroll through a meadow that once served as a U.S. Cavalry remount station and a prisoner of war camp. In between, there are abandoned roads leading to former mountain settlements, a precipitous view from a rocky outcropping, a couple of quiet campsites, ample opportunities to view wildlife, and, of course, a few miles of the "long green tunnel." The only thing missing is a waterfall, but a few stream crossings on the north end provide the sounds and setting to bring out deer and other denizens of the forest for a close look.

Because the majority of the hike leads you on a steady descent, down and out of the park, hikers carrying only day packs can make the trip in about three hours of walking—but what's the hurry? Short side trails along this route lead to, among other diversions, flowering trees and volcanic rock formations. These trails are like anterooms at a favorite museum, each leading to unexpected discoveries worthy of exploration.

The hike begins at the Jenkins Gap trailhead parking area, SDMP 12.4. Descend blue-blazed Jenkins Gap Trail about 50 yd. to its junction with the AT and turn north. In early June, when mountain laurel blooms along the Blue Ridge, the Jenkins Gap Trail reveals plentiful blossoms and a quiet streamside setting in which to view them. More mountain laurel and abundant pink azalea line the level ground of the AT. For a brief period of one to two weeks in late May and early June, flowering azalea and mountain laurel share the stage for a virtual festival of these flowers.

At about 0.5 mi., the trail begins a steep, but graded, climb of Compton Peak, ultimately ascending 500 ft. in half a mile. Compton Springs, two reliable water sources, are just off the trail halfway through the climb. Although this may be early in the hike to refill your water bottles, this is the last water directly on the trail until Tom Floyd Wayside at 4.8 mi. If you plan to stop along the way for lunch, it's a good idea to polish off the contents of your water bottle at Compton Springs and refuel for the day.

The summit of Compton Peak (1.3 mi.) is the day's first reward for a declivitous climb. For the views, blue-blazed trails lead east and west, and both deserve a look. To the west, it is 0.2 mi. over the summit of Compton and down to a stony ledge offering views to the west of the village of Browntown, Buck and Long mountains, and Page Valley along the South Fork Shenandoah River. There are views to the north beyond Possum Rest, where this hike is leading, and of the Piedmont.

The eastern side trail descends 200 ft. in over 0.2 mi. to basalt rock outcroppings, remnants of the volcanic activity that helped build the Blue Ridge. Close examination of these dark columns of fine-grained mineral reveals a concoction that is the basis of over-the-counter mineral supplements: aluminum, magnesium, calcium, and iron. To get the best picture of the columns of rock, careful spelunking to the base is necessary. It's a bit treacherous in wet weather, but experienced rock jumpers (i.e., big kids) in solid hiking shoes can handle it.

Here the Blue Ridge can be imagined as a series of columns with the soils and vegetation draping over them and holding the thousand-mile crest together, as if it were a Roebling suspension bridge—instead of cables there are the eroded remnants of the Catoctin, Pedlar, and other major mountain-building episodes.

As you climb back to the trail, dainty flowers of white Clintonia invite a rest and drink before your descent north into Compton Gap (2.1 mi.) and crossing of Skyline Dr.

at milepost 10.4. From the parking area at Compton Gap, the AT shares the trail with the yellow-blazed former Compton Gap – Chester Gap Rd., which once led to the cabins of mountaineers and now leads to suburban dwellings adjacent to the park border. The combination of white and yellow (Compton Gap Trail) blazes visible on trees here will continue until the AT breaks toward the park boundary at 3.7 mi. Ironically, the proximity of this stretch of trail to adjacent neighborhoods isn't reflected in the human population on the trail.

North of Compton Gap, hikers who keep silent on this section so close to the civilization outside the park can come face to face with the animals that thrive on the edge of the forest. In fact, observant hikers will likely see more wildlife than people on this hike. Perhaps because it seems too close to the civilized world, hikers tend to neglect this section.

At 2.4 mi. the intersection with the Dickey Ridge Trail offers another worthy distraction. Like Skyline Dr., this side trail follows Dickey Ridge some 9 mi. north to the town of Front Royal. Just 350 yd. from the AT is Fort Windham Rocks, where columns of greenstone, a derivative of molten basalt lava, display a 600-million-year-old interplay of heating and cooling that turned the hot, dark lava into a cool, green stone. Climbing and frolicking among the rocks of Fort Windham can be a day-long excursion in itself.

Back on the AT, the trail passes Springhouse Rd. at 2.7 mi., and follows the green tunnel under a canopy of chestnut oak and hickory along level ground for over a mile before breaking north from Compton Gap Trail, formerly the route of the AT, onto a slender footpath in open woods. The oak and hickory forest here and below Possum Rest are inviting habitat for wild turkey. Hikers moving silently, both hushed afoot and sans voice, may be delighted by coming upon a flock of turkeys gorging themselves on fallen acorns. Engrossed in their feast, they sometimes let their guards down enough for hikers to get a good look. More, likely, they will become aware of intruders just before you spy them, and the sudden racket they make will take you by surprise. For the truly patient hiker, taking up station in a blind may be rewarded with the sight of the flock trotting through the woods.

At 4.1 mi., the trail leaves SNP at Possum Rest, close to the halfway point of the hike and a fine spot for lunch before a steep descent. The view across Harmony Hollow to Dickey Ridge gives that feeling that you could almost toss a rock to the opposite ridge or scamper down the ledge and back up the other side lickety-split. To the north, the view is of High Knob on the opposite side of Chester Gap, the route of the AT as it meanders north.

Below and north, tuliptrees, or

yellow-poplars, rise 100 ft. and more above the slope. With leaves up to 8 in. long and magnificent flowers with pink-striped white petals as big as the leaves, the forest below makes a fine show in May. Tuliptrees are not too choosy about the company they keep; they are as at home with willow and alder as with sycamore, white pine or, as you'll see below, white ash. When hiking through the tuliptrees, watch for dogwoods, a common understory sight with tuliptrees, hugging the slopes. Having lunch, or any extended stop at Possum Rest, improves your chances for seeing a soaring raven in mid-air aerobatics or a red-tail hawk on the flying prowl for its own lunch.

Descending the steep steps of Possum Rest, the wonderful craftsmanship of the PATC crews that maintain the trail through the park is apparent. It is as though each stone was carefully carved to perfect shape. In addition to the AT, the PATC, a club older than the park itself, maintains a couple of hundred miles of trails throughout SNP and another 1000 or so in the surrounding region. You may encounter these dedicated souls on the trail; words of praise and thanks are always appreciated.

We encountered a band of another sort of passionate creature on an autumn descent of Possum Rest: an agitated swarm of bees rushing to finish their season's business beneath the greenstone rocks. The dozen stings were enough to warrant a trip to the local hospital, but the mishap probably could have been avoided with a few precautions.

From the bottom of Possum Rest, the trail follows level ground as it makes its way toward the Tom Floyd Wayside. Hikers not fortunate enough to see turkey here may be surprised by the unexpected flight of a grouse stirred from its place in the leaves and thicket. The sudden take-off of the grouse never fails to startle, but a quick recovery from the shock wins a glimpse of the brown-and-white-spotted feathers. At Tom Floyd Wayside at 4.8 mi., via a short, marked pathway, there are a shelter for backpackers, a tent camping area, and Ginger Spring, a reliable water source. The spring is also accessible from a second path 0.2 mi. down the AT, without hiking to the shelter.

The Wayside's namesake and builder is a legend along these parts of the AT. A skilled woodsman, he explored long-forgotten corners of SNP and published a popular history of the Jones Mt. area, *Lost Trails and Forgotten People* (see also Jones Mt. description in Hike #38). Floyd's shelter is owned and maintained by the PATC. His greatest claim to fame was the development of the Big Blue Trail, now known as the Tuscarora to coincide with the Pennsylvania portion of the trail bearing the same name (see Hike #39). We can imagine that Floyd liked a spicebush tea, because in wet weather you can practically taste it in the spring water.

Spicebush is a common understory species in the yellow-poplar (tulip-tree) forest; April and May hikers will spot them by their red berries.

Continuing a descent it generally will follow for two more miles, with a couple of small rises mixed in, the trail joins gravel VA 601 after crossing a stream. This is an exit option for the hike. A blue-blazed trail at 5.1 mi. leads 350 yd. back to VA 601, where there is parking for six cars. If you hike in summer, a shrub with yellow tendril flowers clustered like fingers may catch your attention from the east side of the trail. This is the chinkapin—an oak, you'll discover upon closer inspection of its oblong, tapered leaf. The nut, which drops in autumn, has a sweet, buttery flavor when roasted. But you'll have to get through the prickly burr surrounding it to know. Please be aware the trail is passing through private property here on an easement, and the chinkapin is not common in these parts. Don't harvest the nut!

Traveling through more of the park area's chestnut oak forest, the AT passes a blue-blazed trail at 5.7 mi. leading 0.3 mi. to a 4-H facility, where water can be obtained from a spigot. The trail then finds slightly level ground in a thick meadow, one that would be completely impassable were it not for the vigilant clearing by members of the PATC.

After crossing two small streams, then Moore Run at 6.3 mi., the trail reaches VA 602. If the past 2.8 mi. since leaving SNP have appeared to

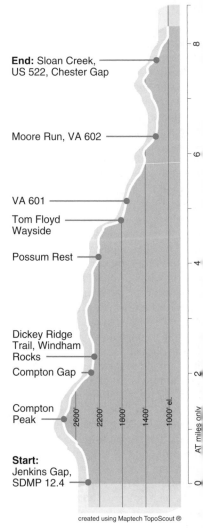

End: Sloan Creek, US 522, Chester Gap

Moore Run, VA 602

VA 601

Tom Floyd Wayside

Possum Rest

Dickey Ridge Trail, Windham Rocks

Compton Gap

Compton Peak

Start: Jenkins Gap, SDMP 12.4

2600' 2200' 1800' 1400' 1000' el.

AT miles only

created using Maptech TopoScout ®

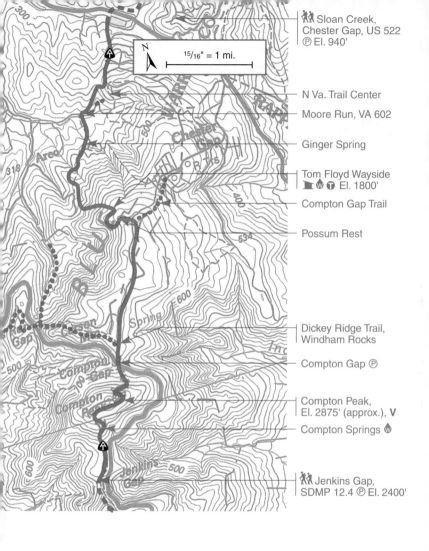

北北 Sloan Creek,
Chester Gap, US 522
Ⓟ El. 940'

N Va. Trail Center

Moore Run, VA 602

Ginger Spring

Tom Floyd Wayside
▰ ⓦ Ⓣ El. 1800'

Compton Gap Trail

Possum Rest

Dickey Ridge Trail,
Windham Rocks

Compton Gap Ⓟ

Compton Peak,
El. 2875' (approx.), **V**

Compton Springs ⓦ

北北 Jenkins Gap,
SDMP 12.4 Ⓟ El. 2400'

be nearly as pristine as the park, it's due to the Harmony Hollow easement that protects the trail through here. Although the park was authorized in the 1930s to acquire more than 500,000 acres, fewer than 200,000 make up the park. Conservation easements, which allow private landowners to retain ownership of their property while donating development rights, have become a principal tool for protecting trail corridors such as that of the AT.

As you ascend from the road, rather steeply after 3 mi. of generally downward hiking, a tall chain-link fence appears to the left of the trail. This intrusion onto the aesthetic of the trail nonetheless indicates another protected area: the wildlife preserve of the National Zoological Park. Hikers in need of a water refill may take the blue-blazed trail at 6.5 mi. to the Northern Virginia Trail Center, one of several PATC properties near the park. A spigot outside is available to hikers.

The last half mile of the hike is a descent through an open meadow, still adjacent to the wildlife center. This is the meadow that was formerly a U.S. Cavalry remount station and a World War II prisoner of war camp. US 522 comes into view below, and the sounds of the modern world with it. The town of Front Royal, the gateway community of the park, is 5 mi. west. Crossing narrow Sloan Creek on a footbridge, the trail finds the road, parking on the shoulder, and level ground at 940 ft.

HIKE #43 Itinerary

Miles N	NORTH	Elev. (ft/m)	Miles S
7.7	**End:** Sloan Creek, at **US 522 in Chester Gap,** 3.5 mi. E of intersection with VA 55 in Front Royal.	940/287	0.0
7.2	Meadow, former POW camp and U.S. Cavalry remount station.		0.5
6.5	To R, trail to **N Va. Trail Center,** water from spigot.		1.2
6.3	Cross **Moore Run, VA 602.**		1.4
5.8	Pass old-growth beech tree.		1.9
5.7	Trail to **N Va. 4-H Educational Center,** water available from spigot (0.3 mi.).		2.0
5.1	Meet **VA 601,** early exit option.		2.6
4.9	0.2-mi. trail to **Ginger Spring.**		2.8
4.8	Short path to **Tom Floyd Wayside Shelter** (self-registration for backcountry permits), tent sites, **Ginger Spring.**	1800/549	2.9
4.1	**Possum Rest** (boundary of SNP); view.		3.6
3.7	AT breaks L onto narrow path; **Compton Gap Trail** continues straight ahead.		3.9
2.6	**Springhouse Rd.**		5.0
2.3	**Dickey Ridge Trail** to Fort Windham Rocks (350 yd.) and Front Royal (9 mi.).		5.3
2.0	**Compton Gap,** SDMP 10.4, early exit option.		5.6
1.2	**Compton Peak;** to W, trail to summit (2909 ft.) and views; to E, trail to rock formations.	approx. 2875/876	6.4
0.8	**Compton Springs**		6.8
0.0	**Start: In Jenkins Gap at SDMP 12.4,** S of US 340 entrance to SNP in Front Royal; trailhead parking area. Descend blue-blazed Jenkins Gap Trail approximately 50 yd. to AT (visible from parking area).	2400/731	7.7

SOUTH

HIKE #44

Chester Gap to Ashby Gap

Map: PATC Va. #8, N Va., S Half

Route: From US 522 N of SNP through the G. R. Thompson Wildlife Management Area and Sky Meadows SP to Ashby Gap

Recommended direction: S to N

Distance: 20.7 mi.

Elevation +/-: 900 to 1900 to 800 to 1950 to 800 ft.

Effort: Easy

Day hike: Yes

Overnight backpacking hike: Yes

Duration: 14 hr. if hiked in its entirety in 1 day (fatigue will slow you down); 10 hr. if broken into 2 days

Early exit options: At 8.4 mi., VA 725; at 10.7 mi., blue-blazed trail; at 12.6 mi., VA 638; at 13.7 mi., dirt road; at 17.1 mi., Sky Meadows SP

Natural history feature: Trillium in bloom in late spring

Trailhead access: *Start:* From VA 55 in Front Royal, go W on US 522 about 3.5 mi., look for trailhead parking on R just beyond Natl. Zoological Park. *Late start from Manassas Gap:* From I-66W, take Exit 13 to VA 55E; in 2.5 mi., go N on VA 725 0.2 mi. Park in PATC lot at junction with AT. *End:* Take US 50 in Paris and go W 1.0 mi. to VA 601; turn R (N) and take an immediate, sharp L and descend a steep gravel driveway to parking area (8 cars).

Camping: Mosby Campsite; Denton Shelter; Manassas Gap Shelter; Dick's Dome Shelter; Sky Meadows SP; and where permitted along trail

---

For most of the year, this forest ramble is not one that draws the crowds to the Blue Ridge. Most "destination hikers" who have journeyed to the Blue Ridge are hiking 10 mi. south in Shenandoah National Park. But in June, when the trillium are blooming along the AT in the G. Richard Thompson Wildlife Area, there is plenty of fellowship in the woods there. However, with the nearness of VA 638 and housing developments along it, hikers are as likely to hear the faint sound of lawnmowers and barking dogs in the dis-

tance as barred owls or songbirds nearby. Still, the hike offers a nice walk in the woods, a splendid view to the south of the high Blue Ridge, and a surprising amount of wildlife given the proximity to housing developments.

For an overnight backpacking trip from US 522 in Chester Gap, backpackers may enjoy a stay at the Denton Shelter, known as the Hiker's Hilton because of generous amenities that include an outdoor shower, a picnic table in a small pavilion, and open grounds that can only be described as a lawn. For a shorter day hike amidst spring trillium, take a late start to the hike, beginning at Manassas Gap (see "Trailhead access," above).

Autumn and winter hikers take note: The Thompson Wildlife Management Area, through which 10 mi. of the hike travels, is managed for hunting. A call to the ATC office to see what's in season is a worthwhile planning precaution. When hiking during hunting season, stay on the trail and dress for safety.

From the trailhead, the AT crosses north across busy US 522 and enters the woods, then cuts hard to the right just north of the road, traveling on land administered by the U.S. Zoological Survey. At 2.3 mi. the trail crests a wide knoll (1900 ft.). A maintenance trail, used for access to the AT, joins from the right, and in 0.3 mi. the trail leaves the USZS property. At 3.2 mi. the trail crosses a fire road, then a small stream. A blue-blazed trail just past 3.3 mi. leads 100 yd. to Mosby Campsite, a 10-acre parcel donated by the PATC to the National Park Service. The Tom Sealock Spring provides water. There are roughly half a dozen sites and no other facilities.

Moving north from the campground access trail, the AT crosses three abandoned farm roads starting at 3.5 mi. Lush in April and May with flowering dogwoods, the state tree of the Virginia Commonwealth, the forest here displays an uncommonly large stand of the species. Usually found in groups in the middle story of oak and beech-maple forests, here, perhaps due the relative youth of this recovering woodland, dogwoods abound.

Flowering dogwoods play a far more important role in the Appalachian forest than merely beautifying the countryside. The high fat content of its red berries are an important source of energy for migrating birds, while its buds are a vital food source for the spring azure butterfly and its larvae. The armies of ants often found on dogwood bark in late winter and early spring are actually following the larvae, which leave a high-protein secretion favored by the ants. In turn, the ants act as protectors for the caterpillars, attacking the tiny flies that plague the larvae.

The dogwood is recognized as much for its usefulness to human culture as for its role in the forest landscape. Native Americans used the root bark in dyes for clothing and accessories, and a boiled concoction of the inner bark to relieve fever and diarrhea. European settlers have used a tonic produced from dogwood bark in prescriptions for malaria and other fevers alternately treated with quinine. As for the name dogwood, noted naturalist John Eastman, in his *Book of Forest and Thicket,* theorizes that the repugnant smell of fresh-cut dogwood, which he describes as resembling dog feces, has given this otherwise graceful tree its name. Before the age of graphite shafts and club heads, the dogwood was the preferred material for golf club heads on drivers and fairway woods.

At 4.1 mi. a power line right-of-way, as is often true on the AT, opens an area for raspberries in spring and blueberries in summer, and here serves as a kind of forest divider between the dogwood thicket and a more mature stand of yellow-poplar and hickory, including the shagbark and bitternut varieties. In modern times, the renowned versatility of hickory wood for fuel and construction materials has somewhat overshadowed its utility as a source of food. The shagbark hickory is one of the most sought after hardwoods, while its effectiveness as heating fuel is unsurpassed in the eastern wood world—a cord of hickory gives heat equivalent to that given by 175 gallons of fuel oil. The smoke produced by hickory has been favored by Native Americans and modern suburbanites for flavoring meats and poultry. As a food source, the hickory nut and its relatives the walnut and pecan are well known. Less known is the sweet syrup derived from tapped trees in spring. The hickory produces far less sap than the famous maple, making hickory syrup less commercially viable, but no less tasty.

At 5.2 mi., just beyond the intersection with an old road and house, is the short spur trail to the left to Denton Shelter and campground. The facility deserves its title of Hiker's Hilton. The shelter sports an outdoor, spring-fed shower, a sheltered picnic table, and a cooking area that must be the envy of many local parks departments and every backyard barbecuer, planted flowers, and a lawn suitable for croquet (although getting the mallets and balls there would present a challenge). To some the shelter may seem out of place, but the proximity of the trail to private land on this stretch of the AT requires concentrating camping to a central location. In addition to the shelter, which accommodates seven, there are tent platforms nearby. The shelter is named for Molly and Jim Denton, noted Potomac Appalachian Trail Club volunteers and authors. The trail was the medium that brought the couple together in their youths and their life together composed a story of romance on and with the AT. Whether you plan to stay at the Hiker's Hilton, a stop to read about the Dentons warms a hiker's heart on even a winter's hike.

A footbridge crosses a small stream at 6.1 mi., and soon after the trail crosses VA 638. Follow the white blazes roughly 100 yd. to the left. The trail leads over a wooden stile onto private farmland, and climbs steeply through the field, offering wide views of High Knob to the south at about 6.3 mi., then again at 6.6 mi. after crossing a farm road.

At 8.1 mi. the trail crosses railroad tracks and a few streams that are headwaters of Goose Creek, one of a few so-named creeks in northern Virginia; at 8.2 mi. it reaches the intersection of VA 55 and VA 725 in Manassas Gap. It crosses VA 55, then

Michael Warren

Timber rattlesnake

follows VA 725 under I-66 through a small settlement before leaving the road at the trailhead at the PATC parking lot. This is an early exit spot for the hike, or a late starting point for a hike to Ashby Gap (see "Trailhead access"). The trail crosses a footbridge and begins the ascent of a low knob. At 8.6 mi. it reaches the top of the knob and descends to cross a dirt farm road; a small fire pond is on the right. The trail passes over a small dam at the base of the pond, meanders through an open field, and climbs again, via switchbacks.

The AT enters the G. Richard Thompson Wildlife Management Area at 10.2 mi. These state-owned game lands of woodlands and streams are home to deer, grouse, turkey, and other game that feast on hickory nuts and sassafras bark under an upper story of yellow-poplar. Another infrequently seen, but often vilified, denizen of the Blue Ridge resides here: the eastern timber rattlesnake. On summer hikes, as the afternoon sun filters through the trees, you may spy a rattler stretched across the trail, warming in the sun as it peeps through the small opening in the canopy made by trail clearing. On one such hike, daydreaming our way along the AT hoping to see the autumn antlers and mating rituals of bucks and does, we nearly stepped on a 5-ft. rattler, glimpsing its black diamond markings just one step before treading on the thing. Annoyed at losing its sunny spot and more frightened of us than we of it (which is saying a lot), the snake disappeared into the grasses.

From the early days of Skyland, the first resort in what is now SNP, there were reports of snakes so plentiful as to pose a fine reason for never hiking after dusk overtook the woods. Now it's rare to see more than one at a time, except in a few out-of-the-way rocky ledges that provide the necessities of sun, shelter, and food. On that day we saw a second rattler straddling the trail at the junction of the AT and the blue-blazed Ted Lake Trail, at the 10.7-mi. mark on this hike (to the left the trail leads 0.8 mi. to trailhead parking on VA 638, an early exit option). The snake lay there, apparently in the lazy aftermath of consuming lunch, so put off by us that it refused to move from the trail. It merely looked at us coolly as if to say: "Go around me, I ain't moving." In balancing the twin leave-no-trace objectives of staying always on the trail and never disturbing wildlife, we yielded the right-of-way to the snake and bushwhacked around it—to the tail end, of course.

Just beyond the junction with Ted Lake Trail, at 10.8 mi., is the 70-yd. access trail to Manassas Gap Shelter, an unassuming structure that accommodates four. A spring nearby provides a reliable, if meager, water supply. Because this section of the AT gets far less traffic than the nearby SNP sections, one can wander into the area in late afternoon and find room at the shelter—except during the May and June rush of AT thru-hikers. For day hikers, the shelter is a cool, quiet place for a nap. A note

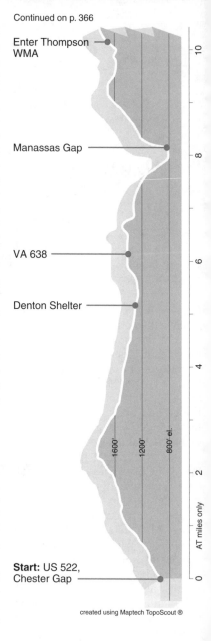

Continued on p. 366

Enter Thompson WMA

Manassas Gap

VA 638

Denton Shelter

1600' 1200' 800' el.

Start: US 522, Chester Gap

AT miles only

created using Maptech TopoScout ®

Ted Lake Trail, VA 638 Ⓟ

Thompson WMA

Manassas Gap,
VA 55, VA 725 Ⓟ El. 800'

VA 638

Denton ⛺ 🏠 💧 🚻
El. 1300'

Mosby Campsite ⛺ 💧

🥾 Chester Gap, US 522
Ⓟ El. 940'

discovered in the shelter logbook said: "Don't worry about rodents at this shelter; the snake will get them." AT backpackers are famous for such musings.

Over the next couple of miles, the AT is alight in spring with acres of trillium, a bloom as delicate as it is fetching. This lily's trademark is its three broad leaves and three resplendent white petals that decorate the forest floor. In late spring, the flowers turn pink. Here, they are everywhere. To keep it that way, stay on the trail and enjoy the view. Simply clipping the leaf or taking a flower can kill the plant, which takes six years above ground to develop to full flower. The flower is a protected species in Virginia and other eastern states. Consider its life cycle and understand why.

The seed spends two winters below the soil surface before developing a root that waits another spring to sprout above ground. Then, for six years, the plant produces a single leaf and the three leaf forms that show the early development of flower petals. In the sixth year, the trillium flowers in all its glory and will continue each spring if left alone. Native Americans used trillium leaves to relieve infections and control bleeding, while the baby leaves of domesticated trillium are sometimes found in gourmet salads. For hikers, they are a memorable part of the AT in northern Virginia.

A blue-blazed trail at 12.6 mi. leads 0.4 mi. to the Trico Fire Tower, another

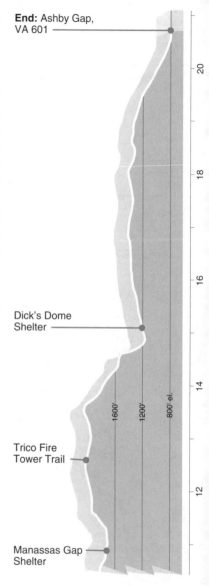

End: Ashby Gap, VA 601

Dick's Dome Shelter

1600' 1200' 800' el.

Trico Fire Tower Trail

Manassas Gap Shelter

Ashby Gap, VA 601 ⓟ
El. 800'

US 50

Sky Meadows SP ▲ ⓣ

Dick's Dome ▰ ⓣ
El. 1200'

Trico Fire Tower Trail,
El. 1950'

Verlin Smith Trail,
Trillium begins ✿

Manassas Gap ▰ ◍ ⓣ

Ted Lake Trail, VA 638 ⓟ

1" = 1 mi.

project of the Civilian Conservation Corps along the Blue Ridge. The tower is locked, but the parking lot, which accommodates fourteen cars, provides easy access from VA 638 to the AT and another exit option for this hike. Several radio and microwave towers are also here. Continue through trillium, which ends just before the trail crosses a dirt road at 13.7 mi. The road leads left 0.3 mi. to another parking lot on VA 638.

A dirt road at 15.1 mi. leads east 0.2 mi. to Dick's Dome Shelter, built by PATC member Dick George on private property. It accommodates four, but there is no reliable water for drinking, despite its proximity to Whiskey Hollow Creek. The privy is a short way up the hill.

Descending, the trail crosses a small creek in Whiskey Hollow, then ascends and leaves the Thompson Wildlife Area briefly and reenters at 15.6 mi. The AT crosses a small spring at 16.2 mi., beyond which a blue-blazed trail leads 0.1 mi. to parking at Signal Knob, named for its use as a link in the confederate communication chain during the Civil War. Native Americans used the knob as an eastern signal summit in a communications network spanning ridges west to the Allegheny Mts. An unmarked trail leads 150 yd. from the lot to views.

The trail arrives at Sky Meadows SP at 17.1 mi. A short trail leads to trailhead parking for 10 cars. In the park are a campground, 1.3 mi. down the blue-blazed North Ridge Trail at 17.4 mi., a nicely groomed system of foot trails, and a farmstead museum. The AT leaves the park at 17.6 mi., beginning a stretch of dirt road junctions and crossings. There are westward views of the valley. Take care to follow the white blazes at the road junctions to avoid wandering down the wrong path.

The trip through the park and northward for the final 3 mile pass through dogwood, hickory, and maple as it descends toward Ashby Gap. At 19.6 mi. the trail crosses an open field that is the corridor over buried telephone lines. Look for blackberry bushes in late summer.

At 20.3 mi., as the trail follows a dirt road, a wooden sign claims that George Washington passed here. If you're hiking with small children, be aware that the sign is a warning that busy US 50 is just ahead. The trail emerges from the woods, passes through a gap in a stone wall, crosses the four-lane highway at 20.5 mi., and continues another 0.2 mi. to parking at the PATC lot, which accommodates eight cars.

HIKE #44   Itinerary

Miles N	NORTH	Elev. (ft/m)	Miles S
20.7	**End:** At **Ashby Gap,** 1.0 mi. W of Paris. Blue-blazed trail leads R 100 ft. to PATC parking at VA 601.	800/244	0.0
20.5	Cross **US 50** (4-lane highway).		0.2
19.6	Cross open corridor over buried telephone cables; blackberries in late summer; descend.		1.1
17.6	Leave SP; good views W; begin stretch of crossing old roads; stay with white blazes.		3.1
17.4	Side trail leads R 1.3 mi. to campground.		3.3
17.1	Enter **Sky Meadows SP.**		3.6
16.2	Spring to R of trail, then path to L leads 0.1 mi. to parking at Signal Knob, unmarked trail from lot leads to views. Views also from AT just past junction.		4.5
15.1	In Whiskey Hollow, blue-blazed trail leads R 0.2 mi. to **Dick's Dome Shelter;** privy; avoid water from spring. Immediately beyond access trail, cross stream and ascend.	1200/366	5.6
14.5	Begin descent into **Whiskey Hollow.**		6.2
13.7	Cross old road as trillium area ends; trail to L leads 0.2 mi. to parking at VA 638.		7.0
12.9	Side trail leads 0.6 mi. L to Trico Fire Tower Trail, another 0.1 further is VA 638.		7.8
12.6	**Trico Fire Tower Trail** leads 0.4 mi. L to VA 638 and parking; early exit option.	1950/594	8.1
11.0	Begin area of protected trillium wildflowers in May; pass Verlin Smith Trail on R, which leads 1.0 mi. to Kettle Run.		9.7
10.8	Blue-blazed trail (70 yd.) to **Manassas Gap Shelter,** spring, privy.	1700/518	9.9
10.7	Merge briefly with **Ted Lake Trail,** which leads L 0.8 mi. to parking lot at VA 638; early exit option.		10.0

(continued on next page)

Miles N	NORTH	Elev. (ft/m)	Miles S
10.2	Enter **G. R. Thompson Wildlife Management Area;** stay on trail during hunting season.	1700/518	10.5
9.2	Blue-blazed trail leads E 100 ft. to view.		11.5
8.7	After crossing old road, cross small dam below former mill pond, then pass through open meadow.		12.0
8.4	**PATC parking lot** on VA 725; early exit option. Linden, with small store open 7 days, is 1.0 mi. W. Leave **VA 725** and begin ascent.		12.3
8.2	Cross **VA 55** in **Manassas Gap;** pick up **VA 725.**	800/244	12.5
8.1	Cross RR tracks, then **Goose Creek.**		12.6
6.9	Reach crest with view of Trumbo Hollow as trail descends into sag.	1500/457	13.8
6.2	Reach **VA 638,** turn L and travel S 100 yd. on road, then cross stile on other side of road and ascend N into field.		14.5
6.1	Cross small stream.		14.6
5.2	Short trail L to **Denton Shelter,** water, latrine, tent sites.	1300/396	15.5
3.5	Cross first of 3 old roads.		17.2
3.3	Cross small stream, then in 200 ft. reach blue-blazed trail to **Mosby Campsite** (100 yd.); spring.		17.4
2.3	Reach crest of knob; leave USZS land.	1900/579	18.4
0.0	**Start:** In **Chester Gap** at US 522, 3.5 mi. E of VA 55 in Front Royal; roadside parking only.	940/287	20.7

SOUTH

Snickers Gap to VA 605

Map: PATC Va. #8, N Va., S Half

Route: From Snickers Gap over Tomblin Hill and Buzzard Hill through Fent Wiley and Reservoir hollows to VA 605 near Ashby Hollow

Recommended direction: N to S

Distance: 6.8 mi.

Elevation +/-: 1000 to 1300 to 1050 ft.

Effort: Strenuous

Day hike: Yes

Overnight backpacking hike: Optional

Duration: 4 to 5 hr.

Early exit option: None

Natural history features: Bears Den Rocks; Lookout Point; Buzzard Hill

Trailhead access: *Start:* From Bluemont, proceed W on VA 7 for 1.8 mi. through Snickers Gap to parking lot at SW corner of intersection of VA 7 and VA 679. Overnight parking at own risk. *End:* From parking area at Start, head E on VA 7 approximately 0.5 mi. to VA 601 and turn R. Proceed S for approximately 4.5 mi. to VA 605, a driveable dirt road, at Mt. Weather. Turn R on VA 605 and head W 1.4 mi. to AT trailhead. There is room for 2 to 3 cars to park on the power line right-of-way at the AT crossing.

Camping: Bears Den Hostel; Sam Moore Shelter; and where permitted along trail

---

This 6.8-mi. stretch of the AT seesaws in and out of a succession of hollows and over numerous side ridges as it crosses through an area once dominated by Confederate Col. John Singleton Mosby. During the Civil War, Mosby and his troops, the Confederate Rangers (also known as Mosby's Confederacy), lived in farmhouses throughout this area. Mosby's reputation for eluding Union soldiers earned him the nickname "the Grey Ghost." The AT climbs to several high lookouts that make it easy to see how someone familiar with the terrain could keep an undetected eye on the enemy.

Several steep, rocky ascents make this one of the most difficult sections of the AT in the northern half of Virginia. There are excellent views of the Shenandoah Valley, from Bears Den Rocks, Lookout Point, and Buzzard Hill, while the dark, cool Fent Wiley Hollow includes a great variety of mature timber and a chance to cool down before climbing the next hill. The trail intersects several creeks throughout the section, offering ample, though unprotected, water sources.

The northern end of this hike is set in Snickers Gap, named for Edward Snicker, a ferry operator who shuttled people across the Shenandoah in the mid–1700s. The hike begins along the VA 7 median. Head east along the south shoulder of VA 7 and proceed 0.1 mi. to a gravel driveway. Turn right onto the driveway and continue as the route becomes a narrow path. As the trail becomes a grassy path it begins a gentle ascent through a forest of dogwood, yellow-poplar, oak, laurel, and sassafras. Continue upward for 0.5 mi. to Bears Den Rocks (1300 ft.) on the right (0.6 mi.). The pile of large boulders stacked to this side of the trail and protruding outward over the side of the mountain offers a panoramic view of the Shenandoah Valley, marred only by the black strip of VA 7 lacing through forested countryside.

Near this site in 1868, Dr. Mahlon Loomis unwittingly operated the first radio antenna—20 years before Hertz demonstrated the existence of radio waves. Believing electricity rippled through the air like waves in the ocean, Loomis set out to develop a form of aerial telegraph. Loomis climbed to this site while a colleague stationed himself on Catoctin Ridge, 18 mi. away. The two men simultaneously raised kites tied with copper gauze and attached to a copper wire. The copper kite string was attached to a galvanometer. Following a pre-arranged sequence, the two men attached one or the other galvanometer to ground wires and

secured readings on the opposite instrument. Hertz followed a similar procedure when he demonstrated radio waves two decades later.

Beyond this scientific site, a path to the left leads 0.2 mi. to the Bears Den Hostel. As you approach the cabin, you're apt to feel like a trespasser. The clothes on the line, children's play set in the yard, volleyball net, and dog-house certainly make the quaint cottage look like someone's getaway home. But a sign tells you you're in the right place. The building, with full amenities, sleeps twenty. It is locked from 9:30 a.m. to 5:00 p.m.; check-in is from 5:00 to 9:00 p.m. Camping is permitted in the yard for a moderate fee ($6 at press time) that also buys you use of the facilities. Hikers are welcome to fill their water bottles from a tap on the left side of the house entrance. A blue-blazed trail to the left of the hostel leads 125 yd. to a spring.

Back on the AT, the trail continues through a forest of oak, pine, and laurel and reaches a wide creek. Cross the creek on a narrow wooden footbridge and continue to a second stream. There is no bridge here, but there are several large stepping stones to help you across. Beyond the stream, the trail crosses an old road. The pine trees taper off as the trail winds through hickory, maple, and chestnut oak.

At 2.4 mi. the AT intersects with Spout Run. This branch of the Shenandoah River is swift and several inches deep in normal conditions, and can rise over a foot high after a good rain shower. With no bridge to help you across, the stream may be a bit intimidating. Don't despair. The AT intersects the river in a deep but narrow ravine and crossing is really much easier than you might first imagine.

Beyond Spout Run, the AT crosses an old road and begins a half-mile ascent to Lookout Point. In the spring, bright yellow buttercups mix with pink phlox along the path. Above, a green canopy of hickory, maple, and oak shades the trail in the spring, then fades to a yellowish hue at the first signs of autumn.

Gaining 600 ft. in just 0.5 mi., the hike to Lookout Point is merciless, but your efforts will be rewarded by the view. When you reach the top at 3.1 mi., look to the left of the AT for an excellent shot of the mountains to the south. A shady, flat area near this point provides a suitable dry campsite. If you're running low on water, and you've packed a water filter, it's OK to deplete your supply here. The AT soon descends 0.5 mi. to another arm of Spout Run.

Beyond the stream, a blue-blazed trail to the left leads to Sawmill Spring and the Sam Moore Shelter, named for a PATC volunteer who oversaw this section of the AT for over 50 years. (As of press time he is still an active volunteer.) The shelter sleeps up to six. Winter hikers will appreciate the fireplace, and those seeking a bit of privacy will be glad for the outhouse. If you're able to purify the water, replenish your water

bottle at one of these sources and get ready for another steep, uphill climb as the trail begins its ascent of Tomblin Hill. As you make the climb, put thoughts of lunch on hold: the peak should be labeled Tomblin Mound. The small sand piles that appear to be moving along the crest of the hill are really large ant colonies working swiftly and silently to fortify the area.

Leaving an airy canopy of oak behind, the AT descends into Fent Wiley Hollow, home to a dark, damp forest of mature timber, where the air turns suddenly cool and thick. The next quarter-mile stretch provides several more opportunities to refill the canteens, and, with several steep climbs ahead, once again you'll be glad you did.

At 4.6 mi. the AT begins the 500-ft. climb to the summit of Buzzard Hill. As you climb, look and, more importantly, listen, for passing owls, which are known to shelter in the dim hollow. At the top of Buzzard Hill (5.0 mi.) a side trail on the right leads 40 yd. to a rocky ledge. The mountainous view to the west makes a nice backdrop for lunch.

From Buzzard Hill, the AT cuts to Reservoir Hollow. The 300-ft. descent is stretched over a mile, allowing a much easier trip down. However, several steep, rocky drops call for caution. As the trail descends, look for the remains of a stone cabin to the right of the trail, near one of the many narrow springs flowing through this section. The AT reaches Reservoir

Hollow at 6.0 mi. and intersects a wide creek. There is a waterfall 160 yd. upstream that is worth checking out, especially for the shutterbugs in the group. Before exploring, make a mental note of the trail blazes and return to this point to proceed.

The trail continues through the hollow, which is again dark and cool, lending a feeling of solitude. However, the loud sound of airplane engines overhead, en route to Dulles Airport, remind you that you are not far from civilization. Apparently, the wildlife in these parts are used to the noise. As you wind through the thick woods, you're apt to catch an owl or a white-tailed deer off guard.

At the 6.8-mi. point the trail intersects with VA 605 and the southern end of this hike. Less than 2 mi. to the east is Mt. Weather. Presently a classified government installation, the site was first utilized in 1900, when Prof. Willis L. Moore, chief of the U.S. Weather Bureau, decided to unite several advanced weather research activities taking place throughout the Blue Ridge area. Mt. Weather began operation in 1901 with the goal of eventually investigating terrestrial magnetism, solar-physical and upper air phenomena, and model weather research. The facility's biggest claim to fame happened in 1907 when researchers sent a kite 5 mi. into the atmosphere—the highest ascent recorded in history, lending new insight to atmospheric studies. The installation is closed to the public.

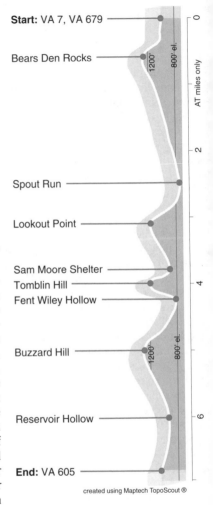

Start: VA 7, VA 679

Bears Den Rocks

1200' 800' el.

AT miles only

0

Spout Run

2

Lookout Point

Sam Moore Shelter
Tomblin Hill
Fent Wiley Hollow

4

Buzzard Hill

1200' 800' el.

Reservoir Hollow

6

End: VA 605

created using Maptech TopoScout ®

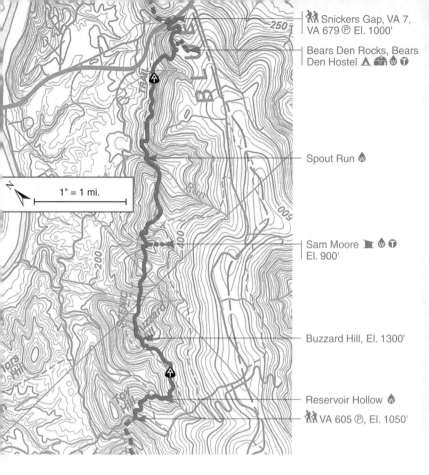

🏃🏃 Snickers Gap, VA 7, VA 679 Ⓟ El. 1000'

Bears Den Rocks, Bears Den Hostel ▲ 🏠 Ⓦ Ⓣ

Spout Run Ⓦ

Sam Moore ▰ Ⓦ Ⓣ El. 900'

Buzzard Hill, El. 1300'

Reservoir Hollow Ⓦ

🏃🏃 VA 605 Ⓟ, El. 1050'

1" = 1 mi.

Optional Extended Hike: Look for blazes on the opposite side of VA 605 and continue following the AT as it descends into Ashby Hollow, across Morgan Mill Stream, and to the top of Piney Ridge, passing through a forest of chestnut oak and pine. From Pine Ridge (8.3 mi.) the trail descends quite steeply into yet another hollow. In Bolden Hollow the trail bears left onto a wide forest road, then makes a quick right onto a series of swiftly ascending switchbacks. This second turn is easy to overlook. If you start to see "no trespassing" signs, turn back; you missed a blaze.

The switchbacks help ease the 400-ft. rise to the next peak. A narrow ridge at the top provides a scenic rest stop before heading back down a steep, rocky outcrop. At 10.5 mi. a blue-blazed trail on the right leads 0.1 mi. to Rod Hollow Shelter and spring. The remaining 3.4 mi. are mostly uphill, but the climb is gradual, and the trail continues to dip in several spots to meet more of the many creeks that bisect this area. At 13.9 mi. a blue-blazed trail to the left leads 85 yd. to a trailhead parking lot on VA 601, in Ashby Gap.

On a cool day in early spring, when daylight is growing longer, this extended version offers the chance to explore additional peaks and hollows. The added views do not disappoint, but they often echo the first half of the hike and camping options are limited.

To access the trailhead parking lot for extended hike, follow US 50 from Paris 1.0 mi. west to VA 601. Turn right (north) on VA 601, then make an immediate and very sharp left and descend a steep gravel driveway into a small PATC parking area (for eight cars).

HIKE #45   Itinerary

Miles N	NORTH	Elev. (ft/m)	Miles S
6.8	**Start:** In **Snickers Gap,** in parking lot at intersection of **VA 7** and **VA 679,** 1.8 mi. W of Bluemont.	1000/305	0.0
6.2	**Bears Den Rocks** and path (L 0.2 mi.) to **Bears Den Hostel,** water, camping (fee), rest rooms for overnighters.	1300/396	0.6
5.6	Footbridge over creek.		1.2
4.4	Cross **Spout Run** in deep, narrow ravine.	700/213	2.4
3.7	**Lookout Point** and dry campsite.	1300/396	3.1
3.2	Cross branch of **Spout Run.**		3.6
3.1	Blue-blazed trail leads L to **Sawmill Spring** and **Sam Moore Shelter,** privy.	900/274	3.7
2.8	**Tomblin Hill,** extensive anthills.	1200/366	4.0
2.5	**Fent Wiley Hollow.**	800/244	4.3
2.2	Ascend steeply.		4.6
1.8	**Buzzard Hill.**	1300/396	5.0
0.8	**Reservoir Hollow;** cross creek; waterfall is 160 yd. upstream.		6.0
0.0	**End:** Roadside parking at **VA 605,** 1.4 mi. W of Mt. Weather on VA 601, approximately 5.0 mi. SW of Bluemont.	1050/320	6.8

SOUTH

Keys Gap to Blackburn Trail Center

Map: PATC Va. #7, N Va.

Route: From Keys Gap to Buzzard Rocks, Deer Lick, and Blackburn Trail Center

Recommended direction: N to S

Distance: 6.5 mi. total; 6.2 mi. on AT

Access trail name and length: Unnamed blue-blazed trail, 0.3 mi.

Elevation +/-: Approx. 850 to 1500 to 1700 ft.

Effort: Moderate to strenuous

Day hike: Yes

Overnight backpacking hike: Optional

Duration: 4 to 6 hr.

Early exit option: None

Natural history feature: Buzzard Rocks

Other features: Excellent views of Shenandoah Valley

Trailhead access: *Start:* From Hillsboro, head W on VA 9 for 6.0 mi. to trailhead parking area on N side of the highway; room for up to 12 cars. Overnight parking at your own risk. *End:* From Hillsboro/VA 9, head S on County Rte. 719 (Woodgrove Rd.) for approximately 3 mi. to County Rte. 713 (AT Rd.) and turn R. Follow signs to Blackburn Trail Center. There is a small parking area with room for 12 cars at site.

Camping: KOA Campground near Harpers Ferry NHP (camping is prohibited in park); David Lesser Shelter; Blackburn Center Campground/Blackburn Trail Center; and where permitted along trail

Following mostly along the ridge crest, this hike offers a number of excellent views of the Shenandoah Valley as it bounces up and down over often rocky terrain. The rocky footing and steep climbs make parts of this hike quite strenuous, but the panoramas that greet you at the top of each crest make the effort worthwhile, perhaps especially for photographers. There are also numerous enticing picnic spots. This hike can be partnered with a trip to Harpers Ferry (see "A Step Back in Time") for a nice weekend getaway or can be enjoyed as a great change of scenery from an extended trip to

Washington, D.C. So pack a lunch, load your camera, fill an extra water bottle, and get ready to climb. *Note:* The 6.3 mi. of the AT from Keys Gap through Harpers Ferry are mostly on streets and sidewalks and therefore have been omitted here. However, the extra miles are worth covering later (or earlier) if you enjoy historic towns.

Formerly known as Vestal's Gap, Keys Gap can be traced to 1747, when it received ferry service from other points along the Shenandoah River and began to flourish as part of the region's early iron industry. George Washington passed through

this area in 1754 during his campaign to Great Meadows and Fort Necessity, Pennsylvania, site of the opening battle of the French and Indian War. This was the only battle in which Washington was forced to surrender during his entire military career.

The access to the AT from VA 9 is easy to miss. Look for the trail marker on the north side of the road and enter on the south. As you enter a small field, you may feel as if you're trespassing, but you're on the right track. There is a white blaze on a tree just ahead. The trail is equally hard to follow once you find it. It enters a wooded area and crosses several other paths. Look for a fire ring on your right and proceed to the left as you begin the first of many uphill climbs. Be on the lookout for the reddish leaves that identify poison ivy—

it is particularly thick in this area in spring and summer.

The AT continues through a thick oak forest, climbing upward over steep, slick, and, in some places, loose rocks and gaining over 600 ft. before reaching 2.1. mi. Here, the AT turns right onto an old road, then veers to the left at a fork just ahead and begins a slight descent. Winter hiking offers views of Purcell Knob to the east, but these are obscured by the thick branches and leaves of the old oaks in spring and summer.

As you climb, look for box turtles, which are common in this area. These reptiles reach up to 9 in. in length and can live to be more than 100 years old. The brownish-black shells have yellow, orange, or olive spots and a hinged lower shell. It you see one of these creatures lying on its back, be a pal and turn it over—turtles who accidentally become flipped often die trying to right themselves.

At 3.0 mi. the AT intersects with a blue-blazed trail on the left that leads 115 yd. to the David Lesser Shelter. The lean-to was built by the PATC in 1991 and still has a relatively new look to it. The site includes a picnic area, room for several tents, a fireplace, and even a porch swing. There is also a privy behind the shelter and a spring just down the hill. This is a nice spot for lunch, but if you can hold out until Buzzard Rocks, less than a mile ahead, you'll be glad you did.

The AT gains about 100 ft. over the next half mile, reaching Buzzard Rocks at 3.6 mi. A blue-blazed trail to the right leads 0.1 mi. to a lookout point. The view from this spot is worth braving the forbidding rocks you'll have to climb over to get there. Even with summer foliage, there is a superb view of the Shenandoah River, rolling through rich, green pastures, and of Shannondale Lake. There is room for one tent near the view, but there is no nearby water source.

The Shenandoah River and its valley were named long ago, and the exact origin of the name cannot be confirmed. However, several guesses are part of the local folklore. One tale has it that "Shenandoah" was a local Native American name meaning "beautiful daughter of the stars." Another story links it to an Iroquois chief named Sherando. It is also possible that the name was derived from

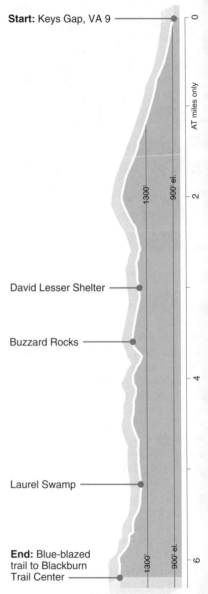

Start: Keys Gap, VA 9

AT miles only

David Lesser Shelter

Buzzard Rocks

Laurel Swamp

End: Blue-blazed trail to Blackburn Trail Center

created using Maptech TopoScout ®

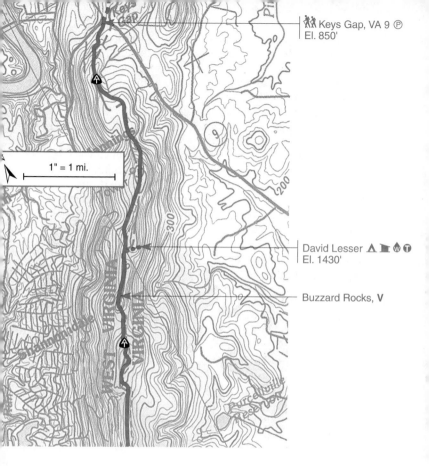

🥾 Keys Gap, VA 9 ℗
El. 850'

1" = 1 mi.

David Lesser ▲ ◣ Ⓦ Ⓣ
El. 1430'

Buzzard Rocks, **V**

a small Algonquin tribe in the lower valley called the Senedo, which was massacred by the Iroquois long before white settlers arrived. Or, "Shenandoah" could be the whites' interpretation of the Iroquois word meaning "big meadow."

The massive stones of Buzzard Rocks are made up of tiny quartz crystals formed from 700-million-year-old volcanic ash. The rocks formed as the continent stretched during the formation of the Iapetos Ocean, an earlier ocean located roughly where we find today's Atlantic.

Leaving Buzzard Rocks, the AT makes a series of steep ascents and descents over the next mile, passing an area known as the Deer Lick at 4.1 mi. This flat, mossy area is not visible from the trail, but you are apt to see deer on and near the AT at this point. At 4.5 mi. the trail bears left onto old Shannondale Rd., then turns right off the road and continues through the woods. Shannondale Rd. once connected Hillsboro to Shannondale Springs, a famous 19th-century resort.

The AT reaches the puzzlingly named Laurel Swamp at 5.2 mi. Despite its name, the area is quite dry and predominantly covered with periwinkle. A house once stood at this spot. For a pleasant diversion from the hike, spend some time tracing the stone walls that outline the former structure and its surrounding yard. If you look hard enough, you will also be able to identify the ruins of the chimney. Since periwinkle does not grow naturally in the wild, it is possible that the former residents planted the tiny blue flowers.

Beyond the ruins, a narrow path leads to the right for a few yards to Laurel Spring. Unless you're hiking after a recent rainfall, don't count on finding water here—the spring is often dry. As the name suggests, there are several laurel thickets throughout the section, blooming with masses of pink, star-shaped flowers in early spring. If you're hiking in spring or summer, look out for honeybees, the flower's main pollinators. Over the next mile, the AT makes a series of steep ascents. But the trail does show a bit of mercy. Just as the climb starts to get tiresome, it tapers off slightly, as if prompted by wishful thinking. A quartzite cliff at 6.1 mi. provides a great view of Wilson Gap to the west with the Shenandoah River cutting a rolling blue ribbon in the distance.

At 6.2 mi. leave the AT with a left turn onto a blue-blazed trail. It descends very steeply, dropping nearly 200 ft. over 0.3 mi. to the Blackburn Trail Center and the southern end of this hike. (A left fork at 0.1 mi. leads to Blackburn Center Campground.) The Blackburn Trail Center consists of a house and two outbuildings owned and maintained by the PATC and used as a work center and recreation site. The house has an inviting air—you may feel as if you are visiting a relative you haven't seen in a while but still feel close to. There is also a pay phone, and the picnic table is a great spot to stop and sit for a bit. You may find PATC

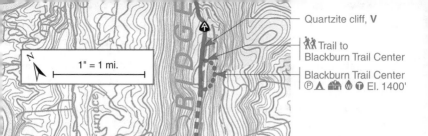

Quartzite cliff, **V**

🏃🏃 Trail to
Blackburn Trail Center

Blackburn Trail Center
Ⓟ 🔺 🏠 💧 🚻 El. 1400'

1" = 1 mi.

members at the site, who are usually happy to tell you stories about the area and nearby attractions. This is also a popular resting spot for AT thru-hikers, many of whom are willing to relate trailside adventures. Overnight accommodations are available for a small fee, but advance reservations are required. Call PATC headquarters at 703-242-0315.

Optional Extended Hike: Make the 200-ft. climb back up to the AT, then descend for 1.5 mi. to reach Wilson Gap. Just before Wilson Gap, the AT begins following an old road. In Wilson Gap (7.4 mi.) the trail cuts onto a path on the right as the old road continues ahead. The turn is easy to miss, but you'll know you've gone too far if you start to see "No Trespassing" signs.

From Wilson Gap, the AT makes a steep climb, gaining nearly 400 ft. in less than half a mile, then traces the top of the ridge for 2 mi. before making an even steeper descent to Devil's Racecourse at 10.2 mi. This is one of at least four Devil's Race-

courses along the AT. In summer, a canopy of red maple and chestnut make this a nice, shady spot for a water break. Beyond Devil's Racecourse, the AT makes a slick, rocky climb up to Crescent Rock, named for the geological fold that forms a crescent in the rock. Although the Shenandoah River and Valley are still evident, the picture now includes the Massanutten Mt. in the distance.

The final leg of the hike consists of more steep upward and downward climbs, passing through strands of yellow-poplars, laurel, native azaleas, young oaks, and pine. A rock outcropping at 12.9 mi. offers a final view of the Shenandoah Valley before you reach County Rte. 679 at 13.4 mi. in Snickers Gap. (For more on Snickers Gap, see Hike #45.) For road access to Snickers Gap, follow VA 7 east from Bluemont for 1.8 mi. to a parking area on the north side of road at the intersection of VA 7 and County Rte. 679. Snickers Gap is 52 mi. west of Washington, D.C.

A Step Back in Time

History buffs, avid sightseers, shutterbugs, and antiquers will enjoy getting to know Harpers Ferry, West Virginia. Here, a step off the AT, which winds through the historic town, is a step back in time. Indeed, if you are easily distracted, you may just lose all track of time. Nestled at the confluence of the Shenandoah and Potomac rivers, Harpers Ferry is a premier attraction of the AT, rich in both history and scenery.

In *Notes on Virginia,* Thomas Jefferson described the view thus:

"You stand on a very high point of land. On your right comes up the Shenandoah, having ranged along the foot of the mountain a hundred miles to seek a vent. On your left approaches the Patowmac, in quest of a passage also. In the moment of their junction they rush together against the mountain, rent it asunder and pass off to the sea."

Robert Harper purchased the land from Lord Fairfax in 1747 and secured a ferry charter from the colony in 1761. Throughout the late 1700s and early 1800s, a surge in the use of water transportation gave a great boost to Harpers Ferry and the town became a commercial and industrial center. Unfortunately, the boom was short lived. John Brown's raid in 1859 set the stage for a downward fall. The city's troubles were furthered by the Civil War, during which it was captured more than twenty-three times by the two armies. The area was plagued by fire, flood, and disease, while technological advancements made water power obsolete.

In 1944, Congress passed an enabling act to designate Harpers Ferry as a national monument. At the time, the area looked more like a national ruin. The first land was acquired in 1952 and the Harpers Ferry National Historical Park was created in 1963, just five years before the enactment of the National Trail System Act and federal recognition of the AT.

Today, the downtown buildings of Harpers Ferry have been restored to their Civil War-era appearance. Quaint shops line the streets, their merchandise plucked right from the 1800s. Tools and other artifacts unearthed during the restoration are on display. Harpers Ferry also plays a significant role in the history of the AT. As you make your way down Shenandoah St., peering in storefront windows, you are tracing the very first segment of the trail. The segment was created by the PATC and opened in 1927. Along this route stands a replica of the firehouse where John Brown made his stand. Old federal arsenal foundations are adjacent.

The Potomac, at Harpers Ferry, from Jefferson Rock

At the edge of town, the historic Hilltop House, built in 1888, sits at the junction of the Potomac and Shenandoah rivers and offers a glimpse of the scene Thomas Jefferson described. In the past, the inn has played host to such distinguished guests as Alexander Graham Bell, Mark Twain, Carl Sandburg, and Woodrow Wilson.

After you've finished exploring the narrow streets of Harpers Ferry, trace the AT through town (north to south), turn right onto High St., and then turn left after the first house on your left. (Park regulations prohibit AT markers and signs on the trail and the streets, so pay attention to street signs; also, a bulletin board at the north end has a map.) After making the left, ascend a very steep staircase. The route continues to take you on a historical tour, winding past Robert Harper's house, the town's oldest, before leading up another set of stairs. Here, a few steps off the trail and to the left, sits Jefferson's "high point of land." The view of the rivers in the endless mountain scenery makes it easy to understand the president's admiration.

HIKE #46   Itinerary

Miles N	**NORTH**	Elev. (ft/m)	Miles S
Total: 6.5 mi. with access			
6.2	**Start:** Trailhead parking on **VA 9 in Keys Gap,** 6.0 mi. NW of Hillsboro.	approx. 850/259	0.0
5.9	Bear L at fire ring and ascend.		0.3
4.1	Begin descent; winter views to E.	1500/457	2.1
3.2	Blue-blazed trail leads L 115 yd. to **David Lesser Shelter,** camping, water.	1430/436	3.0
2.6	**Buzzard Rocks,** view 0.1 mi. to R.	1500/457	3.6
2.1	**Deer Lick.**		4.1
1.7	AT bears L onto **old Shannondale Rd.**		4.5
1.0	**Laurel Swamp.**	1400/427	5.2
0.1	Good views from quartzite cliff.		6.1
0.0	**End:** Turn L onto blue-blazed trail to Blackburn Trail Center. Steep descent.	1700/518	6.2
0.3	**Access: Blackburn Trail Center,** approximately 5 mi. SW of Hillsboro via Appalachian Trail Rd.	1400/427	0.3

Useful Information

US Geological Survey Topographical Maps

USGS maps used in this series are scaled at 1:100,000 (1 cm = 1 km), but in this book we have converted the scale generally to 1"= 1 mi. or a close fraction thereof. The maps listed below are quadrangles covering the area surrounding the named city or other place; approximately 50 mi. E-W and 35 mi. N-S.

> Hagerstown
> Frederick
> Winchester
> Washington West
> Front Royal
> Charlottesville
> Dillwyn
> Buena Vista
> Roanoke
> Radford
> Bluefield
> Wytheville
> Bristol

Appalachian Trail Conference Maps

ATC sells its own 4-color topo hiking maps and some maps published by regional hiking clubs. Together these maps cover the entire AT. Generally these maps are scaled at 1:62,500 (1"= 1 mi.). Maps referred to in this volume are listed here.

Potomac Appalachian Trail Club (PATC) Map 7—West Virginia and Northern Virginia (Potomac River & Harpers Ferry to VA 7 to Snickers Gap)

PATC Map 8—Northern Virginia-South Half (Snickers Gap to Chester Gap)

PATC Map 9—Shenandoah National Park/North District

PATC Map 10—Shenandoah National Park/Central District

PATC Map 11—Shenandoah National Park/South District

ATC—Central Virginia Maps 1 & 2/Rockfish Gap to Bearwallow Gap

ATC—Central Virginia Maps 3 & 4/Bearwallow Gap to New River

ATC—Southwest Virginia Maps 1 & 2/New River to Rich Valley

ATC—Southwest Virginia Maps 3 & 4/Poor Valley to Virginia/Tennessee Line

Definitions

Easy: gentle ups and downs, fairly smooth path, few obstacles.

Moderate: elevation gain or loss of up to 1000 feet; narrower, rocky path; some obstacles (for example, brook crossings with no bridge).

Strenuous: elevation gain or loss of more than 1000 feet; steep ups and downs; difficult, challenging path; numerous obstacles; possibly unsuitable for young children or the infirm.

Hikes

EASY

- #9, Kimberling Creek to Laurel Creek
- #10, Lickskillet Hollow to Kimberling Creek
- #11, Southern End of Brushy Mt.
- #20, Black Horse Gap to VA 652
- #27, Long Mt. Wayside to Little Irish Creek
- #29, Salt Log Gap North to Fish Hatchery Rd.
- #32, Reeds Gap to Cedar Cliff
- #36, Jones Run Trail to Pinefield Gap
- #38, South River Falls to Bearfence Mt.
- #39, Big Meadows and Hawksbill
- #43, Jenkins Gap to Chester Gap
- #44, Chester Gap to Ashby Gap

MODERATE

- #1, Lost Mt. and Whitetop Laurel Creek
- #2, Whitetop Mt. and Buzzard Rock
- #4, Iron Mt. and Brushy Mt.
- #8, Garden Mt. and Little Wolf Creek
- #12, Big Horse Gap to White Pine Horse Campground
- #13, Sugar Run Gap to Pearisburg
- #18, Catawba Mt.
- #21, Black Horse Gap to Bearwallow Gap
- #23, Apple Orchard Falls Trail to Jennings Creek
- #24, Apple Orchard Falls Trail to Petites Gap
- #25, Petites Gap to James River
- #26, Punchbowl Mt. to James River
- #28, Tar Jacket Ridge to Cold Mt.
- #33, Humpback Rocks
- #34, McCormick Gap to Turk Gap
- #35, Blackrock and Wildcat Ridge
- #40, Stony Man Mt. and Marys Rock
- #41, Thornton Gap to Hogback Overlook
- #42, Hogback Overlook to Jenkins Gap

MODERATE TO STRENUOUS

- #14, Stony Creek Valley to Stillhouse Branch
- #31, Reeds Gap to Tye River
- #37, Simmons Gap to South River Falls
- #46, Keys Gap to Blackburn Trail Center

STRENUOUS

#3, Pine Mt. and Mt. Rogers Circuit
#5, Brushy Mt. and Glade Mt.
#6, Tennessee Valley Divide
#7, Garden Mt., Chestnut Ridge,
    and Brushy Mt.
#15, Sinking Creek to Stony Creek

#16, Sinking Creek Mt.
#17, Cove Mt. to Trout Creek
#19, McAfee Knob Loop
#22, Cove Mt. to Jennings Creek
#30, Cash Hollow to Tye River
#45, Snicker's Gap to VA 605

SHELTERS & CAMPSITES

See page 15 for general notes about shelters and campsites on or close to the AT. We list here the shelters (a.k.a. lean-tos) and named campsites (a.k.a. tent sites) described in this book. When shelters have officially designated tent sites, we indicate "campsite" below. Consult the narrative of each hike for information on unofficial tentsites at some shelters and on shelters that are farther off the AT.

Hike #	Shelter	Campsite	Lodge/Cabin	Name
1	x			Saunders
2	x			Whitetop Mt. picnic area
3	x			Wise
		x		Grayson Highlands SP tent camping
4	x			Raccoon Branch
	x			Trimpi
		x		Hurricane Campground
5	x			Louise Chatfield
6		x		Mozer homestead tenting area
	x			Davis Path
7	x			Knot Maul Branch
	x			Chestnut Knob
8		x		Davis Farm Campsite
	x			Jenkins
10	x			Jenny Knob
	x			Helvey's Mill

continues on next page

Hike #	Shelter	Campsite	Lodge/Cabin	Name
12	x			Wapiti
		x		White Pine Horse Campground
13	x			Doc's Knob
14	x			Pine Swamp Branch
	x			Rice Field
15	x			Bailey's Gap
	x			War Spur
	x			Laurel Creek
16	x			Niday
			x	Sarver Cabin
		x		Cabin Branch
17	x			Pickle Branch
19	x			Johns Spring Center
	x			Catawba Mt.
20	x			Willow Creek
	x			Fullhardt Knob
21	x			Bobblet's Gap
22	x			Cove Mt.
23	x			Cornelius Creek
	x			Bryant Ridge
		x		N. Creek Campground
		x		Jellystone Park
24	x			Thunder Hill
25		x		Marble Spring
		x		Grassy Island Ridge
	x			Matts Creek
26	x			Punchbowl
	x			Johns Hollow
27	x			Brown Mt. Creek Trail
28		x		Hog Camp Gap
	x			Cow Camp
29		x		Piney River
		x		Porters Field
	x			Seeley-Woodworth

Hike #	Shelter	Campsite	Lodge/Cabin	Name
30	x			The Priest
31	x			Maupin Field
	x			Harpers Creek
33	x			Paul C. Wolfe
34	x			Calf Mt.
35	x			Blackrock Hut
36			x	PATC Doyle River Cabin
		x		Loft Mt. Campground
	x			Pinefield Hut
37	x			Hightop Hut (thru-hikers only)
38			x	PATC Pocosin Cabin
		x		Lewis Mt. Camping Area
	x			Bearfence Mt. Hut
39		x		Big Meadows Campground
	x			Rock Spring Hut
			x	PATC Rock Spring Cabin
40			x	PATC Corbin Cabin
			x	Skyland cabins
41	x			Pass Mt. Hut
		x		Mathews Arm Campground
			x	PATC Range View Cabin
42	x			Gravel Springs Hut
43	x	x		Tom Floyd Wayside
44		x		Mosby
	x			Manassas Gap
	x			Dick's Dome
		x		Sky Meadows State Park
45			x	Bears Den Hostel
	x			Sam Moore
46		x		KOA Campground
	x			David Lesser
		x	x	Blackburn Center Campground

Day Hikes

Depending on your starting time, physical condition, ambition, and the weather, the following hikes can be manageable day hikes. Check "Duration" and "Distance" in the information block at the beginning of the hike before starting. Many of these hikes work well as sections of longer backpacking hikes, and some appear in the "Overnight Hikes" list as well.

#1, Lost Mt. and Whitetop Laurel Creek

#2, Whitetop Mt. and Buzzard Rock

#3, Pine Mt. and Mt. Rogers Circuit

#4, Iron Mt. and Brushy Mt.

#5, Brushy Mt. and Glade Mt.

#6, Tennessee Valley Divide

#7, Garden Mt., Chestnut Ridge, and Brushy Mt.

#8, Garden Mt. and Little Wolf Creek

#9, Kimberling Creek to Laurel Creek

#10, Lickskillet Hollow to Kimberling Creek

#11, Southern End of Brushy Mt.

#12, Big Horse Gap to White Pine Horse Campground

#13, Sugar Run Gap to Pearisburg

#14, Stony Creek Valley to Stillhouse Branch

#15, Sinking Creek to Stony Creek

#16, Sinking Creek Mt.

#17, Cove Mt. to Trout Creek

#18, Catawba Mt.—West End

#19, McAfee Knob Loop

#20, Black Horse Gap to VA 652

#21, Black Horse Gap to Bearwallow Gap

#22, Cove Mt. to Jennings Creek

#23, Apple Orchard Falls Trail to Jennings Creek

#24, Apple Orchard Falls Trail to Petites Gap

#25, Petites Gap to James River

#26, Punchbowl Mt. to James River

#27, Long Mt. Wayside to Little Irish Creek

#28, Tar Jacket Ridge to Cold Mt.

#29, Salt Log Gap North to Fish Hatchery Rd.

#30, Cash Hollow to Tye River

#31, Reeds Gap to Tye River

#32, Reeds Gap to Cedar Cliff

#33, Humpback Rocks

#34, McCormick Gap to Turk Gap

#35, Blackrock and Wildcat Ridge

#36, Jones Run Trail to Pinefield Gap

#37, Simmons Gap to South River Falls

#38, South River Falls to Bearfence Mt.

#39, Big Meadows and Hawksbill

#40, Stony Man Mt. and Marys Rock

#41, Thornton Gap to Hogback Overlook

#42, Hogback Overlook to Jenkins Gap

#43, Jenkins Gap to Chester Gap

#44, Chester Gap to Ashby Gap

OTHER TRAIL SYSTEMS

Because the majority of AT miles in the Virginias lie within George Washington and Jefferson national forests and Shenandoah National Park, AT hikers are never far from sizable connecting trail systems, some in rugged wilderness and others on the easy grades of rail trails. Many are introduced in this book, but, happily, there are far too many miles to describe in one volume. For hikers looking for a truly off-the-beaten-path hike, the Tuscarora Trail, a little-known 220-mi. route west of the AT offers a less storied, but less traveled, system.

Southern Virginia: Mt. Rogers National Recreation Area and the James River Face Wilderness

Jefferson National Forest, extending nearly 200 mi. south from the James River, offers more than 1000 miles of hiking and riding trails. Two areas of special note are the Mt. Rogers National Recreation Area and, some 250 winding AT miles north, the James River Face Wilderness. Mt. Rogers is a 120,000-acre part of the forest dedicated by Congress for outdoor recreation. A favorite trail here is the Iron Mt. Trail, which, until 1972, was the route of the AT through the region. The trail begins in Damascus, only a few blocks from the AT's passage through the town center. Following a gravel road north, the trail ascends to a junction with the AT 3.5 mi. east of Damascus, continues to the northeast, and follows the Iron Mt. ridge to panoramic views of the Allegheny Mts. from Feathercamp Mt. and the tumbling waters of Feathercamp Branch. It intersects the AT again in Chestnut Flats, 16.8 mi. north of its first junction. Three shelters along the way offer a chance to find solitude on weeknights in summer.

Other premier Mt. Rogers Natl. Rec. Area hikes that intersect with the AT are the Virginia Creeper National Recreation Trail, an easy trail that follows Whitetop and Green Cove creeks on a 34-mi. passage from Abingdon to the North Carolina line; and Mt. Rogers-Pine Mt. circuits, including the Lewis Fork Wilderness, which combines the open mountain meadows of Pine Mt. and the primitive wilderness paths that slab Mt. Rogers. The ATC Southwest Virginia Maps 3 & 4 show these and many more trails in the national recreation area.

James River Face Wilderness is 8903 acres of mixed hardwood forest above the famous James River Gorge. Some 30 miles of trails wander the wilderness, leading to dark, quiet places. Two of the gems in the trail system are Balcony Falls Trail, which offers outstanding views of the gorge, and the Belfast Trail, which leads to an 8-acre boulder field of Antietam quartzite known as the Devils Marbleyard. The ATC Central Virginia Maps 1 & 2 show these and other trails in the James River Face Wilderness.

Shenandoah National Park

More than 500 miles of hiking trails and many miles of dirt roads suitable for hiking traverse the SNP. Utilizing the many north-south trails that parallel the AT and the dozens of trails leading from the AT to river valleys and summits, there is almost no limit to circuit hike possibilities. The South Section of the park is the most remote and, with most of this section designated as wilderness, it is farthest from the crowds. In the Central Section you will find the park's best known hike, to the summit of Old Rag. Accessible from the AT via the Old Rag Fire Road and from the east via the Ridge Trail, Old Rag's 3268-ft. summit is known to welcome visitors at any time of day or night. To many hikers, a flashlight hike up Old Rag gives the ultimate view of the Blue Ridge. The summits and hollows covering the 16 square miles between Old Rag and the AT are home to more than 20 named trails—a network of hikes along creeks and gorges. The renowned Whiteoak Canyon Trail passes 6 waterfalls under cover of virgin hemlock, one of the loveliest sojourns along the entire Blue Ridge by any standard. The PATC's maps 9, 10, and 11 cover SNP's North, Central, and South Sections, respectively.

The Tuscarora Trail

The most significant trail system in the AT vicinity is the Tuscarora Trail. Planned as a western relocation for the AT to escape population pressures growing closer to the trail, the Tuscarora covers 251 miles between its southern junction with the AT in SNP (0.4 mi. S of SDMP 21.9) and its northern junction with the AT near Duncannon, Pennsylvania. Until 1995, the Tuscarora was the name given only to the Maryland-Pennsylvania sections of the trail. Below the Potomac, it was known as the Big Blue, owing its name to the color of ink used in marking various alternative AT routes on planning maps. From its beginning in SNP, it descends the Blue Ridge along Overall Run, a sometimes steep drop that levels off in the South Fork Shenandoah River Valley. Heading west across the valley, the Tuscarora enters Washington NF and climbs the ridge of Massanutten Mt., which defines the western view from the AT in North and Central SNP.

Traveling north, the Tuscarora intersects the fine system of hiking and riding trails in the Massanutten range, crossing into West Virginia for a long, lazy ridge walk. There are several stretches of road walking before the trail crosses the Potomac River in Maryland at Hancock (where a massive, down-home country meal can be had on the cheap at the famous Park 'n' Dine Restaurant). A trail guide and map set for the Tuscarora Trail published by the PATC are available directly from the club.

ADDRESS & TELEPHONE

Appalachian Trail Conservancy, P.O. Box 807, Harpers Ferry, WV 25425-0807; 304-535-6331

National Hiking Organizations
American Hiking Society, 1422 Fenwick La., Silver Spring, MD 20910; 301-565-6714
Appalachian Mountain Club, 5 Joy St., Boston, MA 02108; 617-523-0655. For their hiking guides: Box 298, Gorham, NH 03581; 800-262-4455.
Note: Of particular interest to hikers in northeastern states.

Virginia Regional Hiking and Trail Maintaining Clubs
Mount Rogers Appalachian Trail Club, PO Box 789, Abingdon, VA 24236
Natural Bridge AT Club, P.O. Box 3012, Lynchburg, VA 24503
Old Dominion Appalachian Trail Club, P.O. Box 25283, Richmond, VA 23260
Piedmont Appalachian Trail Hikers, P.O. Box 4423, Greensboro, NC 27404-4423
Potomac Appalachian Trail Club, 118 Park St. SE, Vienna, VA 22180-4609, 703-242-0315
Roanoke Appalachian Trail Club, P.O. Box 12282, Roanoke, VA 24024
Tidewater Appalachian Trail Club, P.O. Box 8246, Norfolk, VA 23503
Virginia Tech Outing Club, P.O. Box 538, Blacksburg, VA 24060

Almost all Web sites addresses begin with http://, preceding www. Most Web sites are updated periodically. Some listed here were still in development when we visited them

Appalachian Trail Conservancy **appalachiantrail.org**

This site is comprehensive, with many lists of and links to regional trail clubs. ATC's "Ultimate Trail Store" has arguably the biggest selection of AT books and maps anywhere (member discounts). Updated trail conditions, permit regulations, and other helpful subjects.

National Hiking Organizations

American Hiking Society **americanhiking.org**

Dedicated to promoting hiking and to protecting and maintaining America's trails, AHS offers programs, publications (magazine), legislative updates, volunteer vacations, and links to many clubs and resources.

Appalachian Mountain Club **www.outdoors.org/**

Granddaddy of the eastern hiking clubs, AMC covers not only the northeastern AT but activities and trail reports on many other trails. AMC Books, AMC Outdoors (magazine), adult and kids' activities (trips and workshops year-round), conservation initiatives, hiking trip planning, AMC hut reservations, and much more.

AT Regional Hiking and Trail Maintaining Clubs
Many regional hiking clubs have their own Web sites, and most of them can be found easily by way of links from the Appalachian Trail Conference Web site listed above. Here are some Web sites concerned with the AT in the states covered by this book.

Natural Bridge AT Club **www.nbatc.org**

Old Dominion AT Club **pages.prodigy.com/VA/cvkr39a/ odatc.html**

The Outdoor Club at Virginia Tech **www.outdoor.org/vt.edu**

Piedmont Appalachian Trail Hikers **www.path-at.org**

| Potomac Appalachian Trail Club | **www.patc.net** |
| Tidewater AT Club | **www.tidewater.com** |

Other AT Web sites

Appalachian Long Distance Hikers Association
www.aldha.org

Aimed primarily at thru-hikers. Savvy advice, networking, forums, volunteering opportunities.

Appalachian Trail Place **www.trailplace.com**

Center for Appalachian Trail Studies. Hosted by Dan "Wingfoot" Bruce, a thru-hiker who maintains a hostel by the trail in Virginia. A spin-off from Wingfoot's *Thru-Hiker's Handbook*. Dozens of searchable databases on AT subjects, many especially helpful to long distance hikers or those with natural history interests. "Mailing lists" of former and would-be thru-hikers, women hikers, teenage hikers, others. Chat rooms. Bibliography. One of the better sites.

The Appalachian Trail Home Page **www.fred.net/kathy/at.html**

The official-sounding name belies the fact that this is a personal home page built by a thru-hiker, Kathy Bilton. Nonetheless, it's one of the better general sites for miscellaneous information about the AT and for connecting with AT people. Links to AT maintaining clubs (also to the AT organizations and to other National Scenic trails), forums for AT issues discussions, advice from thru-hikers, and more.

Commercial and government Web sites

GENERAL

GORP **www.gorp.com**

Great Outdoor Recreation Pages. From various purveyors of travel and outdoor adventure information, services, and supplies. The AT is one small part of this huge, diverse site. Rewarding for those with time to fill.

Magazines

Backpacker   **www.backpacker.com**

Extensive, well researched information about hiking worldwide. Many articles on either the AT specifically or on hiking skills and equipment useful to AT trekkers. "Trail Talk Forums" bring hikers together on-line. "Gearfinder" is a searchable database of hiking/camping products. The site is fueled by links to Backpacker's advertisers, a convenience or a distraction depending on your disposition.

Outside   **www.outsideonline.com**

Most of the magazine, on-line. Hiking per se and the AT specifically are only occasionally featured in *Outside* (whose travel beat is worldwide), but the treatment is usually in depth and colorful. Generally aimed at the under 40 crowd. Good articles on fitness and training. Excellent book reviews.

Bookstores

Amazon   **www.amazon.com**

The leader in on-line bookstores. Search the database on the words "Appalachian Trail" for a long list of titles.

Barnes & Noble   **www.barnesandnoble.com**

They're everywhere and they carry almost everything. If the local store doesn't have it, search on-line under the subject "Appalachian Trail."

Maps

DeLorme Map Co.   **www.delorme.com**

Detailed atlases for the following AT states: North Carolina, Tennessee, West Virginia, Virginia, Maryland, Pennsylvania, New York, Vermont, New Hampshire, Maine. DeLorme, Lower Main St., Box 298, Freeport, ME 04032; 800-452-5931.

Maptech   **www.maptech.com/topo**

Maptech has developed a set of high-quality USGS maps on CD-ROM that cover most of the United States. These TopoScout® CDs, which are available for purchase, facilitate the close examination of the topography of almost any region in the country, including the Appalachian Trail. You can reach Maptech at 655 Portsmouth Ave., Greenland, NH 03840; 800-627-7236.

United States Geological Survey (USGS)

www.usgs.gov/pubprod/products.html

A giant site for both the general public and scientists. This address is for ordering maps. A database facilitates finding the correct map, at the desired scale, for the area you're hiking. 800-USA-MAPS.

Perry-Castaneda Library Map Collection

www.lib.utexas.edu/Libs/PCL/Map_collection/Map_collection.html

An extensive collection of links to on-line map resources around the world. Including not only topographic maps but also historical and weather maps.

Weather

The Weather Underground **www.wunderground.com**

Up-to-the-hour weather reports and forecasts for many cities in the U.S., including numerous smaller cities near the Appalachian Trail.

National Oceanic & Atmospheric Administration

weather.noaa.gov/weather

"NOAA" offers continuously updated weather reports and forecasts all across the country on dedicated radio channels (a lightweight weather-only radio is worth carrying on extended backpacking trips). At home, access NOAA's weather report site at the address above.

Bibliography

Hiking Guides

Adkins, Leonard M. *Walking the Blue Ridge*. 3rd ed. University of North Carolina Press, 2006.

Albright, Jack. *Appalachian Trail Guide to Central Virginia*. Appalachian Trail Conservancy, 2010.

De Hart, Allen. *West Virginia Hiking Trails*. Appalachian Mountain Club Books, 1997.

Dillon, Tom. *Appalachian Trail Guide to Southwest Virginia*. Appalachian Trail Conservancy, 2008.

Golightly, Jean. *Circuit Hikes in the Shenandoah National Park*. Potomac Appalachian Trail Club, 1996.

Hedrick, John. *Appalachian Trail Guide to Shenandoah National Park*. Potomac Appalachian Trail Club, 2012.

Logue, Victoria and Frank. *The Best of the Appalachian Trail Day Hikes*. Menasha Ridge Press, 2004.

Logue, Victoria and Frank. *The Best of the Appalachian Trail Overnight Hikes*. Menasha Ridge Press, 2007.

Myers, Janet. *Appalachian Trail Guide to Maryland and Northern Virginia*. Potomac Appalachian Trail Club, 2008.

Maps & Atlases

DeLorme. *Virginia Atlas & Gazetteer*. DeLorme, 2009.

DeLorme. *West Virginia Atlas & Gazetteer*. DeLorme, 1997.

U.S. Geological Survey, Topographic maps available in printed versions and on CD-ROM. (To contact USGS, see "Map Sources" under "Maps: Legends, Skills, Sources" in the Introduction and see also "Web sites" in "Useful Information.")

Field Guides & Natural History

Chew, V. Collins. *Underfoot: A Geologic Guide to the Appalachian Trail*. Appalachian Trail Conference, 1993.

Conners, John A. *Shenandoah National Park*. McDonald & Woodward, 1988.

Crandall, Hugh. *Shenandoah National Park, The Story Behind the Scenery*. KC Publications, 1990.

Eastman, John Andrews. *The Book of Forest and Thicket*. Stackpole Books, 1995.

Eastman, John Andrews. *The Book of Swamp and Bog*. Stackpole Books, 1995.

Floyd, Tom. *Lost Trails and Forgotten People*. Potomac Appalachian Trail Club, 1985.

Gupton, Oscar W. and Swope, Fred C. *Trees and Shrubs of Virginia.* University Press of Virginia, 1981.

Gupton, Oscar W. and Swope, Fred C. *Wildflowers of the Shenandoah Valley and Blue Ridge Mountains.* University Press of Virginia, 1982.

Lawrence, Eleanor, and Cecilia Fitzsimons. *An Instant Guide to Trees.* Longmeadow Press, 1991.

Newcomb, Lawrence. *Newcomb's Wildflower Guide.* Little, Brown, 1989.

Peattie, Donald Culross. *The Natural History of Trees of Eastern and Central North America.* Houghton Mifflin, 1991.

Peterson, Lee Allen. *A Field Guide to Edible Wild Plants of Eastern and Central North America.* Houghton Mifflin, 1999.

Peterson, Roger Tory. *Peterson First Guide to Birds of North America.* Houghton Mifflin, 2008.

Peterson, Roger Tory. *Peterson First Guide to Wildflowers of Northeastern and North-central North America.* Houghton Mifflin, 2008.

Petty, Robert O. *Wild Plants in Flower: Eastern Deciduous Forest.* Torkel Korling, 1974.

Porter, Randy and Sorrells, Nancy. *A Cyclist's Guide to the Shenandoah Valley.* Shenandoah Odysseys, 1994.

Reid, Fiona. *Peterson First Guide to Mammals of North America.* Houghton Mifflin, 2006.

Rives, Margaret Rose. *Blue Ridge Parkway: The Story Behind the Scenery.* KC Publications, 1982.

Rupp, Rebecca. *Red Oaks and Black Birches: The Science and Lore of Trees.* Garden Way, 1994.

Sutton, Ann, and Myron Sutton. *Eastern Forests.* (Audubon Field Guide). Alfred A. Knopf, 1993.

Watts, May Theilgaard. *Tree Finder.* Nature Study Guild, 1986.

Books About the Appalachian Trail

Appalachian Trail Conference. *Walking the Appalachian Trail Step by Step.* Appalachian Trail Conference, 1993.

Bruce, Dan "Wingfoot." *The Thru-Hiker's Handbook.* Center for Appalachian Trail Studies, 1997. (Updated annually)

Chazin, Daniel D. *Appalachian Trail Data Book 1996.* Appalachian Trail Conservancy, 2013. (Updated annually)

Chase, James B.G. *Backpacker Magazine's Guide to the Appalachian Trail.* Stackpole Books, 2009.

Emblidge, David, ed. *The Appalachian Trail Reader.* Oxford University Press, 1997.

Fisher, Ronald M. *The Appalachian Trail.* National Geographic Society, 1972.

Sylvester, Robert, ed. *Appalachian Trail Thru-Hikers' Companion.* Appalachian Trail Conservancy, 2013. (Updated annually)

Whalen, Christopher. *The Appalachian Trail Workbook for Planning Thru-Hikes,* Appalachian Trail Conference, 1995.

Practical Advice on Hiking & Camping

Berger, Karen. *Hiking & Backpacking: A Complete Guide.* W. W. Norton, 1995.

Cary, Alice. *Parents' Guide to Hiking & Camping.* W.W. Norton, 1997.

Cole, David, and Bruce Hampton. *NOLS Soft Paths.* Stackpole Books, 1995.

Fletcher, Colin and Chip Rowling. *The Complete Walker.* Alfred A. Knopf, 2002.

Long, John, and Hodgson, Michael. *The Day Hiker's Handbook.* Ragged Mountain Press, 1996.

McManners, Hugh. *The Backpacker's Handbook.* Dorling Kindersley, 1995.

Meyer, Kathleen. *How to Shit in the Woods: An Environmentally Sound Approach to a Lost Art.* Ten Speed Press, 1994.

Viehman, John, ed. *Trailside's Hints & Tips for Outdoor Adventures.* Rodale Press, 1993.

Wood, Robert S. *The 2 Oz. Backpacker.* Ten Speed Press, 1982.

Index

Page numbers in *italic* refer to topographic maps and itineraries.

ABOUT THE AUTHORS

DAVID LILLARD has hiked the AT in ten states and lives with his wife, Lauren, within view of the AT's passage over the Blue Ridge. He is a volunteer with the Potomac Appalachian Trail Club and president of American Hiking Society, a national hikers' advocacy organization. Lillard serves on the board of The Land Trust of the Eastern Panhandle, a West Virginia conservation group, and on the corporation council of New York's Adirondack Mountain Club.

GWYN HICKS grew up exploring the hills of northern New Jersey, not far from where the AT cuts through the Delaware Water Gap. Turning trail conservation into a profession, she currently serves as director of communications for American Hiking Society and editor of *American Hiker.* When she is not working to protect trails, she enjoys spending time hiking them with her husband, Steve.

The Exploring the Appalachian Trail™ series

Hikes in the Southern Appalachians: Georgia, North Carolina, Tennessee
by Doris Gove $19.95   400 pages

Hikes in the Virginias: Virginia, West Virginia
by David Lillard and Gwyn Hicks $19.95   432 pages

Hikes in the Mid-Atlantic States: Maryland, Pennsylvania, New Jersey, New York
by Glenn Scherer and Don Hopey $19.95   384 pages

Hikes in Southern New England: Connecticut, Massachusetts, Vermont
by David Emblidge $19.95   304 pages

Hikes in Northern New England: New Hampshire, Maine
by Michael Kodas, Andrew Weegar, Mark Condon, Glenn Scherer $19.95   400 pages

Available from your favorite bookseller or outdoor retailer, or from the publisher.

STACKPOLE BOOKS

5067 Ritter Road, Mechanicsburg, PA 17055 • 800-732-3669
e-mail: sales@stackpolebooks.com
www.stackpolebooks.com